4TH EDITION

Managing and Using Information Systems

A Strategic Approach

KERI E. PEARLSON
KP Partners

CAROL S. SAUNDERS
University of Central Florida

WILEY

JOHN WILEY & SONS, INC.

To Yale & Hana

To Rusty, Russell & Kristin

VICE PRESIDENT & EXECUTIVE PUBLISHER	Don Fowley
EXECUTIVE EDITOR	Beth Lang Golub
EDITORIAL ASSISTANT	Lyle Curry
MARKETING MANAGER	Carly DeCandia
DESIGN DIRECTOR	Harry Nolan
SENIOR DESIGNER	Kevin Murphy
SENIOR PRODUCTION EDITOR	Patricia McFadden
SENIOR MEDIA EDITOR	Lauren Sapira
PRODUCTION MANAGEMENT SERVICES	Pine Tree Composition

This book is printed on acid-free paper. ♾

To order books or for customer service please, call 1-800-CALL WILEY (225-5945).

ISBN 978-0-470-34381-4

Printed in the United States of America

10 9 8 7 6 5 4 3 2

Preface

Information technology and business are becoming inextricably interwoven. I don't think anybody can talk meaningfully about one without the talking about the other.[1]

> Bill Gates
> Microsoft

I'm not hiring MBA students for the technology you learn while in school, but for your ability to learn about, use and subsequently manage new technologies when you get out.

> IT Executive
> Federal Express

Give me a fish and I eat for a day; teach me to fish and I eat for a lifetime.

> Proverb

Managers do not have the luxury of abdicating participation in information systems decisions. Managers who choose to do so risk limiting their future business options. Information systems are at the heart of virtually every business interaction, process, and decision, especially when one considers the vast penetration of the Web in the last few years. Managers who let someone else make decisions about their information systems are letting someone else make decisions about the very foundation of their business. This is a textbook about managing and using information, written for current and future managers as a way of introducing the broader implications of the impact of information systems.

The goal of this book is to assist managers in becoming knowledgeable participants in information systems decisions. Becoming a knowledgeable participant means learning the basics and feeling comfortable enough to ask questions. It does not mean having all the answers nor having a deep understanding of all the technologies out in the world today. No text will provide managers with everything they need to know to make important information systems decisions. Some texts instruct on the basic technical background of information systems. Others discuss applications and their life cycle. Some take a comprehensive view of the management information systems (MIS) field and offer readers snapshots of current systems along with chapters describing how those technologies are designed, used, and integrated into business life.

This book takes a different approach. This text is intended to provide the reader with a foundation of basic concepts relevant to using and managing information. It is not intended to provide a comprehensive treatment on any one aspect of MIS,

---

[1] http://www.woopidoo.com/business_quotes/authors/bill-gates-quotes.htm.

for certainly each aspect is itself a topic of many books. It is not intended to provide readers with enough technological knowledge to make them MIS experts. It is not intended to be a source of discussion of any particular technology. This textbook is written to help managers begin to form a point of view of how information systems will help, hinder, and create opportunities for their organizations.

The idea for this text grew out of discussions with colleagues in the MIS area. Many faculty use a series of case studies, trade and popular press readings, and Web sites to teach their MIS courses. Others simply rely on one of the classic texts, which include dozens of pages of diagrams, frameworks, and technologies. The initial idea for this text emerged from a core MIS course taught at the business school at the University of Texas at Austin. That course was considered an "appetizer" course—a brief introduction into the world of MIS for MBA students. The course had two main topics: using information and managing information. At the time, there was no text like this one, hence students had to purchase thick reading packets made up of articles and case studies to provide them with the basic concepts. The course was structured to provide the general MBA with enough knowledge of the field of MIS that they could recognize opportunities to use the rapidly changing technologies available to them. The course was an appetizer to the menu of specialty courses, each of which went much deeper into the various topics. But completion of the appetizer course meant that students were able to feel comfortable listening to, contributing to, and ultimately participating in information systems decisions.

Today many students are digital natives—people who have grown up using information technologies all of their lives. That means that students come to their courses with significantly more knowledge about things like personal computers, cell phones, texting, the Web, social networking, file downloading, online purchasing, and social media than their counterparts in school just a few years ago. This is a significant trend that is projected to continue; students will be increasingly knowledgeable in personally using technologies. That knowledge has begun to change the corporate environment. Today's digital natives expect to find information systems in corporations that provide at least the functionality they have at home. At the same time, they expect to be able to work in ways that take advantage of the technologies they have grown to depend on for social interaction, collaboration, and innovation. This edition of the text has been completely edited with this new group of students in mind. We believe the basic foundation is still needed for managing and using information systems, but we understand that the assumptions and knowledge base of today's students is significantly different.

This book includes an introduction, 12 chapters of text and minicases, and a set of case studies and supplemental readings on a Web site. The introduction makes the argument introduced in this preface that managers must be knowledgeable participants in information systems decisions. The first few chapters build a basic framework of relationships between business strategy, information systems strategy, and organizational strategy and explore the links between these strategies. Readers will also find a chapter on how information systems relate to business transformation. Supplemental materials, including longer cases from all over the globe, can be found on the Web. Please visit http://www.wiley.com/college/pearlson for more information.

General managers also need some foundation on how IT is managed if they are to successfully discuss their next business needs with IT professionals who can help them. Therefore, the remaining chapters describe the basics of information architecture and infrastructure, the sourcing of information systems, the organization and governance of the MIS function, the ethical issues, the funding of information systems resources, project management, and business analytics and knowledge management.

No text in the field of MIS is current. The process of writing the chapters, coupled with the publication process, makes a text somewhat out-of-date prior to delivery to its audience. With that in mind, this text is written to summarize the "timeless" elements of using and managing information. Although this text is complete in and of itself, learning is enhanced by coupling the chapters with the most current readings and cases. Students are encouraged to search the Web for examples and current events that further clarify the issues at hand. The format of each chapter begins with an example case and the basic language for a set of important management issues. This is followed up with a set of managerial concerns related to the topic. Each chapter then has a food for thought section on an additional, but relatively new, topic. The chapter concludes with a set of study questions, key words, and case studies.

This is the fourth edition of this text, and this version includes several significant additions and revisions. Gone is the chapter on "doing business on the Internet" because after all, virtually every business now uses the Internet. Instead, this edition has a new chapter on sourcing. Major changes include a new focus on Web 2.0 (Chapter 2); new framework of managerial levers (Chapter 3); new discussion on collaboration (Chapter 4); alignment and business processes (Chapter 5); SOA WOA, SaaS, enterprise architecture, and cloud computing (Chapter 6); sourcing (Chapter 7); new IT governance framework (Chapter 8); security and compliance (Chapter 9); new discussion of business cases (Chapter 10); new focus on managing business projects (Chapter 11); and on business analytics and business intelligence (Chapter 12). Many of the older cases have been replaced with newer examples throughout the text, and many of the food for thought issues are new.

Who should read this book? General managers interested in participating in information systems decisions will find this a good reference resource for the language and concepts of MIS. Managers in the information systems field will find this book a good resource for beginning to understand the general manager's view of how information systems affect business decisions. And MIS students will be able to use the readings and concepts in this book as the beginning point in their journey to become informed and successful business people.

The information revolution is here. Where do you fit in?

Keri E. Pearlson and Carol S. Saunders

Acknowledgments

Books of this nature are written only with the support of many individuals. We would like to personally thank several individuals who helped with this text. Although we've made every attempt to include everyone who helped make this book a reality, there is always the possibility of unintentionally leaving some off. We apologize in advance if that is the case here.

Philip Russell Saunders came to our rescue when we were in a pinch by researching various topics, finding cases, and verifying examples from previous editions. We really appreciate his efforts. We also appreciate the considerable efforts of Mihir Parikh at the University of Central Florida. Mihir wrote many of the new cases that appear in this fourth edition of the text. Thanks also go to Craig Tidwell who updated the teaching materials.

We also want to acknowledge and thank pbwiki.com. Without their incredible, and free, wiki, we would have been relegated to e-mailing drafts of chapters back and forth. For this edition, we wanted to use Web2.0 tools as we wrote about them.

We have been blessed with the help of our colleagues in this and in previous editions of the book. They helped us by writing cases and reviewing the text. Our thanks continue to go out to Jonathan Trower, Espen Andersen, Janis Gogan, Ashok Rho, Yvonne Lederer Antonucci, E. Jose Proenca, Bruce Rollier, Dave Oliver, Celia Romm, Ed Watson, D. Guiter, S. Vaught, Kala Saravanamuthu, Ron Murch, John Greenwod, Tom Rohleder, Sam Lubbe, Thomas Kern, Mark Dekker, Anne Rutkowski, Kathy Hurtt, Kay Nelson, and John Butler. In addition, the students of the spring 2008 Technology Management and summer 2008 Information Resource Management classes at the University of Central Florida provided comments that proved helpful in writing some cases and making revisions. Though we cannot thank them by name, we also greatly appreciate the comments of the anonymous reviewers who have made a mark on this edition.

The book would not have been started were it not for the initial suggestion of a wonderful editor at John Wiley & Sons, Inc., Beth Lang Golub. Her persistence and patience have helped shepherd this book through many months of creation, modification, evaluation, and production, and she will shepherd it through translation into other languages. Special thanks go to Maria Guarascio, who very cheerfully and very competently helped us through the revision process. We also appreciate the help of (Jennifer Snyder, Lorraina Raccuia, Gitti Lindner, and Sujin Hong) and others at Wiley, who have made this edition a reality.

From Keri: Thank you to my husband, Dr. Yale Pearlson, and my daughter, Hana Pearlson. Their patience with me while I worked on this project was incredible. They celebrated and commiserated the ups and downs that came with the process of writing this book. I love you guys!

From Carol: Rusty, thank you for being my compass (always keeping me headed in the right direction) and my release valve (patiently walking me through stressful times). I couldn't do it without you. I love you, Russell, and Kristin very much!

About the Authors

Keri E. Pearlson

Dr. Keri E. Pearlson is president of KP Partners, a consultancy specializing in creating leaders skilled in the strategic use of information systems and organizational design in the Web 2.0 world.

Dr. Pearlson has held various positions in academia and industry. She was a member of the information systems faculty at the Graduate School of Business at the University of Texas at Austin, where she taught management information systems courses to MBAs and executives. She was a research director at the Research Board, held positions at the Harvard Business School, CSC-Index's Prism Group, nGenera (formerly the Concours Group), AT&T, and Hughes Aircraft Company.

She is co-author of *Zero Time: Providing Instant Customer Value—Every Time, All the Time* (John Wiley & Sons, 2000). Her work has been published in *Sloan Management Review, Academy of Management Executive, Information Resources Management Journal*, and *Beyond Computing*. Many of her case studies have been published by Harvard Business School Publishing and are used all over the world.

Dr. Pearlson holds a Doctorate in Business Administration (DBA) in Management Information Systems from the Harvard Business School and both a Master's Degree in Industrial Engineering Management and a Bachelor's Degree in Applied Mathematics from Stanford University.

Carol S. Saunders

Dr. Carol S. Saunders is professor of MIS at the University of Central Florida in Orlando, Florida. She served as General Conference Chair of the International Conference on Information Systems (ICIS) in 1999 and Telecommuting in 1996. She was the chair of the ICIS Executive Committee in 2000. She was editor-in-chief of *MIS Quarterly* and is a Fellow of the Association of Information Systems (AIS). Her current research interests include the impact of information system on power and communication, virtual teams, virtual worlds, time, information overload, sourcing, and interorganizational linkages.

Her research is published in a number of journals including *MIS Quarterly, Information Systems Research, Journal of MIS, Communications of the ACM, Academy of Management Journal, Academy of Management Review, Communications Research*, and *Organization Science*.

Contents

► **CHAPTER 3** Organizational Impacts of Information Systems Use **76**

► **CHAPTER 4** Information Technology and the Design of Work **98**

► **CHAPTER 5** Information Technology and Changing Business Processes **134**

▶ **CHAPTER 6** Architecture and Infrastructure   **162**

▶ **CHAPTER 7** Information Systems Sourcing   **190**

▶ **CHAPTER 8** Governance of the Information Systems Organization   **218**

▶ **CHAPTER 9** Using Information Ethically **246**

▶ **CHAPTER 10** Funding IT **278**

▶ **CHAPTER 11** Project Management **309**

▶ **CHAPTER 12** Managing Business Knowledge **346**

Glossary **375**

Index **385**

▶ INTRODUCTION

Why do managers need to understand and participate in the information decisions of their organizations? After all, most corporations maintain entire departments dedicated to the management of information systems (IS). These departments are staffed with highly skilled professionals devoted to the field of technology. Shouldn't managers rely on experts to analyze all the aspects of IS and to make the best decisions for the organization? The answer to that question is no. Managing information is a critical skill for success in today's business environment. All decisions made by companies involve, at some level, the management and use of IS. Managers today need to know about their organization's capabilities and uses of information as much as they need to understand how to obtain and budget financial resources. The ubiquity of personal computers (PCs) and the Internet highlights this fact because together they form the backbone for virtually all new business models. Further, the proliferation of supply chain partnerships has extended the urgent need for business managers to be involved in technology decisions. In addition, the availability of seemingly free (or at least very inexpensive) applications and collaboration in the consumer area has changed the landscape once again, increasing the integration of IS and business processes. A manager who does not understand the basics of managing and using information cannot be successful in this business environment.

Consider the now-historic rise of companies such as Amazon.com and Google. Amazon.com began as an online bookseller and rapidly outpaced traditional brick-and-mortar businesses like Barnes and Noble, Borders, and Waterstones. Management at the traditional companies responded by having their IS support personnel build Web sites to compete. But upstart Amazon.com moved on ahead, keeping its leadership position on the Web by leveraging its new business model into other marketplaces, such as music, electronics, health and beauty products, lawn and garden products, auctions, tools and hardware, and more. It cleared the profitability hurdle in the fourth quarter of 2001 by achieving a good mix of IS and business basics: capitalizing on operational efficiencies derived from inventory software and smarter storage, cost cutting, and effectively partnering with such companies as Toys "R" Us Inc. and Target Corporation.[1] In 2008, Amazon.com once again changed the basis of competition in another market, but this time it was the Web services business. Amazon.com Web services offers clients the extensive technology platform used for Amazon.com, but in an on-demand fashion for developing and running the client's own applications.

---

[1] Robert Hof, "How Amazon Cleared the Profitability Hurdle," *BusinessWeek Online* (February 4, 2002), http://www.businessweek.com/magazine/content/02_05/b3768079.htm (accessed May 23, 2002).

Likewise, Google played an important role in revolutionizing the way information is located and used as well as revolutionizing the world of advertising and publishing. Google began in 1999 as a basic search company but quickly learned that a unique business model was a critical factor for future success. The company changed the way people thought about Web content by making it available in a searchable format with an incredibly fast response time. Further, Google's keyword-targeted advertising program revolutionized the way companies advertise. By 2001, Google announced its first quarter of profitability, solidifying the way the world finds information, publishes, and advertises.[2] By 2008, Google had expanded into a complete suite of Web-based applications, such as calendaring, e-mail, collaboration, shopping, and maps. Further, like Amazon.com, Google also offers clients similar on-demand services.[3]

These and other online businesses are able to succeed where traditional companies were not, in part because their management understood the power of information, IS, and the Web. They did not succeed because their managers could build Web pages or assemble an IS network. Quite the contrary. The executives in these new businesses understood the fundamentals of managing and using information and could marry that knowledge with a sound, unique business vision to achieve domination of their intended market spaces.

The goal of this book is to provide the foundation to help the general business manager become a knowledgeable participant in IS decisions because any IS decision in which the manager does not participate can greatly affect the organization's ability to succeed in the future. This introduction outlines the fundamental reasons for taking the initiative to participate in IS decisions. Moreover, because effective participation requires a unique set of managerial skills, this introduction identifies the most important ones. These skills will be helpful not just in making IS decisions, but all business decisions. We describe how a manager should participate in the decision-making process and outline how the remaining chapters of this book develop this point of view. Finally, the introduction presents current models for understanding the nature of a business and that of an information system to provide a framework for the discussions that follow in subsequent chapters.

▶ THE CASE FOR PARTICIPATING IN DECISIONS ABOUT INFORMATION SYSTEMS

Experience shows that business managers have no problem participating in most organizational decisions, even those outside their normal business expertise. For example, ask a plant manager about marketing problems, and the result will probably be a detailed opinion on both key issues and recommended solutions. Dialogue among managers routinely crosses all business functions in formal as

---

[2] Adapted from information at www.google.com/corporate/history.html (accessed June 17, 2005).

[3] For more information on the latest services by these two companies, see http://www.amazon.com and http://code.google.com/.

Reasons
IS must be managed as a critical resource.
IS enable change in the way people work together.
IS are part of almost every aspect of business.
IS enable business opportunities and new strategies.
IS can be used to combat business challenges from competitors.

FIGURE I.1 Reasons why business managers should participate in information systems decisions.

well as informal settings, with one general exception: IS. Management continues to tolerate ignorance in this area relative to other specialized business functions. Culturally, managers can claim ignorance of IS issues without losing prestige among colleagues. On the other hand, admitting a lack of knowledge regarding marketing or financial aspects of the business will earn colleagues' contempt.

These attitudes are attributable to the historic role that IS played in businesses. For many years, technology was regarded as a support function and treated as administrative overhead. Its value as a factor in important management decisions was minimal. It often took a great deal of technical knowledge to understand even the most basic concepts. However, in today's business environment, maintaining this back-office view of technology is certain to cost market share and could ultimately lead to the failure of the organization. Technology has become entwined with all the classic functions of business—operations, marketing, accounting, finance—to such an extent that understanding its role is necessary for making intelligent and effective decisions about any of them. Furthermore, a general understanding of key IS concepts is possible without the extensive technological knowledge required just a few years ago. Finally, with the robust number of consumer applications available on the Web, many decisions made by the IS group are increasingly being made by individuals.

Therefore, understanding basic fundamentals about using and managing information is worth the investment of time. The reasons for this investment are summarized in Figure I.1 and are discussed next.

A Business View

Information technology (IT) is a critical resource for today's businesses. It both supports and consumes a significant amount of an organization's resources. Just like the other three major types of business resources—people, money, and machines—it needs to be managed wisely.

IT spends a significant portion of corporate budgets. Worldwide IT spending topped $3 trillion in 2007, a jump of 8% from the previous year. It's projected to continue to increase.[4] U.S. corporations spent about $3,500 per worker in 1994

---

[4] www.cio.com/article/144551/IT_Spending_to_Surpass_Trillion (accessed July 31, 2008).

on IT and about \$8,000 in 2005.[5] Industry-level research from the Gartner group found that the typical level of IT operating budget as a percentage of gross revenue ranges from 2.3% to 2.5% for consumer packaged goods companies and even higher for pharmaceuticals (4% to 6%) and logistics companies (5% to 6%).

These resources must return value, or they will be invested elsewhere. The business manager, not the IS specialist, decides which activities receive funding, estimates the risk associated with the investment, and develops metrics for evaluating the performance of the investment. Therefore, the business manager needs a basic grounding in managing and using information. On the flip side, IS managers need a business view.

People and Technology Work Together

In addition to financial issues, a manager must know how to mesh technology and people to create effective work. Collaboration is increasingly common, especially with the rise of social networking. Companies are reaching out to individual customers using social media. In fact, the term **Web 2.0** has emerged to describe the use of the World Wide Web (the Internet) to enhance creativity, information sharing, and collaboration among users.[6] Technology facilitates the work that people do and the way they interact with each other. Correctly incorporating IS into the design of a business enables people to focus their time and resources on issues that bear directly on customer satisfaction and other revenue- and profit-generating activities. Adding IS to an existing organization, however, requires the ability to manage change. The skilled business manager must balance the benefits of introducing new technology with the costs associated with changing the existing behaviors of people in the workplace. Making this assessment does not require a detailed technical knowledge. It does require an understanding of what the short-term and long-term consequences are likely to be and why adopting new technology may be more appropriate in some instances than in others. Understanding these issues also helps managers know when it may prove effective to replace people with technology at certain steps in a process.

Integrating Business with Technology

IS are now integrated with almost every aspect of business. For example, as CEO of Wal-Mart Stores International, Bob L. Martin described IS's role, "Today technology plays a role in almost everything we do, from every aspect of customer service to customizing our store formats or matching our merchandising strategies to individual markets in order to meet varied customer preferences."[7] IS place information in the hands of Wal-Mart associates so that decisions can be made

---

[5] A. McAfee and E. Brynjolfsson, "Investing in the IT that Makes a Competitive Difference," *Harvard Business Review* (2008).

[6] Wikipedia, www.wikipedia.com (accessed July 31, 2008).

[7] "The End of Delegation? Information Technology and the CEO," *Harvard Business Review* (September–October 1995), 161.

closer to the customer. IS help simplify organizational activities and processes such as moving goods, stocking shelves, or communicating with suppliers.

Rapid Change in Technology

The proliferation of new technologies creates a business environment filled with opportunities. The changing demographics of the workforce and the integration of "'digital natives," individuals who have grown up completely fluent in the use of personal technologies and the Web, also increase the rate of adoption of new technologies beyond the pace of traditional organizations. Even today, new uses of the Internet produce new types of online businesses that keep every manager and executive on alert. New business opportunities spring up with little advance warning. The manager's role is to frame these opportunities so that others can understand them, to evaluate them against existing business needs, and finally to pursue any that fit with an articulated business strategy. The quality of the information at hand affects the quality of both the decision and its implementation. Managers must develop an understanding of what information is crucial to the decision, how to get it, and how to use it. They must lead the changes driven by IS.

Competitive Challenges

Competitors come from both expected and unexpected places. General managers are in the best position to see the emerging threats and utilize IS effectively to combat ever-changing competitive challenges. Further, general managers are often called on to demonstrate a clear understanding of how their own technology programs and products compare with those of their competitors.

▶ WHAT IF A MANAGER DOESN'T PARTICIPATE?

Decisions about IS directly affect the profits of a business. The basic formula Profit=Revenue−Expenses can be used to evaluate the impact of these decisions. Adopting the wrong technologies can cause a company to miss business opportunities and any revenues those opportunities would generate. Inadequate IS can cause a breakdown in servicing customers, which hurts sales. On the expense side, a poorly calculated investment in technology can lead to overspending and excess capacity. Inefficient business processes sustained by ill-fitting IS also increase expenses. Lags in implementation or poor process adaptation each reduce profits and therefore growth. IS decisions can dramatically affect the bottom line.

Failure to consider IS strategy when planning business strategy and organizational strategy leads to one of three business consequences: (1) IS that fail to support business goals, (2) IS that fail to support organizational systems, and (3) a misalignment between business and organizational strategies. These consequences are discussed briefly in this section and in more detail in later chapters. While examining IS-related consequences in greater detail, consider their potential effects on an organization's ability to achieve its business goals. How would each consequence change the way people work? Which customers would be most affected and how? Would the organization still be able to implement its business strategy?

Information Systems Must Support Business Goals

IS represent a major investment for any firm in today's business environment. Yet poorly chosen IS can actually become an obstacle to achieving business goals. If the systems do not allow the organization to realize its goals, or if IS lack the capacity needed to collect, store, and transfer critical information for the business, the results can be disastrous. Customers will be dissatisfied or even lost. Production costs may be excessive. Worst of all, management may not be able to pursue desired business directions that are blocked by inappropriate IS. Toys "R" Us experienced such a calamity when its well-publicized Web site was unable to process and fulfill orders fast enough. It not only lost those customers, but it also had a major customer relations issue to manage as a result. Consider the well-intended Web designer who was charged with building a Web site to disseminate information to investors, customers, and potential customers. If the business goal is to do business over the Web, then the decision to build an informational Web site, rather than a transactional Web site, is misdirected and could potentially cost the company customers by not taking orders online. Even though it is possible to redesign a Web site, the task requires expending additional resources that might have been saved if business goals and IS strategy were discussed together.

Information Systems Must Support Organizational Systems

Organizational systems represent the fundamental elements of a business—its people, work processes, and structure—and the plan that enables them to work efficiently to achieve business goals. If the company's IS fail to support its organizational systems, the result is a misalignment of the resources needed to achieve its goals. It seems odd to think that a manager might add functionality to a corporate Web site without providing the training these same employees need to use the tool effectively, and yet this mistake—and many more costly ones—occur in businesses every day. Managers make major decisions, such as switching to a new major IS or implementing a standard that prohibits access to an external Web site, without informing all the affected staff of necessary changes in their daily work. For example, when companies put in an enterprise resource planning (ERP) system, the system often dictates how many business processes are executed. Deploying technology without thinking through how it actually will be used in the organization—who will use it, how they will use it, how to make sure the applications chosen actually accomplish what is intended—results in significant expense without a lot to show for it. In another example, a company may decide to prohibit access to the Internet, thinking that they are prohibiting employees from accessing offensive or unsecure sites. But that decision also means that employees can't access social networking sites, which may be useful for collaboration, or new Web-based applications, which may offer functionality to make the business more efficient. The general manager, who, after all, is charged with ensuring that company resources are used effectively, must ensure that the company's IS support its organizational systems and that changes made in one system are reflected in other related systems. For example, a company that plans to institute a wide-scale telecommuting program needs an information system strategy compatible with its organization strategy. Desktop PCs located within the corporate office are not the right solution for a telecommuting organization. Instead, laptop computers, applications that are accessible online anywhere and anytime, and networks that facilitate information sharing are needed. If the organization only allows the purchase of desktop PCs and only builds systems accessible from desks within the office, the telecommuting program is doomed to failure.

▶ SKILLS NEEDED TO PARTICIPATE EFFECTIVELY IN INFORMATION TECHNOLOGY DECISIONS

Participating in IT decisions means bringing a clear set of skills to the table. Managers are asked to take on tasks that require different skills at different times. Those tasks can be divided into visionary tasks, or tasks that provide leadership and direction for the group; informational/interpersonal tasks, or tasks that provide information and knowledge the group needs to have to be successful; and structural tasks, tasks that organize the group. Figure I.2 lists basic skills required of managers who wish to participate successfully in key IT decisions. This list emphasizes understanding, organizing, planning, and solving the business needs of the organization. Individuals who want to develop fully as managers will find this an excellent checklist for professional growth.

These skills may not look much different from those required of any successful manager, which is the main point of this book: General managers can be successful participants in IS decisions without an extensive technical background. General managers who understand a basic set of IS concepts and who have outstanding managerial skills, such as those listed in Figure I.2, are ready for the digital economy.

How To Participate in Information Systems Decisions

Technical wizardry is not required to become a knowledgeable participant in the IS decisions of a business. What a manager needs includes curiosity, creativity, and the confidence to question in order to learn and understand. A solid framework that identifies key management issues and relates them to aspects of IS provides the background needed to participate.

The goal of this book is to provide that framework. The way in which managers use and manage information is directly linked to business goals and the business strategy that drive both organizational and IS decisions. Business, organizational, and information strategies are fundamentally linked in what is called the Information Systems Strategy Triangle. Failing to understand this relationship is detrimental to a business. Failing to plan for the consequences in all three areas can cost a manager his or her job. This book provides managers with a foundation for understanding business issues related to IS from a managerial perspective.

Managerial Role	Skill
Visionary	**Creativity**—the ability to transform resources and create something entirely new to the organization
	Curiosity—the ability to question and learn about new ideas, applications, technologies, and business models
	Confidence—the ability to believe in oneself and assert one's ideas at the proper time
	Focus on Business Solutions—the ability to bring experience and insight to bear on current business opportunities and challenges
	Flexibility—the ability to change rapidly and effectively, such as by adapting work processes, shifting perspectives on an issue, or adjusting a plan to achieve a new goal
Informational and Interpersonal	**Communication**—the ability to share thoughts through text, images, and speech
	Information gathering—the ability to gather thoughts of others through listening, reading, and observing
	Interpersonal skills—the ability to cooperate and collaborate with others on a team, among groups, or across a chain of command to achieve results
Structural	**Project management**—the ability to plan, organize, direct, and control company resources to effectively complete a project
	Analytical skills—the ability to break down a whole into its elements for ease of understanding and analysis
	Organizational skills—the ability to bring together distinct elements and combine them into an effective whole
	Planning skills—the ability to develop objectives and to allocate resources to ensure objectives are met

FIGURE I.2   Skills of successful managers.

Organization of the Book

To be a knowledgeable participant, managers must know about both using information and managing information. The first five chapters offer basic frameworks to make this understanding easier. Chapter 1 explains the Information Systems Strategy Triangle and provides a brief overview of relevant frameworks for business strategy and organizational strategy. It is provided as background for those who have not formally studied organization theory or business strategy. For those who have studied these areas, this chapter is a brief refresher of major concepts used throughout the remaining chapters of the book. Subsequent chapters provide frameworks and sets of examples for understanding the links between IT and business strategy (Chapter 2), organizational forms (Chapter 3), collaboration and individual work (Chapter 4), and business process transformation (Chapter 5).

The rest of the text looks at issues related to building IS strategy itself. Chapter 6 provides a framework for understanding the four components of IS architecture: hardware, software, networks, and data. Chapter 7 discusses sourcing and where companies look for IS resources. Chapter 8 looks at the governance and organization of IS resources. Chapter 9 presents some of the ethical issues that need to be considered. Chapter 10 focuses on the economics of managing IS. Chapter 11 discusses project management in general and the management of IS projects specifically. Finally, Chapter 12 provides an overview of how companies manage knowledge and create a competitive advantage using business analytics.

► BASIC ASSUMPTIONS

Every book is based on certain assumptions, and understanding those assumptions makes a difference in interpreting the text. The first assumption made by this text is that managers must be knowledgeable participants in the IS decisions made within and affecting their organizations. That means that the general manager must have a basic understanding of the business and technology issues related to IS. Because technology changes rapidly, this text also assumes that the technology of today is different from the technology of yesterday, and most likely, the technology available to readers of this text today differs significantly from that available when the text was written. Therefore, this text focuses on generic concepts that are, to the extent possible, technology independent. It provides a framework on which to hang more current information, such as new uses of the Internet or new networking technologies. It is assumed that the reader will seek out current sources to learn about the latest technology.

Although some may debate this next assumption, a second assumption is that the role of a general manager and the role of an IS manager are distinct. The general manager must have a basic knowledge of IS to make decisions that may have serious implications for the business. In addition to general business knowledge, the IS manager must have more in-depth knowledge of technology to manage IS and to partner with general managers who must use the information. As the digital natives take on increasingly more managerial roles in corporations, this second assumption may have to be altered. But for this text, we will assume a different skill set for the IS manager. Assumptions are also made about how business is done and what IS are in general. Knowing what assumptions are made about each will support an understanding of the material to come.

Assumptions about Management

The classic view of management includes four activities, each dependent on the others: planning, organizing, leading, and controlling (see Figure I.3). A manager

Classic Management Model	
Planning	Managers think through their goals and actions in advance. Their actions are usually based on some method, plan, or logic, rather than a hunch or gut feeling.
Organizing	Managers coordinate the human and material resources of the organization. The effectiveness of an organization depends on its ability to direct its resources to attain its goals.
Leading	Managers direct and influence subordinates, getting others to perform essential tasks. By establishing the proper atmosphere, they help their subordinates do their best.
Controlling	Managers attempt to assure that the organization is moving toward its goal. If part of their organization is on the wrong track, managers try to find out why and set things right.

FIGURE I.3   Classic management model.
Source: Adapted from James A. F. Stoner, *Management*, 2nd ed. (Upper Saddle River, NJ: Prentice Hall, 1982).

performs these activities with the people and resources of the organization to attain the established goals of the business. Conceptually, this simple model provides a framework of the key tasks of management, which is useful for both general business and IS management activities. Although many books have been written describing each of these activities, organizational theorist Henry Mintzberg offers a view that most closely details the perspective relevant to IS management.

Mintzberg's model describes management in behavioral terms by categorizing the three major roles a manager fills: interpersonal, informational, and decisional (see Figure I.4). This model is useful because it considers the chaotic nature of the environment in which managers actually work. Managers rarely have time to be reflective in their approaches to problems. They work at an unrelenting pace, and their activities are brief and often interrupted. Thus, quality information becomes even more crucial to effective decision making. The classic view is often seen as a tactical approach to management, whereas some describe Mintzberg's view as more strategic.

Assumptions about Business

Everyone has an internal understanding of what constitutes a business, which is based on readings and experiences in different firms. This understanding forms a model that provides the basis for comprehending actions, interpreting decisions, and communicating ideas. Managers use their internal model to make sense of otherwise chaotic and random activities. This book uses several conceptual models of business. Some take a functional view and others take a process view.

Type of Roles	Manager's Roles	IS Examples
Interpersonal	Figurehead	CIO greets touring dignitaries.
	Leader	IS manager puts in long hours to help motivate project team to complete project on schedule in an environment of heavy budget cuts.
	Liaison	Chief information officer works with the marketing and human resource vice presidents to make sure that the reward and compensation system is changed to encourage use of new IS supporting sales.
Informational	Monitor	Division manager compares progress on IS project for the division with milestones developed during the project's initiation and feasibility phase.
	Disseminator	Chief information officer conveys organization's business strategy to IS department and demonstrates how IS strategy supports the business strategy.
	Spokesperson	IS manager represents IS department at organization's recruiting fair.
Decisional	Entrepreneur	Division manager suggests an application of a new technology that improves the division's operational efficiency.
	Disturbance handler	Division manager, as project team leader, helps resolve design disagreements between division personnel who will be using the system and systems analysts who are designing it.
	Resource allocator	CIO allocates additional personnel positions to various departments based upon business strategy.
	Negotiator	IS manager negotiates for additional personnel needed to respond to recent user requests for enhanced functionality in a system that is being implemented.

FIGURE I.4   Manager's roles.
Source: Adapted from H. Mintzberg, *The Nature of Managerial Work* (New York: Harper & Row, 1973).

Functional View

The classical view of a business is based on the functions that people perform, such as accounting, finance, marketing, operations, and human resources. The business organizes around these functions to coordinate them and to gain economies of scale within specialized sets of tasks. Information first flows vertically up and down

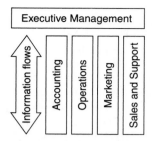

FIGURE I.5 Hierarchical view of the firm.

between line positions and management; after analysis it may be transmitted across other functions for use elsewhere in the company (see Figure I.5).

Process View

Michael Porter of Harvard Business School describes a business in terms of the primary and support activities that are performed to create, deliver, and support a product or service (see Figure I.6). The primary activities of inbound logistics, operations, outbound logistics, marketing and sales, and service are chained together in sequences that describe how a business transforms its raw materials into value-creating products. This value chain is supported by common activities shared across all the primary activities. For example, general management and legal services are distributed among the primary activities. Improving coordination among activities increases business profit. Organizations that effectively manage core processes across functional boundaries will be winners in the marketplace. IS are often the key to this process improvement and cross-functional coordination.

Firm Infrastructure					
Human Resource Management					Margin
Technology Development					
Procurement					
Inbound Logistics	Operations	Outbound Logistics	Marketing & Sales	Service	Margin

FIGURE I.6 Process view of the firm: the value chain.
Source: M. Porter, *Competitive Advantage* (New York: Free Press, 1985).

Both the process and functional views are important to understanding IS. The functional view is useful when similar activities must be explained, coordinated, executed, or communicated. For example, understanding a marketing information system means understanding the functional approach to business in general and the marketing function in particular. The process view, on the other hand, is useful when examining the flow of information throughout a business. For example, understanding the information associated with order fulfillment or product development or customer service means taking a process view of the business. This text assumes that both views are important for participating in IS decisions.

Assumptions about Information Systems

Consider the components of an information system from the manager's viewpoint, rather than from the technologist's viewpoint. Both the nature of information and the context of an information system must be examined to understand the basic assumptions of this text.

Information Hierarchy

The terms *data, information,* and *knowledge* are often used interchangeably, but have significant and discrete meanings within the knowledge management domain (and are more fully explored in Chapter 12). Tom Davenport, in his book *Information Ecology*, pointed out that getting everyone in any given organization to agree on common definitions is difficult. However, his work (summarized in Figure I.7) provides a nice starting point for understanding the subtle but important differences.

The information hierarchy begins with data, or simple observations. **Data** are a set of specific, objective facts or observations, such as "inventory contains 45 units." Standing alone, such facts have no intrinsic meaning, but can be easily captured, transmitted, and stored electronically.

Information is data endowed with relevance and purpose.[8] People turn data into information by organizing it into some unit of analysis (e.g., dollars, dates, or customers). For example, a **mashup** of location data and housing prices adds something beyond what the data provides individually, and that makes it information. Deciding on the appropriate unit of analysis involves interpreting the context of the data and summarizing it into a more condensed form. Consensus must be reached on the unit of analysis.

To be relevant and have a purpose, information must be considered within the context that it is received and used. Because of differences in context, information needs vary across the function and hierarchical level. For example, when considering functional differences related to a sales transaction, a marketing department manager may be interested in the demographic characteristics of buyers, such as their age, gender, and home address. A manager in the accounting department probably won't be interested in any of these details, but instead will

---

[8] Peter F. Drucker, "The Coming of the New Organization," *Harvard Business Review* (January–February 1988), 45–53.

	Data	Information	Knowledge
Definition	Simple observations of the state of the world	Data endowed with relevance and purpose	Information from the human mind (includes reflection, synthesis, context)
Characteristics	• Easily structured • Easily captured on machines • Often quantified • Easily transferred • Mere facts	• Requires unit of analysis • Data that have been processed • Human mediation necessary	• Hard to structure • Difficult to capture on machines • Often tacit • Hard to transfer
Example	Daily inventory report of all inventory items sent to the CEO of a large manufacturing company	Daily inventory report of items that are below economic order quantity levels sent to inventory manager	Inventory manager knowing which items need to be reordered in light of daily inventory report, anticipated labor strikes, and a flood in Brazil that affects the supply of a major component.

FIGURE I.7 Comparison of data, information, and knowledge.
Source: Adapted from Thomas Davenport, *Information Ecology* (New York: Oxford University Press, 1997).

want to know details about the transaction itself, such as method of payment and date of payment. Similarly, information needs may vary across hierarchical levels. These needs are summarized in Figure I.8 and reflect the different activities performed at each level. At the supervisory level, activities are narrow in scope and focused on production or the execution of the business's basic transactions. At this level, information is focused on day-to-day activities that are internally oriented and accurately defined in a detailed manner. The activities of senior management are much broader in scope. Senior management performs long-term planning and needs information that is aggregated, externally oriented, and more subjective. The information needs of middle managers in terms of these characteristics fall between the needs of supervisors and senior management. Because information needs vary across levels, a daily inventory report of a large manufacturing firm may serve as information for a low-level inventory manager, whereas the CEO would consider such a report to be merely data. A report does not necessarily mean information. The context in which the report is used must be considered.

Knowledge is information that is synthesized and contextualized to provide value. It is information with the most value. Knowledge consists of a mix of contextual information, values, experiences, and rules. For example, the mashup of locations and housing prices means one thing to a real estate agent, another

	Top Management	Middle Management	Supervisory and Lower-Level Management
Time Horizon	Long: years	Medium: weeks, months, years	Short: day to day
Level of Detail	Highly aggregated	Summarized	Very detailed
	Less accurate	Integrated	Very accurate
	More predictive	Often financial	Often nonfinancial
Orientation	Primarily external	Primarily internal with limited external	Internal
Decision	Extremely judgmental	Relatively judgmental	Heavy reliance on rules
	Uses creativity and analytical skills		

FIGURE I.8 Information characteristics across hierarchical level.

thing to a potential buyer, and yet something else to an economist. It is richer and deeper than information and more valuable because someone thought deeply about that information and added his or her own unique experience, judgment, and wisdom. Knowledge also involves the synthesis of multiple sources of information over time.[9] The amount of human contribution increases along the continuum from data to information to knowledge. Computers work well for managing data, but are less efficient at managing information.

Some people think there is a fourth level in the information hierarchy, **wisdom**. In this context, wisdom is knowledge, fused with intuition and judgment that facilitates the ability to make decisions. Wisdom is that level of the information hierarchy used by subject matter experts, gurus, and individuals with a high level of experience who seem to "just know" what to do and how to apply the knowledge they gain.

System Hierarchy

An information system comprises three main elements: technology, people, and process (see Figure I.9). When most people use the term *information system*, they actually refer only to the technology element as defined by the organization's infrastructure. In this text the term **infrastructure** refers to everything that supports the flow and processing of information in an organization, including hardware, software, data, and network components, whereas **architecture** refers to the strategy implicit in these components. These ideas will be discussed in greater detail in Chapter 6. **Information system** is defined more broadly as the *combination* of technology (the "what"), people (the "who"), and process (the

[9] Thomas H. Davenport, *Information Ecology* (New York: Oxford University Press, 1997), 9–10.

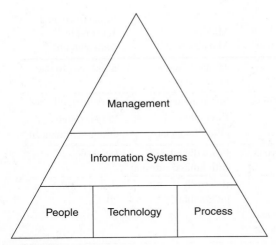

FIGURE I.9 System hierarchy.

"how") that an organization uses to produce and manage information. In contrast, information technology (IT) focuses only on the technical devices and tools used in the system. We define **information technology** as all forms of technology used to create, store, exchange, and use information.

Above the information system itself is management, which oversees the design and structure of the system and monitors its overall performance. Management develops the business requirements and the business strategy that the information system is meant to satisfy. The system's architecture provides a blueprint that translates this strategy into components, or infrastructure.[10]

▶ FOOD FOR THOUGHT: ECONOMICS OF INFORMATION VERSUS ECONOMICS OF THINGS

In their book, *Blown to Bits*, Evans and Wurster argued that every business is in the information business.[11] Even those businesses not typically considered to be information businesses have business strategies in which information plays a critical role. The physical world of manufacturing is shaped by information that dominates products as well as processes. For example, a high-end Mercedes automobile contains as much computing power as a midrange personal computer. Information-intensive processes in the manufacturing and marketing of the automobile include market research, logistics, advertising, and inventory management.

[10] Gordon Hay and Rick Muñoz, "Establishing an IT Architecture Strategy," *Information Systems Management* 14 (Summer 1997), 67–69.

[11] Philip Evans and Thomas Wurster, *Blown to Bits* (Boston: Harvard Business School Press, 2000).

Things	Information
Wear out	Doesn't wear out, can become obsolete or untrue
Are replicated at the expense of the manufacturer	Is replicated at almost zero cost without limit
Exist in a tangible location	Does not physically exist
When sold, possession changes hands	When sold, seller may still possess and sell again
Price based on production costs	Price based on value to consumer

FIGURE I.10   Comparison of the economics of things with the economics of information.

As our world is reshaped by information-intensive industries, it becomes even more important for business strategies to differentiate the timeworn economics of things from the evolving economics of information. Things wear out; things can be replicated at the expense of the manufacturer; things exist in a tangible location. When sold, the seller no longer owns the thing. The price of a thing is typically based on production costs. In contrast, information never wears out, though it can become obsolete or untrue. Information can be replicated at virtually no cost without limit; information exists in the ether. When sold, the seller still retains the information, but this ownership provides little value if the ability of others to copy it is not limited. Finally, information is often costly to produce, but cheap to reproduce. Rather than pricing it to recover the sunk cost of its initial production, its price is typically based on the value to the consumer. Figure I.10 summarizes the major differences between the economics of goods and the economics of information.

Evans and Wurster suggest that traditionally the economics of information has been bundled with the economics of things. However, in this Information Age, firms are vulnerable if they do not separate the two. The Encyclopædia Britannica story serves as an example. Bundling the economics of things with the economics of information made it difficult for Encyclopædia Britannica to gauge the threat posed by Encarta, the encyclopedia on CD-ROM that was given away to promote the sale of computers and peripherals. Britannica focused on its centuries-old tradition of providing information in richly bound tomes sold to the public through a well-trained sales force. Only when it was threatened with its very survival did Encyclopædia Britannica grasp the need to separate the economics of information from economics of things and sell bits of information online. Clearly, Encyclopædia Britannica's business strategy, like that of many other companies, needed to reflect the difference between the economics of things from the economics of information.[12]

---

[12] Ibid.

▶ SUMMARY

The explosive growth of Internet-based businesses highlights the need for all managers to be skilled in managing and using IS. It is no longer acceptable to delegate IS decisions to the management information systems (MIS) department alone. The general manager must be involved to both execute business plans and protect options for future business vision. This chapter makes the case for general managers' full participation in strategic business decisions concerning IS. It outlines the skills required for such participation, and it makes explicit certain key assumptions about the nature of business, management, and IS that will underlie the remaining discussions. Subsequent chapters are designed to build on these concepts by addressing the following questions.

Frameworks and Foundations

- How should information strategy be aligned with business and organizational strategies? (Chapter 1)
- How can a business achieve competitive advantages using its IS? (Chapter 2)
- What does it mean to align IT decisions with organizational decisions? (Chapter 3)
- How is the work of the individual in an organization affected by decisions concerning IS? (Chapter 4)
- How might IS enable business transformation? (Chapter 5)

IS Management Issues

- What are the components of an IT architecture? (Chapter 6)
- How should IS services be provided? (Chapter 7)
- What is an IS organization? How can a manager effectively manage IS? (Chapter 8)
- What ethical and moral considerations bind the uses of information in business? (Chapter 9)
- How are IS funded within an organization? What are the total costs of ownership of IS? (Chapter 10)
- What does it mean to manage a project? (Chapter 11)
- How should knowledge be managed within an organization? (Chapter 12)

▶ KEY TERMS

architecture (p. 15)
data (p. 13)
information (p. 13)
information system (p. 15)

information technology (p. 16)
infrastructure (p. 15)
knowledge (p. 14)

mashup (p. 13)
Web 2.0 (p. 4)
wisdom (p. 15)

▶ DISCUSSION QUESTIONS

1. Why is it important for a general manager to be knowledgeable about information technology?

2. Indicate whether each of the following is information, data, or knowledge:

   a. A daily sales report of each sales transaction that is sent to the chief operating officer

   b. A daily sales report of each sales transaction over $100,000 that is sent to the division marketing manager

   c. A monthly production report that is sent to shop floor supervisors who don't use the report because they believe the figures reported are outdated and inaccurate

   d. An exception report of all accounts that are more than 90 days past-due, which is sent to the Accounts Receivable Manager

   e. A list of Social Security numbers

   f. The contact list in an individual's LinkedIn account

3. Why, in your opinion, did the term Web 2.0 emerge? What is different in the way the Web is used today from the "Web 1.0" world?

CASE STUDY I-1

TERRY CANNON, MBA[13]

Terry Cannon, a typical MBA, was about to graduate from a top-ten business school with an MBA and a desire to change the world while growing a significant savings account. Terry was debating among three job opportunities, each of which would be a big step up the professional ladder from the associates job held when working for Impressive Consulting Group (ICG) prior to returning to school to get an MBA. Terry wasn't sure which job to take, in part because Terry didn't feel the MBA classes at the business school had provided enough preparation in information systems.

Terry started business school after four years of experience at Impressive Consulting Group (ICG), a global consulting organization with practices in virtually every major city in the world. Terry worked in the Dallas office as an associate right out of undergraduate school, with a degree in business with a concentration in marketing. Terry had worked on a number of interesting strategic marketing projects while at ICG. Terry was just completing a standard MBA program after two years of full-time study and a summer working for MFG Corporation, a large manufacturing company in the Midwest. The internship at MFG Corporation involved working with the new Web marketing group, which Terry chose to see just how a company like MFG takes advantage of the Web. At the same time, Terry hoped to become more proficient in Web and Internet technologies. The experience at

---

[13] The names in this case are fictitious. This case is written to highlight administrative issues relevant to general managers, and any resemblance to real individuals or organizations is coincidental.

MFG's Web marketing group, however, only made Terry more anxious, highlighting how much more was involved in information systems and the Web than Terry had previously thought. Terry returned to business school in the fall of the second year wondering just how much information systems knowledge would be needed in future jobs. Further, Terry felt that becoming a knowledgeable participant in information decisions was critical to success in the fast-paced Internet-based business world waiting after graduation.

Terry wondered just what type of information systems knowledge was needed for each of the three jobs under consideration. All three jobs involved a competitive salary, a signing bonus, and stock/retirement benefits, so the decision came down to the knowledge needed to be a success on the job. The three jobs are summarized as follows.

1. *Return to ICG as a consultant.* This job was attractive to Terry because it meant returning to a former employer. Terry had left in good standing and liked the company that rewarded innovation and supported learning and growth among consultants. Terry figured a partnership was possible in the future. As a consultant, Terry could live anywhere and travel to the client site four days a week. The fifth day each week, Terry would be able to work at home, or if desired, in a company office. As a consultant, Terry initially thought engagements in strategic marketing would be the most interesting. ICG had a strong programming group that was brought into each engagement to do the programming and systems analysis work. The consultant role involved understanding client concerns and assisting in building a marketing strategy. Virtually all the projects would have some Internet component, if not entirely about building an Internet presence. This challenge interested Terry, but based on the summer job experience, Terry wondered just how much technical skill would be required of the consultants in this arena.

2. *Join start-up InfoMicro.* Several of Terry's friends from business school were joining together to form a new start-up company on the Internet. This business plan for this company projected that InfoMicro would be one of only two Internet start-ups in their marketplace, giving the company a good position and great opportunity for growth. The business plan showed the company intending to go public through an IPO as early as three years after inception, and Terry believed they could do it. Terry would join as VP of marketing, supplementing the other three friends who would hold president, VP of finance, and VP of operations positions. The friends who would be president and finance VP were just completing a techno-MBA at Terry's school and would provide the technical competence needed to get InfoMicro on the Web. Terry would focus on developing customers and setting marketing strategy, eventually building an organization to support that operation as necessary. Because InfoMicro was a Web-based business, Terry felt a significant amount of information systems knowledge would be required of a successful marketing executive.

3. *Return to MFG Corporation.* The job would be to join the marketing department as a manager responsible for new customer development. Many of MFG corporation's customers were older, established companies like MFG Corporation itself, but new customers were likely to be start-ups and up-and-coming companies, or highly successful new companies like Google or Whole Foods. Terry felt that some knowledge of information systems would be necessary simply to provide innovative interaction mechanisms such as customer Web pages. Terry knew that discussions with the MFG information systems group would be necessary to build these new interfaces. How knowledgeable must Terry be on information systems issues to hold this job?

As spring break approached, Terry knew a decision had to be made. Recruiters from all three companies had given Terry a deadline of the end of break week, and Terry wasn't at all sure which job to take. All sounded interesting, and all were reasonable alternatives for Terry's next career move.

▶ Discussion Questions

1. For each position Terry is considering, what types of information systems knowledge do you think Terry would need?

2. How could Terry be a knowledgeable participant in each of the three jobs? What would it mean to be a knowledgeable participant in each job? Give an example for each job.

3. As a marketing major and an MBA, is Terry prepared for the work world awaiting? Why or why not?

CASE STUDY I-2

ANYGLOBAL COMPANY INC.[14]

Memo

To: Chris Bytemaster, CIO

From: Ms. Hazel Hasslefree, CEO

It seems that the article "IT Doesn't Matter" by Nicholas Carr (*Harvard Business Review*, May 2003) has caught the attention of several members of our Board of Directors. I have been asked to prepare a short presentation about what the article means to our company and whether IT does, in fact, matter in our company.

Would you please prepare a short report, about a page or two, that I can use as a basis for my presentation to them? Would you please summarize the Carr article and respond to the major points that he raises?

Thanks.

[14] We appreciate the suggestions provided to us by Ron Murch at the University of Calgary concerning this case.

CHAPTER 1

THE INFORMATION SYSTEMS STRATEGY TRIANGLE

When the Eastern United States was hit with an ice storm in 2007, most airlines cancelled flights much earlier than JetBlue. JetBlue, overly optimistic about the weather and its ability to fly its planes, wanted to keep the revenues flowing and its customers happy. So it delayed cancelling flights as long as it could. A crisis erupted when it finally had to cancel 1,000 flights over a five-day period. At one point up to nine airplanes full of passengers were stranded on the tarmac at John F. Kennedy International Airport in New York for six hours or more. JetBlue's founder and Chairman, David Neeleman, credited the problems JetBlue experienced to an inadequate reservation system and a shoestring communication system.

The reservation system was hopelessly overwhelmed, and customers were unable to get through to human agents to check on the status of their flight or to obtain an alternative routing. Most reservations agents lived in Salt Lake City—far away from the storm. Many were women who worked from their homes. And yet, they were unavailable to respond to the pleas of stranded passengers. After this crisis, Neeleman realized that JetBlue needed to adjust its work agreement to require reservation agents to work longer hours during difficult periods, such as those created by bad weather.[1]

This case emphasizes the point made in the Introduction: General managers *must* take a role in decisions about information systems (IS). Even though it is not necessary for a general manager to understand all technologies, it is necessary to aggressively seek to understand the consequences of using technologies relevant to the business's environment. General managers who leave IS decisions solely to their IS professionals often put themselves and their companies at a disadvantage. Although IS can facilitate the movement and exchange of information, an information system that is inappropriate for a given operating environment can actually inhibit and confuse that same exchange. This is especially true in crisis

---

[1] Jeff Bailey, "JetBlue's C.E.O. Is 'Mortified' After Fliers are Stranded," *New York Times*, February 19, 2007, www.nytimes.com/2007/19/businesss/19jetblue.html.

environments, such as the ice storm that paralyzed JetBlue's information exchanges. The IS organization is not an island within a firm. The IS organization manages an infrastructure that is essential to the firm's functioning. Further, this case illustrates that a firm's IS must be aligned with the way it manages its employees. In JetBlue's case, it became clear that personnel policies needed to be adjusted to have some, if not most, of JetBlue's 2,000 reservation agents working longer hours in times of crisis.

This chapter introduces a simple framework for understanding the impact of IS on organizations. This framework is called the **Information Systems Strategy Triangle** because it relates business strategy with IS strategy and organizational strategy. This chapter also presents key frameworks from organization theory that describe the context in which IS operate, as well as the business imperatives that IS support. Students with extensive background in organizational behavior and business strategy will find this a useful review of key concepts. The Information Systems Strategy Triangle presented in Figure 1.1 suggests three key points about strategy.

Successful firms have an overriding business strategy that drives both organizational strategy and IS strategy. The decisions made regarding the structure, hiring practices, and other components of the organizational strategy, as well as decisions regarding applications, hardware, and other IS components, are all driven by the firm's business objectives, strategies, and tactics. Successful firms carefully balance these three strategies—they purposely design their organization and their IS strategies to complement their business strategy.

IS strategy can itself affect and is affected by changes in a firm's business and organizational strategies. To perpetuate the balance needed for successful operation, changes in the IS strategy must be accompanied by changes in the organizational strategy and must accommodate the overall business strategy. If a firm designs its business strategy to use IS to gain strategic advantage, the leadership position in IS can only be sustained by constant innovation. The business, IS, and organizational strategies must constantly be adjusted.

IS strategy always involves consequences—intended or not—within business and organizational strategies. Avoiding harmful unintended consequences means remembering to consider business and organizational strategies when designing IS deployment. For example, placing computers on employee desktops without an accompanying set of changes to job descriptions, process design, compensation plans, and business tactics will fail to produce the anticipated productivity

FIGURE 1.1 The Information Systems Strategy Triangle.

improvements. Success can only be achieved by specifically designing all three components of the strategy triangle.

In the JetBlue case discussed earlier, the IS Strategy Triangle was out of alignment at the time of the ice storm. The organizational strategy (e.g., personnel policies about working hours) did not support the IS strategy (e.g., dispersed network of systems that allowed a geographically dispersed workforce, but was not able to handle the high volume of exchanges in a crisis situation). Both of these strategies did not adequately support the business strategy (low cost but a high level of customer service).[2]

Of course, once a firm is out of alignment, it does not mean that it has to stay that way. To correct the misalignment described earlier, JetBlue changed its personnel policy by extending working hours during crisis situations, replaced Neeleman with Dave Barger as CEO, and implemented an "Operational Recovery System." This system offers planners the ability to more easily reroute planes in the case of any disruption. It not only offers a solution to disruptions, but it also calculates the costs of various alternatives.

What does alignment mean? A recently published book entitled *Winning the 3-Legged Race* defines alignment as the situation in which a company's current and emerging business strategy is enabled, supported, and unconstrained by technology. The authors suggest that although alignment is good, there are higher states, namely synchronization and convergence, toward which companies should strive. With synchronization, technology not only enables current business strategy but also anticipates and shapes future business strategy. Convergence goes one step further by exhibiting a state in which business strategy and technology strategy are intertwined and the leadership team members operate almost interchangeably. Although we appreciate the distinction and agree that firms should strive for synchronization and convergence, *alignment* in this text means any of these states, and it pertains to organizational strategy, IS strategy, and business strategy.[3]

A word of explanation is needed here. This chapter and subsequent chapters address questions of IS strategy squarely within the context of business strategy. Studying business strategy alone is something better done in other texts and courses. However, to provide foundation for IS discussions, this chapter summarizes several key business strategy frameworks, as well as organizational theories. Studying IS alone does not provide general managers with the appropriate perspective. To be effective, managers need a solid sense of how IS are used and managed within the organization. Studying details of technologies is also outside the scope of this text. Details of the technologies are relevant, of course, and it is important that any organization maintain a sufficient knowledge base to plan for and operate applications. However, because technologies change so rapidly, keeping a text current is impossible. Therefore this text takes the perspective that understanding

---

[2] We are indebted to a reviewer for this comment

[3] F. Hogue, V. Sambamurthy, R. Zmud, T. Trainer, and C. Wilson, *Winning the 3-Legged Race*, (Upper Saddle River, NJ: Prentice Hall, 2005).

what questions to ask is a skill more fundamental to the general manager than understanding any particular technology. This text provides readers with an appreciation of the need to ask questions, a framework from which to derive the questions to ask, and a foundation sufficient to understand the answers received. The remaining book chapters all build on the foundation provided in the Information Systems Strategy Triangle.

► BRIEF OVERVIEW OF BUSINESS STRATEGY FRAMEWORKS

A **strategy** is a coordinated set of actions to fulfill objectives, purposes, and goals. The essence of a strategy is setting limits on what the business will seek to accomplish. Strategy starts with a mission. A **mission** is a clear and compelling statement that unifies an organization's effort and describes what the firm is all about (i.e., its purpose). In a few words the mission statement sums up what is unique about the firm. Figure 1.2 demonstrates that even though IBM, Dell, and Apple are all in the computer industry, they view their missions quite differently. For example, IBM says it focuses on services and solutions, Dell on customer experiences, and Apple on innovation and personal computing experience.

Are these companies accomplishing their missions? It is hard to determine whether Dell's customers are receiving the "best customer experience." That is why Dell, like other firms, sets measurable objectives and performance targets. Once the objectives and performance targets are set, the measurable objectives

Company	Mission Statement
IBM	At IBM, we strive to lead in the creation, development, and manufacture of the industry's most advanced information technologies, including computer systems, software, networking systems, storage devices, and microelectronics. We translate these advanced technologies into value for our customers through our professional solutions and services businesses worldwide.[a]
Dell	Dell's mission is to be the most successful computer company in the world at delivering the best customer experience in markets we serve.[b]
Apple	Apple ignited the personal computer revolution in the 1970s with the Apple II and reinvented the personal computer in the 1980s with the Macintosh. Apple is committed to bringing the best personal computing experience to students, educators, creative professionals, and consumers around the world through its innovative hardware, software, and Internet offerings.[c]

[a]http://www.ibm.com/investor/company/
[b]http://www.dell.com/content/topics/global.aspx/corp/investor/en/faqs?c=us&l=en&s=corp#faq8
[c]http://www.corporate-ir.net/ireye/ir_site.zhtml?ticker=aapl&script=1800&layout=7#corpinf

FIGURE 1.2 Mission statements of computer companies.

and performance targets can help ensure that a firm is accomplishing its mission. And then the firm needs to decide on a business strategy to meet its objectives and performance targets.

A **business strategy** is a plan articulating where a business seeks to go and how it expects to get there. It is the means by which a business communicates its goals. Management constructs this plan in response to market forces, customer demands, and organizational capabilities. Market forces create the competitive situation for the business. Some markets, such as those faced by airlines, makers of personal computers, and issuers of credit cards, are characterized by many competitors and a high level of competition such that product differentiation becomes increasingly difficult. Other markets, such as those for package delivery and automobiles, are similarly characterized by high competition, but product differentiation is better established. Customer demands comprise the wants and needs of the individuals and companies who purchase the products and services available in the marketplace. Organizational capabilities include the skills and experience that give the corporation a currency that can add value in the marketplace.

Until recently Dell's business strategy was to sell personal computers directly to the customer without going through a middleman. Reaching customers in this way is less expensive and time consuming than selling the computers in retail stores. The Internet, combined with Dell's well-designed IS infrastructure, allows customers to electronically contact Dell, who then designs a PC for a customer's specific needs. Dell's ordering system is integrated with its production system and shares information automatically with each supplier of PC components. This IS enables the assembly of the most current computers without the expense of storing large inventories. Cost savings are passed on to the customer, and the direct-to-customer model allows Dell to focus its production capacity on building only the most current products. With small profit margins and new products arriving quickly to replace existing products, this creative use of IS is aligned with Dell's business strategy. This strategic use of IS ultimately results in cost savings, reflected in the price of systems. In addition, Dell executives achieve a strategic advantage in reducing response time, building custom computers for one of the industry's lowest costs, and eliminating inventories that could become obsolete before they are sold. Thus, this business strategy is consistent with Dell's mission of delivering the best customer experience in the markets it serves.

But things aren't always as they seem. If the direct-to-customer strategy is so effective, why is Dell now also selling its computers at major retail outlets such as Wal-Mart and Best Buy? It is likely that the sales figures and profit margins were not measuring up to Dell's stated objectives and performance targets. Consequently, Dell adjusted its business strategy.

Several well-accepted models frame the discussions of business strategy. We review (1) the Porter generic strategies framework and two variants of its differentiation, and (2) D'Aveni's hypercompetition model.[4] The end of this section introduces key questions a general manager must answer to understand the strategy of the business.

The Generic Strategies Framework

Companies sell their products and services in a marketplace populated with competitors. Michael Porter's framework helps managers understand the strategies they may choose to build a competitive advantage. In his book *Competitive Advantage*, Porter claims that the "fundamental basis of above-average performance in the long run is sustainable competitive advantage."[5] Porter identified three primary strategies for achieving competitive advantage: (1) cost leadership, (2) differentiation, and (3) focus. These advantages derive from the company's relative position in the marketplace, and they depend on the strategies and tactics used by competitors. Figure 1.3 summarizes these three strategies for achieving competitive advantage.

Cost leadership results when the organization aims to be the lowest-cost producer in the marketplace. The organization enjoys above-average performance by minimizing costs. The product or service offered must be comparable in quality to those offered by others in the industry so that customers perceive its relative value. Typically, only one cost leader exists within an industry. If more than one organization seeks an advantage with this strategy, a price war ensues, which eventually may drive the organization with the higher cost structure out of the marketplace.

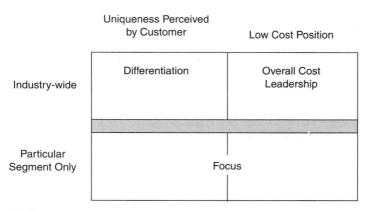

FIGURE 1.3   Three strategies for achieving competitive advantage.
Source: M. Porter, *Competitive Strategies* (New York: Free Press, 1998).

---

[4] Another popular model by Michael Porter, the value chain, provides a useful model for discussing internal operations of an organization. Some find it a useful model for understanding how to link two firms together. This framework is used in Chapter 3 to examine business process design. For further information, see Michael E. Porter, *Competitive Advantage* (New York: Free Press, 1985).

[5] Michael E. Porter, *Competitive Advantage* (New York: Free Press, 1985).

Through mass distribution, economies of scale, and IS to generate operating efficiencies, Wal-Mart epitomizes the cost-leadership strategy.

Through **differentiation**, the organization qualifies its product or service in a way that allows it to appear unique in the marketplace. The organization identifies which qualitative dimensions are most important to its customers and then finds ways to add value along one or more of those dimensions. For this strategy to work, the price charged customers by the differentiator must seem fair relative to the price charged by competitors. Typically, multiple firms in any given market employ this strategy. Progressive Insurance is able to differentiate itself from other automobile insurance companies by breaking out of the industry mold. Its representatives are available 24/7 (i.e., 24 hours a day, 7 days a week) to respond to accident claims. They arrive at an accident scene shortly after the accident with powerful laptops, intelligent software, and the authority to settle claims on the spot. This strategy spurred Progressive's growth and widened its profit margins.

Focus allows an organization to limit its scope to a narrower segment of the market and tailor its offerings to that group of customers. This strategy has two variants: (1) *cost focus*, in which the organization seeks a cost advantage within its segment, and (2) *differentiation focus*, in which it seeks to distinguish its products or services within the segment. This strategy allows the organization to achieve a local competitive advantage, even if it does not achieve competitive advantage in the marketplace overall. As Porter explained,

> The focuser can thus achieve competitive advantage by dedicating itself to the segments exclusively. Breadth of target is clearly a matter of degree, but the essence of focus is the exploitation of a narrow target's differences from the balance of the industry. Narrow focus in and of itself is not sufficient for above-average performance.[6]

Marriott International demonstrates focus in the business and related IS strategies of two of its hotel chains. To better serve its business travelers and cut operational expenses, Marriott properties have check-in kiosks that interface with their Marriott Rewards loyalty program. A guest can swipe a credit card or Marriott Rewards card at the kiosk in the lobby and receive a room assignment and keycard from the machine. She can also print airline boarding passes at the kiosks. Further, the kiosks help the Marriott chain implement its cost focus. The kiosk system is integrated with other systems such as billing and customer relationship management (CRM) to generate operating efficiencies and enhanced corporate standardization.

In contrast, kiosks in the lobby would destroy the feeling that the Ritz-Carlton chain, acquired by Marriott in 1995, is trying to create. To the Ritz-Carlton chain, CRM means capturing and using information about guests, such as their preference for wines, a hometown newspaper, or a sunny room. Each Ritz-Carlton employee is expected to promote personalized service by identifying and recording

---

[6] Michael E. Porter, *Competitive Strategies* (New York: Free Press, 1998).

individual guest preferences. To demonstrate how this rule could be implemented, a waiter, after hearing a guest exclaim that she loves tulips, could log the guest's comments into the Ritz-Carlton CRM system called "Class." On her next visit to a Ritz-Carlton hotel, tulips could be placed in the guest's room after querying Class to learn more about her as her visit approaches. Class, the CRM, is instrumental in implementing the differentiation-focus strategy of the Ritz-Carlton chain.[7] And its strategy allows the Ritz-Carlton chain to live up to its very unique motto (mission): "We are ladies and gentlemen serving ladies and gentlemen."[8] JetBlue appears to have adopted a cost focus strategy. At just over six cents per passenger seat mile, JetBlue has the lowest cost in the airline industry. Even though it is the lowest in the entire industry, it could be argued that JetBlue has far fewer destinations than many of its competitors. These larger competitors are saddled with higher pay scales from having been in the business longer and higher maintenance costs for their fleets of older planes that they needed to acquire to sustain their growth. Should its plans for growth be fully realized, while maintaining its low cost structure, JetBlue could move from its cost focus based on serving a limited, but growing, number of market segments to a cost leadership strategy.[9]

While sustaining a cost focus, JetBlue's chairman believes that JetBlue can compete on more than price. That is why the airline continually strives to keep customers satisfied with frills such as extra leg room, leather seats, prompt baggage delivery, DirectTV, and movies. It has been recognized with many awards for customer satisfaction in the North American airlines industry. Thus, it could be argued that JetBlue also has used a differentiation focus.

Variants on the Differentiation Strategy

Porter's generic strategies are fundamental to an understanding of how organizations create competitive advantage. Several variations of his differentiation strategy, including the shareholder value model and the unlimited resources model, are useful for further analyzing sources of advantage. D'Aveni also described these "arenas of competition" as the timing and know-how advantage and the deep pockets advantage.

The **shareholder value model** holds that the timing of the use of specialized knowledge can create a differentiation advantage as long as the knowledge remains unique.[10] This model suggests that customers buy products or services from an organization to have access to its unique knowledge. The advantage is static, rather than dynamic, because the purchase is a one-time event.

---

[7] Scott Berinato, "Room for Two," CIO.com, May 15, 2002, http://www.cio.com/archive/051502/two_content.html.

[8] http://corporate.ritzcarlton.com/en/About/GoldStandards.htm (accessed February 13, 2008).

[9] Chuck Salter, "And Now the Hard Part," *Fast* Company.com, December 19, 2007, http:www. fastcompany.com/node/48871/print (accessed February 13, 2008).

[10] William E. Fruhan, Jr., "The NPV Model of Strategy—The Shareholder Value Model," in *Financial Strategy: Studies in the Creation, Transfer, and Destruction of Shareholder Value* (Homewood, IL: Richard D. Irwin, 1979).

The **unlimited resources model** utilizes a large base of resources that allows an organization to outlast competitors by practicing a differentiation strategy. An organization with greater resources can manage risk and sustain losses more easily than one with fewer resources. This deep-pocket strategy provides a short-term advantage only. If a firm lacks the capacity for continual innovation, it will not sustain its competitive position over time.

Porter's generic strategies model and its variants are useful for diagnostics, or understanding how a business seeks to profit in its chosen marketplace, and for prescriptions, or building new opportunities for advantage. They reflect a careful balancing of countervailing competitive forces posed by buyers, suppliers, competitors, new entrants, and substitute products and services within an industry. As is the case with many models, they offer managers useful tools for thinking about strategy. However, the Porter models were developed at a time when competitive advantage was sustainable because the rate of change in any given industry was relatively slow and manageable. Since the late 1980s when this framework was at the height of its popularity, several newer models were developed to take into account the increasing turbulence and velocity of the marketplace. In particular, the hypercompetition model offers managers an especially useful tool for conceptualizing their organization's strategy in turbulent environments.

Hypercompetition Framework

Discussions of hypercompetition[11] take a perspective different from the previous models. Those models focus on creating and sustaining competitive advantage, whereas **hypercompetition** models suggest that the speed and aggressiveness of the moves and countermoves in any given market create an environment in which advantages are "rapidly created and eroded."[12] Firms seek to achieve this relatively transitory competitive advantage under hypercompetition in four ways: (1) cost/quality, (2) timing/know-how, (3) strongholds, and (4) deep pockets. The hypercompetition framework is based on the following assumptions:

- Every advantage is eroded. Advantages only last until competitors have duplicated or outmaneuvered them. Once an advantage is no longer an advantage, it becomes a cost of doing business.

- Sustaining an advantage can be a deadly distraction. Some companies can extend their advantages and continue to enjoy the benefits, but sustaining an advantage can take attention away from developing new ones.

- The goal of advantage should be disruption, not sustainability. A company seeks to stay one step ahead through a series of temporary advantages that erode competitors' positions, rather than by creating a sustainable position in the marketplace.

[11] R. D'Aveni, *Hypercompetition: Managing the Dynamics of Strategic Maneuvering* (New York: Free Press, 1994).
[12] Ibid.

- Initiatives are achieved with a series of small steps. Competitive cycles are shorter now, and new advantages must be achieved quickly. Companies focus on creating the next advantage before the benefits of the current advantage erode.

D'Aveni's framework suggests seven approaches an organization can take in its business strategy. Figure 1.4 summarizes this framework. Companies can use these approaches to disrupt competition, depending on their particular capabilities to seize initiative and pursue tactics that can create a series of temporary advantages. For the purposes of this book, we briefly summarize D'Aveni's 7 Ss[13] in Figure 1.5.

JetBlue has clearly implemented some of the 7 Ss. It particularly employed the *superior stakeholder satisfaction* when it installed DirectTV on its planes, provided almonds as a low-carbohydrate snack in response to passenger requests, and

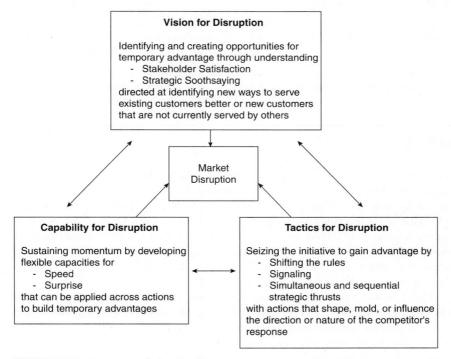

FIGURE 1.4 Disruption and the new 7 Ss.
Source: R. D'Aveni, *Hypercompetition: Managing the Dynamics of Strategic Maneuvering* (New York: Free Press, 1994).

[13] The "old" 7 Ss of competitive advantage—structure, strategy, systems, style, skills, staff, and superordinate goals—entered business literature in a paper by R. Waterman, T. Peters, and J. Phillips, "Structure Is Not Organization," *Business Horizons* (June 1980). D'Aveni used these as a point of reference in deriving his "new" 7 Ss under hypercompetition.

Approach	Definition
Superior stakeholder satisfaction	Understanding how to maximize customer satisfaction by adding value strategically
Strategic soothsaying	Seeking out new knowledge that can predict or create new windows of opportunity
Positioning for speed	Preparing the organization to react as quickly as possible
Positioning for surprise	Preparing the organization to respond to the marketplace in a manner that will surprise competitors
Shifting the rules of competition	Finding new ways to serve customers which transform the industry
Signaling strategic intent	Communicating the intended actions of a company, in order to stall responses by competitors
Simultaneous and sequential strategic thrusts	Taking a series of steps designed to stun and confuse competitors in order to disrupt or block their efforts

FIGURE 1.5   D'Aveni's new 7 Ss.

enacted a policy that the last bag from a flight would be placed on the conveyor belt no later than 20 minutes after the plane arrived at the gate. To *position for speed* and to accommodate its sizable growth plans, JetBlue places on the corporate intranet a checklist of each activity, with deadlines as needed, when JetBlue enters a new market. Another way JetBlue positions itself for speed is its "Operational Recovery System," described earlier as a way to respond quickly to problems. It *shifted the rules of competition* when it issued its Customer Bill of Rights, which clearly defines when customers will receive coupons and vouchers in the event of delays.[14]

The 7 Ss are a useful framework for identifying different aspects of a business strategy and aligning them to make the organization competitive in the hypercompetitive arena of business in the new millennium. This framework helps assess competitors' strengths and weaknesses, as well as build a road map for the company's strategy itself. Using this framework, managers can identify new organizational responses to their competition, as well as new opportunities that extend their current strengths. This framework is particularly useful in markets in which the rate of change makes sustaining a business strategy difficult. It suggests that a business strategy must be continuously redefined to be successful.

---

[14] Salter, "And Now the Hard Part."

Since the 1990s a competitive dynamic has emerged in the marketplace that is characterized by wider gaps between industry leaders and laggards, more concentrated "winner-take-all" environments, and greater churn among sector rivals. This pattern of turbulent "creative destruction" was first predicted over 60 years ago by the economist Joseph Schumpeter. Coincidentally (or maybe not), the accelerated competition has occurred concomitantly with sharp increases in the quality and quantity of information technology (IT) investment. The changes in competitive dynamics are particularly striking in sectors that spend the most on IT.[15]

An application of the hypercompetition model is the destroy your business (DYB) (i.e., "creative destruction") approach to strategic planning that was implemented by Jack Welch at General Electric (GE). Welch recognized that GE could only sustain its competitive advantage for a limited time as competitors attempted to outmaneuver GE. He knew that if GE didn't identify its weaknesses, its competitors would relish doing so. DYB is an approach that places GE employees in the shoes of their competitors.[16] Through the DYB lenses, GE employees develop strategies to destroy GE's competitive advantage. Then, in light of their revelations, they apply the grow your business (GYB) strategy to find fresh ways to reach new customers and better serve existing ones. The goal of the DYB planning approach is the complete disruption of current practices, so that GE can take actions to protect its business before competitors hone in on its weaknesses. The implicit assumption underlying DYB is that GE would not be able to sustain its position in the marketplace over the long term.

Why Are Strategic Advantage Models Essential to Planning for Information Systems?

A general manager who relies solely on IS personnel to make IS decisions may not only give up any authority over IS strategy, but also may hamper crucial future business decisions. In fact, business strategy should drive IS decision making, and changes in business strategy should entail reassessments of IS. Moreover, changes in IS potential should trigger reassessments of business strategy—as in the case of the Internet, where companies that failed to understand or consider its implications for the marketplace were quickly outpaced by competitors who had. For the purposes of our model, the Information Systems Strategy Triangle, understanding business strategy means answering the following questions:

1. What is the business goal or objective?
2. What is the plan for achieving it? What is the role of IS in this plan?
3. Who are the crucial competitors and partners, and what is required of a successful player in this value net?

---

[15] Andrew McAfee and Erik Brynjolfsson "Investing in the IT That Makes a Competitive Difference," *Harvard Business Review* (July 2008), http://harvardbusinessonline.hbsp.harvard.edu (accessed July 27, 2008).

[16] M. Levinson, "Destructive Behavior," *CIO Magazine*, July 15, 2000, http://www.cio.com/archive/071500_destructive_content.html.

Framework	Key Idea	Application to Information Systems
Porter's Generic Strategies Framework	Firms achieve competitive advantage through cost leadership, differentiation, or focus	Understanding which strategy is chosen by a firm is critical to choosing IS to complement the strategy
D'Aveni's Hypercompetition Model	Speed and aggressive moves and countermoves by a firm create competitive advantage	The 7 Ss give the manager suggestions on what moves and countermoves to make. IS are critical to achieving the speed needed for moves and countermoves. IS are in a constant state of flux or development.

FIGURE 1.6   Summary of key strategy frameworks.

Porter's generic strategies and D'Aveni's hypercompetition framework (summarized in Figure 1.6) are revisited in the next few chapters. They are especially helpful in discussing the role of IS in building and sustaining competitive advantages (Chapter 2) and for incorporating IS into business strategy. The next section of this chapter establishes a foundation for understanding organizational strategies.

▶ BRIEF OVERVIEW OF ORGANIZATIONAL STRATEGIES

Organizational strategy includes the organization's design as well as the choices it makes to define, set up, coordinate, and control its work processes. The organizational strategy is a plan that answers the question: "How will the company organize to achieve its goals and implement its business strategy?" A few of the many models of organizational strategy are reviewed in this section.

A simple framework for understanding the design of an organization is the business diamond, introduced by Leavitt and embellished by Hammer and Champy.[17] Shown in Figure 1.7, the **business diamond** identifies the crucial components of an organization's plan as its business processes, its values and beliefs, its management control systems, and its tasks and structures. This simple framework is useful for designing new organizations and for diagnosing organizational troubles. For example, organizations that try to change their cultures but fail to change the way they manage and control cannot be effective.

JetBlue can be used to demonstrate the Business Diamond. *Processes* are obviously are very important at JetBlue. Every morning CEO Barger reviews details about the previous day's flights with the operations team, and each *process* is carefully inspected to see if it can be made more efficient. Based on a list of "focus flights" the operations teams also deconstruct the ten worst delays to find ways to improve problematic processes. *Values and beliefs* are also very important

[17] M. Hammer and J. Champy, *Reengineering the Corporation* (New York: HarperBusiness, 1994).

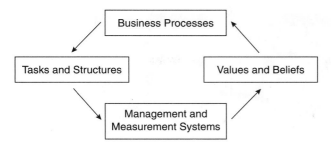

FIGURE 1.7   The business diamond.
Source: M. Hammer and J. Champy, *Reengineering the Corporation* (New York: Harper Business, 1994).

to JetBlue's senior executives, who are actively attempting to infuse the values and beliefs throughout the organization. In particular, Chairman Neeleman uses a visible, "one-on-one" leadership style that allows him to interact freely with the employees. The company is guided by five primary principles: "Treat your people right," "Communicate with your team," "Inspire greatness in others," "Encourage initiative and innovation," and "Do the right thing." When it looked as if growth was negatively affecting the company's *management*, a new training program, Principles of Leadership (POL), was initiated to teach the five primary principles to managers at every level. Another part of the *measurement and management system* is a detailed set of metrics for a variety of operations. For example, the time it takes to deliver bags to the passengers is measured with a goal of delivering them no later than 20 minutes after the plane has reached the gate. Finally, *tasks* are defined such that everyone pitches in and helps. When a plane lands, every employee on the plane from the stewardess, to the pilot, to staff who are deadheading, to the chairman, will pitch in to clean the plane and get it ready for the next set of passengers. Pilots are also expected to participate in the business.[18]

A complementing framework to the business diamond for organizational design can be found in the book by Cash, Eccles, Nohria, and Nolan, *Building the Information Age Organization*.[19] This framework, shown in Figure 1.8, suggests that the successful execution of a business's organizational strategy comprises the best combination of organizational, control, and cultural variables. Organizational variables include decision rights, business processes, formal reporting relationships, and informal networks. Control variables include the availability of data, the nature and quality of planning, and the effectiveness of performance measurement and evaluation systems, and incentives to do good work. Cultural variables comprise the values of the organization. These organizational, control, and cultural variables

[18] Salter, "And Now the Hard Part."

[19] James I. Cash, Robert G. Eccles, Nitin Nohria, and Richard L. Nolan, *Building the Information Age Organization* (Homewood, IL: Richard D. Irwin, 1994).

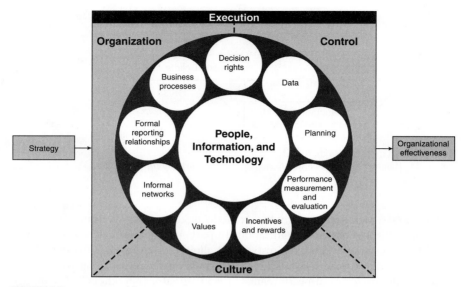

FIGURE 1.8　Managerial levers.
Source: Cash, Eccles, Nohria, and Nolan, *Building the Information Age Organization* (Homewood, IL: Richard D. Irwin, 1994).

are **managerial levers** used by decision makers to effect changes in their organizations. These managerial levers are discussed in detail in Chapter 3.

Our objective is to give the manager a set of frameworks to use in evaluating various aspects of organizational design. Using these frameworks, the manager can review the current organization and assess which components may be missing and what options are available looking forward. Understanding organizational strategy means answering the following questions:

1. What are the important structures and reporting relationships within the organization?
2. Who holds the decision rights to critical decisions?
3. What are the characteristics, experiences, and skill levels of the people within the organization?
4. What are the key business processes?
5. What control systems are in place?
6. What is the culture of the organization?

The answers to these questions inform any assessment of the organization's use of IS. Chapters 3, 4, and 5 use the organizational strategy frameworks, summarized in Figure 1.9, to assess the impact of management information systems (MIS) on the firm. Chapter 8 and 9 look at answers from the first two questions to understand the MIS governance and its impact on ethics.

Framework	Key Idea	Usefulness in IS Discussions
Business diamond	There are 4 key components to an organization: business processes, values and beliefs, management control systems, and tasks and structures.	Using IS in an organization will affect each of these components. Use this framework to identify where these impacts are likely to occur.
Managerial levers	Organizational variables, control variables, and cultural variables are the levers managers can use to affect change in their organization.	This is a more detailed model than the Business diamond and gives specific areas where IS can be used to manage the organization and to change the organization.

FIGURE 1.9   Summary of organizational strategy frameworks.

► BRIEF OVERVIEW OF INFORMATION SYSTEMS STRATEGY

IS strategy is the plan an organization uses to provide information services. IS allow a company to implement its business strategy. JetBlue's vice president for people explains it nicely: "We define what the business needs and then go find the technology to support that."[20]

Business strategy is a function of competition (What does the customer want and what does the competition do?), positioning (In what way does the firm want to compete?), and capabilities (What can the firm do?). IS help determine the company's capabilities. An entire chapter is devoted to IT architecture, but for now a more basic framework will be used to understand the decisions related to IS that an organization must make.

The purpose of the matrix in Figure 1.10 is to give the manager a high-level view of the relation between the four IS infrastructure components and the other resource considerations that are key to IS strategy. Infrastructure includes hardware, such as desktop units and servers. It also includes software, such as the programs used to do business, to manage the computer itself, and to communicate between systems. The third component of IS infrastructure is the network, which is the physical means by which information is exchanged among hardware components, such as through a modem and dial-up network (in which case, the service is actually provided by a vendor such as AT&T), or through a private digital network (in which case the service is probably provided by an internal unit). Finally, the fourth part of the infrastructure is the data. The data includes the bits and bytes stored in the system. In current systems, data are not necessarily stored alongside

---

[20] Hogue et al., Winning the 3-Legged Race, 111.

	What	Who	Where
Hardware	List of physical components of the system	System users and managers	Physical location
Software	List of programs, applications, and utilities	System users and managers	What hardware it resides on and physical location of hardware
Networking	Diagram of how hardware and software components are connected	Systems users and managers; company that provides the service	Where the nodes are located, and where the wires and other transport media are located
Data	Bits of information stored in the system	Owners of data; data administrators	Where the information resides

FIGURE 1.10   Information systems strategy matrix.

the programs that use them; hence, it is important to understand what data are in the system and where they are stored. Many more detailed models of IS infrastructure exist, and interested readers may refer to any of the dozens of books that describe them. For the purposes of this text, the matrix will provide sufficient information to allow the general manager to assess the critical issues in information management.

▶ FOOD FOR THOUGHT: THE HALO EFFECT AND OTHER BUSINESS DELUSIONS

When Dell was flying high in February 2005 and ranked number one among *Fortune* magazine's list of the Most Admired Companies, everyone claimed it was due to their excellent management and strategy. There are even a few such examples in this chapter. However, two years later, when Dell's performance slumped, critics were quick to blame it on a variety of poor management practices: complacency, pride in making acquisitions, being "stuck in a rut," and poor leadership. How could Dell have gone from excellent performance to such problematic performance so quickly?[21]

Phil Rosenzweig suggested that the Dell case illustrates a common error of distortion that many make when evaluating company performance. The error is

---

[21] Phil Rosenzweig, "Misunderstanding the Nature of Company Performance: The Halo Effect and Other Business Delusions," *California Management Review* 49, no. 4, Summer 2007, 6–20.

based on "halo effect," which is "the basic human tendency to make specific inferences on the basis of a general impression"[22] (Rosenzweig, page 7) When Dell was successful, many marveled at its strategy and leadership skills. When it stumbled, things were seen in a negative light. Although the halo effect may seem harmless, it undermines an understanding of the forces that make a company either successful or unsuccessful. Rosenzweig claimed that the error was especially problematic in three popular business books: *In Search of Excellence, Built to Last,* and *Good to Great* because these books have diverted attention from an accurate understanding about successful company performance.

Rosensweig described three misconceptions that are created by the halo effect in general and these three books most specifically.

1. *There exists a formula or blueprint that companies can apply and become high performers.* In fact, many of the causal relationships that were reported were unfounded. Further, business performance is inherently relative, not absolute. For example, Kmart's performance declined steeply in the 1990s, and it declared bankruptcy in 2002. Yet, on several objective measures such as inventory management, procurement, logistics, and automated reordering, it actually improved during this time period. The problem for Kmart was that Wal-Mart and Target improved even more rapidly.

2. *Firm performance is driven entirely by internal factors.* Rosenzweig argued that although strategic choice is important, it is also important to consider what the competition is doing.

3. *Because a decision may turn out badly does not necessarily mean that it was poorly made.* There is much uncertainty in strategic decisions. Decision makers must make decisions under risk—and sometimes things don't always work out well.

Rosenzweig concluded with cautionary notes: Journalists should be more circumspect in what they write; Managers should be skeptical of formulas, recognize that performance is relative, think of business decisions in terms of probabilities, and carefully evaluate decision-making processes and not just their outcomes.

In relating his analysis to Dell, Rosenzweig noted that between 2005 and 2007, Dell was neither complacent nor "stuck in a rut." Rather, it looked for new avenues of growth and sought to leverage its capabilities in other products. Its decline was not absolute, but rather relative. During that same time period, its rival, Hewlett Packard (HP), hired an effective new CEO, and Lenovo became a strong competitor. Rosenzweig suggested that HP and Lenovo's performance was the direct result of Dell's previous excellence. That doesn't mean that Dell can't perform well in the future. It depends on its strategy. That strategy is based on choice, and choice is based on risk.

[22] Ibid., 7.

► SUMMARY

The Information Systems Strategy Triangle represents a simple framework for understanding the impact of IS on businesses. It relates business strategy with IS strategy and organizational strategy and implies the balance that must be maintained in business planning. The Information Systems Strategy Triangle suggests the following management principles.

Business Strategy

Business strategy drives organizational strategy and IS strategy. The organization and its IS should clearly support defined business goals and objectives.

- Definition: A well-articulated vision of where a business seeks to go and how it expects to get there
- Models: Porter's generic strategies model; D'Aveni's hypercompetition model

Organizational Strategy

Organizational strategy must complement business strategy. The way a business is organized either supports the implementation of its business strategy or it gets in the way.

- Definition: The organization's design, as well as the choices it makes to define, set up, coordinate, and control its work processes
- Models: Business diamond; managerial levers

IS Strategy

IS strategy must complement business strategy. When IS support business goals, the business appears to be working well. IS strategy can itself affect and is affected by changes in a firm's business and organizational strategies. Moreover, information systems strategy always has consequences—intended or not—on business and organizational strategies.

- Definition: The plan the organization uses in providing information systems and services
- Models: A basic framework for understanding IS decisions relating architecture (the "what") and the other resource considerations ("who" and "where") that represent important planning constraints

Strategic Relationships

Organizational strategy and information strategy must complement each other. They must be designed so that they support, rather than hinder each other. If a decision is made to change one corner of the triangle, it is necessary to evaluate the other two corners to ensure that balance is preserved. Changing business strategy without thinking through the effects on the organizational and IS strategies will cause the business to struggle until balance is restored. Likewise, changing IS or the organization alone will cause an imbalance.

▶ KEY TERMS

business diamond (p. 34)
business strategy (p. 26)
cost leadership (p. 27)
differentiation (p. 28)
focus (p. 28)
hypercompetition (p. 30)
IS strategy (p. 37)

Information Systems
    Strategy Triangle (p. 23)
managerial levers (p. 36)
mission (p. 25)
organizational strategy
    (p. 34)

shareholder value model
    (p. 29)
strategy (p. 25)
unlimited resources
    model (p. 30)

▶ DISCUSSION QUESTIONS

1. Why is it important for business strategy to drive organizational strategy and IS strategy? What might happen if business strategy was not the driver?

2. Suppose managers in an organization decided to hand out laptop computers to all salespeople without making any other formal changes in organizational strategy or business strategy. What might be the outcome? What unintended consequences might occur?

3. Consider a traditional manufacturing company that wanted to take advantage of the Internet and Web 2.0 tools. What might be a reasonable business strategy, and how would organizational and IS strategy need to change?

4. This chapter describes key components of an IS strategy. Describe the IS strategy of a consulting firm using the matrix framework.

5. What does this tip from *Fast Company* mean: "The job of the CIO is to provide organizational and strategic flexibility"?[23]

CASE STUDY 1-1

ROCHE'S NEW SCIENTIFIC METHOD

For years, the Swiss pharmaceutical giant Roche Group worked hard to create an ultra-competitive culture that pitted scientific teams against one another in fighting for scarce resources. Roche had believed that this culture was instrumental in creating such blockbuster drugs as Valium and Librium. But, on the downside, this approach made it almost impossible for scientists to abandon faltering projects that they felt were pivotal for their careers. Rather, it led them to hoard their technical expertise and findings. In 1998, the company turned to a more collaborative style of teamwork—especially for its teams working in the new field of genomics. Roche began running ads in *Science* magazine for a young new breed of researchers who could reinvent themselves as their job opportunities rapidly changed.

It was the new breakthroughs in genomics and molecular biology that pushed Roche to change the way it hunted for drugs. Roche knew it had to speed up the discovery process

[23] "20 Technology Briefs: What's New? What's Next? What Matters," *Fast Company*, March 2002, http://www.fastcompany.com/online/56/fasttalk.html.

for new drugs and size up toxicity risks earlier than ever. Projects needed to be managed in a totally different way.

Roche can now churn out *1 million* genomics experiments a day. Whereas research teams once spent years looking for a single good idea, they now must consider hundreds or even thousands of candidates daily. The data that is generated is overwhelming not only for the researchers, but also for Roche's large infrastructure of computers.

Despite the daunting task, the potential is too great for Roche to ignore. At a recent media briefing, Roche Group chairman and CEO Franz Humer declared, "Look at this revolution of genetics, genomics, and proteomics. It's becoming ever clearer that we will be able to identify early the predisposition of people to disease—and to monitor and treat them more effectively. We'll develop markers for cancer. That will lead to better test kits and to new pharmaceuticals."

Thus, Roche's U.S. pharmaceuticals headquarters is making adjustments to deal with having 'too much data, too fast.' Roche's management has recognized that it needs to rethink the best ways to build teams, hire people, and create a culture where failure is all right, as long as it is fast. Roche has had to embrace an organizational revolution to accommodate the technological revolution.

Learning to Swim in a Deluge of Data

At the heart of the genomics explosion is the GeneChip. This carefully mounted piece of darkened glass, about the size of a thumbnail, can contain up to 12,000 tiny marks. Each mark represents a human gene—one amino acid at a time. When specific genes are activated in an experiment, they light up against the chip's dark background. The genes that light up might be markers for disease. The GeneChip is a true innovation that must be used effectively throughout Roche.

For example, computer capacity must be used effectively. Each sample run on a GeneChip set generates 60 million bytes of raw data. Basic analysis on each GeneChip set adds 180 million bytes of computer storage for each set. Given that Roche ran 1,000 GeneChip experiments in both 1999 and 2000, it is not hard to believe that the storage requirements were mind-boggling. "Every six months, the IT guys would come to us and say, 'You've used up all of your storage,'" states Jiayi Ding, a Roche scientist. In early 1999, Roche's computer-services experts at Nutley were already concerned that ten researchers working on GeneChip experiments (out of the 300 employees at the site) were hogging 90% of the company's total computer capacity.

Fail Fast, So You Can Succeed Sooner

One of the biggest challenges in drug research—or in any field—is to let go of ideas that are no longer promising and to move on to brighter prospects that aren't being given enough attention. When new hire Lee Babiss arrived from archrival Glaxo to head preclinical research, he preached a simple message: Fail fast. He knew that the best hope of finding the right new drugs was to spend less time on dead-ends.

Screening was needed to sift though the massive number of drugs to find the few promising drugs that offered the greatest likelihood of success. To solve its screening bottleneck, Roche installed an ultra-high-throughput machine made by Carl Zeiss at a cost of more than $1 million. "We can test 100,000 compounds a day," says Larnie Myer, the technical robotics expert who runs and maintains the screening machine. Though most of those compounds don't work out, identifying just a few "hits" within several weeks of testing can speed up Roche's overall efforts. The Zeiss machine ultimately has led to changes in the entire research process.

Change Everything—One Piece at a Time

Genomics could dramatically change things at Roche: In Palo Alto, researcher Gary Peltz built a computerized model of the mouse genome that allows him to simulate classical lab studies in a matter of minutes. In Iceland, Roche teamed up with Decode, a company which researches Icelandic genealogical records. Decode used the data it had collected to identify and locate genes that are associated with stroke and schizophrenia. In Nutley, genomic data is being used to size up a drug's side effects before embarking on lengthy animal experiments.

Each of these initiatives runs on a different timeline. Some parts of Roche will see dramatic business changes in a year or two, while others will not see changes for much longer "This isn't just a matter of turning on a light switch," says Klaus Lindpaintner, Roche's global head of genetics research.

Discussion Questions

1. How does the business strategy affect information systems and organizational decisions?
2. What generic strategy does Roche appear to be using based on this case? Provide a rationale for your response.
3. Apply the hypercompetition model to Roche. Which of the 7 Ss are demonstrated in this case?
4. How do information systems support Roche's business strategy?

Source: Excerpted from G. Anders, "Fresh Start 2002: Roche's New Scientific Method," *Fast Company* (January 2002), available at http://www.fastcompany.com/online/54/roche.html.

CASE STUDY 1-2

GOOGLE

Started in the late 1990s, Google grew rapidly to become one of the leading companies in the world. Google's mission is "to organize the world's information and make it universally accessible and useful." It is operating on a simple but innovative business model of attracting Internet users to its free search services and earning revenue from targeted advertising. In the winner-takes-all business of Internet search, Google has captured considerably more market share than its next highest rival, Yahoo!. This has turned Google's Web pages into the Web's most valuable real (virtual) estate. Through its two flagship programs, AdWords and AdSense, Google has capitalized on this leadership position to capture the lion's share in advertisement spending. AdWords enables businesses to place ads on Google and its network of publishing partners for as low as 25 cents per thousand impressions. On the other hand, it uses AdSense to push advertisements on publishing partners' Web sites targeting specific audience and share ad revenue with the publishing partner. This creates a win–win situation for both advertisers and publishers and developed Google into one giant sucking machine for ad revenue.

Even as a large company, Google continues to take risks and expand into new markets. It currently offers over 120 products or services. Sergey Brin and Larry Page, the founders, declared in Google's IPO prospectus, "We would fund projects that have a 10 percent chance of earning a billion dollars over the long term. Do not be surprised if we place smaller bets in areas that seem very speculative or even strange. As the ratio of reward to risk increases, we will accept projects further outside our normal areas, especially when the initial investment is small."

Google promotes a culture of creativity and innovation in a number of ways. IT encourages innovation in all employees by allowing them to spend 20 percent of their time on a project of their own choosing. In addition, it offers benefits such as free meals, on-site gym, on-site dentist, and even washing machines at the company for busy employees.

Despite open and free work culture, a rigid and procedure-filled structure is imposed for making timely decisions and executing plans. For example, when designing new features, the team and senior managers meet in a large conference room. They use the right side of the conference room walls to digitally project new features and the left side to project any transcribed critique with a timer clock giving everyone 10 minutes to lay out ideas and finalize features. Thus, Google utilizes rigorous, data-driven procedures for evaluating new ideas in the midst of a chaotic innovation process.

Google's vice president for search products and user experience, Marissa Mayer, outlines nine notions of innovations embedded in the organizational culture, processes, and structure of Google (from *BusinessWeek* article, "Champions of Innovation")

1. Ideas come from everywhere: Google expects everyone to innovate, even the finance team.

2. Share everything you can: Every idea, every project, every deadline—it's all accessible to everyone on the intranet.

3. You're brilliant, we're hiring: Founders Larry Page and Sergey Brin approve hires. They favor intelligence over experience.

4. A license to pursue dreams: Employees get a "free" day a week. Half of new launches come from this "20% time."

5. Innovation, not instant perfection: Google launches early and often in small beta tests, before releasing new features widely.

6. Don't politic, use data: Mayer discourages the use of "I like" in meetings, pushing staffers to use metrics

7. Creativity loves restraint: Give people a vision, rules about how to get there, and deadlines.

8. Worry about usage and users, not money: Provide something simple to use and easy to love. The money will follow.

9. Don't kill projects—morph them: There's always a kernel of something good that can be salvaged.

Keeping up with the organizational strategy of Google, its IT department provides free and open access to IT for all employees. Rather than keeping tight control, Google allows employees to choose from several options for computer and operating systems, download software themselves, and maintain official and unofficial blog sites. Google's intranet provides employees information about every piece of work at any part of Google. In this way employees can find and join hands with others working on similar technologies or features.

In building the necessary IT infrastructure, Google's IT department balances buying and making its own software depending on its needs and off-the-shelf availability. For example, it uses Oracle's accounting software, whereas it built its own customer relationship management (CRM) software, which it then integrated with its ad systems. It also supports open source projects both by extensively using open source software within the organization and by paying college students to contribute to them through programs like Summer of Code. In addition, Google also develops generic applications such as GoogleApps for both internal and external use.

Given the nature of business, security of information resources is critical for Google. For instance, its master search algorithm is considered a more valuable secret formula than Coca-Cola's. However, rather than improving IT security by stifling freedom through preventive policy controls, Google puts security in the infrastructure and focuses more on detective and corrective controls. Its network management software tools combined with 150 security engineers constantly look for viruses and spyware, as well as strange network traffic patterns associated with intrusion.

Discussion Questions

1. How is Google's mission statement related to its business strategy?
2. How does Google's information systems strategy support its business strategy?
3. How does Google's organizational strategy support its business strategy?
4. Which of Porter's three generic strategies does Google appear to be using based on this case? Provide a rationale for your response.
5. Using D'Aveni's Hypercompetitive Framework, analyze Google's strategy and the type of market disruption it has created.

Source: Excerpted from: *"Champions of Innovation"* by Michelle Colin, *Business Week*, June 19, 2006, Issue 3989, pp.18–26; and "Pleasing Google's Tech-Savvy Staff" by Vauhini Vara, *Wall Street Journal*, March 18, 2008, p.B6.

CHAPTER 2

STRATEGIC USE OF INFORMATION RESOURCES[1]

Zara is a Spanish manufacturer with a business model that provides them a significant strategic advantage in the highly competitive retail and apparel industry. At the heart of their model is a set of business processes and a simple, some might call outdated, information system that links demand to manufacturing and manufacturing to distribution. The strategy at Zara stores is simply to have a continuous flow of new products that are typically in limited supply. As a result, regular customers visit their stores often—on an average of 17 times a year, whereas most stores can only entice their customers inside on an average of four times a year. If customers see something they like, they buy it on the spot because they know it will probably be gone the next time they visit the store. The result is a very loyal and satisfied customer base and a wildly profitable business model.

How can this be? It is in part made possible because Zara aligns its information system strategy with its business strategy. The entire process from factory to shop floor is coordinated from Zara's headquarters using information systems. The point-of-sale system records the information from each sale, and the information is transmitted to headquarters at the end of each business day. The Zara shop managers also report back daily to the designers at headquarters to let them know what has sold and what the customers wanted but couldn't find. The information is used to determine which product lines and colors should be kept and which should be altered or dropped. The designers communicate directly with the production staff to plan for the incredible number of designs—more than 11,000—that will be manufactured every year.

The shop managers have the option of ordering new designs twice a week using handheld computers. Before ordering, they can use their handheld computers to check out the new designs. Once an order is received at the manufacturing plant at headquarters, a large computer-controlled piece of equipment calculates how

---

[1] The authors wish to acknowledge and thank W. Thomas Cannon, MBA 1999, for his help in researching and writing earlier drafts of this chapter.

to position patterns to minimize scrap and cut up to 100 layers of fabric at a time. The cut fabric is then sent from Zara factories to external workshops for sewing. The completed products are sent to distribution centers, where miles of automated conveyor belts are used to sort the garments and recombine them into shipments for each store. Zara's information technology (IT) department wrote the applications controlling the conveyors, often in collaboration with vendors of the conveyor equipment.

As the Zara example illustrates, innovative use of a firm's information resources can provide companies with substantial advantages over competitors. This chapter uses the business strategy foundation from Chapter 1 to help general managers visualize how to use information resources for competitive advantage. This chapter briefly recounts the evolving strategic use of information resources and highlights the difference between simply using information systems (IS) and using IS strategically. Then, this chapter explores the use of information resources to support the strategic goals of an organization.

The material in this chapter will enable a general manager to understand the link between business strategy and information strategy on the Information Systems Strategy Triangle. General managers want to find answers to questions: Does using information resources provide a sustainable competitive advantage? What tools are available to help shape their strategic use? What are the risks of using information resources to gain strategic advantage?

▶ EVOLUTION OF INFORMATION RESOURCES

The Eras model shows how organizations have used IS over the past decades. Figure 2.1 summarizes this view and provides a road map for a general manager to use in thinking strategically about the current use of information resources within the firm.

IS strategy from the 1960s to the 1990s was driven by internal organizational needs. First came the need to lower existing transaction costs. Next was the need to provide support for managers by collecting and distributing information. An additional need was to redesign business processes. As competitors built similar systems, organizations lost any advantages they held from their IS, and competition within a given industry once again was driven by forces that existed prior to the new technology.

As each era begins, organizations adopt a strategic role for IS to address not only the firm's internal circumstances but its external circumstances as well. Thus, in the ubiquitous era, companies seek those applications that again provide them with an advantage over competition. They also seek applications that keep them from being outgunned by start-ups with innovative business models or traditional companies entering new markets. For example, a plethora of "dot-coms" challenged all industries and traditional businesses by entering the marketplace armed with Internet-based innovative systems.

	Era I 1960s	Era II 1970s	Era III 1980s	Era IV 1990s	Era V 2000 +
Primary role of IT	Efficiency	Effectiveness	Strategic	Strategic	Value creation
	Automate existing paper-based processes	Solve problems and create opportunities	Increase individual and group effectiveness	Transform industry/ organization	Create collaborative partnerships
Justify IT expenditures	ROI	Increasing productivity and better decision quality	Competitive position	Competitive position	Adding value
Target of systems	Organization	Organization/ group	Individual manager/ group	Business processes ecosystem	Customer/ supplier ecosystem
Information models	Application specific	Data-driven	User-driven	Business-driven	Knowledge-driven
Dominate technology	Mainframe, "centralized intelligence"	Minicomputer, mostly "centra-lized intelligence"	Microcomputer, "decentralized intelligence"	Client Server, "distributed intelligence"	Internet, global "ubiquitous intelligence"
Basis of value	Scarcity	Scarcity	Scarcity	Plentitude	Plentitude
Underlying economics	Economics of information bundled with economics of things	Economics of information bundled with economics of things	Economics of information bundled with economics of things	Economics of information separated from economics of things	Economics of information separated from economics of things

FIGURE 2.1 Eras of information usage in organizations.

The Information System Strategy Triangle introduced in Chapter 1 reflects the link between IS strategy and organizational strategy and the internal requirements of the firm. The link between IS strategy and business strategy reflects the firm's external requirements. Maximizing the effectiveness of the firm's business strategy requires that the general manager be able both to identify and use information resources. This chapter looks at how information resources can be used strategically by general managers.

▶ INFORMATION RESOURCES AS STRATEGIC TOOLS

Crafting a strategic advantage requires the general manager to cleverly combine all the firm's resources, including financial, production, human, and information resources, and to consider external resources such as the Internet and opportunities in the global arena. Information resources are more than just the infrastructure. This generic term, **information resources**, is defined as the available data, technology, people, and processes within an organization to be used by the manager to perform business processes and tasks. Information resources can either be assets or capabilities. An **IT asset** is anything, tangible or intangible, that can be used by a firm in its processes for creating, producing, and/or offering its products (goods or services). An **information technology (IT) capability** is something that is learned or developed over time for the firm to create, produce, or offer its products. An IT capability makes it possible for a firm to use its IT assets effectively.[2]

An IS infrastructure (a concept that is discussed in detail in Chapter 6) is an IT asset. It includes each of an information resource's constituent components (i.e., data, technology, people, and processes). The infrastructure provides the foundation for the delivery of a firm's products or services. Another IT asset is an information repository, which is logically related data that is captured, organized, and retrievable by the firm.

In the ever-expanding **Web 2.0** space, the view of IT assets is broadening to include potential resources that are available to the firm, but that are not necessarily owned by the firm. These additional information resources are often available as a service, rather than as a system to be procured and implemented internally. For example, a Web-based software such as SalesForce.com offers managers the opportunity to find new ways to manage their customer information with an externally based IT resource. Social networking systems such as Facebook or Linked-In offer managers the opportunity to find expertise or an entire network of individuals ready to participate in the innovation processes of the corporate using relatively little capital or expense.

The three major categories of IT capabilities are technical skills, IT management skills, and relationship skills. Technical skills are applied to designing, developing, and implementing information systems. IT management skills are critical for managing the IT function and IT projects. They include an understanding of business processes and the ability to oversee the development and maintenance of systems to support these processes effectively. Relationship skills can either be externally focused or spanning across departments. An externally focused relationship skill includes the ability to respond to the firm's market and to work with customers and suppliers. The relationship between a firm's IS managers and its business managers is a spanning relationship skill. Even though it focuses on relationships in the firm, it requires spanning beyond the IT department. Relationship skills develop over time and require mutual respect and trust. They, like the other information resources, can create a unique advantage for a firm. Figure 2.2 summarizes the different types of information resources and provides examples of each.

Committing and developing information resources require substantial financial resources. Therefore, a general manager evaluating an information resource might

---

[2] G. Piccoli and B. Ives, "IT-Dependent Strategic Initiatives and Sustained Competitive Advantage: A Review and Synthesis of the Literature," *MIS Quarterly* 29, no. 4 (2005), 747–776.

Type of Information Resource	Definition	Example
IT ASSET	Anything that can be used by a firm in its processes for creating, producing, and/or offering its products (goods or services)	
IS infrastructure	Base foundation of the IT portfolio shared through the firm[3]	Hardware, software, network, data components, proprietary technology, Web-based services
Information repository	Data that is logically related and organized in a structured form accessible and usable for decision making purposes.	Critical information about customers that can be used to gain strategic advantage. Much of this information is increasingly available on the Web.
IT CAPABILITY	Something that is learned or developed over time and used by the firm to create, produce, or offer its products using IT assets	
Technical skill	Ability applied to designing, developing, and implementing information systems	Proficiency in systems analysis and design; programming skills
IT management skills	Ability to manage IT function and IT projects	Being knowledgeable about business processes and managing systems to support them; evaluating technology options; envisioning creative IS solutions to business problems
Relationship skills	Ability of IS specialists to work with parties outside the IS department.	Spanning: having a good relationship between IT and business managers. Externally focused: have a good relationship with an outsourcing vendor

FIGURE 2.2 Information resources.[4]

consider the following questions to better understand the type of advantage the information resource can create:[5]

- *What makes the information resource valuable?* In Eras I through III, the value of information was tied to the physical delivery mechanisms. In these eras, value was derived from scarcity reflected in the cost to produce the information. Information, like diamonds, gold, and MBA degrees,

[3] Adapted from M. Broadbent, P. Weill, and D. St. Clair, "The Implications of Information Technology Infrastructure for Business Process Redesign," *MIS Quarterly* 23, no. 2 (1999), 163.

[4] Adapted from Piccoli and Ives, "IT-Dependent Strategic Initiatives," 755.

[5] Adapted from David J. Collis and Cynthia A. Montgomery, "Competing on Resources: Strategy in the 1990s," *Harvard Business Review* (July–August 1995), reprint no. 95403.

was more valuable because it was found in limited quantities. However, the networked economy prevalent in Era IV drives a new model of value—value from plenitude. **Network effects** offer a reason for value derived from plenitude. The value of a network node to a person or organization in the network increases when others join the network. For example, an e-mail account has no value without another e-mail account that could receive the e-mail. As e-mail accounts become relatively ubiquitous, the value of having an e-mail account increases as its potential for use increases. Further, copying additional people on an e-mail is done a very low cost (virtually zero) highlighting that as the cost of producing an additional copy of an information product becomes trivial, the value of the network that invents, manufactures, and distributes it increases.[6] Therefore, rather than using the extremely low production costs to guide the determination of price, information products or services must be priced to reflect their value to the buyer. Different organizational buyers have different information needs depending on their competitive position within an industry.

- *Who appropriates the value created by the information resource?* The value chain model can help determine where a resource's value lies and how the appropriation can be improved in a firm's favor. The resource-based view describes the attributes of information resources that make it possible for them to create and sustain competitive advantage.

- *Is the information resource equally distributed across firms?* At the beginning of the life cycle of a new technology, early adopters may experience a competitive advantage from using an information resource. For example, a manager who has mastered the value from internal wikis may find uses for them that give his or her firm a momentary advantage. However in the longer term, a general manager is unlikely to possess a resource that is completely unique. But the experience gained when using the information resource may cause inequities between firms. By surveying the firms within an industry, he or she may establish that the value received by a resource is distributed unequally. The value of a resource that is unequally distributed tends to be higher because it can create strategic advantage. The value of information mushrooms under conditions of information asymmetries. The possessor of information may use it against, or sell it to, companies or individuals who are not otherwise able to access the information.

- *Is the information resource highly mobile?* A reliance on the individual skills of IT professionals exposes a firm to the risk that key individuals will leave the firm, taking the resource with them. Developing unique

---

[6] Kevin Kelly, "New Rules for the New Economy," *Wired* (September 1997), http://www.wired.com/wired/5.09/newrules_pr.html.

knowledge-sharing processes and creating an organizational memory can help reduce the impact of the loss of a mobile employee. Recording the lessons learned from all team members after the completion of each project is one attempt at lowering this risk.

- *How quickly does the information resource become obsolete?* "Things" wear out, whereas information does not. However, information can become obsolete, untrue, or even unfashionable. Like most other assets, information resources lose value over time. A general manager should understand the rate of this decline of value, as well as what factors may speed or slow it. For example, consider a database of customer information. How long, on average, is the current address of each customer valid? What events in the customers' lives might change their purchasing pattern and reduce the forecasting capability of the current information?

Information resources exist in a company alongside other resources. The general manager is responsible for organizing all resources so that business goals are met. Understanding the nature of the resources at hand is a prerequisite to using them effectively. By aligning the organization's IS strategy with its business strategy, the general manager maximizes its profit potential. Meanwhile, the firm's competitors are working to do the same. In this competitive environment, how should the information resources be organized and applied to enable the organization to compete most effectively?

▶ HOW CAN INFORMATION RESOURCES BE USED STRATEGICALLY?

The general manager confronts many elements that influence the competitive environment of his or her enterprise. Overlooking a single element can bring about disastrous results for the firm. This slim tolerance for error requires the manager to take multiple views of the strategic landscape. We discuss three such views that can help a general manager align IS strategy with business strategy. The first view uses the five competitive forces model by Michael Porter to look at the major influences on a firm's competitive environment. Information resources should be directed strategically to alter the competitive forces to benefit the firm's position in the industry. The second view uses Porter's value chain model to assess the internal operations of the organization and partners in its supply chain. Information resources should be directed at altering the value-creating or value-supporting activities of the firm. This chapter explores this view further to consider the value chain of an entire industry to identify opportunities for the organization to gain competitive advantage. The third view specifically focuses on the types of IS resources needed to gain and sustain competitive advantage. These three views provide a general manager with varied perspectives from which to identify strategic opportunities to apply the firm's information resources.

Using Information Resources to Influence Competitive Forces

Porter provides the general manager with a classic view of the major forces that shape the competitive environment of a firm. These five competitive forces are shown in Figure 2.3, along with some examples of how information resources can be applied to influence each force. This view reminds the general manager that competitive forces result from more than just the actions of direct competitors. Each force now will be explored in detail from an IS perspective.

Potential Threat of New Entrants

Existing firms within an industry often try to reduce the threat of new entrants to the marketplace by erecting barriers to entry. Barriers to entry help the firm create a stronghold by offering products or services that are difficult to displace in the eyes of customers based on apparently unique features. Such barriers include controlled access to limited distribution channels, public image of a firm, and government regulations of an industry. Information resources also can be used to build barriers that discourage competitors from entering the industry. For example, Massachusetts Mutual Life Insurance Company created an IS infrastructure that connects the local sales agent with comprehensive information about products and

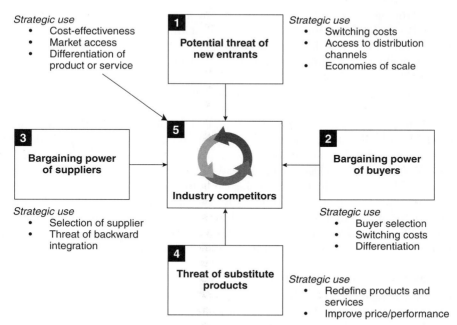

FIGURE 2.3 Five competitive forces with potential strategic use of information resources. Source: Adapted from Michael Porter, *Competitive Strategy* (New York: The Free Press, 1998); and Lynda M. Applegate, F. Warren McFarlan, and James L. McKenney, *Corporate Information Systems Management: The Issues Facing Senior Executives*, 4th ed. (Homewood, IL: Richard D. Irwin, 1996).

customers. An insurance company entering the marketplace would have to spend millions of dollars to build the telecommunications and IS required to provide its sales force with the same competitive advantage. Therefore, the system at Mass Mutual may be a barrier to entry for new companies.

Bargaining Power of Buyers

Customers often have substantial power to affect the competitive environment. This power can take the form of easy consumer access to several retail outlets to purchase the same product or the opportunity to purchase in large volumes at superstores like Wal-Mart. Information resources can be used to build switching costs that make it less attractive for customers to purchase from competitors. Switching costs can be any aspect of a buyer's purchasing decision that decreases the likelihood of "switching" his or her purchase to a competitor. Such an approach requires a deep understanding of how a customer obtains the product or service. For example, Amazon.com's One Click encourages return purchases by making buying easier. Amazon.com stores buyer information, including contact information and credit card numbers, so that it can be accessed with one click, saving consumers the effort of data reentry. Similarly, Apple's iTunes simple-to-use interface and proprietary software on the iPod make it difficult for customers to use other formats and technologies than the iPod.

Another good example of the power of buyers can be found at Facebook. On November 6, 2007, Facebook announced an exciting new service, Beacon. Press releases from Facebook shouted that "users gain ability to share their actions from 44 participating sites with their friends on Facebook." The concept was called "Social Distribution" and gave Facebook information from the participating sites that would be posted on the Facebook customer's page. Customers erupted in protest, and one month later, on December 6, CEO Mark Zuckerberg, personally issued an apology for the way Facebook handled the new feature. "We simply did a bad job with this release, and I apologize for it. While I'm disappointed with our mistakes, we appreciate all the feedback we have received from our users. I'd like to discuss what we have learned and how we have improved Beacon." Zuckerberg continued by sharing why they built Beacon in the first place (to let people share with their friends a lot of information across sites) and why it was designed the way it was (to be as easy to use as possible and so users "didn't have to touch it to make it work."). But the blogosphere quickly lit up with issues of privacy, control, and security as well as general dislike of the strategy, forcing the company to respond.

Bargaining Power of Suppliers

Suppliers' bargaining power can reduce a firm's profitability. This force is strongest when a firm has few suppliers from which to choose, the quality of supplier inputs is crucial to the finished product, or the volume of purchases is insignificant to the supplier. For example, steel firms lost some of their power over the automobile industry because car manufacturers developed technologically advanced quality control systems. Manufacturers can now reject steel from suppliers when it does not meet the required quality levels. Through the Internet, firms continue to provide information for free as they attempt to increase their share of visitors to their Web sites. This decision reduces the power of information suppliers and necessitates finding new ways for content providers to develop and distribute information. Many Internet firms are integrating backward within the industry by creating their own information supply and reselling it to other Internet sites. Well-funded firms simply acquire these content providers, which is often quicker than building the capability from scratch. One example is eBay's acquisition of PayPal, the system used to transact payment for goods and services all over the Web.

Threat of Substitute Products

The potential of a substitute product in the marketplace depends on the buyers' willingness to substitute, the relative price-to-performance of the substitute, and the level of switching costs a buyer faces. Information resources can create advantages by reducing the threat of substitution. For example, Internet auction site eBay used innovative IT to create a set of services for their small businesses, a major source of revenue for the online auctioneer. At a time when customers were beginning to complain, sellers were wondering about the fees, and competition was trying to lure them both away, eBay brought out ProStores, a service to help all sellers build their own Web site. eBay managers noticed that many sellers did not have any Web presence other than eBay, and the move was another way to lock in these customers to the eBay environment. "The more those sellers are locked into an eBay environment, the less likely they will work with rivals," according to one Web site.[7] It seemed to work. One seller, a Tennessee-based, wholesale distributor of ball bearings and chains, reportedly doubled its eBay sales four months after its ProStores site was launched.[8] For competitors to be successful, they needed to offer not just a substitute, but also a better service to these sellers. So far none has.

Substitutes that cause a threat are not just products offered from the initial company or products that are similar but offered by a competitor. The threat often comes from potentially new innovations that make the previous product obsolete. Consider how digital cameras have made film (and the cameras that use them) obsolete. CDs and more recently digitally based MP3 files have made vinyl records (and the record players that use them) obsolete. Free Web-based applications are a threat to software vendors who charge for their products and who do not have Web-based delivery. Managers must watch for potential substitutes from many different sources to fully manage this competitive threat.

Industry Competitors

Rivalry among the firms competing within an industry is high when it is expensive for a firm to leave the industry, the growth rate of the industry is declining, or

---

[7] Evan Shumann, StorefrontBacktalk.com, http://www.storefrontbacktalk.com/story/062605ebay.php

[8] Gwen Moran, " The Pros of Opening an eBay ProStore," www.entrepreneur.com, March 24, 2006.

products have lost differentiation. Under these circumstances, the firm must focus on the competitive actions of a rival to protect market share. Intense rivalry in an industry ensures that competitors respond quickly to any strategic actions. The banking industry illustrates this point. When a large Philadelphia-based bank developed an ATM network, several smaller competitors joined forces and shared information resources to create a competing network. The large bank was unable to create a significant advantage from its system and had to carry the full costs of developing the network by itself. Information resources were committed quickly to achieve neutralizing results due to the high level of rivalry that existed between the local bank competitors in Philadelphia.

As firms within an industry begin to implement standard business processes and technologies—often using enterprisewide systems such as those of SAP and Oracle—the industry becomes more attractive to consolidation through acquisition. Standardizing IS lowers the coordination costs of merging two enterprises and can result in a less-competitive environment in the industry.

One way competitors differentiate themselves with an otherwise undifferentiated product is through creative use of IS. Information provides advantages in such competition when added to an existing product. For example, FedEx adds information to its delivery service helping it differentiate its offerings from those of other delivery services. FedEx customers are able to track their packages, know exactly where their package is in transit, see who signed for the package, and know exactly when it was delivered. Competitors offer some of the same information, but FedEx was able to take an early lead by using information to differentiate their services. Figure 2.4 summarizes these five forces working simultaneously at the retailer and manufacturer Zara.

General managers can use the five competitive forces model to identify the key forces currently affecting competition, to recognize uses of information resources to influence forces, and to consider likely changes in these forces over time. The changing forces drive both the business strategy and IS strategy, and this model provides a way to think about how information resources can create competitive advantage for a business unit and, even more broadly, for the firm. They also can reshape a whole industry—compelling general managers to take actions to help their firm gain or sustain competitive advantage. Consider an example of a large grocery retailer. Because of many factors, including the number of items on the shelves of the store, the complexity of managing customers, and the logistics necessary to keep inventory moving and reordered as necessary, these retailers are no longer are able to compete without information systems. The basis of competition has changed in part because of the innovative use of information systems by industry leaders. Keeping track of inventory is a given, but large chains must also intimately know their customers and find new ways to provide innovative services to keep their loyalties. The entire industry has changed from one of locally providing groceries to one of managing information about every aspect of their business. The alternative perspective presented in the next section provides the general manager with an opportunity to select the proper mix of

Competitive Force	IT Influence on Competitive Force
Threat of New Entrant	Zara's IT supports its tightly knit group of designers, market specialists, production managers, and production planners. New entrants are unlikely to provide IT to support relationships that have been built over time. Further, it has a rich information repository about customers that would be hard to replicate.
Bargaining Power of Buyers	With its constant infusion of new products, buyers are drawn to Zara stores. Zara boasts more than 11,000 new designs a year, whereas competitors typically offer only 2,000–4,000. Further, because of the low inventory that the Zara stores stock, the regular customers buy products they like when they see them because they are likely to be gone the next time they visit the store. More recently Zara has employed laser technology to measure 10,000 women volunteers so that it can add the measurements of "real" customers into its information repositories. This means that the new products will be more likely to fit Zara customers.
Bargaining Power of Suppliers	Its computer-controlled cutting machine cuts up to 1000 layers at a time. It then sends the cut materials to suppliers who sew the pieces together. The suppliers' work is relatively simple, and many suppliers can do the sewing. Thus, the pool of suppliers is expanded, and Zara has greater flexibility in choosing the sewing companies. Further, because Zara dyes 50% of the fabric in its plant, it is less dependent on suppliers and can respond more quickly to midseason changes in customer color preferences.
Industry Competitors	Industry competitors long marketed the desire of durable, classic lines. Zara focuses on meeting customer preferences for trendy, low-cost fashion. It has the highest sales per square foot of any of its competitors. It does so with virtually no advertising and only 10% of stock is unsold. It keeps its inventory levels very low and offers new products at an amazing pace for the industry (i.e., 15 days from idea to shelves). Zara has extremely efficient manufacturing and distribution operations.
Threat of Substitute Products	IT helps Zara offer extremely fashionable lines that are only expected to last for approximately 10 wears. IT enables Zara to offer trendy, appealing apparel at hard-to-beat prices, making substitutes difficult.

FIGURE 2.4   Application of five competitive forces model for zara.

information resources and to apply them to achieve strategic advantage by altering key activities.

Using Information Resources to Alter the Value Chain

The value chain model addresses the activities that create, deliver, and support a company's product or service. Porter divided these activities into two broad

	Inbound Logistics	Operations	Outbound Logistics	Marketing and Sales	Service
	Materials handling Delivery	Manufacturing Assembly	Order processing Shipping	Product Pricing Promotion Place	Customer service Repair

Support activities: Organization, Human Resources, Technology, Purchasing

FIGURE 2.5   Value chain of the firm.
Source: Adapted from Michael Porter and Victor Millar, "How Information Gives You Competitive Advantage," *Harvard Business Review* (July–August 1985), reprint no. 85415.

categories, as shown in Figure 2.5: support and primary activities. Primary activities relate directly to the value created in a product or service, whereas support activities make it possible for the primary activities to exist and remain coordinated. Each activity may affect how other activities are performed, suggesting that information resources should not be applied in isolation. For example, more efficient IS for repairing a product may increase the possible number of repairs per week, but the customer does not receive any value unless his or her product is repaired, which requires that the spare parts be available. Changing the rate of repair also affects the rate of spare parts ordering. If information resources are focused too narrowly on a specific activity, then the expected value increase may not be realized, as other parts of the chain are not adjusted.

The value chain framework suggests that competition stems from two sources: lowering the cost to perform activities and adding value to a product or service so that buyers will pay more. To achieve true competitive advantage, a firm requires accurate information on elements outside itself. Lowering activity costs only achieves an advantage if the firm possesses information about its competitors' cost structures. Even though reducing isolated costs can improve profits temporarily, it does not provide a clear competitive advantage unless a firm can lower its costs below a competitor's. Doing so enables the firm to lower its prices as a way to grow its market share.

Adding value can be used to gain strategic advantage only if a firm possesses accurate information regarding its customer. Which product attributes are valued, and where can improvements be made? Improving customer service when its products fail was a goal behind Otis Elevator's Otisline system. The customer's service call is automatically routed to the field technician with the skill and knowledge to complete the repair. Otis Elevator knows that customers value a fast response to minimize the downtime of the elevator. This goal is achieved by using information resources to move the necessary information between activities.

When customers call for service, their requests are automatically and accurately entered and stored in the customer service database and communicated to the technician linked to that account. This technician is then contacted immediately over the wireless handheld computer network and told of the problem. That way the service technician can make sure he or she has both the parts and knowledge to make repairs. This approach provides Otis with an advantage because the response is fast, and the technician arrives at the job properly prepared to fix the problem.

Although the value chain framework emphasizes the activities of the individual firm, it can be extended, as in Figure 2.6, to include the firm in a larger value system. This value system is a collection of firm value chains connected through a business relationship and through technology. From this perspective, a variety of strategic opportunities exist to use information resources to gain a competitive advantage. Understanding how information is used within each value chain of the system can lead to new opportunities to change the information component of value-added activities. It can also lead to shakeouts within the industry, as the firms that fail to provide value are forced out and as new business models are adopted by the surviving firms.

Opportunity also exists in the transfer of information across value chains. Amazon.com began by selling books directly to customers over the Internet and bypassing the traditional industry channels. Customers who valued the time saved by shopping from home rather than driving to physical retail outlets flocked to Amazon.com's Web site to buy books. Industry competitors Barnes and Noble and Borders Books were forced to develop their own Web sites, thus driving up

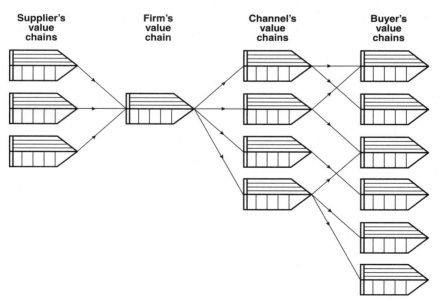

FIGURE 2.6   The value system: interconnecting relationships between organizations.

their cost of doing business. The new paradigm for Barnes and Noble and Borders means rethinking how their value chain works with the value offered to their customers through their traditional business.

CRM is a natural extension of applying the value chain model to customers. **Customer relationship management (CRM)** includes management activities performed to obtain, enhance relationships with, and retain customers. CRM is a coordinated set of activities designed to learn more about customers' needs and behaviors to develop stronger relationships with them and to enhance their value chains. CRM consists of technological components, as well as a process that brings together many pieces of information about customers, sales, marketing effectiveness, responsiveness, and market trends. CRM can lead to better customer service, more efficient call centers, product cross-selling, simplified sales and marketing efforts, more efficient sales transactions, and increased customer revenues. In Chapter 1 we described the Ritz-Carlton's CRM, Class, which captures information about guest preferences and enables providing enhanced customized service during future visits.

In an application of the value chain model to the Zara example discussed earlier in the chapter, Figure 2.7 describes the value added to primary and support activities provided by information systems at Zara. The focus in Figure 2.7 is on value added to Zara's processes, but suppliers and customers in its supply chain also realize the value added by information systems. Most notably, the customer is better served as a result of the information systems. For example, the stores place orders twice a week over personal digital assistants (PDAs). Each night, managers use their PDAs to learn about newly available garments. The orders are received and promptly processed and delivered. In this way Zara can be very timely in responding to customer preferences.

Supply Chain Management

Supply chain management (SCM) is an approach that improves the way a company finds raw components it needs to make a product or service, manufactures that product or service, and delivers it to customers. Technology, especially Web-based technology, allows the supply chains of a company's customers and suppliers to be linked through a single network that optimizes costs and opportunities for all companies in the supply chain. By sharing information across the network, guesswork about order quantities for raw materials and products can be reduced, and suppliers can make sure they have enough on hand if demand for their products unexpectedly rises.

Sharing information across firms requires collaboration and, increasingly, the IT to support its seamless processing across firm boundaries. If a firm wants to limit its collaboration with its trading partners, it can use technologies such as electronic marketplaces where only minimal information such as product characteristics, delivery addresses, and billing addresses need to be exchanged over the Internet. However, when firms start sharing information about production schedules, valued customers, or how complex systems work, a much higher level of collaboration

Activity	Zara's Value Chain
PRIMARY ACTIVITIES	
Inbound Logistics	IT-enabled Just-in-Time (JIT) strategy results in inventory being received when needed. Most dyes are purchased from its own subsidiaries to better support JIT strategy and reduce costs.
Operations	Information systems support decisions about the fabric, cut, and price points. Cloth is ironed and products are packed on hangers so they don't need ironing when they arrive at stores. Price tags are already on the products. Zara produces 60% of its merchandise in-house. Fabric is cut and dyed by robots in 23 highly automated Spanish factories.
Outbound Logistics	Clothes move on miles of automated conveyor belts at distribution centers and reach stores within 48 hours.
Marketing and Sales	Limited inventory allows low percentage of unsold inventory (10%); POS at stores linked to headquarters to track how items are selling; customers ask for what they want, and this information is transmitted daily from stores to designers over handheld computers.
Service	No focus on service on products
SUPPORT ACTIVITIES	
Organization	IT supports tightly knit collaboration among designers, store managers, market specialists, production managers, and production planners.
Human Resources	Managers are trained to monitor what's selling and report data to designers ever day. The manager is key to making customers feel listened to, and to communicating with headquarters to keep each store and the entire Zara clothing line at the cutting edge of fashion.
Technology	Technology is integrated to support all primary activities. Zara's IT staff works with vendors to develop automated conveyor to support distribution activities.
Purchasing	Vertical integration reduces amount of purchasing needed.

FIGURE 2.7 Application of value chain model to Zara.

(and trust) is needed. Such collaboration is often made possible by reengineering operations to mirror or complement each other and working extensively to make one company's computer system talk with the other's.

Collaboration paid off for supply-chain partners Wal-Mart and Procter & Gamble (P&G). Until these two giants linked their software systems in the 1980s, they shared little information. Now their integrated systems automatically alert P&G to ship more P&G products when Wal-Mart's distribution centers run low.

The SCM system also allows P&G to monitor shelves at individual Wal-Mart stores through real-time satellite linkups that send messages to the factory whenever a P&G item is scanned at the register. This real-time information aids P&G in manufacturing, shipping, and displaying products for Wal-Mart. Invoicing and payments are automatically processed. Because of high volumes and operating efficiencies derived from the SCM software, P&G can offer discounted prices to help Wal-Mart offer its "low, everyday prices."

In some cases the collaboration does not pay off equally for all parties in the supply chain. Although Wal-Mart realized operational efficiencies from its use of radio frequency identification (RFID) technology, it will not realize the greatest benefits until all its distribution centers install the technology. Nonetheless, Wal-Mart switched course and decided to first complete the installations of RFID technology in its stores so that it can better collaborate with suppliers that need to monitor the flow of inventory and respond to problems or spikes in demand. Further, it subsidized its smaller suppliers by offering an RFID solution for less than $5,000. Because of economies of scale, Wal-Mart reaped far more benefit from RFID technology than many of its smaller suppliers. Thus, Wal-Mart made it enticing for its more hesitant supply chain partners to adopt RFID by offering them information from its stores or subsidizing their purchase of the technology.[9]

Unlike the five competitive forces model, the focus of the value chain is on activities. Yet, in applying the value chain, competitive forces may be affected to the extent that the proposed technology may add value to suppliers, customers, or even competitors and potential new entrants.

Using the Resource-Based View to Attain and Sustain Competitive Advantage

The **resource-based view**[10] is useful in determining whether a firm's strategy has created value. Unlike Porter' competitive forces framework, this view maintains that competitive advantage comes from the information and other resources of the firm. On the other hand, Porter's competitive forces framework argues that aspects of the firm's industry create sources of competitive advantage. Like the value chain model, the resource-based view concentrates on what adds value to the firm. However, whereas the value chain model focuses on a firm's activities, the resource-based view focuses on the resources that it can manage.

---

[9] Marc L. Songini, Wal-Mart Shifts RFID plans (2007, February 26), Computer World: http://www.computerworld.com/action/article.do?command = viewArticleBasic&articleId = 284115 (accessed April 28, 2008).

[10] The resource-based view was originally proposed by management researchers, most prominently Jay Barney, "Firm Resources and Sustained Competitive Advantage," *Journal of Management* 17, no. 1 (1991), 99–120; and J. Barney, "Is the Resource-Based 'View' a Useful Perspective for Strategic Management Research? Yes," *Academy of Management Review* 26, no. 1 (2001), 41–56. M. Wade and J. Hulland, "Review: The Resource-Based View and Information Systems Research: Review, Extension and Suggestions for Future Research," *MIS Quarterly* 28, no. 1 (2004), 107–142) reviewed its application in the MIS literature and derived a framework to better understand its application to IS resources.

The RBV has been applied in the area of IS to help identify two subsets of information resources: those that enable a firm to *attain* competitive advantage and those that enable a firm to *sustain* the advantage over the long term. In the first subset are both valuable and rare resources that firms must leverage to establish a superior resource position. A resource is considered valuable when it enables the firm to become more efficient or effective. It is rare when other firms do not possess it. For example, many banks today would not think of doing business without ATMs. ATMs are very valuable to the banks in terms of their operations. A bank's customers expect it to provide ATMs in many convenient locations. However, because many other banks also have ATMs, they are not a rare resource, and they do not offer a strategic advantage. Many systems in Eras I and II, and especially Era III, were justified on their ability to provide a rare and valuable resource.

But as many firms moved into subsequent eras, they as quickly learned that gaining a competitive advantage does not automatically mean that you can sustain it over the long term. The only way to do that is to continue to innovate or to protect against resource imitation, substitution, or transfer. For example, Wal-Mart's complex logistics management is deeply embedded in both its own and its supplier's operations that imitations by other firms is unlikely. It was not easy for eBay customers to find a substitute for ProStores, discussed earlier in this chapter. UPS was able to build a competing information system to the one FedEx uses, but by the time it was up and running, FedEx has innovated far beyond and continued to enjoy advantages. Finally, to sustain competitive advantage, resources must be difficult to transfer, or relatively immobile. Some resources such as computer hardware and software can be easily bought and sold. However, technical knowledge, especially that relates to the firm's operation, a gung-ho company culture, and managerial experience in the firm's environment is less easy to obtain and, hence, considered harder to transfer to other firms.

From the IS perspective,[11] some types of resources are better than others for creating attributes that enable a firm to attain and sustain competitive value (i.e., value, rarity, low substitutability, low mobility, low imitability). For example, externally focused relationship skills can build advantages. Consider the ability to work with buyers and suppliers, the ability to read the market, the ability of IS to manage partnerships with the business units (spanning relationship management), and the ability to plan and work with the business units in undertaking change (IT management skills). These relationship resources that span departmental and organizational boundaries tend to have more initial and enduring impact on the firm than resources focused only within IT departments, such as IT infrastructure or technical skills. This is due, in part, because it takes time to develop the trust and respect underlying the relationship.

Some IT management skills are general enough in nature to make them easier to transfer and imitate relationship skills. Although it clearly is important for IS executives to manage internally oriented resources such as IS infrastructure,

---

[11] Ibid.

systems development, and running cost-effective IS operations, these skills can be acquired in many different forums. They are basic IT management skills possessed by virtually all good IS managers. Other skills, however, are unique to a firm and require considerable time and resources to develop. For example, it takes time to learn how the firm operates and to understand critical processes and socially complex working relationships. However, the message posed by the resource-based view is that IS executives must look beyond their own IT shop and concentrate on cultivating resources that help the firm understand changing business environments and allow them to work well with all their external stakeholders.

Even when considering internally oriented information resources, there are differences in the extent to which they add value. Many argue that IS personnel are willing to move, especially when offered higher salaries by firms needing these skills. Yet, some technical skills, such as knowledge of a firm's use of technology to support business processes and technology integration skills are not easily moved to another firm. Further, hardware and many software applications can be purchased or outsourced, making them highly imitable and transferrable, and not very rare over time. Because it is unlikely that two firms will have exactly the same strategic alternatives, resources at one firm have only moderate substitutability in the other firm.

It is harder to rate the value attributes of an information repository. Some information repositories are filled with internally oriented information designed to improve the firm's efficiency. Consistent with our earlier arguments, these repositories are of less value than those that tap the external environment and contain significant knowledge about the industry, the competitors, and the customers. Although most firms have these types of information repositories, not all firms use them effectively. They tend to be unique to the firm and thus less imitable, substitutable, or transferrable.

Figure 2.8 indicates the extent to which the attributes of each information resource may add value to Zara. Zara's advantage does not come from the specific hardware or software technologies they use. Management spends five to ten times less than its rivals on technology. It uses relatively old POS equipment to communicate over modems each night to headquarters. The handheld computers, automated conveyors, and large computer-controlled equipment to cut patterns are used skillfully by Zara, but they could eventually be purchased by or imitated by competitors. If the contractual arrangements exclude the option of selling to competitors, then this makes the externally focused skill more difficult to transfer, but not impossible. Hence, IT infrastructure in terms of value creation (i.e., value and rarity) has a moderate rating. It is easy to imitate and transfer and only moderately difficult to substitute, considering the automated conveyors; hence Zara's infrastructure would not be a particular good resource for maintaining strategic value. The technical skills, although not exceptionally valuable or rare, may offer some sustainable value because they are used to integrate across Zara's range of systems and would thus not be overly easy to imitate, substitute, or transfer.

In contrast, Zara has created considerable value from its information repository with customers' preferences and body types, and from its IT management skills

	VALUE CREATION		VALUE SUSTAINABILITY		
	Value	Rarity	Imitation	Substitution	Transfer
INFORMATION ASSET					
IT Infrastructure	M	M	H	M	H
Information Repository	H	M	M	L	M
INFORMATION CAPABILITY					
Technical Skills	M	L	M	M	M
IT Management Skills	H	H	L	L	M
RELATIONSHIP SKILLS					
Externally Focused	H	M	L	M	L-M
Spanning	H	H	L	L	L

FIGURE 2.8   Information resources at Zara, by attribute.
Source: Adapted from M. Wade and J. Hulland, "The Resource-Based View and Information Systems Research: Review, Extension and Suggestions for Future Research," *MIS Quarterly* 28, no. 1 (2004), 107–142.

and spanning relationships skills. Not only do Zara store managers communicate daily with designers about customer preferences, but also the information, which is stored in Zara's information repository, is easily retrievable by the designers, market specialists, procurement planners, and production managers. It would be a challenge for other companies to develop and apply the rich information not only because of the volume of data, but also because of the working relationships that have been shaped to use it. Thus the information repository has great value to Zara and is relatively rare because of its integration with Zara's operations and personnel. It is also relatively difficult to imitate or transfer, extremely difficult to substitute. The tight-knit teams at headquarters are very unusual and allow Zara the ability to correctly interpret and quickly respond to customers' needs. IT is integrally involved in supporting the way work is performed. These working relationships and managerial skills are not easy to replicate or purchase in the marketplace. They would all be very difficult to imitate. Overall, Zara is able to create high value from its IT management and relationship skills. It would be moderately to extremely difficult to substitute or transfer them.

Most firms don't really have a choice of creating competitive advantage by manipulating industry forces or by adding value, either through their use of information resources or IT-enhanced activities. Rather, all affect the firm, though the relative impact may differ depending on the firm's industry, environment, and executives' choice.

▶ STRATEGIC ALLIANCES

The value chain helps a firm focus on adding value to the chains of its partners. The resource-based view considers the value created using externally oriented relationships skills. The latest era of information resources evolution emphasizes the importance of collaborative partnerships, and the increasing number of Web applications focused on collaboration and social networking only foreshadow even more emphasis. These partnerships can take many forms, including joint ventures, joint projects, trade associations, buyer–supplier partnerships, or cartels. Often such partnerships use information technologies to support strategic alliances and integrate data across partners' information systems. A **strategic alliance** is an interorganizational relationship that affords one or more companies in the relationship a strategic advantage. IT can help produce the product developed by the alliance, share information resources across the partners' existing value systems, or facilitate communication and coordination among the partners. For example, Delta formed a strategic alliance with e-Travel Inc., a travel service software company that targets large corporations, to promote Delta's online reservations system. The alliance was strategic because it helped Delta reduce agency reservation fees and offered e-Travel new corporate leads. As introduced earlier, SCM is another frequently discussed type of IT-facilitated strategic alliance.

Strategic alliances often are based on trust and respect that can only develop over time as a result of a repeating pattern of interactions. Ring and Van de Ven have developed a four-stage model that demonstrates the importance of repeating patterns. The first stage in the cycle is the *negotiation stage*. in which individuals in two or more companies talk with one another and try to understand what each individual is seeking—both as a representative of the company and also as a person with individual goals. An agreement is made that calls for one party to deliver a product or service and to receive payment in return. These agreements, which are created in the *commitment stage*, can be either formal or informal. Formal agreements are called contracts. The product is delivered and payment is received in the *execution stage*. Both parties assess what has happened during the ongoing *assessment stage*, and if happy, they repeat the cycle, sometimes negotiating for even more products or services and receiving more rewards for delivering. With enough repetition, roles are created that continue to be followed, even if the original employees who started the negotiations leave the organization. (See Figure 2.9.)

Co-opetition

Clearly, not all strategic alliances are formed with suppliers or customers as partners. Rather, co-opetition is becoming an increasingly popular alternative model. As defined by Brandenburg and Nalebuff in their book of the same name, **co-opetition** is a strategy whereby companies cooperate and compete at the same

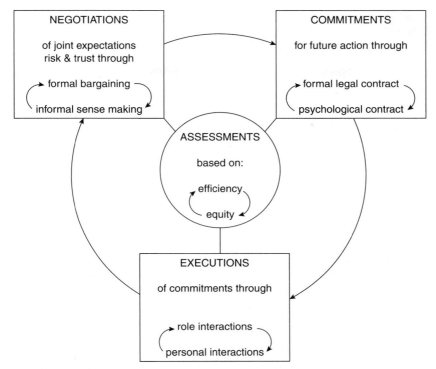

FIGURE 2.9   Four-stage model by Ring and Van de Ven.
Source: Developmental processes of cooperative interorganizational relationships. Ring, Peter S.; Van de Ven, Andrew H., Academy of Management Review. 1994 Jan, Vol 19(1) pg 97.

time with companies in its value net.[12] The value net includes a company and its competitors and complementors, as well as its customers and suppliers, and the interactions among all of them. A complementor is a company whose product or service is used in conjunction with a particular product or service to make a more useful set for the customer. For example, Goodyear is a complementor to Ford and GM because tires are a complementary product to automobiles. Likewise, hardware and software companies are complementors.

Co-opetition, then, is the strategy for creating the best possible outcome for a business by optimally combining competition and cooperation. It frequently creates competitive advantage by giving power in the form of information to other organizations or groups. For example, Covisint, the auto industry's e-marketplace, grew out of a consortium of competitors General Motors, Ford, and Daimler-Chrysler, Nissan and Renault. By addressing multiple automotive functional needs across the entire product life cycle, Covisint offers support for collaboration, supply

---

[12] A. Brandenburg and B. Nalebuff, *Co-opetition* (New York: Doubleday, 1996).

chain management, procurement, and quality management. Thus, co-opetition as demonstrated by Covisint, not only streamlines the internal operations of its backers, but also has the potential to transform the automotive industry.

▶ RISKS

As demonstrated throughout this chapter, information resources may be used to gain strategic advantage, even if that advantage is fleeting. When information systems are chosen as the tool to outpace their firm's competitors, executives should be aware of the many risks that may surface. Some of theses risks include the following:

- *Awaking a sleeping giant.* A firm can implement IS to gain competitive advantage, only to find that it nudged a larger competitor with deeper pockets into implementing an IS with even better features. FedEx offered its customers the ability to trace the transit and delivery of their packages online. FedEx's much larger competitor, UPS, rose to the challenge. UPS not only implemented the same services, but also added a new set of features. Both the UPS and FedEx sites passed through multiple Web site iterations as the dueling delivery companies continue to struggle for competitive advantage. Netflix awoke a sleeping giant and ended up with a new partner. Despite its size and merchandising savvy, Wal-Mart was stymied by Netflix's head start in the rapidly expanding niche of online DVD rentals. Wal-Mart turned over its online DVD business to Netflix in 2005 and still offers access to Netflix from its Web site. Netflix, in turn, reminds its customers that they can purchase DVDs at Wal-mart.com.

- *Demonstrating bad timing.* Sometimes customers are not ready to use the technology designed to gain strategic advantage. For example, Momenta Corp. experienced monumental failure when it attempted to sell pen-based technology in the early 1990s. A decade later pen-based computing is well accepted by PDA users.

- *Implementing IS poorly.* Stories abound of information systems that fail because they are poorly implemented. Typically these systems are complex and often global in their reach. In its zeal to implement a system to streamline supply chain communications and lower operating costs, Nike's implementation team allegedly performed customization that extended beyond the recommendations of its software supplier, i2 Technologies. The resulting missed and duplicated orders may have cost Nike as much as a $100 million. Another implementation fiasco took place at Hershey Foods, when it attempted to implement its supply and inventory system. Hershey developers brought the complex system up too quickly and then failed to test it adequately. Related systems problems crippled shipments during the critical Halloween shopping season, resulting in large declines in sales and net income.

- *Failing to deliver what users want.* Systems that do not meet the needs of the firm's target market are likely to fail. Streamline.com (also called Streamline Inc.) experienced the effects of this risk when using the Web to provide home delivery of groceries and pick-up/drop-off services for movie rentals, dry cleaning, and film. Streamline charged a $30-per-month subscription fee and worked from "personal shopping lists" customers submitted through its Web site. But Streamline failed to convince a large number of shoppers that Streamline's services matched their lifestyle. Streamline may have failed because its once-a-week delivery was too infrequent, or because its customers wanted to inspect the produce when bags were dropped off. More recently, Webvan thought it had learned from Streamline. Webvan invested heavily in an infrastructure that would allow its employees to take customers' orders online and deliver them within 30 minutes. Unfortunately for Webvan, many of its customers worked during the day and wanted their groceries delivered at home at night. This made the 30-minute delivery window—and the related infrastructure expenses—unnecessary.

- *Web-based alternative removes advantages.* With increasingly more applications moving to Web-based platforms, managers must consider the risk of losing any advantage obtained by an information resource that later becomes available as a service on the Web. The Web-based alternative may be much less expensive to use, be more easily available, and include a similar set of advantages.

- *Running afoul of the law.* Using IS strategically may promote litigation if the IS results in the violation of laws or regulations. Years ago, American Airlines' reservation system, Sabre, was challenged by American Airlines' competitors on the grounds that it violated antitrust laws. Napster filed for bankruptcy as a consequence of BMG Entertainment, AOL Time Warner, EMI, Sony, and Vivendi International jointly suing it for copyright infringement. The suit led to Napster's court-ordered shutdown. More recently, Apple experienced a problem over their proprietary software, which violates legislation passed in France and possibly Scandinavia, where governments insist on more open systems.

Every business decision has risks associated with it. However, with the large expenditure of IT resources needed to create sustainable, strategic advantages, the manager will want to carefully identify and then design a mitigation strategy to manage the associated risks.

► FOOD FOR THOUGHT: CO-CREATING IT AND BUSINESS STRATEGY

Throughout this chapter we have discussed the alignment of IT strategy with business strategy. Certainly they must be carefully aligned to ensure that maximum value is achieved from IT investments. However in the fast-paced business environment where information is increasingly a core component of the product or service offered by the firm, we are seeing the co-creating of IT and business strategy. That is to say that IT strategy *is* business strategy; one cannot be created independent of the other. In many cases they are now one in the same.

For companies whose main product is information, such as financial services companies, it's clear that how information is managed is the core of the business strategy itself. How an investment firm manages the clients' account, how their clients interact with the company, and how investments are made are all done through the management of information. A financial services company must co-create business and IT strategy.

But consider a company like FedEx, most well known as the package delivery company. Are customers paying to have a package delivered or to have information about that package's delivery route and timetable? One could argue that they are one in the same, and that increasingly the company's business strategy **is** its information systems strategy. Certainly there are components of the operation that are more than just information. There are actual packages to be loaded on actual trucks and planes, which are then actually delivered to their destinations. However, to make it all work, the company must rely on information systems. Should the information systems go down, FedEx would be unable to do business. A company like this must co-create IT strategy and business strategy.

This was not true a few years ago. Companies could often separate information systems strategy from business strategy, in part because their products or services did not have a large information component. For example, a few years ago, should the information system of a trucking company stop working, the trucks would still be able to take their shipments to their destination and pick up new shipments. It might be slower or a bit more chaotic, but the business wouldn't stop. Today, that's not the case. Complicated logistics are the norm, and information systems are the foundation of the business, such as seen at FedEx.

As the number and type of applications increase on the Web and on future technologies that we can only fantasize at this point, we expect to see only co-creation of business and IT strategy. Managers who think they can build a business model without considering the opportunities and impact of information systems, both the resources owned by the firm and those available on the Web will find they have significant difficulties creating any type of sustainable advantage in their marketplace.

This raises the question, however, of whether IS is always necessary for strategic advantage. Some experts believe that companies do not have to use IT to gain strategic advantage, although many companies will. There are strategies that can be competently executed without a major IT component, where perhaps IT is just a utility like the lights and electricity in a business. IT is necessary to create components of the strategy, but not a major focus of the business strategy. In an increasingly Web-enabled world, this debate is just beginning.

▶ SUMMARY

- Information resources include data, technology, people, and processes within an organization. Information resources can be either assets or capabilities.
- Three major categories of IT capabilities are technical skills, IT management skills, and relationship skills.
- Using IS for strategic advantage requires an awareness of the many relationships that affect both competitive business and information strategies.
- The five competitive forces model implies that more than just the local competitors influence the reality of the business situation. Analyzing the five competitive forces—new entrants, buyers, suppliers, industry competitors, and substitute products—from both a business view and an information view helps general managers use information resources to minimize the effect of these forces on the organization.
- The value chain highlights how information systems add value to the primary and support activities of a firm's internal operations, as well as to the activities of its customers, and other components of its supply chain.
- CRM systems are a coordinated set of activities designed to help an organization better know and understand their customers.
- The resource-based view (RBV) helps a firm understand the value created by their strategy. RBV maintains that competitive advantage comes from the information resources of the firm. Resources enable a firm to attain and sustain competitive advantage.
- IT can facilitate strategic alliances. Supply chain management (SCM) is one example of a mechanism for creating strategic alliances.
- Co-opetition is the complex arrangement through which companies cooperate and compete at the same time with other companies in its value net.
- Numerous risks are associated with using information systems to gain strategic advantage: awaking a sleeping giant, demonstrating bad timing, implementing poorly, failing to deliver what customers want, and running afoul of the law.

▶ KEY TERMS

customer relationship
  management (CRM)
  (p. 60)
co-opetition (p. 66)
information resources
  (p. 48)

IT asset (p. 49)
IT capability (p. 49)
network effects (p. 51)
resource-based view
  (RBV) (p. 62)
strategic alliance (p. 66)

supply chain management
  (SCM) (p. 60)
Web 2.0 (p. 49)

▶ DISCUSSION QUESTIONS

1. How can information itself provide a competitive advantage to an organization? Give two or three examples. For each example, describe its associated risks.

2. Use the five competitive forces model as described in this chapter to describe how information technology might be used to provide a winning position for each of these businesses:

   a. A global airline

   b. A local dry cleaner

   c. An appliance service firm (provides services to fix and maintain appliances)

   d. A bank

   e. A Web-based wine retailer

3. Using the value chain model, describe how information technology might be used to provide a winning position for each of these businesses:

   a. A global airline

   b. A local dry cleaner

   c. An appliance service firm (provides services to fix and maintain appliances)

   d. A bank

   e. A Web-based wine retailer

4. Use the resource-based view as described in this chapter to describe how information technology might be used to provide and sustain a winning position for each of these businesses:

   a. A global airline

   b. A local dry cleaner

   c. An appliance service firm (provides services to fix and maintain appliances)

   d. A bank

   e. A Web-based wine retailer

5. Some claim that no sustainable competitive advantages can be gained from IT other than the capability of the IS organization itself. Do you agree or disagree? Defend your position.

6. Cisco Systems has a network of component suppliers, distributors, and contract manufacturers that are linked through Cisco's extranet. When a customer orders a Cisco product at Cisco's Web site, the order triggers contracts to manufacturers of printed circuit board assemblies when appropriate and alerts distributors and component suppliers. Cisco's contract manufacturers are aware of the order because they can log on to Cisco's extranet and link with Cisco's own manufacturing execution systems. What are the advantages of Cisco's strategic alliances? Does this Cisco example demonstrate SCM? Why or why not?

7. Tesco, the UK retail grocery chain, used their CRM system to generate annual incremental sales of £100 million. Using a frequent-shopper card, a customer got discounts at the time of purchase, and the company got information about their purchases, creating a detailed database of customer preferences. Tesco then categorized customers and customized discounts and mailings, generating increased sales and identifying new products to expand their offerings. At the individual stores, data showed which products must be priced below competitors, which products had fewer price-sensitive customers, and which products must have regular low prices to be successful. In some cases, prices are store-specific, based on the customer information. The information system has enabled Tesco to expand beyond groceries to books, CDs, DVDs, consumer electronics, flowers, and wine. The chain also offers services such as loans, credit cards, savings accounts, and travel planning. What can Tesco management do now that they have a CRM that they

could not do prior to the CRM implementation? How does this system enable Tesco to increase the value provided to customers?

CASE STUDY 2-1

LEAR WON'T TAKE A BACKSEAT

For decades, Lear Corp. made car seats. Today, with the help of virtual reality and other digital technologies, Lear makes a whole lot more—and makes it a whole lot faster. Lear Corp. used virtual reality to envision the interior of the Chevrolet Express LT, a new luxury van that Lear helped design and build. Within two years, the first models started coming off a GM assembly line near St. Louis.

In the automotive world, that kind of turnaround time is almost impossibly quick. Even when the shell of a vehicle already exists, as it did in this case, the vehicle design schedule traditionally spans about three years. Between the initial concept and the production-ready design lies a painstaking clay-modeling process that typically involves at least a half-dozen costly iterations. But by shifting much of that process to a virtual reality environment, Lear cut the product development period to a year and a half.

GM awarded Lear the lucrative contract for the Express LT largely because of the speed and flexibility that Lear's use of technology makes possible. "We always thought of Lear as a great seating company," says Linda Cook, 45, GM's planning director for commercial trucks and vans. "We didn't realize how much else it could do. Lear really needed that technology to get our attention."

Lear, based in Southfield, Michigan, has roots that go back to 1917. By the 1990s, it had become the world's biggest manufacturer of automotive seating. (If you've sat in anything from a Chevy to a Ferrari recently, then you've probably enjoyed the comfort of a Lear product.) But in the mid-1990s, the auto parts industry entered a period of aggressive consolidation. Instead of relying on thousands of small vendors to make each part separately, automakers wanted to buy complete systems from a few big suppliers. So Lear snapped up smaller companies and combined them into an operation that was capable of making an entire vehicle interior. It also invested heavily in the latest computer-aided design (CAD) software and in other new technologies. By 2000, thanks to acquisitions and expansion into new product areas, sales had climbed to $14.1 billion.

CAD first appeared in the auto industry in the late 1970s, but it didn't reach a critical mass of power and capability until the mid-1990s. That's when Lear decided to invest in an animated virtual reality package from Alias|Wavefront, a software subsidiary of Silicon Graphics. By 1998, the Reality Center was under construction, complete with a triple-projection screen and three digitized drawing boards. Out went the chisel; in came the cursor. Thanks to this technology, Lear has all but eliminated the slow, muck-filled process of building prototype after prototype from brownish-orange sculpting clay. However, Lear typically makes at least one physical prototype of every product that it develops in the Reality Center in order to test tactile issues.

In exploring new technologies, the Lear team was tempted at first by the prospect of using them to change long-standing ways of working together. Take the Internet. By digitizing much of the design process, Lear made it possible for designers to send their work back and forth over the Net—thereby creating a virtual workplace that brings together people from all around the world. In November 1998, for example, Rothkop traveled to a Volvo design center in Sweden and used the Net to work with colleagues at the Reality Center back in Southfield. Where the Internet extends or enhances communication, the Lear team has embraced it. For the most part, though, the real work of designing auto parts remains an up-close-and-personal business.

For that reason, when it came to building the Reality Center, Lear put a premium on creating an environment that would foster collaboration. The team considered a stereoscopic "cave," a space in which people can sit and be completely surrounded by a screen. While that arrangement simulates being in a car, "it can kind of make people nauseated," Rothkop says. Worse yet, only one or two people at a time can sit in the cave—a situation that has dismal implications for collaboration. Instead, the Lear team chose a simpler design for its virtual reality room, one that has a flatter screen and a more open space. There's even room in front of the screen for a full-sized truck, so Lear designers can bring together the real and the virtual whenever their work calls for that.

Another temptation that Lear executives faced was to think that CAD and VR would let them break down traditional job barriers and combine the roles of designer, sculptor, and animator into a single worker. But, in Lear's experience, the seemingly artificial barriers between jobs often turn out to be quite natural. So Lear drew back from the notion of combining jobs.

Discussion Questions

1. What is the strategic advantage afforded to Lear from virtual reality? How does this technology help it compete?
2. How long is Lear's window of opportunity for the strategic advantage given by the virtual reality system? That is, do you think that competitors will follow suit and implement a similar system. If yes, when?
3. Do you think the CAD system offers Lear strategic advantage? Explain.
4. Apply the value chain to demonstrate how the virtual reality system adds value for Lear and for General Motors.
5. What other types of competitive advantages might Lear executives seek from IS in general?

Source: Adapted from Fara Warner, "Lear Won't Take a Backseat," *Fast Company* 47 (June 2001), p. 178, available at http://www.fastcompany.com/online/47/bestpractice.html.

CASE STUDY 2-2

ZIPCAR

Zipcar was an answer for customers who want to rent a car for a few hours in their home city, rather than for a few days from a traditional rental agency. Car reservations were for a specific pick up time and location around the city, often in neighborhoods so the customers need only to walk to pick up their reserved car. Customers applied for a Zipcard, which enabled them to reserve a car online and unlock their car when they arrive at the car's location.

The company operated with a very small staff compared to traditional rental agencies. Very little human interaction was required between the customer and Zipcar for a transaction. A customer reserved a car online, entered into the reserved car by waving the RFID-enabled Zipcard against the card reader mounted behind the windshield on the driver side, returned the car to the same location, and was billed on the credit card already on file. The customer could check all rental records and print receipts from the online reservation system. The system also had a color-coded time chart showing availability and location of all rental cars in the vicinity. This transparent information exchange allows a customer to pick the car he or she wants, if available, or delay the reservation until the car was returned by another customer. Zipcar also created and installed a GPS-enabled wireless device in each car, which allowed members to find and reserve a nearest vehicle using a cell phone.

All the cars were outfitted with patented wireless technology. Their proprietary IT platform carried information flow between customers, vehicles, and the company. It was used to monitor car security, fulfill reservations, record hourly usage, and maintain mileage information. It also relayed vital technical information such as battery voltage and fuel level. It even informed the central system if a customer forgot to turn off headlights, which can quickly drain battery power.

This business model provided unique advantages over traditional car rentals. The customer did not have to stand in line or fill out papers to rent a car. The customer knew exactly which make and model he or she would be getting. Unlike most off-airport rental agency locations, which were only open during business hours, Zipcar locations were open 24 hours. The Zipcar rates also included the cost of gas and insurance, as well as reserved parking spots at some locations.

Additionally, the company used social networking technologies to develop an online community of Zipcar members—Zipsters. It encouraged Zipsters to talk about their Ziptrips (i.e., share their personal experiences with Zipcar).

Thus, information technology was not only the key enabler of this business model but also was a facilitator in creating a buzz and encouraging community development around the concept. Zipcar changed the rules of the rental car industry by bringing the new Web 2.0 mind-set of focusing on automation, customer empowerment, transparency, and community. Zipcar has been very successful, with over 200,000 paying members and renting over 5,000 vehicles in 50 markets in the United States, Canada, and the UK.

Discussion Questions

1. Analyze the business model of Zipcar using Porter's five forces model.
2. Discuss the synergy between the business strategy of Zipcar and information technology.
3. What *network effects* are part of the strategy of Zipcar? How do they add value?
4. As the CEO of Zipcar, where is your most threatening competition? What would you do to sustain a competitive advantage?

Source: Adapted from "A Self-Service Rental Car," by Paul Boutin, *BusinessWeek*, May 4, 2006; "RFID: A Ticket to Ride," by Mary K. Pratt, *ComputerWorld*, December 18, 2006; www.zipcar.com.

3

ORGANIZATIONAL IMPACTS OF INFORMATION SYSTEMS USE

Started in mid-1990s, Cognizant Technology Solutions grew quickly to become a $1.4 billion revenue company providing IT outsourcing services. However, growing at such a breakneck speed, it had to reinvent its organization structure multiple times. Initially, its India-centric structure located the managers of each group in India along with software engineers. Employees at customer locations worldwide reported to the managers. As the company grew and its focus shifted from simple, cost-based solutions to complex, relationship-based solutions, this model had to be changed. Under the redesigned reporting structure, the managers were moved to customer locations, while software engineers remained in India. This change improved customer relations but brought in new headaches on the technical side. Under the new arrangement, managers had to spend daytime with customers and unexpectedly ended up spending nighttime with software engineers to clarify customer requirements and fix bugs. This placed a tremendous strain on managers, who threatened to quit. Thus, either type of organizational structure was not working. According to Francisco D'Souza, CEO, "Frankly, we were out of ideas [about what to do]."

However, they found that despite these problems, some groups were working well and providing solid performance. After an extensive analysis of those groups, the company decided to adopt their informal management structure of comanagement throughout the company. In this matrix structure, each project has two managers equally responsible for the project. One manger is in India, and the other is at the client site. They work out among themselves how and when to deal with issues. And both are equally responsible for customer satisfaction, project deadlines and group revenue.[1]

The point is simple: Information systems (IS) comprise a fundamental organizational component that affects the way managers design their organizations.

[1] Excerpted from J. McGregor "For Cognizant, Two's Company." *BusinessWeek*, January 17, 2008.

When used appropriately, IS and information technology (IT) leverage human resources, capital, and materials to create an organization that optimizes performance. A synergy results from designing organizations with IT in mind that cannot be achieved when IT is just added on.

Chapter 1 introduced a simple framework for understanding the impact of IS on organizations. The Information Systems Strategy Triangle relates business strategy with IS strategy and organizational strategy. In an organization that operates successfully, an overriding business strategy drives both organizational strategy and information strategy. The most effective businesses optimize the interrelationships between the organization and IT, thus maximizing efficiency and productivity.

Organizational strategy includes the organization's design, as well as the managerial choices that define, set up, coordinate, and control its work processes. As discussed in Chapter 1, many models of organizational strategy are available, such as the business diamond, which identifies four primary components of an organization: its business processes, its tasks and structures (or organizational design), its management and measurement (control) systems, and its values and beliefs (culture). Figure 3.1 summarizes complementary design variables from the managerial levers framework. Optimized organizational design and management control systems support the most advantageous business processes, and they, in turn, reflect the firm's values and culture.

This chapter builds on the managerial levers model. Of primary concern is the ways in which IT can improve organizational design, management control, and organizational culture. This chapter looks at some innovative organizational designs that made extensive use of IT, explores how IT can facilitate management control at the organizational and individual levels, and concludes with some ideas about how culture affects organizational design. It focuses on organizational-level issues related to strategy. The next two chapters complement it with a discussion of new approaches to work and organizational processes.

▶ INFORMATION TECHNOLOGY AND ORGANIZATIONAL DESIGN

This section examines how IT enables or inhibits the design of an organization's physical structure. Ideally an organization is designed to facilitate the communication and work processes necessary for it to accomplish its goals. In this section we will talk about decision rights that underlie formal structures, formal reporting relationships, and information network. Also of importance are organizational processes. We will study processes in more detail in Chapter 5.

Decision Rights

Decision rights indicate who in the organization has the responsibility to initiate, supply information for, approve, implement, and control various types of decisions. Ideally the individual who has the most information about a decision and who is in

Variable	Description
Organizational variables	
Decision rights	Authority to initiate, approve, implement, and control various types of decisions necessary to plan and run the–business.
Business processes	The set of ordered tasks needed to complete key objectives of the business.
Formal reporting relationships	The structure set up to ensure coordination among all units within the organization; reflects allocation of decision rights.
Informal networks	Mechanism, such as ad hoc groups, which work to coordinate and transfer information outside the formal reporting relationships.
Control variables	
Data	The facts collected, stored, and used by the organization.
Planning	The processes by which future direction is established, communicated, and implemented.
Performance measurement and evaluation	The set of measures that are used to assess success in the execution of plans and the processes by which such measures are used to improve the quality of work.
Incentives	The monetary and nonmonetary devices used to motivate behavior within an organization.
Cultural variables	
Values	The set of implicit and explicit beliefs that underlies decisions made and actions taken; reflects aspirations about the way things should be done.

FIGURE 3.1 Organizational design variables.
Source: James I. Cash, Robert G. Eccles, Nitin Nohria, and Richard L. Nolan, *Building the Information Age Organization* (Homewood, IL: Richard D. Irwin, 1994).

the best position to understand all the relevant issues should be the person who has the decision right for the decision. Much of the discussion of IT governance in Chapter 8 is based on who has the decision right for critical IT decisions. And, when talking about accountability and responsibility in the chapter on ethics (Chapter 9), one has to start with the person who is responsible for the decision—that is, the person who has the decision right for the decision. Organizational design is all about making sure that decision rights are properly allocated—and reflected in the structure of formal reporting relationships.

Consider the case of Zara from Chapter 2. Each of its 1,000 stores order clothes in the same way, using the same digital form, using the same outdated PDAs, following a rigid weekly timetable for ordering. Most other large retailers use forecasting and inventory control models to determine what clothes should be sent to the stores. That is, the ordering decisions are made at headquarters. However, with Zara, the decision rights for ordering have been moved to the

Zara store managers. By giving them the decision rights for ordering, Zara store managers can place orders that reflect the tastes and preferences of customers in their localized areas.[2]

Formal Reporting Relationships and Organization Structures

Organization structure is the way of designing an organization so that decision rights are correctly allocated. The structure of reporting relationships typically reflects the flow of communication and decision making throughout the organization. Traditional organization structures are hierarchical, flat, or matrix (see Figure 3.2).

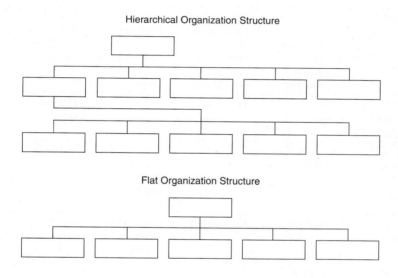

Hierarchical Organization Structure

Flat Organization Structure

Matrix Organization Structure

Industry \ Regions	Region 1	Region 2	Region 3
Industry 1	Position for industry 1 in region 1	Position for industry 1 in region 2	Position for industry 1 in region 3
Industry 2	Position for industry 2 in region 1	Position for industry 2 in region 2	Position for industry 2 in region 3
Industry 3	Position for industry 3 in region 1	Position for industry 3 in region 2	Position for industry 3 in region 3

FIGURE 3.2   Hierarchical, flat, and matrix organization structures.

[2] Andrew McAfee and Erik Brynjolfsson, "Investing in the IT That Makes a Competitive Difference," *Harvard Business Review*, http://harvard businessonline.hbsp.harvard.edu 2008 (accessed July 21, 2008).

	Hierarchical	Flat	Matrix	Networked
Description	Bureaucratic form with defined levels of management	Decision making pushed down to the lowest level in the organization	Workers assigned to two or more supervisors in an effort to make sure multiple dimensions of the business are integrated	Formal and informal communication networks that connect all parts of the company
Characteristics	Division of labor, specialization, unity of command, formalization	Informal roles, planning and control; often small and young organizations	Dual reporting relationships based on function and purpose	Known for flexibility and adaptability
Type of Environment Best Supported	Stable Certain	Dynamic Uncertain	Dynamic Uncertain	Dynamic Uncertain
Basis of Structuring	Primarily function	Primarily function	Functions and purpose (i.e., location, product, customer)	Networks
Power Structure	Centralized	Centralized	Distributed (matrix managers)	Distributed (network)
Key Technologies Supporting This Structure	Mainframe, centralized data and processing	Personal computers	Networks	Intranets and Internet

FIGURE 3.3 Comparison of organizational structures.

The networked structure is a newer organizational form. A comparison of these four types of organization structures may be found in Figure 3.3.

Hierarchical Organization Structure

As business organizations entered the twentieth century, they found themselves growing and needing to devise systems for processing and storing information. A new class of worker—the clerical worker—flourished. From 1870 to 1920 alone, the number of clerical workers mushroomed from 74,200 to more than a quarter of a million.[3] Factories and offices structured themselves using the model that Max Weber observed when studying the Catholic Church and the German army. This model, called a bureaucracy, was based on a hierarchical organization structure.

Hierarchical organization structure is an organizational form based on the concepts of division of labor, specialization, and unity of command. Decision rights are highly specified and centralized. When work needs to be done, it typically comes from the top and is segmented into smaller and smaller pieces until it reaches the level of the business in which it will be done. Middle managers do the primary information processing and communicating, telling their subordinates what to do and telling senior managers the outcome of what was done. Jobs within the organization are specialized and often organized around particular functions, such as marketing, accounting, manufacturing, and so on. Unity of command means that each person has a single supervisor, who in turn has a supervisor, and so on. A number of rules are established to handle the routine work performed by employees of the organization. When in doubt about how to complete a task, workers turn to rules. If a rule doesn't exist to handle the situation, workers turn to the hierarchy for the decision. Key decisions are made at the top and filter down through the organization in a centralized fashion. IS are typically used to store and communicate information along the lines of the hierarchy and to support the information management function of the managers. Hierarchical structures are most suited to relatively stable, certain environments where the top-level executives are in command of the information needed to make critical decisions.

Two common organizational forms are based on the hierarchical organization structure: functional and divisional. The **functional form** is a structure that groups common activities together. The division of labor is based on key functions, such as accounting, marketing, finance, engineering, and production. Because the training, work, and values are typically similar for people in the same function, their collaboration and efficiency is promoted within the function. This creates economies of scale and enables in-depth knowledge and skill development. At the same time, coordination and cooperation with other departments is more difficult. The functional form was used in practically every business up to World War II. It is still used in many small and medium-sized companies, especially if they only have one or a few products or services. In contrast is the divisional form that was "invented" by General Motors and DuPont. The **divisional form** cuts across functional lines and, instead, organizes according to outputs. Each division is responsible for a different set of customers, products, geographical markets, and so forth. Within the divisional unit, diverse functions such as manufacturing and marketing are represented, but employees tend to relate more to their division than to the functional area. The divisional form is good for coordinating organizational activities across functions, especially in unstable or dynamic environments. Typically it is more customer focused. Cognizant's original

---

[3] Frances Cairncross, *The Company of the Future* (London: Profile Books, 2002).

India-centric organizational structure described at the beginning of the chapter is an example of a divisional form.

Flat Organization Structure

In contrast, in the **flat organization structure**, decision making is centralized, with the power often residing in the owner or founder. In flat organizations, everyone does whatever needs to be done to complete business. For this reason, flat organizations can respond quickly to dynamic, uncertain environments. Entrepreneurial organizations often use this structure because they typically have fewer employees, and even when they grow, they initially build on the premise that everyone must do whatever is needed. To increase flexibility and innovation, decision rights may not be clearly defined. As the work grows, new individuals are added to the organization, and eventually a hierarchy is formed where divisions are responsible for segments of the work processes. Many companies strive to keep the "entrepreneurial spirit," but in reality work gets done in much the same way as with the hierarchy described previously. Flat organizations often use IS to off-load certain routine work to avoid hiring additional workers. As a hierarchy develops, the IS become the glue tying together parts of the organization that otherwise would not communicate.

Matrix Organization Structure

The third popular form, the **matrix organization structure**, typically assigns workers to two or more supervisors in an effort to make sure multiple dimensions of the business are integrated. Each supervisor directs a different aspect of the employee's work. For example, a member of a matrix team from marketing would have a supervisor for marketing decisions and a different supervisor for a specific product line. The team member would report to both, and both would be responsible in some measure for that member's performance and development. That is, the marketing manager would oversee the employee's development of marketing skills, and the product manager would make sure that the employee developed skills related to the product. Thus, decision rights are shared between the managers. In some cases the matrix might even reflect still a third dimension (or more), such as the customer relations segment. IS reduce the operating complexity of matrix organizations by allowing information sharing among the different managerial functions. For example, a salesperson's sales would be entered into the information system and appear in the results of all managers to whom he or she reports. The matrix structure allows organizations to concentrate on both functions and purpose. It is especially suited to dynamic, uncertain environments and to complex decision making. Cognizant likely moved to the matrix structure from the hierarchical, divisional structure because the complexity of its projects had increased.

The matrix organization structure carries its own set of weaknesses. Though theoretically each boss has a well-defined area of authority, employees often find the matrix organization structure frustrating and confusing because they are often subjected to dual authority. Consequently, working in a matrix organization structure can be time consuming because confusion must be dealt with through frequent meetings and conflict resolution sessions. Matrix organizations also often make it difficult for managers to achieve their business strategies because they flood managers with more information than they can process.

Networked Organization Structure

Made possible by new IS, a fourth type of organizational structure emerged: the **networked organization structure** (see Figure 3.4). Networked organizations characteristically feel both flat and hierarchical at the same time. An article published in the *Harvard Business Review* describes this type of organization: "Rigid hierarchies are replaced by formal and informal communication networks that connect all parts of the company.... [This type of organizational structure] is well known for its flexibility and adaptiveness."[4] It is particularly suited to dynamic, unstable environments.

Networked organization structures are those that rely on highly decentralized decision rights and utilize distributed information and communication systems to replace inflexible hierarchical controls with controls based in IS. Networked organizations are defined by their ability to promote creativity and flexibility while maintaining operational process control. Because networked structures are distributed, many employees throughout the organization can share their knowledge and experience and participate in making key organizational decisions. IS are fundamental to process design; they improve process efficiency, effectiveness, and

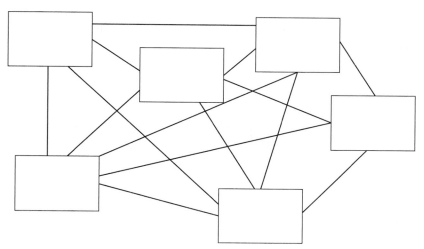

FIGURE 3.4 The networked organization.

[4] L. M. Applegate, J. I. Cash, and D. Q. Mills, "Information Technology and Tomorrow's Manager," *Harvard Business Review*, (November–December 1988), 128–136.

flexibility. As part of the execution of these processes, data are gathered and stored in centralized data warehouses for use in analysis and decision making. In theory, at least, decision making is more timely and accurate because data are collected and stored instantly. The extensive use of communications technologies and networks also renders it easier to coordinate across functional boundaries. In short, the networked organization is one in which IT ties together people, processes, and units.

The organization feels flat when IT is used primarily as a communication vehicle. Traditional hierarchical lines of authority are used for tasks other than communication when everyone can communicate with everyone else, at least in theory. The term used is *technological leveling* because the technology enables individuals from all parts of the organization to reach all other parts of the organization.

Some organizations take the networked structure one step further. When IT is used extensively as a design tool for the organization, a different organizational form called the T-form organization is possible. The "T" stands for "technology-based" or "technology-oriented." In T-form organizations, IT is combined with traditional organizational components to form new types of components, such as electronic linking, production automation, electronic workflows, electronic customer/supplier relationships, and self-service Internet portals. Although the original T-form organization was created long before the Internet was popular, this structure has been adopted by many Internet-based companies today. Work is often coordinated automatically in the T-form organization. Systems enable information to more easily move around an organization and among individuals, making decisions possible wherever they are needed, rather than only at senior levels of the organization. Business processes are typically designed differently, relying on the technology for more mundane, repetitive tasks and enabling employees to take on more people-oriented and unstructured responsibilities. Technology is integrated with all components of the business, not just communications networks, as in a traditional networked organization.

Informal Networks

The organization structure reflects the authority derived from formal reporting relationships. However, informal relationships also exist and can play an important role in the functioning of an organization. Some informal relationships are designed by management. For example, when working on a special project, an employee might be asked to let the manager in another department know what is going on. This is considered an informal reporting relationship. Or a company may have a job rotation program. Part of the rationale for such programs is that it allows employees to get a broad-based training in a variety of areas. That way the employees can learn about and appreciate the work that is done in the multiple departments where they have worked. It also allows them to make contacts, and even friends, in these departments where they work. Long after they have moved on to another job, they may keep in touch informally or call on their past coworkers when a situation arises in which their input may be helpful.

Not all informal relationships are a consequence of a plan by management. Some networks unintended by management develop because of a variety of other factors, including work proximity, friendship, shared interests, and family ties. They can also arise for political reasons. Employees can cross over departmental, functional, or divisional lines in an effort to create political coalitions to further their goals.

Some informal networks even cross organizational boundaries. As computer and information technologies facilitate collaboration across distances, social networks are formed. Many of these prove useful in getting a job done, even if not all members of the network belong to the same organization.

► INFORMATION TECHNOLOGY AND MANAGEMENT CONTROL SYSTEMS

Not only does IT change the way organizations are structured, it also profoundly affects the way managers control their organizations. By management control, we mean how planning is performed in organizations and how people and processes are monitored, evaluated, and compensated or rewarded. Management control is similar to room thermostats. Thermostats register the desired temperature. A sensing device within the thermostat determines if the temperature in the room is within a specified range of the desired temperature. If the temperature is beyond the desired range, a mechanism is activated to adjust the temperature. For instance, if the thermostat is set at 78 and the temperature in the room is 76, then the heater can be activated (if it is winter) or the air conditioning can be turned off (if it is summer).

Similarly management control systems must respond to the goals established through planning. Measurements must be taken periodically, and if the variance is too great, adjustments must be made to organizational processes or practices. For example, operating processes might need to be changed to achieve the desired goals.

IS plays three important roles in management control processes:

1. *Data Collection* They enable the collection of information that may not be collectible other ways. This information helps managers determine if they are satisfactorily progressing toward realizing the organization's mission as reflected in its stated goals.

2. *Evaluation* They facilitate the analysis of information in ways that may not be possible otherwise. The evaluation compares actual performance with the desired performance that is established as a result of planning.

3. *Communication* They speed the flow of information from where it is generated to where it is needed. This allows an analysis of the situation and a determination about what can be done to correct the situation.

Managers need to control work done at the process level. The process itself needs continuous improvement, and although the various methods of process improvement lie outside the scope of this book, it is important to understand that IS can play a crucial role. IS provide decision models for scenario planning and evaluation. For example, the airlines routinely use decision models to study the effects of changing routes or schedules. IS collect and analyze information from automated processes, which can then be used to make automatic adjustments to the processes. For example, a paper mill uses IS to monitor the mixing of ingredients in a batch of paper and to add more ingredients or change the temperature of the boiler as necessary. IS collect, evaluate, and communicate information, leaving managers free to make decisions.

Planning and Information Technology

In the first chapter, the importance of aligning organizational strategy with the business strategy was discussed. An output of the strategizing process is a plan to guide in achieving the strategic objectives. Information technology can play a role in planning in three ways:

- IS can provide the necessary data to develop the strategic plan. They can be especially useful in collecting data from organizational units and transforming the data into information for the strategic decision makers.

- Some IS actually automate the planning process.

- In some instances, IS can lie at the heart of a strategic initiative. That is, as discussed in Chapters 1 and 2, information systems can be used to gain strategic advantage.

Data Collection and Information Technology

In addition to focusing on organizational-level planning and control, the next three subsections in this chapter focus on the individual level. An important part of management control lies in making sure individuals perform appropriately. At the individual level, IS can streamline the process of data collection (i.e., monitoring) and support performance measurement and evaluation, as well as compensation through salaries, incentives, and rewards.

Monitoring work can take on a completely new meaning with the use of information technologies. IS make it possible to collect such data as the number of keystrokes, the precise time spent on a task, exactly who was contacted, and the specific data that passed through the process. For example, a call center that handles customer service telephone calls is typically monitored by an information system that collects data on the number of calls each representative received and the length of time each representative took to answer each call and then to respond to the question or request for service. Managers at call centers can easily and nonintrusively collect data on virtually any part of the process. In contrast, a manager of field representatives might also use IS to monitor work, but the use may be more obvious and, thus, more intrusive. For example, having field sales personnel complete documents detailing their progress adds work for them.

The organizational design challenge in data collection is twofold: (1) to embed monitoring tasks within everyday work, and (2) to reduce the negative impacts to workers being monitored. Workers perceive their regular tasks as value adding, but have difficulty in seeing how value is added by tasks designed to provide information for management control. Often these tasks are avoided, or worse, data recorded are inaccurate, falsified, or untimely. Collecting monitoring data directly from work tasks—or embedding the creation and storage of performance information into software used to perform work—renders them more reliable.

A large number of software products are available for companies to monitor employees. Software monitoring products are installed by companies to obtain specific data about what employees are doing. Although the intention may seem both ethical and in the best interest of business, in practice the reverse may actually be true. In many cases employees are not informed that they are being monitored or that the information gleaned is being used to measure their productivity. In these cases, monitoring violates both privacy and personal freedoms. To protect their freedoms and to gain their acceptance, employees should be informed when they are monitored, and their bonuses or other rewards should be linked to increases in productivity derived from the monitoring.

However, prior notice about monitoring may heighten employee stress levels and highlight an increase in the level of control that employers are exerting over their employees. As employees become aware of monitoring activities, productivity and morale may fall. Also, tracking job performance in terms of discrete, measurable tasks can serve to disconnect workers from the larger business process in which they are involved, giving them less opportunity to broaden their skills and advance in the organization. Breaking down jobs into simple tasks counters an organizational philosophy that seeks to empower individuals to make significant contributions to the company as a whole. Although the side effects of monitoring may seem peripheral or minor, its importance can only increase as technology further intrudes into the workplace and shapes working conditions. Today's managers must be concerned with creating a work atmosphere that is amenable to IS and responsive to employees' needs.

Performance Measurement, Evaluation, and Information Technology

IS make it possible to evaluate data against reams of standard or historical data as desired. Models can be built and simulations designed. Thus, managers can more easily and completely understand work progress and performance. In fact, the ready availability of so much information catches some managers in "analysis paralysis": analyzing too much or too long. In our example of the call center, a manager can compare a worker's output to that of colleagues, to earlier output, and to historical outputs reflecting similar work conditions at other times. Even though evaluation constitutes an important use of IS, how the information is used has significant organizational consequences. Information collected for evaluation may be used to provide feedback so the worker can improve personal performance; it also can be used to determine rewards and compensation. The former use—for improvement in performance—is nonthreatening and generally welcome. Using the same information for determining compensation or rewards, however, can be threatening. Suppose the call center manager is evaluating the number and duration of calls that service representatives answer on a given day. The manager's goal is to make sure all calls are answered quickly, and he or she communicates that goal to his or her staff. Now think about how the evaluation information is used. If the manager simply provides the workers with information about numbers and duration, then the evaluation is not threatening. Typically, each worker will make his or her own evaluation and respond by improving call numbers and duration. A discussion may even occur in which the service representative describes other important dimensions, such as customer satisfaction and quality. Perhaps the representative takes longer than average on each call because of the attention devoted to the customer. On the other hand, if the manager uses the information about number of calls and duration to rank workers so that top workers are rewarded, then workers may feel threatened by the evaluation and respond accordingly. The representative not on the top of the list may shorten calls or deliver less quality, consequently decreasing customer satisfaction. The lesson for managers is to take care concerning what is monitored and how the information the systems make available is used. Metrics for performance must be meaningful in terms of the organization's broader goals, but these metrics are harder to define when work is decentralized and monitored electronically.

How feedback is communicated in the organization plays a role in affecting behavior. Some feedback can be communicated via IS themselves. A simple example is the feedback built into an electronic form that will not allow it to be submitted until it is properly filled out. For more complex feedback, IS may not be the appropriate vehicle. For example, no one would want to be told they were doing a poor job via e-mail or voice mail. Negative feedback of significant consequence often is best delivered in person.

IS can allow for feedback from a variety of participants who otherwise could not be involved. Many companies do a "360-degree" feedback, into which the individual's supervisors, subordinates, and coworkers all provide input. IS make it relatively easy to solicit feedback from anyone who has access to the system. Because that feedback is received more quickly, improvements can be made faster.

Incentives and Rewards and Information Technology

Incentives and rewards are the ways organizations encourage good performance. A clever reward system can make employees feel good without paying them more money. IS can affect these processes, too. Some organizations use their Web sites to recognize high performers. Others reward them with new technology. At one organization, top performers get new computers every year, whereas lower performers get the "hand-me-downs."

IS make it easier to design complex incentive systems, such as shared or team-based incentives. An information system facilitates keeping track of contributions of team members and, in conjunction with qualitative inputs, can be used to allocate rewards according to complex formulas. For example, in the call center example, tracking metrics, such as "average time per call" and "number of calls answered," allows the manager to monitor agents' performance. This quantitative data makes for useful comparisons, but it cannot account for qualitative variables: for example, agents who spend more time handling calls may be providing better customer service. Agents who know they will be evaluated by the volume of calls they process may rush callers and provide poorer service to maximize their performance according to the narrow metric. Agents providing the poorest service could, in fact, be compensated best if the firm's performance evaluation and compensation strategy is linked only to such metrics. The manager must consider both the metrics and qualitative data in assigning compensation and rewards.

▶ INFORMATION TECHNOLOGY AND CULTURE

The third managerial lever is culture. Culture is playing an increasingly important role in information system development and use. Hence, it is important to consider culture when devising organizational strategy. **Culture** is defined as a shared "set of values and beliefs about what is desirable and undesirable in a community of people."[5] **Beliefs** are the perceptions that people hold about how things are done in their community, whereas **values** reflect the community's aspirations about the way things should be done.

Culture has been compared to an iceberg because, like an iceberg, only part of the culture is visible from the surface. It is possible to see formal ceremonies, traditional dress, symbols in art, and other cultural artifacts. What is not visible are unspoken rules, values, and beliefs that are so deep-seated they are hard to express.[6] Further, culture is something of a moving target because it is not static. It evolves over time.

There are different levels of culture. Culture can occur across countries, across organizations, or even within organizations. For instance, Google works hard to create a culture of creativity throughout its organization. Employees get a "free" day a week to pursue their dream project and are encouraged to share their ideas with other employees. They can do so with technology or during one of the free meals at the company cafeteria or in the company laundry room when they move their clothes from the washer to the dryer.

An example at the organizational level is when IS developers have different values from the clients in the same organization for whom they are developing systems. Clients may favor computer-based development practices that encourage reusability of components that allow flexibility and fast turnaround. Developers, on the other hand, may prefer a development approach that favors stability and control, but tends to be slower.

---

[5] Mansour Javidan and R. J. House, "Cultural Acumen for the Global Manager," *Organizational Dynamics* 29, no. 4 (2001), 292.

[6] E. Schein, *Organizational Change and Leadership*, 3rd ed. (New York: Wiley, 2004).

Differences in national culture may also affect system development and use. For example, when one of this book's authors was designing a database in Malaysia, she asked questions that required a "yes" or "no" response. In trying to reconcile the strange set of responses she received, the author learned that Malaysians are hesitant to ever say "No." Cultural differences have been noted in terms of development practices, Web design, change request strategies, adherence to schedules, incentive schemes, and many other aspects of IS development and use.

Certainly one of the best-known (and prolific) researchers in the area differences in the values across national cultures is Geert Hofstede. Hofstede[7] originally identified four major dimensions of national culture: power distance, uncertainty avoidance, individualism-collectivism, and masculinity-femininity. To correct for a possible bias toward Western values, a new dimension, Confucian Work Dynamism, also referred to as "short-term vs. long-term orientation," was later added.[8] Many others have used, built upon, or tried to correct problems related to Hofstede's four dimensions. One notable project is the GLOBE (Global Leadership and Organizational Behavior Effectiveness) research program which is a team of 150 researchers who have collected data on cultural values and practices and leadership attributes from over 18,000 managers in 62 countries. The GLOBE project has uncovered nine cultural dimensions, six of which have their origins in Hofstede's pioneering work. The GLOBE dimensions and their relationship to Hofstede's dimensions are summarized in Figure 3.5.

Even though the world may be becoming "flatter," cultural differences have not totally disappeared. When people from different cultures come together, they may converge on some things. Yet, culturally based idiosyncrasies may surface. Having an understanding and appreciation for cultural values, practices, and subtleties can help in smoothing the challenges that occur in dealing with these idiosyncrasies. An awareness of the Hofstede or GLOBE dimensions may help improve communications and reduce conflict.

Effective communication means listening, framing the message in a way that is understandable to the receiver, and responding to feedback. Effective cross-cultural communication involves all of these plus searching for an integrated solution that can be accepted and implemented by members of diverse cultures. This may not be as simple as it sounds. For instance typical American managers, noted for their high-performance orientation, prefer direct and explicit language full of facts and figures. However, managers in lower-performance-oriented countries like Russia or Greece tend to prefer indirect and vague language that encourages the exploration of ideas.[9] In countries with high levels of uncertainty avoidance, such as Switzerland and Austria, meetings should be planned in

[7] G. Hofstede, *Culture's Consequences: International Differences in Work-Related Values* (London: Sage, 1980).

[8] G. Hofstede and M. H. Bond, The Confucius Connection: From Cultural Roots to Economic Growth, *Organizational Dynamics* 16 (1988), 4021.

[9] Javidan and House, "Cultural Acumen for the Global Manager."

GLOBE Dimensions	Description	Relationship to Hofstede Dimension
Uncertainty Avoidance	Extent to which members of an organization or society strive to avoid uncertainty by reliance on social norms, rituals, and bureaucratic practices to alleviate the unpredictability of future events.	Same as Uncertainty Avoidance
Power Distance	Degree to which members of an organization or society expect and agree that power should be equally shared.	Same as Power Distance
Collectivism I: Societal Collectivism	Degree to which organizational and societal institutional practices encourage and reward collective distribution of resources and collective action.	Same as Individualism/Collectivism
Collectivism II: In-Group Collectivism	Degree to which individuals express pride, loyalty, and cohesiveness in their organizations or families	Type of Collectivism focused on small in-groups
General Egalitarianism	Extent to which an organization or society minimizes gender role differences and gender discrimination	Modified version of Masculinity/Femininity
Assertiveness	Degree to which individuals in organizations or societies are assertive, confrontational, and aggressive in social relationships	Modified version of Masculinity/Femininity
Future Orientation	Degree to which individuals in organizations or societies engage in future-oriented behaviors such as planning, investing in the future, and delaying gratification	Similar to Confucian Work Dynamism by Hofstede and Bond (1988)
Performance Orientation	Extent to which an organization or society encourages and rewards group members for performance improvement and excellence	
Humane Orientation	Degree to which individuals in organizations or societies encourage and reward individuals for being fair, altruistic, friendly, generous, caring, and kind to others.	Similar to Kind Heartedness by Hofstede and Bond (1988)

FIGURE 3.5 National Cultural Dimensions.
Source: Adapted from R. House, M. Javidan, P. Hanges, and P. Dorfman, "Understanding cultures and implicit leadership theories across the globe: An introduction to project GLOBE," *Journal of World Business* 37. no. 1 (2002), 3–10.

advance with a clear agenda. The managers in Greece or Russia who come from low uncertainty avoidance cultures often shy away from agendas or planned meetings.

Knowing that a society tends to score high or low on certain dimensions helps a manager anticipate how a person from that society might react. However, it only provides a starting point, because each person is different. Without being aware of cultural differences, though, a manager is sure to have a hard time in dealing effectively with members of other cultures.

► FOOD FOR THOUGHT: IMMEDIATELY RESPONSIVE ORGANIZATIONS

IS in general, and the Web in particular, have enabled organizations to speed up the way they operate. Organizations are now able to create the ability to respond instantly to customer demands, supplier issues, and internal communication needs. IS are enabling even more advanced organization forms such as the adaptive organization, the horizontal organization and a relatively new form, the zero time organization.[10] Common to all these designs is the idea of agile, responsive organizations that can configure their resources and people quickly and are flexible enough to sense and respond to changing demands.

The zero time organization, for example, describes the concept of instant "customerization," or the ability to respond to customers immediately. To accomplish this goal, the organization must master five disciplines:

1. *Instant value alignment* understanding the customer so well that the company anticipates and is therefore ready to provide exactly what the customer wants.

2. *Instant learning* building learning directly into the company's tasks and processes and making sure that requisite information is readily at hand when it is needed.

3. *Instant involvement* using IS to communicate all relevant information to suppliers, customers, and employees and making sure everyone is prepared to deliver their products, services, or information instantly.

4. *Instant adaptation* creating a culture and structure that enable all workers to act instantly and to make decisions to respond to customers.

5. *Instant execution* building business processes that involve as few people as possible (no touch), electronically cross organizational boundaries, and result in cycle times so short that they appear to execute instantly when the customer needs their outputs.

Building in the capability to respond instantly means designing the organization so that each of the key structural elements are able to respond instantly. For example, instant learning means building learning into the business processes. It

[10] R. Yeh, K. Pearlson, and G. Kozmetsky, *Zero Time: Providing Instant Customer Value Everytime — All the Time* (Hoboken, NJ: John Wiley & Sons, 2000).

means using IS to deliver small modules of learning directly to the point where the process is being done. For example, at Dell Computers, assembly line workers have access to a terminal directly above their workstations. As an assembly comes to their stations, its bar code tells the information system what type of assembly it is and which instructions to display. When the assembly reaches the table, the instructions are already there. The worker does not have to ask for the instructions, nor go anyplace to find them. IS allow this type of instant learning to happen.

Further, Web-based applications that are easily configured by the user, rather than by an IS specialist, enable organizations to quickly build systems that meet the businesses needs, then to reconfigure or completely redesign the systems as the business needs change.

Few companies qualify as zero time organizations with all of their processes designed in a way that allows them to respond instantly to every interaction. However, as described in Chapter 6, Web-based architectures combined with human resources from the net-generation (those who have grown up using the Internet and have the ability to conduct most of their professional life on the Net) create the foundation for instantly responsive organizations. As IS and agile technologies become ubiquitous and customers demand increasingly instant service, zero time characteristics will become even more common in business.

▶ SUMMARY

- Incorporating information systems as a fundamental organizational design component is critical to company survival. Organizational strategy includes the organization's design, the organization's culture, and the manager's choices that define, set up, coordinate, and control its work processes.
- Organizational designers today must have a working knowledge of what information systems can do and how the choice of information system will affect the organization itself.
- Organization structures can facilitate or inhibit information flows.
- Organizational design should take into account decision rights, organization structure, and informal networks.
- Structures such as flat, hierarchical, and matrix organizations are being enhanced by information technology resulting in networked organizations that can better respond to dynamic, uncertain organizational environments. IT supports networked organizations.
- Information technology affects managerial control mechanisms: planning, data, performance measurement and evaluation, and incentives and rewards.
- Management control at the individual level is concerned with monitoring (i.e., data collection), evaluating, providing feedback, compensating, and rewarding. It is the job of the manager to ensure the proper control mechanisms are in place and the interactions between the organization and the information systems do not undermine the managerial objectives.
- Organizational and national culture should be taken into account when designing and using IS.

► KEY TERMS

beliefs (p. 89)
culture (p. 89)
decision rights (p. 77)
divisional form (p. 81)
flat organization structure
    (p. 82)

functional form (p. 81)
hierarchical organization
    structure (p. 81)
matrix organization
    structure (p. 82)

networked organization
    structure (p. 83)
organizational strategy
    (p. 77)
values (p. 89)

► DISCUSSION QUESTIONS

1. How might IT change a manager's job?

2. Is monitoring an employee's work on a computer a desirable or undesirable activity from a manager's perspective? From the employee's perspective? Defend your position.

3. Consider the brief description of the zero time organization. What is an example of a control system that would be critical to manage for success in the zero time organization? Why?

4. Mary Kay, Inc., sells facial skin care products and cosmetics around the globe. The business model is to provide one-on-one, highly personalized service. More than 500,000 Independent Beauty Consultants (IBCs) sell in 29 markets worldwide. Each IBC runs his or her own business by developing a client base and then providing services and products for sale to those clients. Recently the IBCs were offered support through an e-commerce system with two major components: mymk.com and Mary Kay InTouch. Mymk.com allows IBCs to create instant online sites where customers can shop anytime directly with their personal IBC. Mary Kay InTouch streamlines the ordering process by automatically calculating discounts, detecting promotion eligibility, allowing the IBCs to access up-to-date product catalogs, and providing a faster way to transact business with the company.[11]

   a. How would the organizational strategy need to change to respond to Mary Kay's new business strategy?

   b. What changes would you suggest Mary Kay, Inc. managers make in their management systems order to realize the intended benefits of the new systems? Specifically, what types of changes would you expect to make in the evaluation systems, reward systems, and feedback systems?

CASE STUDY 3-1

US AIR AND AMERICA WEST MERGER CASE

Facing increasingly tough competition from low-fare airlines and high operational cost structure, US Airways agreed to be acquired by America West to create synergies and reduce cost through enhanced economies of scale. Termed as the largest low-cost airline in

[11] Adapted from "Mary Kay, Inc.," *Fortune*, Microsoft supplement (November 8, 1999), 5.

the world, the merger was initially deemed a success and heralded a path for other airlines to follow. However, the problems started unraveling within few months. Even two and half years after the merger, the succeeding airline, US Airways, failed to operate as one airline. The new airline needed to first consolidate diverse IS across the both airlines and then integrate them to receive a single operating certificate from the Federal Aviation Agency. However, in addition to feuding pilot unions of both airlines, IS integration issues had been a key reason behind the problems. The IS integration issues were a result of underlying organizational issues: different organizational structures and cultures at the two airlines and different IT department management styles.

Although the resulting airline retained the name of the acquired airline, US Airways, most of the management team came from America West, including CEO Doug Parker. The headquarters was moved from Arlington, Virginia, to Tempe, Arizona. Experienced in operating a small airline with mostly West Coast operations, the management team failed to adjust its organizational structure and processes to accommodate the complexity involved in operating a large airline on the East Coast. The result was delayed baggage, unexpected overtime expenses, less-than-optimal hiring of airport workers, and added hotel expenses for accommodating stranded passengers. Additionally, unresolved seniority issues led to nightmares in rescheduling shifts and routes. Even if the aircraft were identical, the crew could not be switched because a joint contract had not been signed, and crew rankings had not been finalized.

The two airlines had extremely different organizational cultures. US Airways had an older workforce with highly structured bureaucracy, whereas America West had a much younger workforce with an entrepreneurial culture. During past financial difficulties, US Airways laid off thousands of workers and sought concessions from employees. On the other hand, America West protected employees and sought concessions from vendors and the government.

Even IT departments at the two airlines had radically different approaches to IT management; one centered on insourcing; the other excelled at outsourcing. Most IT activities, such as application support, systems support, desktop support, HR, payroll, financial systems, reporting, and accounting, were handled in-house at America West. These activities, however, were outsourced to EDS at the old US Airways. Thus, the IT department at America West was structured to handle IT issues internally, whereas the old US Airways IT department's role was primarily to oversee the work performed by EDS staff. These differences in IT management styles led to completely different department structures and processes. Rather than choosing one or the other approach, the new company decided to take a hybrid approach by outsourcing some work and insourcing others. This added to even more difficulties.

Key information systems used by the two airlines also differed. For example, old US Airways had been using the SABRE reservation system, whereas America West used the SHARES system. New US Airways decided to switch over from SABRE to the SHARES system. EDS, which provides infrastructure for both systems, was brought in to facilitate the integration of different reservation systems of the predecessor airlines. Given the millions of transactions per year, integrating the two systems is not easy, especially when they both must continue to operate in real-time during the integration process. Out of 7 million reservations transferred to the new system, about 1.5 million "didn't sync up" correctly. The airline executives blamed the troubles on the legacy architecture of the reservations systems. However, external experts blamed the airline for failing to recognize the complexity and resource requirements of integrating two systems.

With the separate procedures of the predecessor airlines and the lack of experience in integrating two diverse organizational and IS cultures, the company lacked "a common focus as to what's important to fix," as COO Robert Isom put it. Recently, the airline set concrete metrics and goals for each work group through a standard departure checklist—"Countdown to Departure." It also centralized some key operational decision making. For example, airport station managers can no longer arbitrarily delay a flight for connecting passengers. They have to clear those decisions through a centralized operations control center. This resulted in a significant improvement in on-time performance metrics. CEO Parker acknowledged, "Just putting two airlines together doesn't automatically create value."

Discussion Questions

1. How did different organizational structures create problems in the merger? What steps did the new US Airways take to reduce these problems?
2. When two companies merge, what steps should be taken to combine organizational structures and processes?
3. How did the differences in culture create problems for the new US Airways? What, if anything, could the executives have done to lessen these problems?
4. If you were a consultant brought in to advise on the merger, what advice you have given to CEO Parker?

Sources: Melanie Trottman, "Can US Airways Pass Test of Time?" *The Wall Street Journal*, December 26, 2007, P. A6; Stan Gibson, "Airline Flies with Hybrid IT Plan," *eWeek*, October 24, 2005; and Stephanie Overby, "How to Save an Airline," *CIO*, February 15, 2006.

CASE STUDY 3-2

THE FBI

The Federal Bureau of Investigation of the U.S. government, the FBI, was forced to scrap its $170 million virtual case file (VCF) management system. Official reports blamed numerous delays, cost overruns, and incompatible software. But a deeper examination of the cause of this failure uncovered issues of control, culture, and incompatible organizational systems.

Among its many duties, the FBI is charged with the responsibility to fight crime and terrorism. To do so requires a large number of agents located within the Unites States and around the world. That means agents must be able to share information among themselves within the bureau and with other federal, state, and local law enforcement agencies. But sharing information has never been standard operating procedure for this agency. According to one source, "agents are accustomed to holding information close to their bulletproof vests and scorn the idea of sharing information."

Enter the FBI's efforts to modernize its infrastructure, code-named "Trilogy." The efforts included providing agents with 30,000 desktop PCs, high-bandwidth networks to connect FBI locations around the world, and the VCF project to facilitate sharing of case information worldwide. The FBI director explained to Congress that VCF would provide "an electronic means for agents to globally send field notes, documents, pieces of intelligence and other evidence so they could hopefully act faster on leads." It was designed to replace a paper-intensive process with an electronic, Web-based process. With such a reasonable goal, why didn't it work?

The CIO of the FBI offered one explanation. He claimed that "the FBI must radically change the agency's culture if the Bureau is ever going to get the high-tech analysis and surveillance tools it needs to effectively fight terrorism. We must move from a decentralized amalgam of 56 field offices that are deeply distrustful of technology, outsiders and each other to a seamlessly integrated global intelligence operation capable of sharing information and preventing crimes in real-time."

A former project manager at the FBI further explained, "They work under the idea that everything needs to be kept secret. But everything doesn't have to be kept secret. To do this right, you have to share information."

The VCF system has been shut down, but the CIO is working on a new approach. He is busy trying to win buy-in from agents in the field so that the next case management system will work. In addition, he is working to establish a portfolio management plan that will cover all of the FBI's IT projects, even those begun in decentralized offices. His team has been designing an enterprise architecture that will lay out standards for a bureauwide information system. The Director of the FBI has helped too. He reorganized the governance of IT, taking IT budget control away from the districts and giving total IT budget authority to the CIO.

The FBI announced that it will build a new case management system called Sentinel in four phases. The new system, according to the CIO, will include workflow, document management, record management, audit trails, access control, and single sign-on. To manage the expectations of the agents, the CIO plans to communicate often and significantly increase the training program for the new system. The CIO commented, "We want to automate those things that are the most manually cumbersome for the agents so they can see that technology can actually enhance their productivity. That is how to change their attitudes."

Discussion Questions

1. What do you think were the real reasons why the VCF system failed?
2. What were the points of alignment and misalignment between the Information Systems Strategy and the FBI organization?
3. What do you think of the CIO's final comment about how to change attitudes? Do you think it will work? Why or why not?
4. If you were the CIO, what would you do to help the FBI modernize and make better use of information technology?

Source: Adapted from Allan Holmes, "Why the G-Men Aren't IT Men," *CIO Magazine* (June 15, 2005), 42–45.

CHAPTER 4

INFORMATION TECHNOLOGY AND THE DESIGN OF WORK[1]

Best Buy, the leading U.S. retailer in electronics, completely transformed its view of the ordinary workday. Once known for killer hours and herd-riding bosses, it ushered in a new approach to work: Results-Only Work Environment (ROWE). ROWE was the brainchild of two passionate employees who thought that Best Buy managers were mired in analog-age inertia and did not recognize that employees could use technology to perform work from a variety of places. The ROWE developers thought implementing a flextime program "stigmatizes those who use it . . . and keeps companies acting like the military (fixated on schedules) when they should behave more like MySpace (social networks where real-time innovation can flourish)."[2]

ROWE is a program that allows limitless flexibility when it comes to work hours. Employees can choose where and when they will do their work—as long as project goals are satisfied. Employee decisions about working hours and location are framed by 13 guideposts—the most surprising of which is "Every meeting is optional."

Can Best Buy's approach work? Best Buy claims that productivity soared 41% between 2005 and 2007 on ROWE teams, and voluntary turnover plummeted 90%. This helped Best Buy save $16 million each year. Is their approach unusual? Best Buy clearly has adopted one of the most accommodating approaches to work hours, but 79% of employers now allow their employees some flexibility. A third or more of IBM and AT&T employees have no official office, and Sun Microsystems Inc. calculates that it has saved over $400 million in real estate costs by allowing nearly half of its employees to work anywhere they want.[3]

---

[1] The authors wish to acknowledge and thank David K. Wolpert, MBA 1999, for his help in researching and writing early drafts of this chapter.

[2] M. Conlin, "Smashing the Clock," *BusinessWeek*, December 11, 2006, www.businessweek.com/print/magazine/content/06_50/b4013001.htm?chan=gl downloaded 6/25/2008

[3] "Finding Freedom at Work," *Time*, May 30, 2008, www.time.com/time/printout/0,8816,1810690,00.html downloaded June 25, 2008.

The Best Buy example illustrates how the nature of work is changing before our eyes—and information technology is supporting, if not propelling, the changes. In preindustrial societies, work was seamlessly interwoven into everyday life. Activities all revolved around nature's cyclical rhythms (i.e., the season, day and night, the pangs of hunger) and the necessities of living. The Industrial Revolution changed this. With the advent of clocks and the ability to divide time into measurable, homogeneous units for which they could be paid, people started to separate work from other spheres of life. Their workday was distinguished from family, community and leisure time by punching a time clock or responding to the blast of a factory whistle. Work was also separated into space as well as time as people started going to a particular place to work.[4]

Technology has now brought the approach to work full circle in that the time and place of work are increasingly blended with other aspects of living. People now can do their work in their own homes at times that accommodate home life and leisure activities. They are able to enter cyberspace—a virtually unlimited space full of opportunities.[5] Paradoxically, however, they want to create a sense of belonging within that space. That is, they wish to create a sense of "place," which is a bounded domain in space that structures their experiences and interactions of others that they meet in this "place." People learn to identify with these places, or locations in space, based on a personal sharing of experiences with others within the space. Over time visitors to the place associate with it a set of appropriate behaviors. Increasingly places are being constructed in space with Web 2.0 tools that encourage collaboration, allowing people to easily communicate on an ongoing basis.

The Information Systems Strategy Triangle, discussed in Chapters 1 and 3, suggests that changing information systems (IS) results in changes in organizational characteristics. Because work and organizing are highly interdependent, significant changes in the nature of work are bound to coincide with significant changes in the way that organizations are structured and how people experience work in their daily lives.[6] Virtual organizations provide one of the clearest examples of this. A **virtual organization** is a structure that makes it possible for individuals to work for an organization and live anywhere. The Internet and corporate intranets create the opportunity for individuals to work from any place they can access a computer—from home, satellite offices, customer sites, and hotel rooms.

The structure of a virtual organization is networked. Everyone has access to everyone else using technology. Hierarchy may be present in the supervisory roles, but work is done crossing boundaries. For work that can be done on a computer or work that makes extensive use of telecommunications and the Internet make it possible to design a work environment anywhere. E-mail is the most widely used means of communication, making it possible for even the newest member of a

---

[4] S. Barley and G. Kunda, "Bringing Work Back In," *Organizational Science* 12, no. 1 (2001), 76–95.

[5] S. Harrison and P. Dourish, "Re-Place-ing Space: The Roles of Place and Space in Collaborative Systems," *CSCW Proceedings* (1996), 1–11.

[6] Barley and Kunda, "Bringing Work Back In."

team to communicate with the most senior person in the organization. Increasingly popular are social networking tools that not only enhance communication and collaboration, but also help employees get to know each other and identify each other's skills and experiences.

The basis of success in a virtual organization is the amount of collaboration that takes place between individuals. In a traditional organization, individuals mainly collaborate by holding face-to-face meetings. They use IS to communicate and to supplement these meetings, but the culture requires "looking at eyeballs" to get work done. By contrast, a virtual organization uses its IS as the basis for collaboration.

VeriFone, a leading manufacturer of credit verification systems, is well known for its virtual organization.[7] The company was founded in 1981 by an entrepreneur who hated bureaucracy. By 1990, it was the leading company for transaction automation with products and services used in more than 80 countries. VeriFone's office building in northern California houses a nominal corporate headquarters. In several plants around the world, its processing systems are made, and its distribution centers facilitate rapid delivery to customers. Most corporate functions, however, occur at multiple global locations, including Texas, Hawaii, India, and Taiwan. The company seeks to put its people in close proximity to customers and emerging markets, which results in about a third of the employees traveling roughly half of the time. This strategy gives VeriFone firsthand information about business opportunities and competitive situations worldwide.

At the heart of the company culture is constant and reliable sharing of information. It is a culture that thrives on the chief executive officer's ban on secretaries and paper correspondence. Every day the chief information officer (CIO) gathers yesterday's results and measures them against the company's plans. Systems post travel itineraries of everyone in the company and track which people speak what languages. Using IS for simulation and analysis, the CIO pulls together information from databases around the company for an e-mail newsletter to everyone in the company. The newsletter describes the latest products, competitive wins, and operating efficiencies. The top 15 salespeople are often listed, along with their sales figures. More than just managing the IS, VeriFone's CIO provides the "information glue" that holds the virtual organization together.

A story is told of a new salesperson who was trying to close a particularly big deal. He was about to get a customer signature on the contract when he was asked about the competition's system. Being new to the company, he did not have an answer, but he knew he could count on the company's information network for help. He asked his customer for 24 hours to research the answer. He then sent a note to everyone in the company asking the questions posed by the customer. The next morning, he had several responses from others around the company. He went to his client with the answers and closed the deal.

---

[7] Hossam Galal, Donna Stoddard, Richard Nolan, and Jon Kao, "VeriFone: The Transaction Automation Company," Harvard Business School case study 195–088.

What is interesting about this example is that the "new guy" was treated as a colleague by others around the world, even though they did not know him personally. He was also able to collaborate with them instantaneously. It was standard procedure, not panic time, because of the culture of collaboration in this virtual organization. The information infrastructure provided the means, but the organization built on top of it consisted of processes designed for individuals at a geographical remove.

Chapter 3 explored how IT influences organizational design. This chapter examines how IT is related to changing the nature of work, the rise of new work environments, and IT's impact on different types of workers and how they work with one another. This chapter looks at how IT enables and facilitates a shift toward collaborative work. It examines how work has changed, how work supports communication and collaboration, where work is done, and how work is managed. The terms *IS* and *IT* are used interchangeably in this chapter, and only basic details are provided on technologies used. The point of this chapter is to look at the impact of IS on the way work is done by individuals and teams. This chapter should help managers understand the challenges in designing technology-intensive work and develop a sense of how to address these challenges and overcome resistance to IT.

► WORK DESIGN FRAMEWORK

As the place and time of work becomes less distinguishable from other aspects of people's lives, the concept of "jobs" is changing and being replaced by the concept of work. Prior to the Industrial Revolution, a job meant a discrete task of a short duration with a clear beginning and end.[8] By the mid-20th century the concept of job had evolved into an ongoing, often unending stream of meaningful activities that allowed the worker to fulfill a distinct role. More recently organizations are moving away from organization structures built around particular jobs to a setting in which a person's work is defined in terms of what needs to be done.[9] In many organizations it is no longer appropriate for people to establish their turfs and narrowly define their jobs to only address specific functions. Yet, as jobs "disappear," IT can enable workers to better perform in tomorrow's workplace; that is, IT can help workers function and collaborate in accomplishing work that more broadly encompasses all the tasks that need to be done.

In this chapter a simple framework is used to assess how emerging technologies may affect work. As suggested by the Information Systems Strategy Triangle (in Chapter 1), this framework links the organizational strategy with IS decisions. This framework is useful in designing key characteristics of work by asking key questions and helping identify where IS can affect how the work is done. Consider the following questions:

---

[8] William Bridges, *JobShift: How to Prosper in a Workplace without Jobs* (New York: Addison-Wesley, 1995).
[9] Ibid.

- *What work will be performed?* Understanding what tasks are needed to complete the process being done by the worker requires an assessment of specific desired outcomes, inputs, and the transformation needed to turn inputs into outcomes. Understanding changes in tasks helps better understand changes in the nature of work.

- *What is the best way to do the work?* Some things are best done by people, and other things are best done by computers. For example, dealing directly with customers is often best done by people because the unpredictability of the interaction may require a complex set of tasks that cannot be automated. Further, most people want to deal directly with other people. On the other hand, computers are much better at keeping track of inventory, calculating compensation, and many other repetitious tasks that are opportunities for human error. ITs provide increasing support for communication and collaboration tasks among workers.

- *Who is going to do the work?* If a person is going to do the work, who should that person be? What skills are needed? From what part of the organization should that person come? If a team is going to do the work, many of these same questions need to be asked. However, they are asked within the context of the team: Who should be on the team? What skills do the team members need? What parts of the organization need to be represented by the team?

- *Where will the work be performed?* With the increasing availability of networks, Web 2.0 tools, and the Internet, managers can now design work for workers who are not physically near them. Does the work need to be performed locally? Remotely? By a geographically dispersed work group?

- *How can IT increase the effectiveness of the workers doing the work?* How can IT help workers communicate with other workers to get the work done? How can IT support collaboration? What can be done to increase the acceptance of IT-induced change?

Figure 4.1 shows how these questions can be used in a framework to incorporate IS into the design of work. Although it is outside the scope of this chapter to discuss the current research on either work or job design, the reader is encouraged to read these rich literatures.

▶ HOW INFORMATION TECHNOLOGY SUPPORTS COMMUNICATION AND COLLABORATION

Though it may seem like putting the cart before the horse, the discussion will respond to the last question in Figure 4.1 first. This is because many of the changes that are described in later sections of this chapter have been supported, if not propelled, by IT. Some of these technologies such as social networking and blogs seem to have been introduced into the workplace by digital natives when they

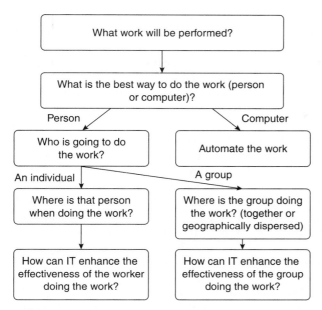

FIGURE 4.1 Framework for work design.

started their first full-time jobs. This section describes major technologies that have affected communications and collaboration in today's work environment.

IT to Facilitate Communication

The IT support for communication is considerable and growing. It includes e-mail, intranets, instant messaging, VoIP, video teleconferencing, unified communications, RSS, virtual private networks, and file transfer.

E-mail (electronic mail) is a way of transmitting messages over communication networks. It was one of the first uses of the Internet and still constitutes a good portion of Internet traffic. Most e-mail messages consist strictly of text, but e-mail can also be used to transfer images, video clips, sound clips, and other types of computer files. A permutation of e-mail is the mailing list server. Users subscribe to a mailing list; when any user sends a message to the server, a copy of the message is sent to everyone on the list. This service allows for restricted-access discussion groups; only subscribed members can participate in or view the discussions that are transmitted via e-mail. Popular mailing list providers include ListServ and Majordomo.

An **intranet** looks and acts like the Internet, but it is comprised of information used exclusively with a company and unavailable to the general public via the Internet. It is a password-protected set of interconnected nodes that is under the company's administrative control. Employees at AT&T, for example, can use company computers to access an employee handbook (containing links to such things as employee data, benefit information and procedures for dealing with irate callers) via the company's intranet that is separated from the Internet by a security "firewall."

Instant messaging (IM) is an Internet protocol (IP)–based application that provides convenient communication between people using a variety of different device types, including computer-to-computer and mobile devices, such as digital cellular phones.[10] It can identify which "buddies" have a "presence" and are able to receive messages at the moment. If a "buddy" is available, the sender's typed message pops up on the receiver's computer screen. Failing to respond quickly to the message typically is perceived to be rude. Although initially a communication tool used exclusively by teenagers, IM now serves as an internal communication systems in large companies and even allows managers to verify whether their telecommuting employees are logged on to their computer at their homes. With most systems, people need to agree to be on a potential sender's buddy list, and they can set their status to "busy" or "away" if they do not want to be disturbed. Even then, IM is sometimes criticized for being distracting and reducing privacy, especially by people who are not good at doing a number of things at the same time.

Voice over Internet Protocol (VoIP) is "a method for taking analog audio signals, like the kind you hear when you talk on the phone, and turning them into digital data that can be transmitted over the Internet."[11] It is rapidly gaining in popularity because the free VoIP software that is available with proprietary systems such as Skype allows people to make free Internet phone calls without using the phone company. VoIP also reduces costs to organizations because numerous calls can be transmitted over the same Internet connection, and phone connections are shared on the same network as personal computers. For example, Western Digital, which sells hard drives, uses VoIP as a way of reducing the costs of worldwide telephone calls.[12] VoIP is especially beneficial for organizations with underused network capacity that can accommodate adding VoIP to their current network. It is also being used increasingly to communicate with remote workers. Although there are no complaints about its costs, there are some about VoIP's reliability and inability to function in power outages.

Video teleconference (also called videoconference) is "a set of interactive telecommunication technologies which allow two or more locations to interact via two-way video and audio transmissions simultaneously."[13] Although analog and digital conferencing has been available for decades, video teleconferencing (and

---

[10] IEC definition of instant messaging available from http://www.iec.org/online/tutorials/instant_msg/ (accessed on September 9, 2002)

[11] Adapted from http://computer.howstuffworks.com/ip-telephony (accessed August 3, 2005

[12] Microsoft Case Studies, "Western Digital Improves Productivity, www.microsoft.com/uc/voipasyouare/default.aspx

[13] "Videoconferencing," Wikipedia http://en.wikipedia.org/wiki/Videoconferencing downloaded July 15, 2008.

also Web conferencing) using Internet Protocol made its debut in the mid-1990s. Advanced video teleconferencing technologies gave birth to the field known as "telemedicine." Telemedicine enables doctors working on virtual teams to confer with distant colleagues, share data, and examine patients in remote locations without losing the time and money to travel. For example, Arizona's Telemedicine Program has a teletrauma service that recently helped save a young child's life. A bad car crash near Douglas left three persons dead and an 18-month-old baby with severe trauma to the head and multiple fractures. A skilled trauma surgeon in Tucson utilized the teletrauma connection to provide direct supervision miles away to the local Douglas physician through multiple interventions. Another part of the Arizona Telemedicine Program enables the delivery of medical services to prisoners in ten Arizona rural prisons. This program saves not only lives, but also millions of dollars.[14]

Unified communications (UC) are an "evolving communications technology architecture which automates and unifies all forms of human and device communications in context, and with a common experience."[15] Unified communications offer a streamlined interface in which such technologies as cell phones, fax machines, personal computers, VoIP, instant messaging, file transfers, collaborative workspaces, teleconferencing, e-mail, and videoconferencing meld together to form a collaborative communications environment. Nissan's UC includes VoIP desk and cell phones, Web conferencing, telepresence, and networked collaborative workspaces provided by Cisco.[16] As a result, its employees are more accessible to one another, and its collaborative workspaces for tasks like concept car drafting afford a level of coordination not previously available.

Really Simple Syndication or RSS (also called Web feeds) refers to a structured file format for porting data from one platform or information system to another. It is an umbrella term that refers to several different XML (Extensible Markup Language) formats. The main benefit of RSS Web feeds is that the user can aggregate frequently updated data such as news, blog entries, changing stock prices, and recent changes on wiki pages into one easily manageable location. Thus, the user does not have to go to each individual Web site to lookup that data or have multiple browsers open to view each of the Web sites. Second, the user receives regular data updates at timely intervals. For example, the user can receive a summary of articles from a publisher on a prespecified topic of interest. Once alerted, the user can choose to link to and read the full version. Third, RSS Web feeds provide a cheaper electronic alternative to mailing lists for publishers.

[14] *Arizona Telemedicine: Telemedicine Updates* (June 16, 2005), available at http://www.telemedicine.arizona.edu/updates/page1.htm.

[15] "Unified Communications." Wikipedia. 27 June 2008 http://en.wikipedia.org/wiki/Unified_communications.

[16] "Global Automobile Company Collaborates Using UC," newsroom.cisco.com, 14 Apr 2008. Cisco Systems, Inc. 27 Jun 2008, http://newsroom.cisco.com/Newsroom/flash/evp/Flash7/main.html?videoXML=../xml/high/453B633ED75C6173310E2198711889B6_video.xml&defaultTopic=Technologies&defaultSubTopic=Unified%20Communications.

A **virtual private network (VPN)** is a private network that uses a public network such as the Internet to connect remote sites or users. With a VPN, users at remote sites are treated as if they were on a local network. If the various sites of the VPN are owned by a single company, they are often referred to as a corporate intranet; However, if they are owned by different companies, the VPN may be called an extranet.[17] A VPN maintains privacy through the use of a tunneling protocol and security procedures.Until fairly recently companies had to use the much more expensive dedicated connections such as leased lines instead of VPN's "virtual" connections. VPNs are also used to support both remote access to an intranet and connections between multiple intranets within the same organization. Telecommuters often use a Virtual Private Network (VPN) requiring Secure Socket Layer (SSL) authentication as a way of enhancing security.

File transfer consists simply of transferring a copy of a file from one computer to another on the Internet. The most common procedure, file transfer protocol (FTP), allows entire files—even large ones—to be transferred over the Internet more quickly and securely than with e-mail. Besides dedicated file transfer services such as FTP, there are numerous ways to transfer files over a network (e.g., file transfers over instant messaging systems or between computers and peripheral systems, distributed file transfers over peer-to-peer networks).

IT to Facilitate Collaboration

Collaboration is a key task in many work processes, and IS greatly changes how collaboration is done. It is important for an organization's survival. Thomas Friedman argues that collaboration is the way that small companies can "act big" and flourish in today's flat world. The key to success is for such companies is "to take advantage of all the new tools for collaboration to reach farther, faster, wider and deeper."[18] Collaboration tools include social networking sites, virtual worlds, web logs (blogs), wikis, and groupware.

A **social networking site** is a Web-based service that allows its members to create a public profile with their interests and expertise, post text and pictures and all manner of data, list other users with whom they share a connection, and view and communicate openly or privately with their list of connections and those made by others within the system. These sites are particularly useful for forming ad hoc groups. Popular social networking services for personal uses are MySpace and Facebook. LinkedIn, which boasts over 23 million users in 150 countries,[19] invites members to create profiles summarizing their professional accomplishments so that they can be contacted for business opportunities. It also can be used to locate potential business allies or search for jobs.

---

[17] "Extranets," Wikipedia, retrieved from http://en.wikipedia.org/wiki/Extranet. on September 26, 2008.

[18] Thomas L. Friedman, *The World is Flat* (New York: Farrar, Straus and Giroux, 2005), 145.

[19] Jessica Guynn, "Professional Networking Site LinkedIn Valued at $1 Billion," June 18, 2008, http://www.latimes.com/business/la-fi-linkedin18-2008jun18,0,6631759.story.

A **virtual world** is "a computer-based simulated environment intended for its users to inhabit and interact via avatars."[20] These avatars are usually depicted as two-dimensional or three-dimensional graphical representations capable of interacting with other avatars, manipulating objects, and moving about the virtual world. Most virtual worlds are characterized by creativity, interactivity, collaboration, and three-dimensionality.[21] Sites like Second Life allow users to collaborate virtually by having their avatars meet and talk on the screen.

Web logs (blogs) are online journals that link together into a very large network of information sharing. Blogs discuss topics ranging from poetry to vacation journals to constitutional law to political opinions. Blogs provide news and information in the moment to potentially thousands of individuals connected with an event or situation. For example, when the tsunami hit Thailand, early reports were from blogs. *Business Week* calls it "Micro-news" when a blog is devoted to a niche topic. Companies such as Plaxo, an Internet-contact management company, use blogs as a key part of their marketing and promotion strategy. General Motors uses them to connect with the press. The vice chairman has launched his own blog site and receives numerous suggestions and criticisms from customers. Further, when a conflict arose between an outside company and GM, journalists were sent to a blog run by GM for details. GM is taking a lead in experimenting with this technology to manage the media. But the biggest application for blogs is advertising. Some companies have even begun to create fake blogs, using made-up names, to jump-start the buzz around products or services. For example, Captain Morgan, the rum distributor, was said to have created a fake blog for its rum drinks.

A **wiki** is software that allows users to work collaboratively to create, edit, and link web pages easily. Anyone who has access to the wiki can contribute or modify content. They are especially good for their ability to support multimedia content and for keeping track of multiple revisions of a document. The best known wiki effort is the collaborative encyclopedia Wikipedia.

Groupware[22] is software that enables group members to work together on a project, even from remote locations, by allowing them to simultaneously access the same files. Calendars, documents, e-mail messages, databases, and meetings are popular applications. Groupware is often broken down into categories describing whether the members work together in real-time (i.e., synchronously) or at different times (i.e., asynchronously). For example, products such as Lotus Notes, Lotus Domino, and Microsoft Exchange enable groups to share information asynchronously, whereas products such as Microsoft Office Groove and Webex enable groups to share information, such as an electronic presentation, synchronously.

[20] "Virtual World," Wikipedia http://en.wikipedia.org/wiki/Virtual_world downloaded July 16, 2008

[21] Doing Business in Second Life http://blip.tv/file/242816 downloaded July 16, 2008.

[22] Adapted from http://whatis.techtarget.com (accessed August 3, 2005)

▶ HOW INFORMATION TECHNOLOGY CHANGES THE NATURE OF WORK

Advances in IT provide an expanding set of tools that make individual workers more productive and broaden their capabilities. They transform the way work is performed—and the nature of the work itself. This section examines three ways in which new IT alters employee life: by creating new types of work, by creating new ways to do traditional work, and by presenting new challenges in human resource management brought about by the use of IT.

Creating New Types of Work

IT often leads to the creation of new jobs or redefines existing ones. The high-tech field emerged in its entirety over the past 60 years and has created a wide range of positions in the IT sector, such as programmers, analysts, IT managers, hardware assemblers, Web site designers, software sales personnel, and IT consultants. A study based on the Bureau of Labor Statistics places the number of IT workers in the United States at 3.7 million workers in 2006, with projections for this number to grow 25.2% to 4.0 million by 2016.[23] Even within traditional non-IT organizations, the growing reliance on IS creates new types of jobs, such as knowledge managers who manage firms' knowledge systems (see Chapter 12 for more on knowledge management). IS departments also employ individuals who help create and manage the technologies, such as systems analysts, database administrators, network administrators, and network security advisors. The Internet has given rise to many other types of jobs, such as Web masters and site designers. Virtually every department in every business has someone who "knows the computer" as part of their job.

New Ways to Do Traditional Work

Changing the Way Work Is Done

IT has changed the way work is done. Many traditional jobs are now done by computers. For example, computers can check spelling of documents, whereas traditionally that was the job of an editor or writer. Jobs once done by art and skill are often greatly changed by the introduction of IT, such as the jobs described at the beginning of this chapter. Workers at one time needed an understanding of not only what to do, but also how to do it; now their main task often is to make sure the computer is working because the computer does the task for them. Workers once were familiar with others in their organization because they passed work to them; now they may never know those coworkers because the computer routes the work. In sum, the introduction of IT into an organization can greatly change the day-to-day tasks performed by the workers in the organization.

---

[23] Ray Panko, "IT Employment Prospects: Beyond the Dotcom Bubble, " *European Journal of Information Systems* (2008).

Zuboff describes a paper mill, where papermakers' jobs were radically changed with the introduction of computers.[24] The papermakers mixed big vats of paper and knew when the paper was ready by the smell, consistency, and other subjective attributes of the mixture. For example, one worker could judge the amount of chlorine in the mixture by sniffing and squeezing the pulp. They were masters at their craft, but they were not able to explicitly describe to anyone else exactly what was done to make paper. The company, in an effort to increase productivity in the paper-making process, installed an information and control system. Instead of the workers looking at and personally testing the vats of paper, the system continuously tested parameters and displayed the results on a panel located in the control room. The papermakers sat in the control room, reading the numbers, and making decisions on how to make the paper. Many found it much more difficult, if not impossible, to make the same quality paper when watching the control panel instead of personally testing, smelling, and looking at the vats. The introduction of the information system resulted in different skills needed to make paper. Abstracting the entire process and displaying the results on electronic readouts required skills to interpret the measurements, conditions, and data generated by the new computer system.

In another example, salespeople have portable terminals that not only keep track of inventory, but also help them in the selling function. Prior to the information system, the salespeople used manual processes to keep track of inventory in their trucks. When visiting customers, it was only possible to tell them what was missing from their shelves and to replenish any stock they wanted. With IT, the salespeople have become more like marketing and sales consultants, helping the customers with models and data of previous sales, floor layouts, and replenishment as well as forecasting demand based on analysis of the data histories stored in the IS. The salespeople need to do more than just be persuasive. They now must also do data analysis and floor plan design, in addition to using the computer. Thus, the skills needed by the salespeople have greatly changed with the introduction of IT.

The Internet enables changes in many types of work. For example, within minutes, financial analysts can download an annual report from a corporate Web site and check what others have said about the company's growth prospects. They can automatically receive RSS Web feeds for stock updates from Google every few seconds. Librarians can check the holdings of other libraries online and request that particular volumes be routed to their own clients, or download the articles from a growing number of databases. Marketing professionals can pretest the reactions of consumers to potential products in virtual worlds such as Second Life. Sales jobs are radically changing to complement online ordering systems. Technical support agents diagnose and resolve problems on client computers using the Internet and software from Motive Communications. The cost and time required to access information has plummeted, increasing personal productivity and giving workers new tools.

---

[24] Shoshana Zuboff, *In the Age of the Smart Machine: The Future of Work and Power* (New York: Basic Books, 1988), 211.

Changing Communication Patterns

All one has to do is observe people walking down a busy downtown street or a college campus to note changes in communication patterns over a period as short as the last decade. Many of the people are talking on their cell phones. Or observe what happens when a plane lands. It is possible that as many as half the people on the plane whip out their BlackBerrys or cell phones as soon as the plane touches down. They are busy making arrangements to meet the people who are picking them up at the airport or checking to see the calls they missed while in flight. Finally, consider meeting a friend at a busy subway station in Hong Kong. It is virtually impossible, without the aid of a cell phone, to locate one another.

Similarly, IT is changing the communication patterns of workers. There are still some workers who do not need to communicate with other workers for the bulk of their workday; however, that workday is defined. For example, many truck drivers do not interact with others in their organization. But consider the example of a Wal-Mart driver who picks up goods dropped off by manufacturers at the Wal-Mart distribution center and then delivers those goods in small batches to each of the Wal-Mart stores. Wal-Mart has connected its drivers with radios and satellites so that they can pick up goods from manufacturers on the return trip after they have dropped off their goods at the Wal-Mart stores. In this way, Wal-Mart saves the delivery charges from that manufacturer and conserves energy in the process. Wal-Mart drivers use IT to save money by enhancing their communications with suppliers.[25]

Changing Organizational Decision Making and Information Processing

IT changes not only organizational decision-making processes, but also the information used in making those decisions. Data processed to create more accurate and timely information are being captured earlier in the process. Through technologies such as RSS Web feeds, information that they need to do their job can be pushed to them.

IT can change the amount and type of information available to workers. For example, salespeople can use technology to get quick answers to customer questions, much as the new VeriFone salesman at the beginning of this chapter did. Further, Web 2.0 tools allow salespeople to search for best practices on a marketing topic over a social network and to benefit from blogs and wikis written by informed employees in their company. Furthermore, organizations now maintain large historical business databases, called data warehouses, which can be mined by using tools to analyze patterns, trends, and relationships in the data warehouses. For example, Fingerhut, a $2 billion mail-order business, maintains a data warehouse generated from 50 years of sales transactions. Using data-mining techniques, Fingerhut's marketing team recently found that customers who change their residence triple their purchasing in the 12 weeks after their move,

---

[25] Friedman, *The World is Flat*.

with the most buying taking place in the first 4 weeks They purchase furniture, telecommunications equipment, and decorations, but abstain from jewelry and home electronics purchase. Marketers at Fingerhut now offer a customized "mover's catalog" to movers and don't send other catalogs during that 12-week window.[26] Thus, the work of marketers at Fingerhut changed to reflect the greater information available to them.

In their classic 1958 *Harvard Business Review* article, Leavitt and Whisler boldly predicted that IT would shrink the ranks of middle management by the 1980s.[27] Because of IT, top-level executives would have access to information and decision-making tools and models that would allow them to easily assume tasks previously performed by middle managers. Other tasks clearly in the typical job description of middle managers at the time would become so routinized and programmed because of IT that they could be performed by lower-level managers. As Leavitt and Whisler predicted, the 1980s saw a shrinking in the ranks of middle managers. This trend was partly attributable to widespread corporate downsizing. However, it was also attributable to changes in decision making induced by IT. Since the 1980s, IT has become an even more commonly employed tool of executive decision makers. IT has increased the flow of information to these decision makers and provided tools for filtering and analyzing the information.

Changing Collaboration

Whereas decision making in organizations is often viewed as deliberate and distinct acts, an increasing amount of work being performed by teams is definitely more fluid.[28] Teams have learned to collaborate by continually structuring and restructuring their work—constantly adjusting their highly entwined actions—to respond to their ever-evolving environments.

IT helps make work more team oriented and collaborative. Workers can more easily share information with their teammates. They can send documents over computer networks to others, and they can more easily ask questions using e-mail or instant messaging. The president of a New York-based marketing firm, CoActive Digital, recently decided to implement a wiki to have a common place where 25 to 30 people could go to share a variety of documents ranging from large files to meeting notes and PowerPoint presentations.[29] An added benefit is that the wiki is encrypted, protected, and used with a VPN. The president recognized that the challenge for implementing the wiki would be to change a culture in which e-mail

---

[26] David Pearson, "Marketing for Survival," *CIO Magazine* (April 15, 1998), available at http://www.cio.com/archive/041598/finger_content.html.

[27] Harold Leavitt and Thomas Whisler, "Management in the 1980s," *Harvard Business Review* (November–December 1958), 41–48.

[28] Barley and Kunda, "Bringing Work Back In."

[29] C. G. Lynch, "How a Marketing Firm Implemented an Enterprise Wiki," CIO.com retrieved from www.cio.com/artilce/print/413063 (accessed on July 9, 2008).

had long been the staple for communication. Consequently, he decided to work closely with the business leader of the business development group. This group handles inquiries from customers and coordinates how the work (i.e., marketing campaigns) will get done internally. The group has lots of meetings and lots of work that needs to be shared. He populated the wiki site with documents that had been traded over e-mail, such as meeting notes, and with relevant documents and asked the business leader to encourage her group members to use the wikis. It took some effort, but eventually the group learned to appreciate the benefits of the wiki for collaboration.

The Internet greatly enhances collaboration. Technologies, such as blogs, virtual worlds, wikis, social networking, and video teleconferencing, provide collaborative applications that facilitate creating groups that form around a large number of goals at a rate much faster than ever before. One might say that with the lowered transaction costs of group formation (with many of the social networking sites, it's virtually free), there are many more possible social connections.[30] For example, Wachovia is implementing a social networking service to link over 110,000 of its employees.[31] It allows users to upload pictures as well as personal and professional background information. In this way, employees can get to know a more personal side of others in their organization with whom they communicate on a daily basis. Networking in this way can give employees insight about whom they should contact to get an answer for varying types of questions, as well as to determine their availability at a given moment.

Beyond sharing and conversation, teams can also use the Internet and Web 2.0 to create something together. An example here is the well-known Web-based site Wikipedia. Further, teams can undertake collective action or the behavior that creates a situation for its members to share something and make something happen. Collective action was taken in 2007 when the international bank HSBC was the recipient of a large number of complaints after they removed a free overdraft policy and began charging students a new fee. Hundreds of angry students posted their feelings on a Facebook group set up by one disgruntled person. Within a very short time, 6,000 graduates signed onto the page to protest the new fees. The bank was forced to rescind their new policy shortly afterwards.[32]

The preceding examples show how IS are a key component in the design of work. IT can greatly change the day-to-day tasks, which in turn change the skills needed by workers. The examples show that adding IS to a work environment changes the way work is done.

[30] Clay Shirky, *Here Comes Everybody: The Power of Organizing without Organizations* (Johannesburg, South Africa: The Penguin Press, 2008).

[31] Edward Cone, "Social Networks at Work Promise Bottom-Line Results," *CIO Insight*, October 8, 2007. http://www.cioinsight.com/c/a/Trends/Social-Networks-at-Work-PromisebrBottomLine-Results/.

[32] Fay Schlesinger, "Swivelchair Activism," *The Guardian*, December 11 2007, http://www.guardian.co.uk/education/2007/dec/11/students.studentpolitics, Accessed 7/29/08.

New Challenges in Managing People

New working arrangements create new challenges in how workers are supervised, evaluated, compensated, and even hired. When most work was performed individually in a central location, supervision and evaluation were relatively easy. A manager could directly observe the salesperson who spent much of his or her day in an office. It was fairly simple to ascertain whether the employee was present and productive.

Now modern organizations, especially virtual organizations, often face the challenge of managing a workforce that is spread across the world, working in isolation from direct supervision, and working more in teams. Rather than working in a central office, many salespeople work remotely and rely on laptop computers, Web 2.0, cellular phones, and pagers to link them to customers and their office colleagues. The technical complexity of certain products, such as enterprise software, necessitates a team-based sales approach combining the expertise of many individuals; it can be difficult to say which individual closed a sale, making it difficult to apportion individual-based rewards.

One technological solution, electronic employee monitoring (introduced in Chapter 3), replaces direct supervision by automatically tracking certain activities, such as the number of calls processed, e-mail messages sent, or time spent surfing the Web. Direct employee evaluation can be replaced, in part, by pay-for-performance compensation strategies that reward employees for deliverables produced or targets met, as opposed to subjective factors such as "attitude" or "teamwork." These changes are summarized in Figure 4.2.

The introduction of ROWE at Best Buy illustrates the need to change from an approach where managers watch employees and count the hours they spend at their desks, to one that focuses instead on the work they actually do. Best Buy's Senior Vice President, John "J.T." Thompson admitted, "For years I had been focused on the wrong currency. I was always looking to see if people were here. I should have been looking at what they were getting done."[33] He changed his mind when he realized that the benefits the ROWE program offered—and the managerial changes that it commanded.

Hiring is also different because of IT for three reasons. First, in IT-savvy firms, workers must either know how to use the technologies that support the work of the firm before they are hired, or they must be trainable in the requisite skills. Hiring procedures incorporate activities that determine the skills of applicants. For example, a company may ask a candidate to sit at a computer to answer a basic questionnaire, take a short quiz, or simply browse the Web to evaluate the applicant's skill level, or they may only accept applications submitted to a Web site. Second, IT utilization affects the array of nontechnical skills needed in the organization. Certain functions—many clerical tasks, for example—can be handled more expeditiously, so fewer workers adept in those skills are required.

---

[33] Conlin, "Smashing the Clock."

	Traditional Approach: Subjective Observation	Newer approach: Objective Assessment
Supervision	Personal and informal. Manager is usually present or relies on others to ensure employee is present and productive.	Electronic or assessed by deliverable. As long as the employee is producing value, he does not need formal supervision.
Evaluation	Focus is on process through direct observation. Manager sees how employee performs at work. Subjective (personal) factors are very important.	Focus is on output by deliverable (e.g., produce a report by a certain date) or by target (e.g., meet a sales quota). As long as deliverables are produced and/or targets achieved, the employee is meeting performance expectations adequately. Subjective factors may be less important and are harder to gauge.
Compensation and Rewards	Often individually based.	Often team-based or contractually spelled out.
Hiring	Personal with little reliance on computers. Often more reliance on clerical skills.	Often electronic with recruiting Web sites and electronic testing. More informated work that requires a higher level of IT skills.

FIGURE 4.2   Changes to supervision, evaluations, compensation, and hiring.

IT-savvy companies can eliminate clerical capabilities from their hiring practices and focus on more targeted skills. Third, IT has become an essential part of the hiring process for many firms. Advertisements for positions are posted on the Web, and applicants send their resumes over the Web or send potential employers to their Web sites. Companies, when researching candidates, often look at their Facebook or MySpace pages (and in many cases, they do not like what they see). Social networking also involves informal introductions and casual conversations in cyberspace. Virtual interviews can be arranged in virtual worlds to reduce recruiting costs. A face-to-face interview is eventually required, but recruiters can significantly increase their chances of finding the right applicant with initial virtual interviews. Not surprisingly, the new CEO of Linden Labs (the company that created Second Life) was interviewed virtually in Second Life.[34]

The design of the work needed by an organization is a function of the skill mix required for the firm's work processes and of the flow of those processes themselves. Thus, a company that infuses technology effectively and employs a

---

[34] Alana Semuel, " 'Second Life' operator Linden Lab gets new CEO," *Los Angeles Times*, April 24, 2008.

workforce with a high level of IT skills designs itself differently from another company that does not. The skill mix required by an IT-savvy firm reflects greater capacity for using the technology itself. It requires less of certain clerical and even managerial skills that are leveraged by technical capacity. It may also deploy skills according to different ratios in central and local units.

New IT also challenges employee skills. Employees who cannot keep pace are increasingly unemployable. As many lower-level service or clerical jobs become partially automated, only those workers able to learn new technologies and adapt to changing work practices can anticipate stability in their long-term employment. Firms institute extensive training programs to ensure their workers possess the skills to use IT effectively.

As workforce demographics shift, so too do the IT needs and opportunities to change work. Digital natives, those employees who have grown up using computers, texting, and the Web as a normal, integrated part of their daily lives, are finding new and innovative ways to do their work. There are all sorts of impacts from the skills these employees bring to their work, including how to do their work in a new, and often more efficient, manner.

IT has drastically changed the landscape of work today. As a result of IT, many new jobs were created. In the next section, we examine how IT can change where work is done and who does it.

▶ HOW INFORMATION TECHNOLOGY CHANGES WHERE WORK IS DONE AND WHO DOES IT

This section examines another important effect of IT on work: the ability of some workers to work anywhere, at any time. At the individual level, we focus on telecommuters and mobile workers. At the group level we focus on virtual teams.

Telecommuting and Mobile Work

The terms *telecommuting* and *mobile worker* are often used to describe these types of work arrangements. **Telecommuting**, sometimes called teleworking, refers to work arrangements with employers that allow employees to work from home, at a customer site, or from other convenient locations instead of coming into the corporate office. The term *telecommute* is derived from combining "telecommunications" with "commuting," hence these workers use telecommunications instead of commuting to the office. **Mobile workers** are those who work from wherever they are. They are outfitted with the technology necessary for access to coworkers, company computers, intranets, and other information sources.

Factors Driving Telecommuting and Mobile Work

Telecommuting has been around since the 1970s, but since the late 1990s it has steadily been gaining popularity. In 2006, according to World at Work, more than 45 million Americans telecommuted in some fashion. This number is expected to increase to 100 million in 2010 as more work is performed from remote locations.[35] A recent survey indicates that currently 12% of organizational workforces are at remote locations, and this number is expected to grow.[36] Several factors that drive this trend are shown in Figure 4.3.

First, work is increasingly knowledge based. The U.S. and many other world economies continue to shift from manufacturing to service industries. Equipped with the right IT, employees can create, assimilate, and distribute knowledge as effectively at home as they can at an office. The shift to knowledge-based work thus tends to minimize the need for a particular locus of activity.

Second, telecommuters often time-shift their work to accommodate their lifestyles. For instance, parents modify their work schedules to allow time to take their children to school and extracurricular activities. Telecommuting provides an attractive alternative for parents who might otherwise decide to take leaves of absence from work for child rearing. Telecommuting also enables persons housebound by illness, disability, or the lack of access to transportation to join the workforce.

Telecommuting also may provide employees with enormous geographic flexibility. The freedom to live where one wishes, even at a location remote from one's corporate office, can boost employee morale and job satisfaction. As a workplace policy, it may also lead to improved employee retention. For example, Best Buy workers use the ROWE program as part of its recruiting pitch. Further, productivity and employee satisfaction for those on the ROWE program are markedly

Driver	Effect
Shift to knowledge-based work	Eliminates requirement that certain work be performed in a specific place.
Changing demographics and lifestyle preferences	Provides workers with geographic and time-shifting flexibility.
New technologies with enhanced bandwidth	Makes remotely performed work practical and cost effective
Reliance on Web	Provides workers with the ability to stay connected to coworkers and customers, even on a 24/7 basis.
Energy concerns	Reduces the cost of commuting for telecommuters and reduces energy costs associated with real estate for companies

FIGURE 4.3   Driving factors of telecommuting and virtual teams.

[35] The actual statistics for the number of telecommuters is hard to find. The figures were obtained from Suite Commute, http://www.suitecommute.com/Statistics.htm downloaded on July 15, 2008.

[36] IDG Research Services with Custom Solutions Group, *Today's Enterprise Workforces: Remote but Not Isolated*, retrieved from www.interactive-intelligence.com/re.cfm.

higher, and voluntary turnover is down. Many employees can be more productive at home, and they actually work more hours than if they commuted to an office. Furthermore, such impediments to productivity as traffic delays, canceled flights, bad weather, and mild illnesses become less significant. Companies enjoy this benefit, too. Those who build in telecommuting as a standard work practice are able to hire workers from a much larger talent pool than those companies who require geographical presence. JetBlue's entire force of 550 reservation agents, for instance, work from their homes, generating savings that helped the airline report its first profit a mere six months after its first flight.[37]

The third driving factor of telecommuting is that the new technologies, which make work in remote locations viable, are becoming better and cheaper. For example, prices of personal computers continue to drop, and processing power roughly doubles every 18 months.[38] The drastic increase in capabilities of portable technologies make mobile work more effective and productive. Telecommunication speeds are increasing exponentially at the same time that the costs for connectivity are plummeting. The Web offers an easy-to-use "front-end" to sophisticated "back-office" applications used by major corporations, such as those that run on mainframe computers.

A fourth driving factor is the increasing reliance on Web-based technologies by all generations, but especially the younger generations. The younger generations are at ease with Web-based social relationships and are adept at using social networking tools to grow these relationships. Web-based tools allow them to stay connected with their coworkers and customers. Further, as more and more organizations turn to flexible working hours such as the ROWE program implemented by Best Buy and as 24/7 becomes the norm in terms of service, the Web becomes the standard platform to allow workers to respond to customers' increasing demands.

A fifth factor is the mounting emphasis on conserving energy. As the cost of gasoline continues to skyrocket, employees are looking for ways to save money. Telecommuting is quite appealing in such a scenario, especially when public transportation is not readily available. Companies can also experience lower energy costs from computing. Many telecommuters no longer need to be tethered to official desks. Thus, real estate needs of their employers are shrinking. Further, energy is no longer needed to heat or cool these office spaces. Companies are realizing that they can comply with the Clean Air Act and be praised for their "green computing" practices at the same time they are reaping considerable cost savings.

Disadvantages of Telecommuting and Mobile Work

Telecommuting also has some disadvantages. Remote work challenges managers in addressing performance evaluation and compensation. Managers of telecommuters

---

[37] Joan Raymond, "Next Frontiers: Moving into the Future," *Newsweek* (April 29, 2002), 40, 42.

[38] Gordon Moore, head of Intel, observed that the capacity of microprocessors doubled roughly every 12 to 18 months. Even though this observation was made in 1965, it still holds true. Eventually, it became known in the industry as Moore's law.

must evaluate employee performance in terms of results or deliverables. Virtual offices make it more difficult for managers to appreciate the skills of the people reporting to them, which in turn makes performance evaluation more difficult. For the many telecommuting tasks that do not produce well-defined deliverables or results, or those where managerial controls typically prove inadequate, managers must rely heavily on the telecommuter's self-discipline. As a result, managers may feel they are losing control over their employees, and some telecommuting employees do, in fact, abuse their privileges. Managers accustomed to traditional work models in which they are able to exert control more easily may strongly resist telecommuting. In fact, managers are often the biggest impediment to implementing telecommuting programs.

Workers who go to an office or who must make appearances at customer locations have a structure that gets them up and out of their home. Telecommuters, on the other hand, must exert a high level of self-discipline to ensure they get the work done. Working from home, in particular, is full of distractions such as personal phone calls, visitors, and inconvenient family disruptions. A remote worker must carefully set up a home work environment and develop strategies to enable quality time for the work task.

Telecommuters often opt for the increased flexibility in work hours that remote work offers them. They are lured by the promise of being able to work around the schedules of their children or other family members. Paradoxically, because of their flexible work situation, it is often difficult for them to separate work from their home life. Consequently, they may work many more hours than the standard nine-to-five worker, or experience the stress of trying to separate work from play. As a matter of fact, one of the reasons higher-ups at Best Buy were not immediately informed about the ROWE experiment is because employees were concerned that overbearing bosses would expect them to always be working, and middle of the night phone calls would become routine.[39]

Working remotely can disconnect an employee from his or her company's culture and make them feel isolated. The casual, face-to-face encounters that take place in offices transmit extensive cultural, political, and other organizational information. These encounters are lost to an employee who seldom, if ever, works at the office. Consequently, telecommuters need to undertake special efforts to stay connected. They must engage in forms of conversation to replace "water cooler" talk. This could take the form of instant messaging, telephone calls/conferences, e-mail, blogs, or even video conferencing or unified communications.

Virtual work also raises the specter of **offshoring**, or foreign outsourcing of software development and computer services. Once a company establishes an infrastructure for remote work, the work often can be performed abroad as easily as domestically. U.S. immigration laws limit the number of foreigners who may work in the United States since the terrorist attacks in New York City and Washington, D.C., on September 11, 2001. However, no such limitations exist on work performed outside this country by workers who then transmit their work to

---

[39] Conlin, "Smashing the Clock."

Employee Advantages of Telecommuting	Potential Problems
Reduced stress due to increased ability to meet schedules and less work-related distractions	Increased stress from inability to separate work life from home life
Higher morale; lower absenteeism	Harder to evaluate performance
Geographic flexibility	Employee may become disconnected from company culture
Higher personal productivity	Telecommuters are more easily replaced by offshore workers
Housebound individuals can join the workforce	Not suitable for all jobs or employees

FIGURE 4.4   Advantages and disadvantages of telecommuting.

the United States electronically. Because such work is not subject to minimum wage controls, companies may have a strong economic incentive to outsource work abroad. Companies find it particularly easy to outsource clerical work related to electronic production, such as data processing and computer programming. Benefits and drawbacks of telecommuting are summarized in Figure 4.4.

Managerial Issues in Telecommuting and Mobile Work

Telecommuting requires managers to undertake special planning, staffing, and supervising activities. In terms of planning, business and support tasks must be redesigned to support mobile and remote workers. Everyday business tasks such as submitting employee expense reports in person (as is common when an original signature is needed on the form) and attending daily progress meetings are inappropriate if most of the workers are remote. Support tasks such as fixing computers by dispatching someone from the central IS department may not be feasible if the worker is in a hotel in a remote city. Basic business and support processes must be designed with both the remote worker and the worker remaining in the office in mind. Because telecommuters may not be able to deal with issues requiring face-to-face contact, nontelecommuters may find that they are asked to assume additional tasks. Training should be offered to telecommuters and nontelecommuters alike so that they can anticipate and understand the new work environment.

Not all jobs are suitable for telecommuting. Some jobs may require the worker to be at the work location. Basically only those job aspects that can be performed independently at remote locations are the most suitable for telecommuting. Further, the employees selected to staff telecommuting jobs must be self-starters. They must be responsible for completing work tasks without being in the corporate office. New employees who need to be socialized into the organization's practices and culture are not good candidates for mobile or remote work.

Managers must find new ways to evaluate and supervise those employees without seeing them every day in the office. Typically this means judging their work on the basis of targeted output, and not based on how telecommuters do the work. They must also work to coordinate schedules, ensure adequate communication among all workers, establish policies about use of different technologies to support communications, and help their organizations adapt by building business processes to support mobile and remote workers.

▶ VIRTUAL TEAMS

Employees are not only working remotely on an independent basis, but also on teams with remote members called virtual teams. **Virtual teams** are defined as "geographically and/or organizationally dispersed coworkers that are assembled using a combination of telecommunications and information technologies to accomplish an organizational task."[40] This definition includes teams whose members seldom meet face-to-face. The members of virtual teams may be in different locations, organizations, time zones, or time shifts. Further, virtual teams may have distinct, relatively permanent membership, or they may be relatively fluid as they evolve to respond to changing task requirements and as members leave and are replaced by new members.

Factors Driving Virtual Teams

The same drivers that apply to telecommuting, listed in Figure 4.3, can also be applied to virtual teams. Virtual teams clearly offer advantages in terms of expanding the knowledge base through team membership. Thanks to new and ever-emerging communication and information technologies, managers can draw team members with needed skills or expertise from around the globe, without having to commit to huge travel expenses. That is, difficulties in getting relevant stakeholders together physically are relaxed. Further, virtual teams can benefit from *following the sun*. In an example of following the sun, London team members of a virtual team of software developers at Tandem Services Corporation initially code the project and transmit their code each evening to U.S. team members for testing. U.S. members forward the code they tested to Tokyo for debugging. London team members start their next day with the code debugged by their Japanese colleagues, and another cycle is initiated.[41] Increasingly, growing pressure for offshoring has resulted in systems development by global virtual teams whose members are located around the world.

Disadvantages and Challenges of Virtual Teams

There are some clear disadvantages to virtual teams. For example, different time zones, although helpful when following the sun, can work against virtual team

[40] A. M. Townsend, S. DeMarie, and A. R. Hendrickson, "Virtual Teams: Technology and the Workplace of the Future," *Academy of Management Executive* 12, no. 3 (1998), 17–28.

[41] Marie-Claude Boudreau, Karen Loch, Daniel Robey, and Detmar Straub, "Going Global: Using Information Technology to Advance the Competitiveness of the Virtual Transnational Organization," *Academy of Management Executive* 12, no. 4 (1998), 120–128.

members when they are forced to stay up late or work in the middle of the night to communicate with team members in other time zones. Further, security is harder to ensure with distributed workers. There also are a considerable number of challenges, that if not correctly managed could turn into disadvantages. A summary of these challenges in comparison with more traditional teams can be found in Figure 4.5.

A major communication challenge that virtual teams face stems from the limitations of having to primarily communicate electronically via e-mail, tele-conferences, or messaging systems. Electronic media allow team members to transcend the limitations of space and even store messages for future reference. But, electronic communications may not allow team members to convey the nuances that are possible with face-to-face conversations. Thus, conflict may be more likely to erupt in virtual environments, and trust may be slower to form. In addition, virtual teams differ from traditional teams in terms of technological and diversity challenges. For example, traditional teams, unlike virtual ones, may not have to deal with the hassles of learning new technologies or selecting the technology that is most appropriate for the task at hand. Perhaps the greatest challenges that virtual teams face in comparison to their more traditional counterparts arise from the diversity of the team members. Virtual teams enable members to come from many different cultures and nations. Even though this diversity allows managers to pick team members from a wider selection of experts, global virtual teams are more likely than more traditional teams to be stymied by team members who have different native languages and cultures.

Managerial Issues in Virtual Teams

Managers cannot manage virtual teams in the same way that they manage more traditional teams. The differences in management control activities are particularly pronounced. Leaders of virtual teams cannot easily observe the behavior of virtual team members. Thus, monitoring of behavior is likely to be more limited than in traditional teams. As is the case with telecommuters and mobile workers, performance is more likely to be evaluated in terms of output than on displays of behavior. Because the team members are dispersed, providing feedback is especially important—not just at the end of a team's project, but throughout the team's life. To encourage the accomplishment of the team's goal, compensation should be based heavily on the team's performance, rather than just on individual performance. Compensating team members for individual performance may result in "hot-rodding" or lack of cooperation among team members. Organizational reward systems must be aligned with the accomplishment of desired team goals. This alignment is especially difficult when virtual team members belong to different organizations, each with their own unique reward and compensation systems. Each compensation system may affect individual performance in a different way. Managers need to be aware of differences and discover ways to provide motivating rewards to all team members. Further, policies about the selection, evaluation, and compensation of virtual team members may need to be enacted.

Challenges	Virtual Teams (VT)	Traditional Teams
Communication	• Multiple time zones can lead to greater efficiencies when leveraged, but can also create communication difficulties in terms of scheduling meetings and interactions. • Communication dynamics such as facial expressions, vocal inflections, verbal cues, and gestures are altered.	• Teams are collocated in same time zone. Scheduling is less difficult. • Teams may use richer communication media, including face-to-face discussions.
Technology	• Team members must have proficiency across a wide range of technologies; VT membership may be biased toward individuals skilled at learning new technologies. • Technology offers an electronic repository that may facilitate building an organizational memory. • Work group effectiveness may be more dependent on the ability to align group structure and technology with the task environment.	• Technology is not critical for group processes. Technological collaboration tools, while possibly used, are not essential for communications. Team members may not need to possess these skills. • Electronic repositories are not typically used. • Task technology fit may not be as critical.

Team Diversity	• Members typically come from different organizations and/or cultures. This makes it:
	
	  • Harder to establish a group identity
	  • Necessary to have better communication skills
	  • More difficult to build trust, norms, and shared meanings about roles, because team members have fewer cues about their teammates' performance
	  • More likely that they have different perceptions about time and deadlines
		• Because members are more homogeneous, group identity is easier to form.
		
		• Because of commonalities, communications are easier to complete successfully.

FIGURE 4.5 Comparison of challenges facing virtual teams and traditional teams.

Looking beyond these management control activities, we see that prescriptions for managing the communications and information technologies in virtual team environments are limited. The rest of this section is devoted to managing the challenges highlighted in Figure 4.5: communication, technology and diversity.

Communication Challenges   Perhaps the most research has focused on ways to overcome communication challenges. Because the distances are often great, managers clearly need to keep the channels of communication open to allow team members to get their work done. Some communication tasks lend themselves to certain technologies. This means that they must have the necessary technological support. For instance, if a team leader wants to have a meeting of team members but has neither the budget nor the lead time to plan for extensive travel to the meeting, video teleconferencing may be a viable alternative. E-mails are excellent for short messages to one or all group members. Team leaders may decide to initiate a team's activity with a face-to-face meeting so that the seeds of trust can be planted and team members feel as if they know one another on a more personal basis.

Face-to face meetings also appear to be the heartbeat of successful global virtual teams.[42] An in-depth study of three global virtual teams, found that the two effective teams created a rhythm organized around regularly scheduled face-to-face meetings. Before each meeting there was a flurry of communication and activity as team members prepared for the meeting. After the meeting there were a considerable number of follow-up messages and tasks. The ineffective team did not demonstrate a similar pattern. Because not all teams can meet face-to-face, synchronous meetings using video teleconferencing, or possibly in a virtual world, can activate the heartbeat.

Because team leaders cannot always see what their team members are up to or if they are experiencing any problems, frequent communications are important. If team members are quiet, the team leader must reach out to them to encourage their participation and to ensure that they feel their contributions are appreciated. Even though a majority of team members are in one location, the team leader should rotate meeting times to alternate the convenience among team members. Further, in the event that there is a larger group of team members in one or several places, the team leader should encourage these subgroups to have all their discussions online so remote members will not feel isolated.

Technology Challenges   Having the needed communication and information technologies available means that all team members have the same or compatible technologies at their locations. The support staff to maintain and update the systems must be in place. Managers must ensure that seamless telephone transfers to the home office, desktop support, network connectivity, and security support are

---

[42] M. L. Maznevski and K. Chudoba, "Bridging Space Over Time: Global Virtual Team Dynamics and Effectiveness," *Organization Science* 11, no. 5 (2000), 373–392.

provided to the remote workers. Team members (like telecommuters) must have access to the files and applications they need to do their work. The importance of security for remote work cannot be overstated.

Further, managers must also provide the framework for using the technology. Policies and norms, or unwritten rules, need to be established about how the team members should use the technology to work with one another.[43] These should include norms about telephone, e-mail, and videoconferencing etiquette (i.e., how often to check for messages, the maximum time to wait to return e-mails, warning team members about absences or national holidays), work to be performed, and so on. Such norms are especially important when team members are not in the same office and cannot see when team members are unavailable.

Diversity Challenges Managers may also seek to provide technologies to support diverse team member characteristics. For example, team members from different parts of the globe may have different views of time.[44] Team members from Anglo-American cultures (i.e., U.S., U.K., Canada, Australia, New Zealand) may view time as a continuum from past, to present and future. For such team members, each unit of time is the same, and thus they can be interchanged with one another or used as a basis for pay. These team members are likely to be concerned with deadlines and often prefer to complete one task before starting another (i.e., monochronous). For team members who are conscious of deadlines, planning and scheduling software may be especially useful. In contrast, team members from India often have a cyclical view of time. They do not get excited about deadlines and there is no hurry to make a decision because it is likely to cycle back—at which time the team member may be in a better position to make the decision. Many people from India tend to be polychronous. Team members who are polychronous and prefer to do several activities at one time may want to have instant messaging or Skype (a voice-over-IP support system) available to them so that they can communicate with their teammates and still work on other tasks.

In addition to providing the appropriate technologies, managers with team members who have different views of time need to be aware of the differences and try to develop strategies to motivate those who are not concerned with deadlines to deliver their assigned tasks on time. Or the managers may wish to assign these team members to do tasks that are not sensitive to deadlines.

Of course, views of time are only one dimension of diversity. Although diversity has been demonstrated to lead to more creative solutions, it also makes it harder for team members to learn to trust one another, to communicate, and to form a group identity. Through open communications, managers may be able to uncover and deal with other areas of diversity that negatively affect the team.

---

[43] C. Saunders, C. Van Slyke, and D. R. Vogel, "My Time or Yours? Managing Time Visions in Global Virtual Teams," *Academy of Management Executive* 18, no. 1 (2004), 19–31.

[44] C. S. Saunders, C. Van Slyke, and D. Vogel, "My Time or Yours? Managing Time Visions in Global Virtual Teams," *Academy of Management Executive* 18, no. 1 (2004), 19–31.

▶ GAINING ACCEPTANCE FOR IT-INDUCED CHANGE

The changes described in this chapter no doubt alter the frames of reference of organizational employees and may be a major source of concern for them. Employees may resist the changes if they view the changes as negatively affecting them. In the case of a new information system that they do not fully understand or are not prepared to operate, they may resist in several ways:

- They may deny that the system is up and running.
- They may sabotage the system by distorting or otherwise altering inputs.
- They may try to convince themselves, and others, that the new system really will not change the status quo.
- They may refuse to use the new system where its usage is voluntary.

To avoid the negative consequences of resistance to change, system implementers and managers must actively manage the change process and gain acceptance for new IS. To help explain how to gain acceptance for a new technology, Professor Fred Davis and his colleagues developed the Technology Acceptance Model (TAM). Many variations of TAM exist, but its most basic form is displayed on the right-hand side in Figure 4.6. TAM suggests that managers cannot get employees to use a system until they want to use it. To convince employees to want to use the system, managers may need to change employee attitudes about the system. Employee attitudes may change if employees believe that the system will allow them to do more or better work for the same amount of effort (perceived usefulness), and that it is easy to use. Training, documentation, and user support consultants are external variables that may help explain the usefulness of the system and make it easier to use.

TAM has many variants. For example, one variant considers subjective norms,[45] whereas another adds attitudes toward behaviors.[46] The Unified Theory of Acceptance and Use of Technology makes a valiant effort to integrate the many fragmented findings about TAM.[47] Another attempt to integrate the many findings is TAM3.[48] A simplified version of TAM3 is shown in Figure 4.6. The left hand side of Figure 4.6 provides the four categories of determinants of perceived usefulness and perceived ease of use. Specifically, they are *individual differences* (e.g., gender, age), *system characteristics* (such things as output quality and job relevance that help individuals develop favorable or unfavorable views about the system), *social*

[45] V. Venkatesh and F. D. Davis, "A Theoretical Extension of the Technology Acceptance Model: Four Longitudinal Field Studies," *Management Science* 45, no. 2 (2000), 186–204.

[46] S. Taylor and P. Todd, "Assessing IT Usage: The Role of Prior Experience," *MIS Quarterly* 19, no. 2 (1995), 561–570.

[47] Venkatesh, V., Morris, M. G., Davis, G. B., & Davis, F. D. (2003). User acceptance of information technology: Toward a unified view. *MIS Quarterly*, 27(3), 425–478.

[48] V. Venkatesh and H. Bala, "Technology Acceptance Model 3 and a Research Agenda on Interventions, *Decision Sciences*, 39, No. 2, 2008, 273-315.

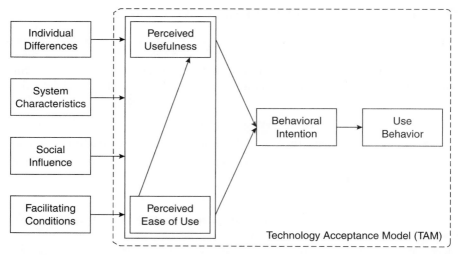

FIGURE 4.6 Simplified technology acceptance model 3(TAm3).
Source: Viswanath Venkatest and Hillol Bala, "Technology Acceptance Model 3 and a Research Agenda on Interventions," *Decision Sciences*, 39:2 (2008), pg.276.

influence (e.g., subjective norms), and facilitating conditions (e.g. top management support). The interrelationships described in UTAUT and TAM3 are very complex. For example, although social influences are important, they are likely to be important *only* for older works and women, and then *only* when they start using the system. The more complex models (UTAUT and TAM3) are useful for experts who are trying to take into account the nuances when trying to figure out the best way to implement systems. However, the parsimonious TAM model is clearly easier for practitioners trying to grasp the major issues involved in user acceptance.

TAM and all of these variants assume that system use is under the control of the individuals. When employees are mandated to use the system, they may use it in the short run, but over the long run the negative consequences of resistance may surface. Thus, gaining acceptance of the system is important, even in those situations where it is mandated.

TAM assumes that technology will be accepted if people's attitudes and beliefs support its use. One way to make sure that employees' attitudes and beliefs are favorable toward the system is to have them participate in its design and implementation. When future users of the system participate in its design and implementation, they can more easily tell the designers what they need from the system. Being involved in the development also makes them more aware of the trade-offs that inevitably occur during a system implementation. They may be more willing to accept the consequences of the trade-offs. Finally, being involved in the design and development allows users to better understand how the system works, and thus may make it easier for them to use the system.

Microsoft recently applied the concept of participation when it invited hackers to a little-publicized security conference dubbed "Blue Hat" for the express purpose of exploiting flaws in Microsoft computing systems. The unusual summit of delegates of the hacking community and their primary corporate target illustrates the importance of security breaches to the world's most powerful software company. Bill Gates, Microsoft's chairman at the time, estimated that security-related issues cost the company $2 billion a year—more than a third of its research budget. It is likely that Microsoft was using the event to woo an influential group to report security flaws discreetly rather than to go public with them. Both the hackers and the corporate engineers appreciated each other's technical knowledge and agreed to meet again.[49]

▶ FOOD FOR THOUGHT: SECURITY WITH REMOTE WORKERS

In May of 2006, the Department of Veterans Affairs (VA) announced that a laptop carrying unencrypted, sensitive personal information on more that 2.2 million active-duty military personnel was stolen from an employee's home.[50] This security breach highlights the importance of posting and enforcing proper telecommuting (and remote work) policies. Although the VA claims that there is a policy in place that does not allow workers to take their laptops home, it would seem that the policy is not strictly enforced and/or that employees are not educated about the agency's telecommuting policies and the importance of adhering to them.

The development, posting, and enforcement of telecommuting policies are vital in a world where security breaches are commonplace. These policies should incorporate such simple rules as never store information on a laptop, encrypt all information once it leaves the office, and provide telecommuters with dedicated computers that can only be used for work. If an organization does not wish to adhere to these strict guidelines, then it at least needs to develop telecommuting policies that define what software will be allowed on the home-based computer and what data will be stored on the computer. Further, employees must be made aware of the policies through a well-planned education program.[51] One approach to make sure that remote workers understand the telecommuting policy, and to make them accountable, is to have them sign an

---

[49] Ina Fried, "Microsoft Asks for Help from Hackers," *ZD Net News* (June 16, 2005), available at http://news.zdnet.com/2100-1009_22-5749234html?tag=st.num.

[50] Robert Lemos, "VA Data Theft Affects Most Soldiers," *Security Focus*, June 7, 2006 http://www.securityfocus.com/brief/224.

[51] Mary J. Culnan, Ellen R. Foxman, and Amy W. Ray, "Why IT executives Should Help Employees Secure Their Home Computers," *MIS Quarterly Executive* 7, no. 1 (March 2008), 49–56, http://test.misqe.org/ojs/index.php/misqe/article/view/161.

agreement with employers on exactly how their computers are to be used and maintained.[52]

As the physical corporate walls are torn down and more workers work from remote locations, technology advances to keep up with their business and network security needs. Some of these technologies are the following.

- Probably the most basic security tactic is to deploy antivirus and antispyware software on computers used by remote workers. There should be a related organization policy about how often the computers should be updated with the latest virus definitions and system patches.

- Basic security protections that are often overlooked include adding a desktop firewall and SSL (Security Socket Layer) for authentication.

- Many government-issued computers are equipped with Absolute Software's Computrace—"the LoJack of computer hardware" to trace the location of a missing or stolen computer.[53]

- Centennial Software's DeviceWall prevents USB mass-storage devices or iPods from accessing data on home-based computers. DeviceWall also lets machines work in read-only mode and can limit Wi-Fi connections and use of CDs.[54]

- A terminal server (without Internet access) allows remote workers to log on to a server where all their applications and data are available. In this scenario, because all the applications are running on data center computers, remote client security software is unnecessary.[55]

- A relatively new category of technology, data-leak prevention technology, is designed to ensure that sensitive corporate data is not being printed out, e-mailed, or saved to removable media without the proper authorization, even on remote endpoints.[56]

Remote workers pose a threat to office workers because if they come into the office with an infected computer and plug into the network, perimeter security technology is unable protect all the other workers connected to the network. Further, as demonstrated by the VA example earlier, remote workers can be the source of a security breach if their computers are stolen. It is impossible for organizations to make remote workers totally secure. However, managers need to get more involved in assessing the areas and severity of risk and take appropriate

---

[52] Ellen Messmer, "Telecommuting Security Concerns Grow," *Network World*, April 24, 2006, http://www.networkworld.com/news/2006/042406-telecommuter-security.html.

[53] Cara Garretson, "Heightened Awareness, Reinforced Products Advance Teleworker's Security," *Network World*, February 20, 2007, http://www.networkworld.com/news/2007/022007-heightened-awareness.html?ap1=rcb.

[54] Ibid.

[55] Ibid.

[56] Ibid.

steps, via policies, education and technology, to reduce the risks and make those remote workers as secure as possible.

▶ SUMMARY

- The nature of work is changing, and IT supports, if not propels, these changes.
- Organization structures have responded to changes in work. One new organizational form is the virtual organization, or a structure that makes it possible for individuals to work for an organization and live anywhere. They are made possible through information and communication technologies.
- Communication and collaboration are becoming increasingly important in today's work. Technology to support communication includes e-mail, intranets, instant messaging (IM), Voice over Internet Protocol (VoIP), unified communications, RSS (Web feeds), virtual private networks (VPN), and file transfers. Technology to support collaboration includes social networking sites, Web logs (blogs), virtual worlds, wikis, and groupware.
- IT affects work by creating new work, creating new working arrangements, and presenting new managerial challenges in employee supervision, evaluation, compensation, and hiring.
- Newer approaches to management reflect greater use of computer and information technology in hiring and supervising employees, a greater focus on output (compared to behavior), and a greater team orientation.
- The shift to knowledge-based work, changing demographics and lifestyle preferences, new technologies, growing reliance on the Web, and energy concerns all contribute to the growth in remote work.
- Companies find that building telecommuting capabilities can be an important tool for attracting and retaining employees, increasing worker productivity, providing flexibility to otherwise overworked individuals, reducing office space and associated costs, responding to environmental concerns about energy consumption, and complying with the Clean Air Act. Telecommuting also promises employees potential benefits: schedule flexibility, higher personal productivity, less commuting time and fewer expenses, and greater geographic flexibility.
- Disadvantages of telecommuting include difficulties in evaluating performance, greater feelings of isolation among employees, easier displacement by offshoring, and limitations of jobs and workers in its application.
- Virtual teams are defined as "geographically and/or organizationally dispersed coworkers that are assembled using a combination of telecommunications and information technologies to accomplish an organizational task." They are increasingly common organizational phenomenon and must be managed differently than more traditional teams.
- Managers of virtual teams must focus on overcoming the challenges of communication, technology, and diversity of team members.
- To gain acceptance of a new technology, potential users must exhibit a favorable attitude toward the technology. In the case of information systems, the users' beliefs about its perceived usefulness and perceived ease of use color their attitudes about the system.

▶ KEY TERMS

e-mail (p. 103)
file transfer (p. 106)
groupware (p. 107)
instant messaging (IM)
  (p. 104)
intranet (p. 103)
mobile workers (p. 115)
offshoring (p. 118)
RSS (Web feed) (p. 105)

social networking site
  (p. 106)
telecommuting (p. 115)
unified communications
  (p. 105)
video teleconference
  (p. 104)
virtual teams (p. 120)
virtual organization (p. 99)

virtual private network
  (VPN) (p. 106)
virtual world (p. 107)
Voice over Internet
  Protocol (VoIP) (p. 104)
Web logs (blogs) (p. 107)
wiki (p. 107)

▶ DISCUSSION QUESTIONS

1. Why might a worker resist the implementation of a new technology? What are some of the possible consequences of asking a worker to use a computer or similar device in his or her job?

2. How can IT alter an individual's work? How can a manager ensure that the impact is positive rather than negative?

3. What current technologies do you predict will show the most impact on the way work is done? Why?

4. Given the growth in telecommuting and other mobile work arrangements, how might offices physically change in the coming years? Will offices as we think of them today exist by 2012? Why or why not?

5. How is working at an online retailer different from working at a brick-and-mortar retailer? What types of jobs are necessary at each? What skills are important?

6. Paul Saffo, director of the Institute for the Future, noted, "Telecommuting is a reality for many today, and will continue to be more so in the future. But beware, this doesn't mean we will travel less. In fact, the more one uses electronics, the more they are likely to travel."[57] Do you agree with this statement? Why or why not?

7. The explosion of information-driven self-serve options in the consumer world is evident in the gas station, where customers pay, pump gas, and purchase a car wash without ever seeing an employee; in the retail store such as Wal-Mart, Home Depot, and the local grocery, where self-service checkout stands mean customers can purchase a basket of items without ever speaking to a sales agent; at the airport, where customers make reservations and pay for and print tickets without the help of an agent; and at the bank, where ATMs have long replaced tellers for most transactions. But a backlash is coming, experts predict. Some say that people are more isolated than they used to be in the days of face-to-face service, and they question how much time people are really saving if they have to continually learn new processes, operate new machines, and overcome new glitches. Laborsaving technologies were supposed to liberate people from mundane tasks, but it appears that these technologies are actually shifting the boring tasks to the customer. On

---

[57] "Online Forum: Companies of the Future," available at http://www.msnbc.com/news/738363.asp (accessed June 11, 2002).

the other hand, many people like the convenience of using these self-service systems, especially because it means customers can visit a bank for cash or order books or gifts from an online retailer 24 hours a day. Does this mean the end of "doing business the old-fashioned way?" Will this put a burden on the elderly or the poor when corporations begin charging for face-to-face services?[58]

CASE STUDY 4-1

AUTOMATED WASTE DISPOSAL, INC.

Ciro Viento is responsible for 110 of Automated Waste Disposal, Inc.'s (AWD's) garbage trucks. Automated Waste Disposal is a commercial and household trash hauler in Connecticut and New York. When a caller recently complained to Viento that a blue and white Automated Waste Disposal truck was speeding down Route 22, Viento turned to the company's information system. He learned that the driver of a company front-loader had been on that very road at 7:22 a.m., doing 51 miles per hour (mph) in a 35 mph zone. Was the driver of that truck ever in trouble!

This AWD system uses a global positioning system not only to smooth its operations, but also to keep closer track of its workers, who may not always be doing what they are supposed to be doing during work hours. Viento pointed out, "If you're not out there babysitting them, you don't know how long it takes to do the route. The guy could be driving around the world, he could be at his girlfriend's house."

Before AWD installed the GPS system, the drivers of his 22 front-loaders clocked in approximately 300 hours a week of overtime at 1.5 times pay. Once AWD started monitoring the time they spent in the yard before and after completing their routes and the time and location of stops that they made, the number of overtime hours plummeted to 70 per week. This translated to substantial savings for a company whose drivers earn about $20 an hour.

AWD also installed GPS receivers, which are the size and shape of cans of tuna, in salesmen's cars. Viento was not surprised to learn that some of the company's salespeople frequented a local bar around 4 p.m. when they were supposed to be calling on customers. Viento decided to set digital boundaries around the bar.

Not surprisingly, the drivers and salespeople aren't entirely happy with the new GPS-based system. Tom McNally, an AWD driver, admits: "It's kind of like Big Brother is watching a little bit. But it's where we're heading in this society . . . I get testy in the deli when I'm waiting in line for coffee, because it's like, hey, they're (managers) watching. I've got to go."

Viento counters that employers have a right to know what their employees are up to: "If you come to work here, and I pay you and you're driving one of my vehicles, I should have the right to know what you're doing."

Discussion Questions

1. What are the positive and negative aspects of Viento's use of the GPS-based system to monitor his drivers and salespeople?

---

[58] Stevenson Swanson, "Are Self-Serve Options a Disservice?" *Austin American Statesman* (May 8, 2005), Section H, p. 1. Reprinted from *Chicago Tribune*.

2. What advice do you have for Viento about the use of the system for supervising, evaluating, and compensating his drivers and salespeople?

3. As more and more companies turn to IS to help them monitor their employees, what do you anticipate the impact will be on employee privacy? Can anything be done to ensure employee privacy?

Source: Adapted from MSNBC News (Associated Press), "Bosses Keep Sharp Eye on Mobile Workers" (December 30, 2004), available at http://www.msnbc.msn.com/id/6769377/(downloaded June 18, 2005).

CASE STUDY 4-2

VIRTUALLY THERE?

Dr. Laura Esserman leans forward and speaks with conviction, making broad gestures with her hands. "Over the past couple of decades, I've watched industries be transformed by the use of information systems and incredible visual displays," she says. "What we could do is to completely change the way we work—just by changing the way we collect and share information."

Sounds familiar, right? But Esserman isn't championing yet another overzealous Silicon Valley start-up—she's envisioning how cancer patients will interact with their doctors. If Esserman, a Stanford-trained surgeon and MBA, has her way, patients won't sit passively on an exam table, listening to impenetrable diagnoses and memorizing treatment instructions. Instead, they'll have access to a multimedia treasure chest of real-time diagnosis, treatment, and success-rate data from thousands of cases like their own. Better still, they won't meet with just one doctor. There will be other doctors on the case—some from the other side of the hospital and some, perhaps, from the other side of the world.

Esserman and her colleagues at the University of California, San Francisco's Carol Franc Buck Breast Care Center are pioneers in the new world of virtual teams and virtual tools, a world in which there will be real change in the way highly trained people whose work depends on intense collaboration get things done. Her goal at the Buck Breast Care Center is to use virtual tools to bring more useful information (and more doctors) into the exam room. Why? Because two heads really are better than one. She explains that when patients see their doctors after a breast cancer diagnosis, for example, they are handed a recommended course of treatment that involves serious choices and trade-offs. Of course, most patients don't know enough about the merits of, say, a lumpectomy versus a mastectomy to make an informed choice, so they trust their doctors to tell them what to do.

But a single doctor isn't always equipped to make the best decision, especially because different procedures can have very different long-term physical and emotional impacts—but may not be all that different in their short-term medical outcomes. "Very often," Esserman says, "doctors recommend a particular treatment because they're more familiar with it. But we should be advocates for our patients, rather than our specialties."

Although her full-blown program is a long way off, Esserman has run a pilot project with 24 patients. She worked with both Oracle, the Silicon Valley database giant, and MAYA Viz, a Pittsburgh company that develops "decision community" software, to allow doctors across the country to collaborate virtually. Through Esserman's approach, when a patient arrives at the doctor's office to receive treatment instructions, instead of listening to a physician's monologue, she's handed a printout. On the top left side of the page is the diagnosis, followed by patient-specific data: the size and spread of the tumor, when it was discovered, and the name of the treating doctor. Below that is statistical information generated from clinical-research databases, such as the number of similar cases treated each year and details about survival rates.

A set of arrows points to treatment options. Next, the patient reads the risks and benefits associated with each treatment. She can follow along as the doctor explains the chances that the cancer will recur after each option and the likelihood that a particular treatment will require follow-up procedures, as well as a comparison of survival rates for each one.

At this point, the patient has an opportunity to voice concerns about treatment options, and the physician can explain her experiences with each one. "When you share this kind of information, patients and doctors can make decisions together according to the patient's values," Esserman says. This is where the network tools come into play. Drawing from stored databases of both clinical trials and patient-treatment histories local to the hospital, the physician can compare courses of action and results far beyond her own personal experience. "A medical opinion is really just one physician's synthesis of the information," notes Esserman. "So you need a way to calibrate yourself—a way to continually ask, Are there variations among the group of doctors that I work with? Am I subjecting people to procedures that turn out not to be useful?"

With a real-time, shared-data network, these questions can be answered at the touch of a button instead of after hours, weeks, or months of research. But that's just the beginning. A real-time network also presents the possibility of seeking help from other specialists on puzzling cases, even if those specialists are on the other side of the world.

Discussion Questions

1. Why does this case offer an example of a virtual team? In what ways are the team members on this team dispersed (i.e., location, organization, culture)?
2. What are the advantages of the virtual team described in this case?
3. What technological support is needed for the virtual team to meet its goals?
4. What suggestions can you offer Dr. Esserman for managing this virtual team?

Source: Excerpted from Alison Overholt, "Virtually There," *Fast Company* 56 (March 2002), 108, available at http://www.fastcompany.com/online/56/virtual.html.

CHAPTER 5

INFORMATION TECHNOLOGY AND CHANGING BUSINESS PROCESSES[1]

Executives at concrete company Cemex faced a challenge as they confronted their second century of existence. As a 100-year-old multinational cement corporation, based in Monterrey, Mexico, they sought new ways to operate, innovate, and manage their vast organization. It took them 16 years, but they completely changed the key processes that affect their customers.

Prior to their transformation, the company looked like any other regional cement company with autonomous plants, secluded local management, and a dependency on factors they felt were beyond their control. Customers were regularly caught without their shipments. But that was standard practice in the industry, so it was tolerated.

The new CEO began by revisiting their business strategy and challenged his team to solve the issues of inefficient delivery and unforecastable demand. At the time, the IT department was only supporting back-office accounting applications. The transformation team looked at best practice ways of using information technology (IT) to serve production and delivery operations and built the IT capability they needed to be completely aligned with the business process redesign. They built Cemexnet to link all their cement plants and to keep the plants updated on changes in supply and demand. They redesigned their delivery processes while installing a logistics information system that used GPS technology to help dispatchers manage their fleet of trucks. Now the closest trucks were used to make deliveries, and rerouting was possible in extreme circumstances. Management also redesigned and created a set of global processes so customers, suppliers, and distributors could manage their orders.

---

[1] The authors wish to acknowledge and thank Jeff Greer, MBA 1999, for his help researching and writing early drafts of this paper.

134

The results were dramatic. Delivery windows went from 3 hours to 20 minutes, and Cemex made that window 98% of the time. They meet this window because they have control over their processes and information about issues that might affect their processes. Sales increased 19% in the first quarter after all the components and redesigned processes were put in place. And their reputation was greatly enhanced because they were able to transform themselves from just another regional cement company into a highly differentiated, service-oriented, customer-friendly organization. Cemex reset the bar for all others in the industry with their customer orientation, their use of technology, and their process redesign.[2]

IS can enable or impede business change. The right design coupled with the right technology can result in changes such as Cemex experienced. The wrong business process design or the wrong technology, however, can force a company into oblivion.

To a manager in today's business environment, an understanding of how IS enable business change is essential. The terms *management* and *change management* are used almost synonymously: To manage effectively means to manage change effectively. As IS become ever more prevalent and more powerful, the speed and magnitude of the changes that organizations must address to remain competitive will continue to increase. To be a successful manager, one must understand how IS enable change in a business, one must gain a process perspective of business, and one must understand how to transform business processes effectively. This chapter provides the manager with a view of business process change. It provides tools for analyzing how a company currently does business and for thinking about how to effectively manage the inevitable changes that result from competition and the availability of IS. This chapter also describes an IT-based solution commonly known as enterprise IS (information systems).

A brief word to the reader is needed. The term *process* is used extensively in this chapter. In some instances, it is used to refer to the steps taken to change aspects of the business. At other times, it is used to refer to the part of the business to be changed: the business process. The reader should be sensitive to the potentially confusing use of the term *process*.

▶ SILO PERSPECTIVE VERSUS BUSINESS PROCESS PERSPECTIVE

When effectively linked with improvements to business processes, advances in IS enable changes that make it possible to do business in a new way, better and more competitive than before. On the other hand, IS can also inhibit change, which occurs when managers fail to adapt business processes because they rely on inflexible systems to support those processes. Finally, IS can also drive change, for better or for worse. Examples abound of industries that were fundamentally

---

[2] Adapted from "BPR at Cemex" from www.cio.com/article/print/30445 (accessed February 28, 2008).

changed by advances in IS and of companies whose success or failure depended on the ability of their managers to adapt. This chapter considers IS as an enabler of business transformation, a partner in transforming business processes to achieve competitive advantages. We begin by comparing a process view of the firm with a functional view.

Transformation requires discontinuous thinking—recognizing and shedding outdated rules and fundamental assumptions that underlie operations. "Unless we change these rules, we are merely rearranging the deck chairs on the *Titanic*. We cannot achieve breakthroughs in performance by cutting fat or automating existing processes. Rather, we must challenge old assumptions and shed the old rules that made the business under perform in the first place."[3]

Functional (or Silo) Perspective

Many think of business by imagining a hierarchical structure organized around a set of functions. Looking at a traditional organization chart allows an understanding of what the business does to achieve its goals. A typical hierarchical structure, organized by function, might look like the one shown in Figure 5.1.

In a hierarchy, each department determines its core competency and then concentrates on what it does best. For example, the operations department focuses on operations, the marketing department focuses on marketing, and so on. Each major function within the organization usually forms a separate department to ensure that work is done by groups of experts in that function. This functional structure is widespread in today's organizations and is reinforced by business education curricula, which generally follow functional structures—students take courses in functions (i.e., marketing, management, accounting), major in functions, and then are predisposed to think in terms of these same functions.[4]

Even when companies use the perspective of the value chain model (as discussed in Chapter 2), they still focus on functions that deliver their portion of

Typical Hierarchical Organization Structure

FIGURE 5.1   Hierarchical structure.

---

[3] Michael Hammer, "Reengineering Work: Don't Automate, Obliterate," *Harvard Business Review* (July–August 1990), 4.

[4] Thomas Davenport and John Beck, *The Attention Economy* (Boston: Harvard Business School Press, 2001), 173.

the process and "throwing it over the wall" to the next group on the value chain. These **silos**, or self-contained functional units, are useful for several reasons. First, they allow an organization to optimize expertise. For example, instead of having marketing people in a number of different groups, all the marketing people belong to the same department, which allows them to informally network and learn from each other and allows the business to leverage its resources. Second, the silos allow the organization to avoid redundancy in expertise by hiring one person who can be assigned to projects across functions on an as-needed basis instead of hiring an expert in each function. Third, with a functional organization, it is easier to benchmark with outside organizations, utilize bodies of knowledge created for each function, and easily understand the role of each silo. For example, it is clear that the marketing department produces and executes marketing plans, but it may not be clear what a customer-relationship department does. (It typically has some marketing, some sales, some services, and some accounting processes.)

On the other hand, silo organizations can experience significant suboptimization. First, individual departments often recreate information maintained by other departments. Second, communication gaps between departments are often wide. Third, as time passes, the structure and culture of a functionally organized business can become ingrained, creating a complex and frustrating bureaucracy. Fourth, handoffs between silos are often a source of problems, such as finger-pointing and lost information, in business processes. Finally, silos tend to lose sight of the objective of the overall organization goal and operate in a way that maximizes their local goals.

A firm's work changes over time. In a functionally organized silo business, each group is primarily concerned with its own set of objectives. The executive officers jointly seek to ensure that these functions work together to create value, but the task of providing the "big picture" to so many functionally oriented personnel can prove extremely challenging. As time passes and business circumstances change, new work is created that relies on more than one of the old functional departments. Departments that took different directions must now work together. They negotiate the terms of any new work processes with their own functional interests in mind, and the "big picture" optimum gets scrapped in favor of suboptimal compromises among the silos. These compromises then become repeated processes; they become standard operating procedures.

Losing the big picture means losing business effectiveness. After all, a business's main objective is to create as much value as possible for its shareholders and other stakeholders by satisfying its customers to the greatest extent possible. When functional groups duplicate work, when they fail to communicate with one another, when they lose the big picture and establish suboptimal processes, the customers and stakeholders are not being well served.

Process Perspective

A manager can avoid such bureaucracy—or begin to "fix" it—by managing from a process perspective. A **process perspective** keeps the big picture in view and allows the manager to concentrate on the work that must be done to ensure the optimal creation of value. A process perspective helps the manager avoid or reduce duplicate work, facilitate cross-functional communication, optimize business processes, and ultimately, best serve the customers and stakeholders.

In business, a **process** is defined as an interrelated, sequential set of activities and tasks that turns inputs into outputs, and includes the following:

- A beginning and an end
- Inputs and outputs
- A set of tasks (subprocesses) that transform the inputs into outputs
- A set of metrics for measuring effectiveness

Metrics are important because they focus managers on the critical dimensions of the process. Metrics for a business process are things like throughput, which is how many outputs can be produced per unit time; or cycle time, which is how long it takes for the entire process to execute. Some use measures are the number of handoffs in the process or actual work versus total cycle time. Other metrics are based on the outputs themselves, such as customer satisfaction, revenue per output, profit per output, and quality of the output.

Examples of business processes include customer order fulfillment, manufacturing planning and execution, payroll, financial reporting, and procurement. A typical procurement process might look like Figure 5.2. The process has a beginning and an end, inputs (requirements for goods or services) and outputs (receipt of goods, vendor payment), and subprocesses (filling out a purchase order, verifying the invoice). Metrics of the success of the process might include turnaround time and the number of paperwork errors.

The procurement process in Figure 5.2 cuts across the functional lines of a traditionally structured business. For example, the requirements for goods might originate in the operations department based on guidelines from the finance department. Paperwork would likely flow through the administration department, and the accounting department would be responsible for making payment to the vendor.

Focus on the process by its very nature ensures focus on the business's goals (the "big picture") because each process has an "endpoint" that is usually a deliverable to a customer, supplier, or other stakeholder. A process perspective recognizes that processes are often cross-functional. In the diagram in Figure 5.3, the vertical bars represent functional departments within a business. The horizontal bars represent processes that flow across those functional departments. A process

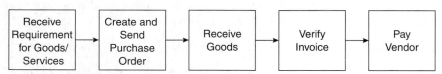

FIGURE 5.2 Sample business process.

Functions

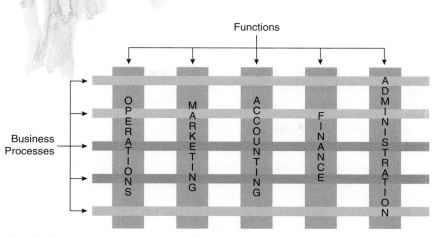

FIGURE 5.3 Cross-functional nature of business processes.

perspective requires an understanding that processes properly exist to serve the larger goals of the business, and that functional departments must work together to optimize processes in light of these goals.

For example, Nokia Telecommunications, the telecommunications manufacturing division of the Finnish company Nokia, built its order fulfillment process to include tendering, order delivery, implementation, and after-sales service tasks.[5] The company built cellular systems, switching systems, and transmission systems worldwide to companies offering mobile and fixed telecommunications services. Their order fulfillment process crossed division and product group boundaries, making it a cross-functional business process.

When managers take the process perspective, they lead their organizations to optimize the value that customers and stakeholders receive. These managers begin to question the status quo. They do not accept "because we have always done it that way" as an answer to why business is conducted in a certain way. They concentrate instead on specific objectives and results. They begin to manage processes by:

- Identifying the customers of processes
- Identifying these customers' requirements
- Clarifying the value that each process adds to the overall goals of the organization
- Sharing their perspective with other organizational members until the organization itself becomes more process focused

[5] For more details about Nokia's efforts, see S. Jarvenpaa and Ilkka Tuomi, "Nokia Telecommunications: Redesign of International Logistics," Harvard Business School case study 9-996-006 (September 1995).

The differences between the silo and process perspective are summarized in Figure 5.4. Unlike a silo perspective, a process perspective recognizes that businesses operate as a set of processes that flow across functional departments. It enables a manger to analyze the business's processes in light of its larger goals, as compared to the functional orientation of the silo perspective. Finally, it provides a manager with insights into how those processes might better serve these goals.

Zara's Cross-Functional Processes

Consider Spanish clothing retailer Zara (see Chapter 2). With 650 stores in 50 countries around the world and a well-designed set of cross-functional processes, Zara is able to design, produce, and deliver a garment within 15 days. For this to happen, Zara managers must regularly create and rapidly replenish small batches of goods all over the world. Zara's organization, operational procedures, performance measures, and even its office layout are all designed to make information transfer easy.

Zara's designers are colocated with the production team, including marketing, procurement, and production planners. Prototypes are created nearby, facilitating easy discussion about the latest design. Large circular tables in the middle of the production process encourage impromptu meetings where ideas are readily exchanged among the designers, market specialists, and production planners. The speed and quality of the design process is greatly enhanced by the colocation of the entire team. That is because the designers can quickly check their ideas with others on their cross-functional teams. For example, the market specialists can quickly respond to their designs in terms of the style, color, and fabric, whereas the procurement and production planners can update them about manufacturing costs and available capacity.

Information technology provides a platform but does not preclude informal face-to-face conversations. Retail store managers are linked to marketing specialists through customized handheld computers but just as often use the telephone to share order data, sales trends, and customer reactions to a new style. The flat

	Silo Perspective	Business Process Perspective
Definition	Self-contained functional units such as marketing, operations, finance, and so on	Interrelated, sequential set of activities and tasks that turns inputs into outputs
Focus	Functional	Cross-functional
Goal Accomplishment	Optimizes on functional goals, which might be a suboptimal organizational goal	Optimizes on organizational goals, or "big picture"
Benefits	Highlighting and developing core competencies; functional efficiencies	Avoiding work duplication and cross-functional communication gaps; organizational effectiveness

FIGURE 5.4 Comparison of silo perspective and business process perspective.

organization structure and cross-functional teams enable information sharing among everyone who needs to know and therefore offers the opportunity to change directions quickly to respond to new market trends.

▶ THE TOOLS FOR CHANGE

Two techniques are used to transform a business: (1) radical process, which is sometimes called **business process reengineering (BPR)** or simply reengineering, and (2) incremental, continuous process improvement, sometimes referred to using the term **total quality management (TQM)**. Every manager needs to know about both of these concepts. In fact, we would venture to say that every company uses both of these methods of improvement someplace in their operations. Some businesses have made radical process reconfiguration a core competency so that they can better serve customers whose demands are constantly changing. Both concepts are important; they continue to be two different tools a manager can use to effect change in the way his or her organization does business. The basis of both approaches is viewing the business as a set of business processes, rather than using a silo perspective.

Incremental Change

At one end of the continuum, managers use incremental change approaches to improve business processes through small, incremental changes. This improvement process generally involves the following activities:

- Choosing a business process to improve
- Choosing a metric by which to measure the business process
- Enabling personnel involved with the process to find ways to improve it based on the metric

Personnel often react favorably to incremental change because it gives them control and ownership of improvements and, therefore, renders change less threatening. The improvements grow from their grassroots efforts. One popular management approach to incremental change is called **six-sigma**. This approach uses incremental change activities within a larger structure of tools and processes to continually improve processes.

Radical Change

Incremental change approaches work well for tweaking existing processes, but more major changes require a different type of management tool. At the other end of the change continuum, radical change enables the organization to attain aggressive improvement goals (again, as defined by a set of metrics). The goal of radical change is to make a rapid, breakthrough impact on key metrics.

The difference in the incremental and radical approaches over time is illustrated by the graph in Figure 5.5. The vertical axis measures, in one sense, how well

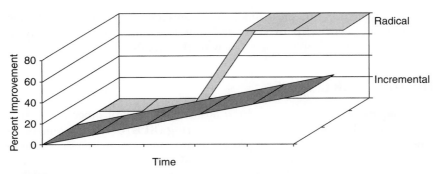

FIGURE 5.5 Comparison of radical and incremental improvement.

a business process meets its goals. Improvements are made either incrementally or radically. The horizontal axis measures time.

Not surprisingly, radical change typically faces greater internal resistance than does incremental change. Therefore, radical change processes should be carefully planned and only used when major change is needed in a short time. Some examples of situations requiring radical change are when the company is in trouble, when it imminently faces a major change in the operating environment, or when it must change significantly to outpace its competition. Key aspects of radical change approaches include the following:

- The need for major change in a short amount of time
- Thinking from a cross-functional process perspective (or, as consultants like to say, "thinking outside the box")
- Challenging old assumptions
- Networked (cross-functional) organizing
- Empowerment of individuals in the process
- Measurement of success via metrics tied directly to business goals

The Process for Radical Redesign

Many different and effective approaches can be taken to achieve radical process change. Each consultant or academic has a pet method, but all share three main elements:

1. They begin with a vision of which performance metrics best reflect the success of overall business strategy.
2. They make changes to the existing process.
3. They measure the results using the predetermined metrics.

The diagram in Figure 5.6 illustrates a general view of how radical redesign methods work. A new process is envisioned, the change is designed and implemented, and its impact is measured. A more specific method for changing a

**Transformation
Methodology**

FIGURE 5.6 Conceptual flow of process design.

business process is illustrated in Figure 5.7. In this process, feedback from each step can affect any of the previous steps

Using a BPR methodology (Figure 5.7), a manager begins by stating a case for action. The manager must understand what it is about current conditions that makes them unfavorable and, in general terms, how business processes must change to address them. Next, the manager must assess the readiness of the organization to undertake change. Only after stating a compelling case for action and addressing organizational readiness should the manager identify those business processes that he or she believes should change to better support the overall business strategy and build a redesign team.

Once the case for action is made, the current process is analyzed. Some experts believe that it is only necessary to do a cursory study of the existing process, just enough to understand the problems, the key metrics, and the basic flow. Others believe a detailed study helps to clearly identify how the process works. Although detail is sometimes helpful, many BPR projects get derailed at this step because of "analysis paralysis," spending an overabundance of time and effort understanding every detail of the process. Such detail is not necessary, but nevertheless is comforting to the manager and may help build credibility with the rest of the organization.

The tool used to understand a business process is a **workflow diagram**, which shows a picture, or map, of the sequence and detail of each process step. More than 200 products are available for helping managers diagram the workflow. The objective of process mapping is to understand and communicate the dimensions of the current process. Typically, process engineers begin the process mapping procedure by defining the scope, mission, and boundaries of the business process.

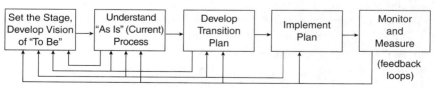

FIGURE 5.7 Method for redesigning a business process.

Next, the engineer develops a high-level overview flowchart of the process and a detailed flow diagram of everything that happens in the process. The diagram uses active verbs to describe activities and identifies all actors, inputs, and outputs of the process. The engineer verifies the detailed diagram for accuracy with the actors in the process and adjusts it accordingly.

Another key task at this stage is to identify metrics of business success that clearly reflect both problems and opportunities in the status quo and that can measure the effectiveness of any new processes. It is vitally important that the metrics chosen relate to the key business drivers in any given situation. Examples include cost of production, cycle time, scrap and rework rates, customer satisfaction, revenues, and quality.

The manager's next step is to develop a transition plan. The plan should include a clearly stated vision, an initial design of the new process that directly addresses the metrics that, in turn, address the goals of the business, and an implementation plan.

The Risk of Radical Redesign

The original concept of reengineering described a theory of radical change through process design. In his famous *Harvard Business Review* article, reengineering guru Michael Hammer described the concept of process design as one of starting with a "clean sheet of paper." The idea was not to let the existing process, nor any of the potential constraints in the environment, get in the way of the redesign. Starting with a greenfields approach allowed, in theory, the process designers to create the best possible design. The implementation of these new processes, however, proved more difficult than most organizations were willing to tolerate.

Dozens of stories tell of companies that attempted reengineering, only to fail to realize the advantages they sought. Radically changing a business is not an easy task. Research done to determine why companies failed to reach their goals reveal some of the more common reasons, which are summarized here.

- *Lack of senior management support at the right times and the right places.* Some estimates suggest that 50% or more of a senior manager's time is necessary to make radical change successful.

- *Lack of a coherent communications program.* Radical change can scare many employees who are unsure about whether they will have a job when the changes are completed. Companies that fail to communicate regularly, clearly, and honestly experience an increased risk of failure.

- *Introducing unnecessary complexity into the new process design.* For example, some companies try to introduce new IS that are unproven or need extensive customization and training. Such an approach adds a level of complexity to a reengineering project that is often difficult to manage.

- *Underestimating the amount of effort needed to redesign and implement the new processes.* Companies, of course, do not stop operation while they reengineer, and therefore, many companies find themselves spread too thin when trying to reengineer and continue operations. Some compare it to "changing airplanes in midair"—not impossible, but definitely not easy.

- *Combining reengineering with downsizing.* Many organizations really just want to downsize their operations and get rid of some of their labor costs. They call that initiative reengineering rather than downsizing and think their employees will understand that the new business design just takes fewer people. Employees are smarter than that and often make the implementation of the radical design impossible.

The benefits of radical change are seductive, but the risks are high. The transformation is not just a change in technology, but a change in organization structure and talent, often more challenging than the process redesigners anticipated. To mitigate this risk, some propose undertaking a revolutionary design approach but an evolutionary implementation approach. Although evolutionary implementation may reduce the risk of rejection, ease the adaptation of the new process, and allow more individuals to participate in the business change, it also means taking longer to realize the benefits of the redesign.

Agility and Constantly Redesigning Processes

To stay competitive and consistently meet changing customer demands, some organizations build **agile processes**, or processes that iterate through a constant renewal cycle of design, deliver, evaluate, redesign, and so on. The ultimate goal for some is agile processes that reconfigure themselves as they "learn" and are utilized in the business. For a process to be agile necessitates a high degree of the use of IT. The more of the process that can be done with software, the easier it is to change, and the more likely it can be designed to be agile and constantly redesigning itself.

Examples of this type of process are often found in manufacturing operations, where production lines are reconfigured regularly to accommodate new products and technologies. For example, automobile production lines produce large quantities of cars, but very few are identical to the car before or after it on the production line. The design of the line is such that many changes in design, features, or options are just incorporated into the assembly of the car at hand. More recently, with the use of the Internet and Web 2.0 technologies, building agility into business processes is increasingly common. Processes run entirely on the Internet, such as order-management, service provisioning, software development, and human resource support are candidates for agile designs that take advantage of the latest innovations offered by the vendors on the Internet.

► SHARED SERVICES

Business executives increasingly expect IT to not just provide technologies but to also provide the engine for efficiency. As companies look for new and different ways to become more efficient and to add more business value, leaders increasingly expect to use IT as a key component of the solution. The term **horizontal integration** is often used as the all-encompassing term for looking beyond individual business processes and considering the bigger, cross-functional picture of the corporation. How can increased efficiencies be had once all business processes themselves are highly efficient? Horizontal integration makes the parts of the corporation work more effectively and efficiently by considering a larger scope than any one business process redesign would consider. Integrated databases, Web 2.0 technologies and services, and common infrastructure are the tools IT brings to the implementation of horizontal integration.

Consider a company with multiple business units, each of which is highly efficient in carrying out the business processes necessary to make their business work. What is the next opportunity for further reducing costs and increasing efficiency? Many organizations have restructured their common business processes into a **shared services** model. For example, IT services, human resources, procurement, and finance are often services needed by all business units of a corporation. Instead of each business unit building and supporting their own organization for each of these functions, a shared services model would consolidate all the individuals from all the business units into a single organization, run centrally, and utilized by each business unit. Often shared services organizations have relationship managers who work with individual business units to facilitate alignment of services to business needs.

Business Process Management (BPM) Systems

Thinking about the business as a set of processes has become commonplace for most organizations. Managing their processes is another story. A class of software systems called **Business Process Management (BPM)** systems is used to solve this management challenge. In the 1990s, a class of systems emerged to help manage workflows in the business. They primarily helped track document-based processes where people executed the steps of the workflow. BPM systems go way beyond the document-management capabilities and include features that manage person-to-person process steps, system-to-system steps, and those processes that include a combination. Systems include process modeling, simulation, code generation, process execution, monitoring, and integration capabilities for both company-based and Web-based systems. The tools allow an organization to actively manage and improve its processes from beginning to end.

BPM systems are a way to build, execute and monitor automated processes that may go across organizational boundaries. Some of the functionality of a BPM may be found in enterprise applications such as ERP, CRM, and financial software because these systems also manage processes within a corporation. But BPM systems go outside a specific application to help companies manage across processes. Some BPM systems manage front office applications that are often person-to-person processes such as a sales or ordering process. These processes

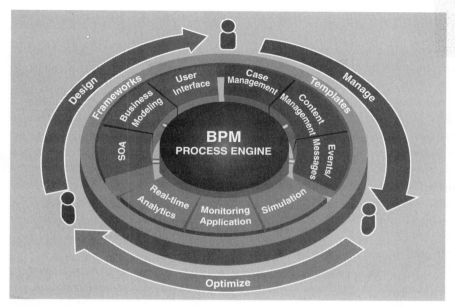

FIGURE 5.8   Sample BPM Architecture: Appian Enterprise.
Source: Adapted from www.appian.com/product/enterprise.

are humancentric. Other BPM systems support back-office processes that often are more system-to-system oriented and possibly extend outside the corporation to include Web-based components.

BPM systems are not meant for all processes. They are very useful when all the activities are in a predetermined order. They are less useful when steps vary each time the process is executed. One example of a BPM is the system by Appian. Their BPM product includes three components to help companies design, manage, and optimize core business processes. Figure 5.8 shows a diagram of the architecture of their BMP.

▶ ENTERPRISE SYSTEMS

Information technology is a critical component of most every business process today because information flow is at the core of most every process. A class of IT applications called **enterprise systems** is a set of information systems tools that many organizations use to enable this information flow within and between processes.

Computer systems in the 1960s and early 1970s were typically designed around a specific application, with each application using its own set of inputs. These early systems did not interface well with each other and often had their own version of data, even though these data were used in other systems. The systems were designed to support a silo approach, and they did so very effectively.

Organizational computing groups were faced with the challenge of linking and maintaining the patchwork of loosely overlapping, redundant systems. In the 1980s and 1990s, software companies in a number of countries, including the United States, Germany, and the Netherlands, began developing integrated software packages that used a common database and cut across organizational systems. Some of these packages were developed from administrative systems (e.g., finance and human resources) and others evolved from materials resource planning (MRP) in manufacturing. These comprehensive software packages that incorporate all modules needed to run the operations of a business are called enterprise systems or, alternatively, enterprise information systems (EIS). **Enterprise resource planning (ERP)** software packages are the most frequently discussed type of enterprise system. Other enterprise systems may be developed in-house to integrate organizational processes.

ERPs were designed to help large companies manage the fragmentation of information stored in hundreds of individual desktop, department, and business unit computers across the organization. They offered the management information system (MIS) department in many large organizations an option for switching from underperforming, obsolete mainframe systems to client-server environments designed to handle the changing business demands of their operational counterparts. The threat of the year 2000 problem (Y2K), a problem in which computers used two digits instead of four digits to represent the year, making it impossible to distinguish between years such as 2000 and 1900, pushed many senior managers to outside vendors who offered Y2K-compliant enterprise systems as the solution for their companies. In some cases, business processes were so untamed that managers thought installing an enterprise system would be a way to standardize processes across their businesses. These managers wanted to transform their business processes by forcing all to conform to a software package.

By far the most widely used enterprise system was offered by a German company, SAP. Their product, R/3, was installed in almost every large global corporation. Many other competitors, including PeopleSoft, Baan, and Oracle, and many other vendors also offered a selection of software systems that, when integrated, formed an enterprise system.

The next generation of enterprise system emerged, ERP II systems. Whereas an ERP makes company information immediately available to all departments throughout a company, ERP II makes company information immediately available to *external stakeholders*, such as customers and partners. ERP II enables e-business by integrating business processes between an enterprise and its trading partners.

Characteristics of Enterprise Systems

Enterprise systems have several characteristics:[6]

- *Integration*. Enterprise systems are designed to seamlessly integrate information flows throughout the company. Enterprise systems are configured by installing various modules, such as:

  - Manufacturing (materials management, inventory, plant maintenance, production planning, routing, shipping, purchasing, etc.)

  - Accounting (general ledger, accounts payable, accounts receivable, cash management, forecasting, cost accounting, profitability analysis, etc.)

  - Human resources (employee data, position management, skills inventory, time accounting, payroll, travel expenses, etc.)

  - Sales (order entry, order management, delivery support, sales planning, pricing, etc.)

- *Packages*. Enterprise systems are commercial packages purchased from software vendors. Unlike many packages, enterprise systems usually require long-term relationships with software vendors because the complex systems must typically be modified on a continuing basis to meet the organization's needs.

- *Best practices*. Enterprise systems reflect industry best practices for generic business processes. To implement them, business process reengineering is often required.

- *Some assembly required*. The enterprise system is software that needs to be integrated with the organization's hardware, operating systems, databases, and telecommunications. Further, enterprise systems often need to be integrated with proprietary legacy systems. It often requires that **middleware** (software used to connect processes running in one or more computers across a network) or "bolt-on" systems be used to make all the components operational.

- *Evolving*. Even though enterprise systems were designed first for mainframe systems and then client-server architectures, many systems now are being designed for Web-enabled or object-oriented versions. A major challenge facing many firms is to integrate Internet ERP applications with supply chain management software. One important problem in meeting this challenge is to allow companies to be both more flexible in sourcing from multiple (or alternative) suppliers, while also increasing

---

[6] M. Lynne Markus and Cornelis Tanis, "The Enterprise System Experience—From Adoption to Success," in R. Zmud (ed.), *Framing the Domains of IT Management: Projecting the Future Through the Past* (Cincinnati, OH: Pinaflex Educational Resources, Inc., 2000), 176–179.

the transparency in tightly coupled supply chains. A second problem is to integrate ERP's transaction-driven focus into a firm's workflow.[7]

Benefits and Disadvantages of Enterprise Systems

The major benefit of an enterprise system is that all modules of the information system easily communicate with each other, offering enormous efficiencies over stand-alone systems. In business, information from one functional area is often needed by another area. For example, an inventory system stores information about vendors who supply specific parts. This same information is required by the accounts payable system, which pays vendors for their goods. It makes sense to integrate these two systems to have a single accurate record of vendors.

Because of the focus on integration, enterprise systems are useful tools for an organization seeking to centralize operations and decision making. One of the benefits of centralization is the effective use of organizational databases. Redundant data entry and duplicate data may be eliminated; standards for numbering, naming, and coding may be enforced; and data and records can be cleaned up through standardization. Further, the enterprise system can reinforce the use of standard procedures across different locations.

The obvious benefits notwithstanding, implementing an enterprise system represents an enormous amount of work. Using the same simple example as previously, if an organization has allowed both the manufacturing and the accounting departments to keep their own records of vendors, then most likely these records are kept in somewhat different forms (one department may keep the vendor name as "IBM," the other as "International Business Machines" or even "IBM Corp.," all of which make it difficult to integrate the databases). Such data inconsistencies must be addressed for the enterprise system to provide optimal advantage.

Moreover, even though enterprise systems are flexible and customizable to a point, most also require business processes to be redesigned to achieve optimal performance of the integrated modules. The flexibility in an enterprise system comes from being able to change parameters in a process, such as the type of part number the company will use. However, all systems make assumptions about how the business processes work, and at some level, customization is not possible. For example, one major *Fortune* 500 company refused to implement a vendor's enterprise system because the company manufactured products in lots of "one," and the vendor's system would not handle the volume this company generated. If they had decided to use the ERP, a complete overhaul of their manufacturing process in a way that executives were unwilling to do would have been necessary.

 Organizations are expected to conform to the approach used in the enterprise system, arguably because the enterprise system represents a set of industry

---

[7] Amit Basu and Akhil Kumar, "Research Commentary: Workflow Management Issues in e-Business," *Information Systems Research* 13, no. 1 (March 2002), 1–14.

best practices. Implementing enterprise systems requires organizations to make changes in their organization structure and often in the individual tasks done by workers. Recall in Chapter 1, the Information Systems Strategy Triangle suggests that implementing an information system must be accompanied with appropriate organizational changes to be effective. Implementing an enterprise system is no different. For example, who will now be responsible for entering the vendor information that was formerly kept in two locations? How will that information be entered into the enterprise system? The answer to such simple operational questions often requires managers at a minimum to modify business processes and more likely to redesign them completely to accommodate the information system.

Furthermore, enterprise systems and the organizational changes they induce tend to come with a hefty price tag. A Meta Group survey of 63 small, medium, and large companies found the average total cost of ownership (TCO) of an ERP to be $15 million.[8] The TCOs ranged from $400,000 to $30 million. As discussed in Chapter 10, TCO numbers included hardware, software, professional services, and internal staff costs as well as installing the software and maintaining, upgrading, and optimizing it for two years. Because they are so complex, the cost of professional services and internal staff tend to be quite high. Further, additional hidden costs in the form of technical and business changes are likely to be necessary when implementing an enterprise system.

One of the reasons that enterprise (ERP) systems are so expensive is that they are sold as a suite, such as financials or manufacturing, and not as individual modules. Because buying modules separately is difficult, companies implementing ERP software often find the price of modules they won't use hidden in the cost of the suite.

Enterprise systems are also risky. The number of enterprise system horror stories demonstrates this risk. For example, Kmart wrote off its $130 million ERP investment. American LaFrance (ALF), the manufacturer of highly customized emergency vehicles and a spinoff from Freightliner, declared bankruptcy in early 2008, blaming their IT vendor and their ERP implementation. The problems with the implementation kept ALF from being able to manufacture many preordered vehicles. The Los Angeles Unified School District implemented an enterprise system only to find their payroll process completely messed up. In June 2007, the worst month for problems, about 30,000 paychecks were issued with errors, and the problems continued well into the next school year. One executive said the problem occurred because the system was rolled out too quickly and without sufficient testing.[9] Oftentimes, installing an enterprise system means the business must

---

[8] Christopher Koch, "The ABCs of ERP," *CIO Magazine*, http://www.cio.com/research/erp/edit/erpbasics.html (accessed February 7, 2002).

[9] For additional examples of IT failures in general, and enterprise systems failures in particular, please visit the blog written by Michael Krigsman, http://blogs.zdnet.com/projectfailures/

reengineer its business processes. Because the enterprise system is an automation of the major business processes such as financial, manufacturing, and human resource management and because most enterprise systems are purchased from vendors such as SAP, PeopleSoft, and Oracle, it is rare that an off-the-shelf system is perfectly harmonious with an existing business process. More typical is that either the software requires significant modification or customization to fit with the existing processes, or the processes must change to fit the software. In most installations of enterprise systems, both take place. The system is customized when it is installed in a business by setting a number of parameters, and in the worst case, by modifying the code itself. The business processes are changed, often through a radical change project, as described earlier in this chapter. Many of these projects are massive undertakings, requiring formal, structured project management tools (as discussed in Chapter 11).

▶ INTEGRATED SUPPLY CHAINS

Another type of enterprise system in common use is the supply chain management system, which manages the **integrated supply chain** (as introduced in Chapter 2). Business processes are not just internal to a company. With the help of information technologies, many processes are linked across companies with a companion process at a customer or supplier, creating an integrated supply chain

The supply chain of a business is the process that begins with raw materials and ends with a product or service ready to be delivered (or in some cases actually delivered) to a customer. It typically includes the procurement of materials or components, the activities to turn these materials into larger subsystems or final products, and the distribution of these final products to warehouses or customers. But with the increase in information systems use, it may also include product design, product planning, contract management, logistics, and sourcing. Globalization of business and ubiquity of communication networks and information technology has enabled businesses to use suppliers from almost anywhere in the world. At the same time, this has created an additional level of complexity for managing the supply chain. Supply chain integration is the approach of technically linking supply chains of vendors and customers to streamline the process and to increase efficiency and accuracy.

Integrated supply chains have several challenges, primarily resulting from different degrees of integration and coordination among supply chain members.[10] At the most basic level, there is the issue of **information integration**. Partners must agree on the type of information to share, the format of that information, the technological standards they will both use to share it, and the security they will use to ensure that only authorized partners access it. Trust must be established so the

---

[10] Adapted from Hau Lee and Seungjin Whang, "E-Business and Supply Chain Integration," Stanford University Global Supply Chain Management Forum, November 2001.

partners can solve higher-level issues that may arise. At the next level is the issue of **synchronized planning**. At this level, the partners must agree on a joint design of planning, forecasting, and replenishment. The partners, having already agreed on what information to share, now have to agree on what to do with it. The third level can be described as **workflow coordination**—the coordination, integration, and automation of critical business processes between partners. For some supply chains, this might mean simply using a third party to link the procurement process to the preferred vendors or to communities of vendors who compete virtually for the business. For others it might be a more complex process of integrating order processing and payment systems. Ultimately, the integration of supply chains is leading to new business models, as varied as the visionaries who think them up. These business models are based on new ideas of coordination and integration made possible by the Internet and information-based supply chains. In some cases, new services have been designed by the partnership between supplier and customer, such as new financial services offered when banks link up electronically with businesses to accept online payments for goods and services purchased by the businesses' customers. In other cases, a new business model for sourcing has resulted, such as one in which companies list their supply needs, and vendors electronically bid to be the supplier for that business.

Demand-driven supply networks are the next step for companies with highly evolved supply chain capabilities. Kimberly Clark, the 135-year-old consumer products company, is one such example. Their vision is for a highly integrated suite of supply chain systems that provide end-to-end visibility of the supply processes in real time. Key processes included in their demand-driven supply network are both forecast-to-stock and order-to-cash. Using an integrated suite of systems allowed their users to share the same information in as close to real time as possible, and to use the data in their systems for continually updating their supply chain, category management, and consumer insight processes. IT has allowed management to reduce the problems of handing off data from one system or process to another (because now everything is in one system), having workers work from different databases (because it's now one database), and of working off old data (because it's as real time as possible). This has improved their ability to see what's going on in the marketplace and evaluate the impact of promotions, production, and inventory much more quickly.

Integrated supply chains are truly global in nature. Thomas Friedman, in his book *The World is Flat*, describes how the Dell computer that he had ordered to write his book was developed from the contributions of an integrated supply chain that involved about four hundred companies in North America, Europe, and, primarily, Asia. However, the globalization of integrated supply chains faces a growing challenge from skyrocketing transportation costs. For example, Tesla Motors, a pioneer in electric-power cars, had originally planned the production of a luxury roadster for the American market based on an integrated global supply chain. The 1,000-pound battery packs for the cars were to be manufactured in Thailand, shipped to Britain for installation, and then shipped to the United States, where they would be assembled into cars. However, because of the extensive costs associated with shipping the batteries more than 5,000 miles, Tesla decided to make the batteries and assemble the cars near its headquarters in California. Darryl Siry, Tesla's senior vice president of global sales, marketing, and service explains: "It was kind of a no-brain decision for us. A major reason was to avoid the transportation costs, which are terrible." Economists warn managers to expect the "neighborhood effect" in which factories may be built closer to components suppliers and consumers to reduce transportation costs. This effect may apply not only to cars and steel, but also to chickens and avocados and a wide range of other items.[11]

When the System Drives the Change

When is it appropriate to use the enterprise system to drive business process redesign, and when is it appropriate to redesign the process first, then implement an enterprise system? In several instances, it is appropriate to let the enterprise system drive business process redesign. First, when an organization is just starting out and processes do not yet exist, it is appropriate to begin with an enterprise system as a way to structure operational business processes. After all, most of the processes embedded in the "vanilla" enterprise system from a top vendor are based on the best practices of corporations who have been in business for years. Second, when an organization does not rely on its operational business processes as a source of competitive advantage, then using an enterprise system to redesign these processes is appropriate. Third, it is reasonable for an organization to let the enterprise system drive business process change when the current systems are in crisis and there is not enough time, resources, or knowledge in the firm to fix them. Even though it is not an optimal situation, managers must make tough decisions about how to fix the problems. A business must have working operational processes; therefore, using an enterprise system as the basis for process design may be the only workable plan. It was precisely this situation that many companies faced with Y2K.

Likewise, it is sometimes inappropriate to let an enterprise system drive business process change. When an organization derives a strategic advantage through its operational business processes, it is usually not advisable to buy a vendor's enterprise system. Using a standard, publicly available information system that both the company and its competitors can buy from a vendor may mean that any competitive advantage is lost. For example, consider a major computer manufacturer that relied on its ability to process orders faster than its competitors to gain strategic advantage. It would not have been to that organization's benefit to use an enterprise system to drive the redesign of the order fulfillment system because doing so would force the manufacturer to restrict its process to that which is available from enterprise system vendors. More important,

[11] Larry Rohter, "Shipping Costs Start to Crimp Globalization," *New York Times*, August 3, 2008, pp. 1, 10.

any other manufacturer could then copy the process, neutralizing any advantages. Furthermore, the manufacturer believed that relying on a third party as the provider of such a strategic system would be a mistake in the long run. Should the system develop a bug or need to be redesigned to accommodate unique aspects of the business, the manufacturer would be forced to negotiate with the enterprise system vendor to get it to modify the enterprise system. With a system designed in-house, the manufacturer was able to ensure complete control over the IS that drives its critical processes.

Another situation in which it would be inappropriate to let an enterprise system drive business process change is when the features of available packages and the needs of the business do not fit. An organization may use specialized processes that cannot be accommodated by the available enterprise systems. For example, many ERPs were developed for discrete part manufacturing and do not support some processes in paper, food, or other process industries.[12]

A third situation would result from lack of top management support, company growth, a desire for strategic flexibility, or decentralized decision making that render the enterprise system inappropriate. For example, Dell stopped the full implementation of SAP R/3 after only the human resources module had been installed because the CIO did not think that the software would be able to keep pace with Dell's extraordinary growth. Enterprise systems were also viewed as culturally inappropriate at the highly decentralized Kraft Foods.

Challenges for Integrating ERP between Companies

With the widespread use of ERP systems, the issue of linking supplier and customer systems to the business's systems brings many challenges. As with integrated supply chains, there are the issues of deciding what to share, how to share it, and what to do with it when the sharing can take place. There are also issues of security and agreeing on encryption or other measures to protect data integrity as well as to ensure that only authorized parties have access.

Some companies have tried to reduce the complexity of this integration by insisting on standards, either at the industry level or at the system level. An example of an industry-level standard is the bar coding used by all who do business in the consumer products industry. An example of a system-level standard is the use of SAP or Oracle as the ERP system used by both supplier and customer.

► FOOD FOR THOUGHT: IS ERP A UNIVERSAL SOLUTION?

Building a business process that crosses functional or even business unit boundaries is often a difficult exercise for executives. Managers and workers may resist change simply because the new process differs significantly from the old process and makes their job more complex or difficult. But imagine the impact when a business

---

[12] Markus and Tanis, "The Enterprise System Experience."

process change, such as an ERP system, crosses country boundaries. That is, when the cultures within which a process must operate are significantly different, there is the potential for not only difficulty in implementation but also total rejection of the new process.

Consider an ERP system in the context of cultural differences. Each firm may have specific requirements for the ERP system that reflects its own organizational structure, management style, and business processes. There are likely to also be unique regulatory and social practices. For example, the record of successful global ERP system implementations in state-owned businesses in China has been abysmal. The problems are due, in part, to the misfit between the ERP systems and traditional Chinese management systems, which favor personal relationships.[13]

ERP systems are usually designed around best practices—but whose best practices? SAP and Oracle, the leading vendors of ERP systems, have a decided Western bias. More specifically, best practices at the heart of their systems are based on business processes that are found in successful companies in Germany and North America. However, when these systems are transplanted into Asian companies, problematic "misfits" have been found to occur.

Take, for example, the use of ERP systems designed for hospitals. Western health-care models are decidedly different from those used in Singapore. Much of the health care in Western countries is privately delivered. The government or insurance companies pay for the major portion of health-care services, with insured patients bearing only a fraction of the costs. In contrast, Singaporean health care is based on a model of individual responsibility, with community support and government subsidies provided only to the limited extent needed to keep the health care affordable. How does this affect processes embedded in the ERP system? The Western-based ERP billing and collections modules cater to complex claims submission processes and insurance verification and not to over-the-counter payment or installment payments by individual patients. Further, "bed class" is a big deal in Singapore, where patients in public hospitals can choose from a variety of plans ranging from one bed to six or more per room. The Western model is simpler because single-bedded rooms are more common.

A survey of Singaporean hospitals with an ERP system revealed that to accommodate the major differences between their processes and those embedded in the ERP, the hospitals typically developed add-on modules rather than changing package source codes. Customizing the source code was considered by the hospitals to be prohibitively costly and to lead to difficulties in maintaining future upgrades from the vendor.[14]

---

[13] M. G. Martinson, "ERP in China: One Package, Two Profiles," *Communications of the ACM* 47, no. 7 (July 2004), 65–68.

[14] C. Soh, S. K. Sia, and J. Tay-Yap, "Cultural Fits and Misfits: Is ERP a Universal Solution?" *Communications of the ACM* 43, no. 4 (April 2000), 47–51.

Because of differences and "misfits," businesses in many non-Western companies are turning to local vendors that have developed systems reflecting local best practices. For example, local ERP vendors in Taiwan have developed ERP systems to support the majority of firms in the market space—small to medium-sized Taiwanese companies with sophisticated, adaptive logistic networks. The local ERP vendors have adopted a strategy of customization and are more willing to modify their systems to satisfy local needs than are their large, global competitors.[15]

These examples suggest that another factor needs to be considered when designing and implementing an ERP. The ERP should not be implemented if the system is based on a cultural model that conflicts with the local customs and that cannot easily be accommodated by the ERP.

▶ SUMMARY

- IS can enable or impede business change. IS enables change by providing both the tools to implement the change and the tools on which the change is based. IS can also impede change, particularly when the desired information is mismatched with the capabilities of the IS.

- To understand the role IS plays in business transformation, one must take a business process, rather than a functional, perspective. Business processes are a well-defined, ordered set of tasks characterized by a beginning and an end, a set of associated metrics, and cross-functional boundaries. Most businesses operate business processes, even if their organization charts are structured by functions rather than by processes.

- Making changes in business processes is typically done through either TQM or BPR techniques. TQM techniques tend to imply an evolutionary change, where processes are improved incrementally. BPR techniques, on the other hand, imply a more radical objective and improvement. Both techniques can be disruptive to the normal flow of the business; hence strong project management skills are needed.

- To stay competitive, organizations must consistently meet changing customer demands and build processes that are agile and self-renewing. Agile processes often require a high degree of IT; the more the process can be done with software, the easier it is to change and the more agile the design becomes.

- BPM systems are used to help managers design, control, and document business processes and ultimately workflow in an organization.

- Enterprise systems are large information systems that provide the core functionality needed to run a business. These systems are typically implemented to help organizations share data between divisions. However, in some cases enterprise systems are used to affect organizational transformation by imposing a set of assumptions on the business processes they manage.

---

[15] E. T. G. Wang, G. Kleing, and J. J. Jiang, "ERP Misfit: Country of Origin and Organizational Factors," *Journal of Management Information Systems* 23, no. 1 (Summer 2006), 263–292.

- An integrated supply chain is often managed using an enterprise system that crosses company boundaries and connects vendors and suppliers with organizations to synchronize and streamline planning and deliver products to all members of the supply chain.

- Information systems are useful as tools to both enable and manage business transformation. The general manager must take care to ensure that consequences of the tools themselves are well understood and well managed.

▶ KEY TERMS

agile processes (p. 145)

business process
   management (BPM)
   (p. 146)

business process
   reengineering (BPR)
   (p. 141)

enterprise resource
   planning (ERP) (p. 148)

enterprise systems (p. 147)

horizontal integration
   (p. 146)

information integration
   (p. 152)

integrated supply chain
   (p. 152)

middleware (p. 149)

process (p. 138)

process perspective
   (p. 137)

shared services (p. 146)

silos (p. 137)

six-sigma (p. 141)

synchronized planning
   (p. 153)

total quality management
   (TQM) (p. 141)

workflow coordination
   (p. 153)

workflow diagram (p. 143)

▶ DISCUSSION QUESTIONS

1. Why was radical design of business processes embraced so quickly and so deeply by senior managers of so many companies? In your opinion, and using hindsight, was its popularity a benefit for businesses? Why or why not?

2. Off-the-shelf enterprise IS often forces an organization to redesign its business processes. What are the critical success factors to make sure the implementation of an enterprise system is successful?

3. Have you been involved with a company doing a redesign of its business processes? If so, what were the key things that went right? What went wrong? What could have been done better to minimize the risk of failure?

4. What do you think that Jerry Gregoire, former CIO of Dell, meant when he said, "Don't automate broken business processes"?[16]

5. What, in your opinion, are the advantages and the disadvantages of a shared services model for IT? What are some example activities done by a relationship manager from a shared services organization?

6. What might an integrated supply chain look like for a financial services company such as an insurance provider or a bank? What are the components of the process?

---

[16] "Technology: How Much? How Fast? How Revolutionary? How Expensive?" *Fast Company* 56, p. 62, http://www.fastcompany.com/online/56/fasttalk.html (accessed May 30, 2002).

SANTA CRUZ BICYCLES

Bicycle enthusiasts not only love the ride their bikes provide, but they also are often willing to pay for newer technology especially when it will increase their speed or comfort. Innovating new technologies for bikes is only half the battle for bike manufacturers. Designing the process to manufacture the bikes is often the more daunting challenge.

Consider the case of Santa Cruz Bicycles. It digitally designs and builds mountain bikes and tests them under the most extreme conditions to bring the best possible product to their customers. A few years back, the company designed and patented the Virtual Pivot Point (VPP) suspension system, a means to absorb the shocks that mountain bikers encounter when on the rough terrain of the off-road ride. One feature of the new design allowed the rear wheel to bounce 10 inches without hitting the frame or seat, providing shock absorption without feeling like the rider was sitting on a coiled spring.

The first few prototypes did not work well; in one case, the VPP joint's upper link snapped after a quick jump. The experience was motivation for a complete overhaul of the design and engineering process to find a way to go from design to prototype faster. The 25-person company adopted a similar system used by large, global manufacturers: product life cycle management (PLM) software.

The research and development team had been using computer-aided-design (CAD) software, but it took 7 months to develop a new design, and if the design failed, starting over was the only solution. This was not only a drain on the company's time but also on finances. The design team found a PLM system that helped them analyze and model capabilities in a much more robust manner. The team uses simulation capabilities to watch the impact of the new designs on rough mountain terrain. The software tracks all the variables the designers and engineers need so they can quickly and easily make adjustments to the design. The new system allows them to run a simulation in a few minutes, which is a very large improvement over their previous design software, which took 7 hours to run a simulation.

The software was just one component of the new process design. The company also hired a new master frame builder to build and test prototypes in-house and they invested in a van-size machine that can fabricate intricate parts for their prototypes, a process they used to outsource. The result was a significant decrease in their design-to-prototype process. What used to average about 28 months from start of design to shipping of the new bike now takes 12 to 14 months.

Discussion Questions

1. What, in your opinion, was the key factor in Santa Cruz Bicycles' successful process redesign? Why was that factor the key?
2. What outside factors had to come together for Santa Cruz Bicycles to be able to make the changes they did?
3. Why is this story more about change management that software implementation?

Source: Adapted from Mel Duvall, "Santa Cruz Bicycles," available at www.baselinemag.com, retrieved February 24, 2008.

BOEING 787 DREAMLINER

Delivery of Boeing's 787 Dreamliner project was delayed, in part, because of their global supply chain network, which was touted to reduce cost and development time. In reality, this turned out to be a major cause for problems. Boeing decided to change the rules of the way large passenger aircraft were developed through its Dreamliner program; rather than simply relying on technological know-how, it decided to use collaboration as a competitive tool embedded into a new global supply chain process.

With the Dreamliner project, Boeing not only attempted to create a new aircraft through the innovative design and new material, but it also radically changed the production process. It built an incredibly complex supply chain involving over 50 partners scattered in 103 locations all over the world. The goal was to reduce the financial risks involved in a $10 billion-plus project for designing and developing a new aircraft and reduce the new product development cycle time. It tapped expertise of various firms in different areas such as composite materials, aerodynamics, and IT infrastructure to create a network in which partners' skills complement each other. This changed the basis of competition to skill set rather than the traditional basis of low cost. In addition, this was the first time Boeing had outsourced the production on the two most critical parts of the plane—the wings and the fuselage.

The first sign of problems showed up just six months into the trial production. Engineers discovered unexpected bubbles in the skin of the fuselage during baking of the composite material. This delayed the project a month. Boeing officials insisted that they made up the time and all things were under control. But next to fail was the test version of the nose section. This time a problem was found in the software programs, which were designed by various manufacturers. They failed to communicate with each other, leading to a breakdown in the integrated supply chain. Then problems popped up in the integration of electronics. The Dreamliner program entered the danger zone when Boeing declared that it was having trouble getting enough permanent titanium fasteners to hold together various parts of the aircraft. The global supply network did not integrate well for Boeing and left it highly dependent on a few suppliers.

This case clearly underscores the hazards in relying on an extensive supply chain in which information exchange problems may create extended problems and seriously compromise a company's ability to carry out business as planned. Creating a radically different process can mean encountering unexpected problems. In some cases, it would put a company so far behind their competition that they were doomed to fail. However, in this case, the major competitor to the Dreamliner, the Airbus 380 program, was also using a global supply-chain model, and its program was delayed by a couple of years. Their competition continued.

Discussion Questions

1. Why did Boeing adopt the radical redesign for designing and developing the 787 Dreamliner? In your opinion, was it a good move? Defend your choice.

2. Using the Silo Perspective versus Business Process Perspective, analyze the Dreamliner program.

3. Develop a risk analysis scenario using the Risks of Radical Redesign framework discussed in the chapter.

4. If you were the program manager, what would you have done different to avoid the problems faced by the Dreamliner program?

Source: Adapted from J. Lynn Lunsford, "Boeing Scrambles to Repair Problems with New Plane," *Wall Street Journal*, December 7, 2007, pp. A1, 13; and Stanley Holmes, "The 787 Encounters Turbulence," *BusinessWeek*, June 19, 2006, pp. 38–40.

CHAPTER 6

ARCHITECTURE AND INFRASTRUCTURE[1]

Valero Energy, the North American oil and gas refiner, has experienced hyper-growth for the past 10 years, mostly through acquisitions.[2] The company's revenue has grown from $29 billion to $90 billion, but with this growth came a mixture of different information technology (IT) systems and applications that were difficult and expensive to manage, and that did not easily integrate into their corporate enterprise resource planning (ERP) system and their business applications suite. Further, in the future, managers wanted to implement a self-service model where business units could create applications themselves in an easy, low-cost manner. For the managers to execute their business strategy, their IT architecture had to be redesigned and their infrastructure updated.

The architecture had to be flexible, able to grow with the company, and easily reused as new systems were needed. The MIS organization decided to use an SOA (service-oriented architecture) design in which applications and computing resources were available as components. For example, an order management component might be used by both a customer service application and a profitability analysis application.

The infrastructure for the ERP and business applications suite was SAP's R/3 system. The newer components included a set of 90 services built on SAP's development environment. Further, these core services have been used to create 40 different composite applications, helping management attain their reusability goal and keeping application development costs down. For example, one of the new applications was designed to let wholesale clients view account information via the Internet. The infrastructure used SAP NewWeaver Portal interface to connect to the SAP R/3 CRM (customer relationship management) system data warehouse and to other non-SAP systems. This design gives users a single view into the integrated information.

---

[1] The authors wish to acknowledge and thank Vince Cavasin, MBA 1999, for his help in researching and writing early drafts of this chapter.

[2] This case was adapted from http://www.cioinsight.com—CIOInsight Ziff Davis Enterprise Holdings Inc., Accessed 24 February 2008.

The results were dramatic. Savings added up for Valero because they did not have to build interfaces between all the independent systems they inherited through the acquisitions. New applications made operations more efficient and effective. One application saved the company a half-million dollars in fees that are charged when a ship sits idle at the dock. Before this new application, the managers did not have a way to monitor tankers as they unloaded oil, and therefore sometimes ships had to wait to unload their cargo. The new application provides visibility to the tankers and communications with employees at the refineries and helps the company avoid scheduling conflicts and the ensuing costs.

So far, this text explored the organizational, tactical, and strategic importance of IS. As illustrated with the Valero story, this chapter examines the mechanisms by which business strategy is transformed into tangible IS architecture and infrastructure. The terms *architecture* and *infrastructure* are often used interchangeably in the context of IS. This chapter discusses how the two differ and the role each plays in realizing a business strategy.

► FROM VISION TO IMPLEMENTATION

As shown in Figure 6.1, architecture translates strategy into infrastructure. Building a house is similar: the owner has a vision of how the final product should look and function. The owner must decide on a strategy about where to live—in an apartment or in a house. The owner's strategy also includes deciding how to live in the house in terms of taking advantage of a beautiful view, having an open floor plan, or planning for special interests by designing such special areas as a game room, study, music room, or other amenities. The architect develops plans based on this vision. These plans, or blueprints, provide a guide—unchangeable in some areas, but subject to interpretation in others—for the carpenters, plumbers, and electricians who actually construct the house. Guided by past experience and by industry standards, these builders select the materials and construction techniques

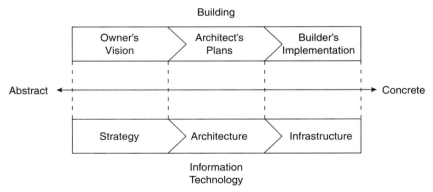

FIGURE 6.1 From the abstract to the concrete—building vs. IT.

best suited to the plan. The plan helps them determine where to put the plumbing and wiring. When the process works, the completed house fulfills its owner's vision, even though he or she did not participate in the actual construction. As finishing touches, the owner adds window coverings, light fixtures, and furniture to make the new house livable.

An information technology (IT) **architecture** provides a blueprint for translating business strategy into a plan for IS. An information technology (IT) **infrastructure** is everything that supports the flow and processing of information in an organization, including hardware, software, data, and network components. It consists of components, chosen and assembled in a manner that best suits the plan and therefore best enables the overarching business strategy.[3] Infrastructure in an organization is similar to the plumbing, wiring, and furnishings in a house.

The Manager's Role

Even though he or she is not drawing up plans or pounding nails, the homeowner in this example needs to know what to reasonably expect from the architect and builders. The homeowner must know enough about architecture, specifically about styling and layout, to work effectively with the architect who draws up the plans. Similarly, the homeowner must know enough about construction details such as the benefits of various types of siding, windows, and insulation to set reasonable expectations for the builders.

Like the homeowner, the manager must understand what to expect from IT architecture and infrastructure to be able to make full and realistic use of them. The manager must effectively communicate his or her business vision to IT architects and implementers and, if necessary, modify the plans if IT cannot realistically support them. For without the involvement of the manager, IT architects could inadvertently make decisions that limit the manager's business options in the future.

For example, a sales manager for a large distribution company did not want to partake in discussions about providing sales force automation systems for his group. He felt that each individual salesperson could buy a laptop, if he or she wanted one, and the IT group would be able to provide support. No architecture was designed, and no long-range thought was given to how IT might support or inhibit the sales group. Salespeople did buy laptops, and other personal organizing devices. Soon, the IT group was unable to support all the different systems the salespeople had, so they developed a set of standards for systems they would support, based on the infrastructure they used elsewhere in the company. Again, the manager just blindly accepted that decision, and salespeople with systems outside the standards bought new systems. Then the sales manager wanted to change the way his group managed sales leads. He approached the IT department for help, and in the discussions that ensued, he learned that earlier infrastructure decisions made by

---

[3] Gordon Hay and Rick Muñoz, "Establishing an IT Architecture Strategy," *Information Systems Management* (Summer 1997).

the IT group now made it expensive to implement the new capability he wanted. Involvement with earlier decisions and the ability to convey his vision of what the sales group wanted to do might have resulted in an IT infrastructure that provided a platform for the changes the manager now wanted to make. The IT group-built infrastructure lacked an architecture that met the business objectives of the sales and marketing management.

▶ THE LEAP FROM STRATEGY TO ARCHITECTURE TO INFRASTRUCTURE

The huge number of IT choices available, coupled with the incredible speed of technology advances, makes the manager's task of designing an IT infrastructure seem nearly impossible. However in this chapter, the task is broken down into two major steps: first, translating strategy into architecture and, second, translating architecture into infrastructure. This chapter describes a simple framework to help managers sort IT issues. This framework stresses the need to consider business strategy when defining an organization's IT building blocks. Although this framework may not cover every possible architectural issue, it does highlight major issues associated with effectively defining IT architecture and infrastructure.

From Strategy to Architecture

The manager must start out with a strategy, and then use the strategy to develop more specific goals, as shown in Figure 6.2. Then detailed business requirements are derived from each goal. In the Valero case, the strategy was to provide a single face to customers, and the goal was to integrate all the acquisitions. The business requirements were to integrate the information systems into a single, flexible system. By outlining the overarching business strategy and then fleshing out the business requirements associated with each goal, the manager can provide the architect with a clear picture of what IS must accomplish and the governance arrangements needed to ensure their smooth development, implementation, and use. The governance arrangements specify who in the company retains control of, and responsibility for, the IS. Preferably this is somebody at the top. Of course, the manager's job is not finished here. He or she must work with the architect to translate these business requirements into a more detailed view of the systems requirements, standards, and processes that shape an IT architecture. This more detailed view includes consideration of such things as data and process demands, as well as security objectives. This process is depicted in Figure 6.2

From Architecture to Infrastructure

Valero's decision to use a service-oriented architecture led to the design of a number of services and composite applications. This illustrates the next step, translating the architecture into infrastructure. This task entails adding yet more detail to the architectural plan that emerged in the previous phase. Now the detail comprises actual hardware, data, networking, and software. Details extend

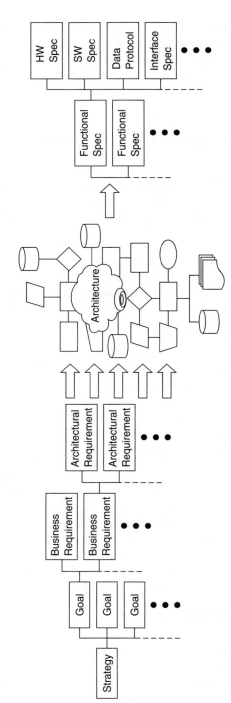

FIGURE 6.2 From strategy to architecture to infrastructure.

to location of data and access procedures, location of firewalls, link specifications, interconnection design, and so on. This phase is also illustrated in Figure 6.2.

When we speak about infrastructure we are referring to more than the components. Plumbing, electrical wiring, walls, and a roof do not make a house. Rather, these components must be assembled according to the blueprint to create a structure in which people can live. Similarly, hardware, software, data, and networks must be combined in a coherent pattern to have a viable infrastructure. This infrastructure can be considered at several levels. At the most global level infrastructure may focus on the enterprise and refer to the infrastructure for the entire organization. Infrastructure may also focus on the interorganizational level by laying the foundation for communicating with customers, suppliers, or other stakeholders across organizational boundaries. Sometimes infrastructure refers to those components needed for an individual application. When considering the structure of a particular application, it is important to consider databases and program components, as well as the devices and operating environments on which they run. The application-level infrastructure reflects decisions made at the enterprise level. The following discussion relates to infrastructure and architecture at the enterprise level.

A Framework for the Translation

When developing a framework for transforming business strategy into architecture and then into infrastructure these basic components should be considered:

- *Hardware:* The physical components that handle computation, storage, or transmission of data (e.g., personal computers, servers, mainframes, hard drives, RAM, fiber-optic cabling, modems, and telephone lines).

- *Software:* The programs that run on hardware to enable work to be performed (e.g., operating systems, databases, accounting packages, word processors, sales force automation, and enterprise resource planning systems). Some software, such as an operating system like Windows Vista or XP, Apple's Leopard, or Linux, provides the **platform** on which other software, the applications, run. Applications, on the other hand, are software that automate tasks such as storing data, transferring files, creating documents, and calculating numbers. Applications include generic software, such as word processors and spreadsheets, and specific software, such as sales force automation systems, human resource management systems, payroll systems, and manufacturing management systems.

- *Network:* Software and hardware components, such as switches, hubs, and routers, that create a path for communication and data sharing according to a common protocol.

- *Data:* The electronic representation of the numbers and text on which the IT infrastructure must perform work. Here, the main concern is the quantity and format of data, and how often it must be transferred from one piece of hardware to another or translated from one format to another.

The framework that guides the analysis of these components was introduced in the first chapter, in Figure 1.10. This framework is simplified to make the point that initially understanding an organization's infrastructure is not difficult. Understanding the technology behind each component of the infrastructure and the technical requirements of the architecture is a much more complex task. The main point is that the general manager must begin with an overview that is complete and that delivers a big picture.

This framework asks three types of questions that must be answered for each infrastructure component: what, who, and where. The "what" questions are those most commonly asked and that identify the specific type of technology. The "who" questions seek to understand what individuals, groups, and departments are involved. In most cases, the individual user is not the owner of the system nor even the person who maintains it. In many cases, the systems are leased, not owned, by the company, making the owner a party completely outside the organization. In understanding the infrastructure, it is important to get a picture of the people involved. The third set of questions address "where" issues. With the proliferation of networks, many IS are designed and built with components in multiple locations, often even crossing oceans. Learning about infrastructure means understanding where everything is located.

We can expand the use of this framework to also understand architecture. To illustrate the connections between strategy and systems, the table in Figure 6.3 has been populated with questions that typify those asked in addressing architecture and infrastructure issues associated with each component.

The questions shown in Figure 6.3 are only representative of those to be asked; the specific questions managers would ask about their organizations depend on the business strategy the organizations are following. However, this framework can help managers raise appropriate questions as they seek to translate business strategy into architecture and ultimately into infrastructure in their organizations. The answers derived with IT architects and implementers should provide a robust picture of the IT environment. That means that the IT architecture includes plans for the data and information, the technology (the standards to be followed and the infrastructure that provides the foundation), and the applications to be accessed via the company IT system.

There are three common configurations of IT architecture. A **mainframe architecture** uses a large central computer that handles all the functionality of the system. Users only need a very simple terminal to access the computer. Applications run on the mainframe, and data is stored there. This was the common architecture of every enterprise for a long time. Microprocessors and the technologies necessary for smaller computers were not available. Computer vendors such as IBM, Digital Equipment Company (DEC) and many others built systems with this architecture in mind. Enterprises liked the idea of a centralized data center where the IT assets were managed, and technology at the time was not able to put all the components into small systems. In addition, since virtually every enterprise had a large data center with mainframe architecture, there are a significant number of legacy

Component	What		Who		Where	
	Architecture	Infrastructure	Architecture	Infrastructure	Architecture	Infrastructure
Hardware	Does fulfillment of our strategy require thick or thin clients?	What size hard drives do we equip our thick clients with?	Who knows the most about servers in our organization?	Who will operate the server?	Does our architecture require centralized or distributed servers?	Must we hire a server administrator for the Tokyo office?
Software	Does fulfillment of our strategy require ERP software?	Shall we go with SAP or Oracle Applications?	Who is affected by a move to SAP?	Who will need SAP training?	Does our geographical organization require multiple database instances?	Does Oracle provide the multiple-database functionality we need?
Network	What kind of bandwidth do we need to fulfill our strategy?	Will 10baseT Ethernet suffice?	Who needs a connection to the network?	Who needs an ISDN line to his or her home?	Does our WAN need to span the Atlantic?	Shall we lease a cable or use satellite?
Data	Do our vendors all use the same EDI format?	Which VAN provides all the translation services we need?	Who needs access to sensitive data?	Who needs encryption software?	Will backups be stored on-site or off-site?	Which storage service shall we select?

FIGURE 6.3 Infrastructure and architecture analysis framework with sample questions.

mainframe environments still in operation today. However, one large computer at the center of the IT architecture is not used as regularly today as it was even as recently as five years ago. Instead, many computers are linked together to form a centralized IT core that operates very much like the mainframe architecture. The idea of a centralized IT core, where the bulk of the processing is done, is a viable, and common architecture design.

A more common configuration is a client/server architecture. **Client/server architecture** is one in which one software program (the **client**) requests and receives data and sometimes instructions from another software program (the **server**) running on a separate computer. The hardware, software, networking, and data are arranged in a way that distributes the processing and functionality between multiple small computers.

Although some would debate this point, a third increasingly common configuration is **service-oriented architecture (SOA)**, the architecture that Valero decided to use. In this text, SOA is defined as an architecture in which larger software programs are broken down into services that are then connected to each other, in a process called orchestration, to form the applications for an entire business process. Sometimes IT architects consider SOA a philosophy rather than an architecture and argue that it's really a type of Web-based architecture. That is because in SOA, the service components reside on different computers, often on the Internet. An example of a service might be an online employment form that, when completed, generates a file with the data for use in another service. Another example might be a ticket processing service that identifies available concert seats and allocates them. These relatively small chunks of functionality are available for many applications, or **reuse**. SOA is increasingly popular because the design enables large units of functionality to be built almost entirely from existing software service components. It offers managers a modular, and therefore a more easily modifiable, approach to building applications, The type of software used in an SOA architecture is often referred to as **software-as-a-service** or SaaS. Another term for these applications, when delivered over the Internet, is **Web services**.

A key differentiator in these configurations is the degree of centralization versus decentralization. A manager must be aware of the trade-offs when considering architecture decisions. For example, client/server architectures are more modular than the mainframe architectures, allowing additional servers to be added with relative ease and provide greater flexibility for adding clients with specific functionality for specific users. Decentralized organizational governance, such as that associated with the networked organization structure (discussed in Chapter 3) is consistent with client/server architectures. In contrast, a mainframe architecture is easier to manage in some ways because all functionality is centralized in the main computer instead of distributed throughout all the clients and servers. A mainframe architecture tends to be a better match in companies with highly centralized governance, for example, those with hierarchical organization structures.

An example of an organization making these trade-offs is the Veterans Health Administration (VHA), a part of the Department of Veterans Affairs of the U.S. federal government.[4] The organization included 14 different business units that served various administrative and organizational needs. The primary objective of the organization was to provide health care for veterans and their families. In addition, the VHA was a major contributor to medical research, allowing medical students to train at VHA hospitals. The medical centers operated independently and sometimes competed against each other. In 1996, however, the U.S. Congress passed an act that enabled the VHA to restructure itself from a system of hospitals to a single health-care system. The IT architecture was reconfigured from a very centralized design, which enabled the Office of Data Management and Telecommunications to retain control, to a decentralized hospital-based architecture that gave local physicians and administrators the opportunity to deploy applications addressing local needs, while ensuring that standards were developed across the different locations. The VA then introduced the "One-VA" architecture to unify the decentralized systems and "to provide an accessible source of consistent, reliable, accurate, useful, and secure information and knowledge to veterans and their families. . . ."

---

[4] Adapted from V. Venkatesh, H. Bala, S. Venkatraman, and J. Bates, "Enterprise Architecture Maturity: The Story of the Veterans Health Administration," *MIS Quarterly Executive* 6, no. 2 (June 2007), 79–90.

Recent technological advances make designs possible such as peer-to-peer and wireless or mobile infrastructures. These designs do not necessarily need to be the firm's exclusive infrastructure. For example, a wireless infrastructure may operate separately or may be built on a mainframe or client/server backbone. **Peer-to-peer** allows networked computers to share resources without a central server playing a dominant role. Kazaa, the Web site for sharing music, movies, games, and more, used a peer-to-peer architecture. **Wireless (mobile) infrastructures** allow communication from remote locations using a variety of wireless technologies (e.g., fixed microwave links, wireless LANs, data over cellular networks, wireless WANs, satellite links, digital dispatch networks, one-way and two-way paging networks, diffuse infrared, laser-based communications, keyless car entry, and global positioning systems).

Web-oriented architectures (WOAs) are architectures in which significant hardware, software, and possibly even data elements reside on the Internet. WOA offers greater flexibility when used as a source for **capacity-on-demand**, or the availability of additional processing capability for a fee. IT managers like the concept of capacity on demand to help manage peak processing periods when additional capacity is needed. It allows them to use the Web-available capacity as needed, rather than purchasing additional computers to handle the larger loads.

▶ ARCHITECTURAL PRINCIPLES

Any good architecture is based on a set of principles, or fundamental beliefs about how the architecture should function. Architectural principles must be consistent with both the values of the enterprise as well as with the technology used in the infrastructure. They are designed by considering the key objectives of the organization, and then translated into principles to apply to the design of the IT architecture. The number of principles vary widely, and there is no set list of what must be included in a set of architectural principles. However, a guideline for developing architectural principles is to make sure they are directly related to the operating model of the enterprise and IS organization. Principles should define the desirable behaviors of the IT systems and the role of the organization(s) that support it. A sample of architectural principles is shown in Figure 6.4

▶ ENTERPRISE ARCHITECTURE

Many companies apply even more complex frameworks than those described earlier for developing an IT architecture and infrastructure, employing an **enterprise architecture**, or the "blueprint" for all IS and their interrelationships in an enterprise. Enterprise architecture is the term used for the organizing logic for the entire organization, often specifying how information technologies will support business processes. It differs from an IT architecture in its level of analysis, although it shares some design principles of the lower-level architectures. It identifies the core processes of the company and how they will work together, how the IT systems

Principle	Description
Ease of use	The IT architecture will promote ease of use in building and supporting the architecture and solutions based on the architecture.
Single point of view	The IT architecture will enable a consistent, integrated view of the business, regardless of access point.
Buy over Build	Business applications, system components, and enabling frameworks will be purchased unless there is a competitive reason to develop them internally.
Speed and Quality	Architectural decisions will be made with an emphasis on accelerating time to market for solutions, while still maintaining required quality levels.
Flexibility and Agility	The IT architecture will incorporate flexibility to support changing business needs and enable evolution of the architecture and the solutions built on it.
Innovative	The IT architecture will support incorporation of new technologies and facilitate innovation.
Data Security	Data is protected from unauthorized use and disclosure.
Common Data Vocabulary	Data is defined consistently throughout the enterprise, and the definitions are understandable and available to all users.
Data Quality	Each data element will have a trustee accountable for data quality.
Data Asset	Data must be managed like other assets that have value to the enterprise.

FIGURE 6.4 Sample architectural principles.
Source: Adapted from examples of IT architecture from IBM, TOGAF, the US Government, and the State of Wisconsin.

will support the processes, the standard technical capabilities and activities for all parts of the enterprise, and guidelines for making choices. As experts Jeanne Ross, Peter Weill, and David Robertson describe in their book, *Enterprise Architecture as Strategy*,

> Top-performing companies define how they will do business (an operating model) and design the processes and infrastructure critical to their current and future operations (enterprise architecture), which guide the evolution of their foundation for execution. Then these smart companies exploit their foundation, embedding new initiatives to make that foundation stronger and using it as a competitive weapon to seize new business opportunities.[5]

[5] Jeanne W. Ross, Peter Weill, and David C. Robertson, *Enterprise Architecture as Strategy* (Boston: Harvard Business School Press, 2006), viii–ix.

The components of an enterprise architecture typically include four key elements:

- Core business processes—the key enterprise processes that create the capabilities the company uses to execute its operating model and create market opportunities
- Shared data—the data that drives the core processes
- Linking and automation technologies—the software, hardware, and networking technologies provide the links between applications (applications themselves are part of the IT architecture, but the way applications will link together is part of the bigger picture of the enterprise architecture)
- Customer groups—key customers to be served by the architecture[6]

One example of an enterprise architecture framework is the **TOGAF** (The Open Group Architecture Framework).[7] TOGAF is an open architecture that has been developing and continuously evolving since the mid-1990s. It seeks to provide a practical, standardized methodology (called Architecture Development Methodology) to successfully implement an enterprise architecture into a company. The architect implements the Enterprise Architecture by setting up the foundation architecture, which is composed of services, functions, and standards. Subsets of the enterprise architecture are the business, data, application, and technology architectures. Like the framework in this book, the TOGAF is designed to translate strategy into architecture and then into a detailed infrastructure; however, it supports a much higher level of architecture that includes more components of the enterprise.[8]

Other examples of enterprise architecture frameworks are Zachman, Federal Enterprise Architecture, and the Gartner Methodology. The **Zachman Framework** determines architectural requirements by providing a broad view that helps guide the analysis of the detailed view. Its perspectives range from the company's scope to its critical models and, finally, to very detailed representations of the data, programs, networks, security, and so on. The models it uses are the conceptual business model, the logical system model, and the physical technical model.[9]

Because enterprise architecture is more about how the company will operate than how the technology is designed, building an enterprise architecture is a joint exercise to be done with business leaders and IT leaders. IT leaders cannot and should not do this alone. Because virtually all business processes today involve some component of IT, the idea of trying to align IT with business processes is outdated. Instead, business processes are designed concurrently with IT systems.

---

[6] Ibid., 50–52.

[7] The Open Group at http://www.opengroup.org.

[8] For more information on the TOGAF framework, visit www.togaf.org, the home site for the Open Group.

[9] For more information on the Zachman framework, visit www.zifa.com, the Web site of the Zachman Institute.

Building an enterprise architecture is more than just linking the business processes to IT. It starts with organizational clarity of vision and strategy and places a high value on consistency in approach as a means of optimal effectiveness. The consistency manifests itself as some level of standardization—standardization of processes, deliverables, and/or people Every enterprise architecture has elements of all these types of standardization; however, the degree and proportion of each vary with the organizational needs, making it dynamic. A good enterprise architect understands this and looks for the right blend for each activity the business undertakes. That means that because organizational groups and individuals are resources for business processes, the organizational design decisions should be part of the enterprise architecture. However, this is a sophisticated capability, and new enterprise architects often seek to put more rigid standards in place and do not attempt to tackle the more complex organizational design issues.

▶ OTHER MANAGERIAL CONSIDERATIONS

The framework guides the manager toward the design and implementation of an appropriate infrastructure. Defining an IT architecture that fulfills an organization's needs today is relatively simple; the problem is, by the time it is installed, those needs change. The primary reason to base an architecture on an organization's strategic goals is to allow for inevitable future changes—changes in the business environment, organization, IT requirements, and technology itself. Considering future impacts should include an analysis of the existing architecture, the strategic time frame, technological advances, and financial constraints.

Understanding Existing Architecture

At the beginning of any project, the first step is to assess the current situation. Understanding existing IT architecture allows the manager to evaluate the IT requirements of an evolving business strategy against current IT capacity. The architecture, rather than the infrastructure, is the basis for this evaluation because the specific technologies used to build the infrastructure are chosen based on the overall plan, or architecture. As previously discussed, it is these architectural plans that support the business strategy. Assuming some overlap is found, the manager can then evaluate the associated infrastructure and the degree to which it can be utilized going forward.

Relevant questions for managers to ask include the following:

- What IT architecture is already in place?
- Is the company developing the IT architecture from scratch?
- Is the company replacing an existing architecture?
- Does the company need to work within the confines of an existing architecture?
- Is the company expanding an existing architecture?

Starting from scratch allows the most flexibility in determining how architecture will enable a new business strategy, and a clean architectural slate generally translates into a clean infrastructure slate. However, it can be a challenge to plan effectively even when starting from scratch. For example, in a resource-starved start-up environment, it is far too easy to let effective IT planning fall by the wayside. Sometimes, the problem is less a shortcoming in IT management and more one of poorly devised business strategy. A strong business strategy is a prerequisite for IT architecture design, which is in turn a prerequisite for infrastructure design.

Of course, managers seldom enjoy the relative luxury of starting with a clean IT slate. More often, they must deal in some way with an existing architecture, infrastructure, and legacy systems already in place. In this case, they encounter both opportunity—to leverage the existing architecture and infrastructure and their attendant human resource experience pool—and the challenge of overcoming or working within the old system's shortcomings. By implementing the following steps, managers can derive the most value and suffer the least pain when working with legacy architectures and infrastructures.

1. *Objectively analyze the existing architecture and infrastructure.* Remember, architecture and infrastructure are separate entities; managers must assess the capability, capacity, reliability, and expandability of each.

2. *Objectively analyze the strategy served by the existing architecture.* What were the strategic goals it was designed to attain? To what extent do those goals align with current strategic goals?

3. *Objectively analyze the ability of the existing architecture and infrastructure to further the current strategic goals.* In what areas is alignment present? What parts of the existing architecture or infrastructure must be modified? Replaced?

Whether managers are facing a fresh start or an existing architecture, they must ensure that the architecture will satisfy their strategic requirements, and that the associated infrastructure is modern and efficient. The following sections describe evaluation criteria including strategic time frame, technical issues (adaptability, scalability, standardization, maintainability, security), and financial issues.

Assessing Strategic Time Frame

Understanding the life span of an IT infrastructure and architecture is critical. How far into the future does the strategy extend? How long can the architecture and its associated infrastructure fulfill strategic goals? What issues could arise and change these assumptions?

Answers to these questions vary widely from industry to industry. Strategic time frames depend on industrywide factors such as level of commitment to fixed resources, maturity of the industry, cyclicality, and barriers to entry. As discussed in Chapter 1, hypercompetition has increased the pace of change to the point that requires any strategic decision be viewed as temporary.

Architectural longevity depends not only on the strategic planning horizon, but also on the nature of a manager's reliance on IT and on the specific rate of advances affecting the information technologies on which he or she depends. Hypercompetition implies that any architecture must be designed with maximum flexibility and scalability to ensure it can handle the imminent business changes. Imagine the planning horizon for a dot-com company in an industry in which Internet technologies and applications are changing daily, if not more often. Even oil giant Valero found that flexibility and agility were critical to their business and hence to their IT architecture

Assessing Technical Issues: Adaptability

With the rapid pace of business, it is no longer possible to build a static information system to support businesses. Instead adaptability is a core design principle of every IT architecture. A manager may think of technological advances as primarily affecting IT infrastructure, but the architecture must be able to support any such advance. Can the architecture adapt to emerging technologies? Can a manager delay the implementation of certain components until he or she can evaluate the potential of new technologies?

At a minimum, the architecture should be able to handle expected technological advances, such as innovations in storage capacity and computing power. An exceptional architecture also has the capacity to absorb unexpected technological leaps. Both hardware and software should be considered when promoting adaptability. For example, new Web-based applications emerge daily that may benefit the corporation. The architecture must be able to integrate these new technologies without violating the architecture principles or significantly disrupting business operations.

The following are guidelines for planning adaptable IT architecture and infrastructure. At this point, these two terms are used together, because in most IT planning they are discussed together. These guidelines are derived from work by Meta Group.[10]

- *Plan for applications and systems that are independent and loosely coupled rather than monolithic.* This approach allows managers to modify or replace only those applications affected by a change in the state of technology.

- *Set clear boundaries between infrastructure components.* If one component changes, others are minimally affected, or if effects are unavoidable, the impact is easily identifiable and quantifiable.

- *When designing a network architecture, provide access to all users when it makes sense to do so (i.e., when security concerns allow it).* A robust and

[10] Larry R. DeBoever and Richard D. Buchanan, "Three Architectural Sins," *CIO Magazine* (May 1, 1997).

consistent network architecture simplifies training and knowledge sharing and provides some resource redundancy. An example is an architecture that allows employees to use a different server or printer if their local one goes down.

Note that requirements concerning reliability may mitigate the need for technological adaptability under certain circumstances. If the architecture requires high reliability, a manager seldom is tempted by bleeding-edge technologies. The competitive advantage offered by bleeding-edge technologies is often eroded by downtime and problems resulting from pioneering efforts with the technology. For example, despite Microsoft's virtual monopoly in providing PC operating systems, its Web server runs on only 20% of sites; the Linux-based Apache server dominates this reliability-sensitive market with nearly 70% of Web sites.[11]

Assessing Technical Issues: Scalability

A large number of other technical issues should also be considered when selecting an architecture or infrastructure. A frequently used criterion is scalability. To be **scalable** refers to how well an infrastructure component can adapt to increased, or in some cases decreased, demands. A scalable network system, for instance, could start with just a few nodes but could easily be expanded to include thousands of nodes. Scalability is an important technical feature because it means that an investment can be made in an infrastructure or architecture with confidence that the firm will not outgrow it.

What is the company's projected growth? What must the architecture do to support it? How will it respond if the company greatly exceeds its growth goals? What if the projected growth never materializes? These questions help define scalability needs.

Consider a case in which capacity requirements were poorly anticipated. In early 2007, an ice storm on the East Coast of the United States forced JetBlue Airlines to scramble to take care of stranded customers, grounded planes, checked luggage, and cancelled flights. In the aftermath, executives told investors that the computers didn't fail. Indeed, they did not fail, but the system failed to scale as needed. The system was set up to accommodate 650 agents and was able to be increased to 950, but no more.[12] It's unlikely that JetBlue, or its software provider, would have had to do any serious systems redesign to respond to the increase in demand; it simply needed to increase its infrastructure capacity. Ultimately, this planning failure cost JetBlue millions to recover from the failure and even more in defending its image, which suffered severe negative word of mouth from the poor service that resulted. JetBlue's plight underscores the importance of analyzing the impact of strategic business decisions on IT architecture and infrastructure and

---

[11] Web server survey at http://news.netcraft.com/archives/web_server_survey.html (accessed June 2005).

[12] Mel Duvall, "What Really Happened to JetBlue," www.cioinsight.com (July 2008).

at least ensuring a contingency plan exists for potential unexpected effects of a strategy change.

Assessing Technical Issues: Standardization

Another important feature deals with commonly used **standards**. Hardware and software that uses a common standard, as opposed to a proprietary approach, are easier to plug into an existing or future infrastructure or architecture because interfaces often accompany the standard. For example, many companies use Microsoft Office software, making it an almost de facto standard. Therefore, a number of additional packages come with translators to the systems in the Office suite to make it easy to move data between systems.

Assessing Technical Issues: Maintainability

How easy is the infrastructure to maintain? Are replacement parts available? Is service available? Maintainability is a key technical consideration because the complexity of these systems increases the number of things that can go wrong, need fixing, or simply need replacing. In addition to availability of parts and service people, maintenance considerations include issues such as the length of time the system might be out of commission for maintenance, how expensive and how local the parts are, and obsolescence. Should a technology become obsolete, costs skyrocket for parts and expertise.

Assessing Technical Issues: Security

Security is a major concern for business managers and IT managers alike. Businesses feel vulnerable to attack. IT managers worry about protecting key data and process elements of the IT infrastructure. Security is a concern that extends outside the corporate boundaries; for example, customers wonder how safe their credit card numbers are when typed into a vendor's order form. Technologies have come a long way to provide security. Innovations encrypt or otherwise disguise sensitive information, financial information, and business information.

Architectures have different inherent security profiles. Securing assets in a highly centralized, mainframe architecture means building protection around the centralized core. Because data and software are stored and executed on the mainframe computer, methods of protecting these assets revolve around protecting the mainframe itself. Client/server architecture are more difficult to secure due to the dispersion of servers. Security is a matter of protecting every server instead of one centralized system. A Web-based architecture that utilizes SaaS and capacity on demand raises a whole new set of security issues. The data and applications not only reside on servers in the various vendor systems around the Web, but also the linking mechanism, the network that ties the Web together, introduces another level of security concerns.

What if, for example, someone were to steal a file of credit card numbers as they were relayed over the Internet? The risk of the interception of e-commerce data may be no greater than the risks of paper transactions: credit card receipts (and credit cards themselves) are stolen and the numbers used fraudulently. Checkbooks are stolen and signatures are fraudulently forged. Transactions with a paper trail are hardly foolproof and may indeed be riskier than e-commerce transactions. The difference is in the speed of the communication. A file with secure information can be sent anywhere in the world in a matter of seconds over the Internet, whereas the paper-based file takes longer to reach a destination. The good news is that the security of networks continues to improve. Innovations such as authentication, passwords, digital signatures, encryption, secure servers, and firewalls are already in place, and new schemes for security, such as securing specific assets instead of just securing the perimeter of a system, are being explored.

Managing security is often a matter of managing risk. It is virtually impossible to be totally secure regardless of the security model employed. Hackers and thieves will find a way around just about any security system. Therefore, managing risk often means assessing the likelihood of a breach and the cost of that breach in terms of loss and recovery. For example, one forward-thinking executive suggested that instead of trying to protect all his employees' Social Security numbers from theft, he preferred to purchase insurance to cover any losses that might result from the identity theft. He chose a service, LifeLock, that closely monitors its customers identity, proactively takes steps to minimize identity theft, and offers a $1 million service guarantee to cover any losses that do occur.

Assessing Financial Issues

Like any business investment, IT infrastructure components should be evaluated based on their expected financial value. Unfortunately, payback from IT investments is often difficult to quantify; it can come in the form of increased productivity, increased interoperability with business partners, improved service for customers, or yet more abstract improvements. For this reason, the Gartner Group suggests focusing on how IT investments enable business objectives rather than on their quantitative returns.[13]

Still, some effort can and should be made to quantify the return on infrastructure investments. This effort can be simplified if a manager works through the following steps with the IT staff.

1. *Quantify costs:* The easy part is costing out the proposed infrastructure components and estimating the total investment necessary. Don't forget to include installation and training costs in the total.

2. *Determine the anticipated life cycles of system components:* Experienced IT staff or consultants can help establish life cycle trends both for a company and an industry to estimate the useful life of various systems.

3. *Quantify benefits:* The hard part is getting input from all affected user groups, as well as the IT group—which presumably knows most about

---

[13] B. Rosser, "Key Issues in Strategic Planning and Architecture [Gartner Group research note]," *Key Issues* (April 15, 1996).

the equipment's capabilities. If possible, form a team with representatives from each of these groups and work together to identify all potential areas in which the new IT system may bring value.

4. *Quantify risks:* Work with the IT staff to identify cost trends in the equipment the company proposes to acquire. Also, assess any risk that might be attributable to delaying acquisition, as opposed to paying more to get the latest technology now.

5. *Consider ongoing dollar costs and benefits:* Examine how the new equipment affects maintenance and upgrade costs associated with the current infrastructure.

Once this analysis is complete, the manager can calculate the company's preferred discounted cash flow (i.e., net present value or internal rate of return computation) and payback horizon. Approaches to evaluating IT investments are discussed in greater detail in Chapter 10.

Differentiating between Architecture and Infrastructure

Figure 6.5 shows the extent to which current and future requirements, associated financial issues, and technical criteria can be used to evaluate architecture and infrastructure. All these criteria are important for decisions about architecture. However, issues regarding the infrastructure and the components chosen to implement the architecture are primarily about adaptability, scalability, standardization, maintainability, security, and financial considerations (such as the cost of infrastructure components). The strategic time frame is an issue that is decided before the infrastructure discussion begins. The example in the following section demonstrates the steps that must be taken to derive these components.

| | Applicability | |
Criteria	Architecture	Infrastructure
Strategic time frame	Very applicable	Not applicable
Adaptability	Very applicable	Very applicable
Scalability/Growth Requirements	Very applicable	Very applicable
Standardization	Very applicable	Very applicable
Maintainability	Very applicable	Very applicable
Security	Very applicable	Very applicable
Assessing financial issues	Somewhat applicable	Very applicable
Net present value		
Payback analysis		
Incidental investments		

FIGURE 6.5 Applicability of evaluation criteria to discussion of architecture and infrastructure.

▶ FROM STRATEGY TO ARCHITECTURE TO INFRASTRUCTURE: AN EXAMPLE

This section considers a simple example to illustrate the application of concepts from preceding sections. The case discussed is TennisUp, a fictitious maker of tennis rackets.

Step 1: Define the Strategic Goals

The managers at TennisUp recognize the increasing popularity of tennis; in fact, they can hardly keep up with demand for their rackets. At the same time, however, TennisUp's president, Love Addin, is concerned that tennis mania may end. Addin wants to ensure that TennisUp can respond to sudden changes in demand for rackets. Along with the board of directors, Addin sets TennisUp's strategic goals:

- To lower costs by outsourcing racket manufacturing
- To lower costs by outsourcing racket distribution
- To improve market responsiveness by outsourcing racket manufacturing
- To improve market responsiveness by outsourcing racket distribution

Step 2: Translate Strategic Goals to Business Requirements

To keep things simple, consider more closely only one of TennisUp's strategic goals: To lower costs by outsourcing racket manufacturing. How can TennisUp's architecture enable this goal? Its business requirements must reflect the following key interfaces to the new manufacturing partners:

- Sales to manufacturing partners: Send forecasts, confirm orders received.
- Manufacturing partner to sales: Send capacity, confirm orders shipped.
- Manufacturing partner to accounting: Confirm orders shipped, electronic invoices, various inventory levels, returns.
- Accounting to manufacturing partner: Transfer funds for orders fulfilled.

Step 3: Apply Strategy-Architecture-Infrastructure Framework

To support the business requirements, an architecture needs to be established. One major component of the architecture deals with how to obtain, store, and use data to support those business requirements. The database can be designed to provide the sales data to support sales applications such as sending forecasts and confirming orders received. The database can also be designed to support manufacturing applications that confirm orders shipped, manage inventory, and estimate capacity. The database also needs to be designed to support accounting applications for invoicing, handling returns, and transferring funds.

Step 4: Translate Architecture to Infrastructure

With the architecture goals in hand, apply the framework presented in the first section of this chapter to build the infrastructure. Figure 6.6 lists questions raised when applying the framework to TennisUp's architecture goals and related infrastructure. Note that not all questions apply in a given situation. Figure 6.7 lists possible infrastructure components.

Component	What		Who		Where	
	Architecture	Infrastructure	Architecture	Infrastructure	Architecture	Infrastructure
Hardware	What kind of supplemental server capacity will the new EDI transactions require?	Will TennisUp's current dual-CPU NT servers handle the capacity, or will the company have to add additional CPUs and/or disks?	NA	Who is responsible for setting up necessary hardware at partner site?	Where does responsibility for owning and maintaining EDI hardware fall within TennisUp?	Which hardware components will need to be replaced or modified to connect to new EDI hardware?
Software	What parts of TennisUp's software architecture will the new architecture affect?	Will TennisUp's current Access database interface adequately with new EDI software?	Who knows the current software architecture well enough to manage the EDI enhancements?	Who will do any new SQL coding required to accommodate new software?	NA	Where will software patches be required to achieve compatibility with changes resulting from new software components?
Network	What is the anticipated volume of transactions between TennisUp and its manufacturing partners?	High volume may require leased lines to carry transaction data; dial-up connections may suffice for low volume.	Who is responsible for additional networking expense incurred by partners due to increased demands of EDI architecture?	NA	Where will security concerns arise in TennisUp's current network architecture?	Where will TennisUp house new networking hardware required for EDI?
Data	Will data formats supporting the new architecture be compatible with TennisUp's existing formats?	Which formats must TennisUp translate?	Who will be responsible for using sales data to project future volumes to report to manufacturing partner?	Who will be responsible for backing up additional data resulting from new architecture?	Where does the current architecture contain potential bottlenecks given changes anticipated in data flows?	Does the new architecture require TennisUp to switch from its current 10Base-T Ethernet to 100Base-T?

FIGURE 6.6   Framework application to TennisUp.

Hardware	Software	Network	Data
3 servers: • manufacturing • sales • accounting Storage systems	ERP system with modules for: • manufacturing • sales • accounting • inventory Enterprise application integration (EAI) software	Cable modem to ISP Dial-up lines for backup Routers Hubs Switches Firewalls	Database: • sales • manufacturing • accounting

FIGURE 6.7   TennisUp's infrastructure components.

Only a few questions that the framework could lead TennisUp to ask are provided; a comprehensive, detailed treatment of this situation would require more information than we can contrive in a simple example.

Step 5: Evaluate Additional Issues

The last task is to weigh the managerial considerations outlined in the second section of this chapter. Weigh them against the same architectural goals outlined in step 2. Figure 6.8 shows how these considerations apply to TennisUp's situation.

Again, note that not every issue in the evaluation criteria was addressed for TennisUp, but this example shows a broad sampling of the kinds of issues that will arise.

► FOOD FOR THOUGHT: CLOUD COMPUTING

Flexibility, agility, and cost management are increasingly important attributes of the enterprise's infrastructure. Managing peak demand, infrequently used applications, and very specialized applications that require extensive computing resources can completely overtake existing servers and resources, slowing down daily transactional and operational business. What can a manager do to increase the capacity in the infrastructure? Replacing locally managed stacks of hardware and software resources with an Internet-based utility is called **cloud computing**.

Cloud computing is the availability of entire computing infrastructure over the Internet. Initially, clouds were a community of SaaS applications built with commodity technologies and open systems. Initial implementations ended up being so proprietary or applications-dependent that they were not widely adopted. Salesforce.com is an example. Salesforce clients use the Internet-based applications provided by Salesforce.com to manage their sales and marketing activities. Today the vision is a build-out of IT infrastructure that is increasingly useful for a variety of applications. Companies like Salesforce.com, Google, and Amazon.com are

Criteria	Architecture	Infrastructure
Strategic time frame	Indefinite: Addin's strategic goal is to be able to respond to fluctuations in market demand.	NA
Technology advances	EDI technology is fairly stable though the impact of Internet-EDI, XML, and VPNs on EDI transactions needs to be assessed, especially with smaller suppliers and customers.	NA
Financial issues: NPV of investment	NA—In this limited case, NPV analysis applies only to infrastructure.	TennisUp will analyze NPV of various hardware and software solutions and ongoing costs before investing.
Payback analysis	TennisUp expects the new architecture to pay for itself within three years.	Various options will be evaluated using conservative sales growth projections to see how they match the three-year goal.
Incidental investments	The new architecture represents a radical shift in the way TennisUp does business and will require extensive training and work force adjustment.	Training costs for each option will be analyzed. Redeployment costs for employees displaced by the outsourcing must also be considered.
Growth requirements/scalability	Outsourcing should provide more scalability than TennisUp's current model, which is constrained by assembly line capacity. Both primary and secondary vendors will be identified to provide scalability of volume.	The scalability required of various new hardware and software components is not significant, but options will be evaluated based on their ability to meet scalability requirements.
Standardization	NA	TennisUp will adopt the ANSI X12 EDI standard, and make it a requirement of all manufacturing partners.
Maintainability	The new architecture raises some maintenance issues, but also eliminates those associated with in-house manufacturing.	Various options will be evaluated for their maintenance and repair costs.
Staff experience	The new model will displace some current employees. The cost and effect on morale needs to be analyzed.	Current staff is not familiar with EDI. Training and work force adjustment will be needed. Some new staff will be hired.

FIGURE 6.8 TennisUp's managerial considerations.

looking for ways to leverage their gigantic infrastructures, and providing basic computing services to clients over the Internet is one option.

Consumers of cloud computing purchase computing capacity on-demand and are not generally concerned with the underlying technologies. It's the next step in **utility computing** or purchasing entire capability as needed. Much like the distribution of electricity, the vision of utility computing is that computing infrastructure would be available when needed in as much quantity as needed. When the lights and appliances are turned off in a home, the electricity is not consumed. Ultimately, the customer is billed only for what is used. In utility computing, a company uses a third-party infrastructure to do their processing or transactions and pay only for what they use. And as in the case of the electrical utility, the economies of scale enjoyed by the computing utility enable very attractive financial models for their customers. As the cost of connectivity falls, models of cloud computing emerge.

Managers considering cloud computing as a component of their architecture have three choices of what to do in the cloud. They can choose to use the infrastructure, a platform, or an entire application. Using the cloud to provide infrastructure means that the cloud is essentially a large cluster of virtual servers or storage devices. Using the cloud for a platform means that the manager will use an environment with the basic software available, such as Web software, applications, database, and collaboration tools. Using the cloud for an entire application generally means that the software is custom designed or custom configured for the business but resides in the cloud.

Cloud computing provides significant incentives for handling peak or new computing needs. In 2007, the *New York Times* decided to make all public domain articles from 1851 to 1922 available on the Internet. To do that they decided to create PDF files of all the articles using the original papers in their archives. This meant they had to scan each column of the story, create a series of graphic pictures of the scanned image, and then cobble them together to create the single PDF for each story. This was a lot of work and required significant computing power. Once this batch of articles was converted and added to their existing library, the *New York Times* would have 11 million stories from 1851 to 1989 available free on the Internet.

The manager of this project had an idea to try using the cloud. He selected a service offered by Amazon.com, Amazon EC2, wrote some code to do the project he envisioned, and tested it on the Amazon servers. He used his credit card to charge the $240 it cost him to do this conversion. He calculated it would have taken him at least a month to do the conversion if he used only the few servers available to him in the *New York Times* network. However using the Amazon cloud services, he was able to use a virtual server cluster of 100 servers, and it took just under 24 hours to do the entire 11 million articles.[14]

The business case for cloud computing includes better managed server costs, energy costs, and staff costs. As described in the example earlier, purchasing the

[14] Galen Gruman, "Early Experiments in Cloud Computing," *InfoWorld*, www.infoworld.com (accessed July 25, 2008); and Derek Gottfrid, "Self-Service, Prorated Super Computing Fun," Blog "Open All the Code that's Fit to Print," November 1, 2007, at open.nytimes.com (accessed July 25, 2008).

computing power needed at a fraction of the cost of purchasing new equipment is at the core of the economic model of cloud computing. In the day of the "green computing," companies focus on reducing their carbon footprint and their energy consumption. Energy consumption, and hence costs, associated with running new computers are eliminated with cloud computing. Because the processing is done at the third-party vendor, the enterprise does not incur the cost to literally keep the lights on. And because cloud computing vendors have multiple clients using their infrastructure, they enjoy economies of scale that result. Staff costs shift from data center maintenance staff to applications integration staff. Staff who normally must maintain the hardware and corporate infrastructure are not needed to maintain the infrastructure in the cloud; that is done by the staff at the vendor's location. Resources inside the corporation can be shifted to focus on more value-added applications for the business.

But managers considering cloud computing must also understand the risks. First is the dependence on the third-party supplier. Building applications that work in the cloud may mean retooling existing applications for the cloud's infrastructure. As of the writing of this text, there were no standards for the infrastructures offered by the various vendors. That means that applications running on one vendor's infrastructure may not port easily to another vendor's environment.

Architectures are increasingly including cloud computing as an alternative to the in-house infrastructures. As coordination costs drop, and platforms in the cloud open up, cloud computing utilization will increase.

▶ SUMMARY

- Strategy drives architecture, which drives infrastructure. Strategic business goals dictate IT architecture requirements. These requirements provide an extensible blueprint suggesting which infrastructure components will best facilitate the realization of the strategic goals.

- Enterprise architecture is the broad design that includes both the information systems architecture and the interrelationships in the enterprise. Often this plan specifies the logic for the entire organization. It identifies core processes, how they work together, how IT systems will support them, and the capabilities necessary to create, execute, and manage them.

- Three configurations for IT architecture are mainframe, client/server, and SOA (or Web-based) architectures. Applications are increasingly being offered as a service, reducing the cost and maintenance requirements for clients.

- The manager's role is to understand how to plan IT to realize business goals. With this knowledge, he or she can facilitate the process of translating business goals to IT architecture and then modify the selection of infrastructure components as necessary.

- Frameworks guide the translation from business strategy to IS design. This translation can be simplified by categorizing components into broad classes (hardware, software, network, data), which make up both IT architecture and infrastructure.

- While translating strategy into architecture and then infrastructure, it is important to know the state of any existing architecture and infrastructure, to weigh current against future architectural requirements, and strategic time frame, and to analyze the financial consequences of the various systems options under consideration. Monitor the performance of the systems on an ongoing basis.

► KEY TERMS

architecture (p. 164)
capacity-on-demand
  (p. 171)
client (p. 169)
client/server architecture
  (p. 169)
cloud computing (p. 183)
enterprise architecture
  (p. 171)
infrastructure (p. 164)
mainframe architecture
  (p. 168)

peer-to-peer (p. 171)
platform (p. 167)
reuse (p. 170)
scalable (p. 177)
server (p. 169)
service-oriented
  architecture (SOA)
  (p. 169)
software-as-a-service
  (SaaS) (p. 170)
standards (p. 178)
TOGAF (p. 173)

utility computing (p. 185)
web-oriented
  architectures (p. 171)
Web services (p. 170)
wireless (mobile)
  infrastructures (p. 171)
Zachman Framework
  (p. 173)

► DISCUSSION QUESTIONS

1. Think about a company you know well. What would be an example of IT architecture at that company? An example of the IT infrastructure?

2. What, in your opinion, is the difference between a client/server architecture and a mainframe architecture? What is an example of a business decision that would be affected by the choice of the architecture?

3. How does the Internet affect an organization's architecture?

4. Saab Cars USA, with its network of 212 dealerships and 30 service centers, dedicated itself to providing its customers a level of service reflective of the high quality of its cars. To improve productivity and reduce costs, Saab wanted to facilitate dealer access to corporate information and applications through the Internet using Web browsers. Saab knew it needed to leverage both its legacy hardware and code to make it a cost-effective e-business initiative. It outsourced to IBM Global Services to build its Intranet Retailer Information System (IRIS). IRIS is written in Java, using IBM DB2 Universal Database running on Saab's existing IBM AS/400 server. Lotus Domino is the middleware that leverages the existing infrastructure. Using a standard Web browser, any authorized employee at a Saab dealership or service center in the United States has access to enterprise applications stored on the AS/400 server at the Saab U.S. headquarters. The applications make use of a consolidated repository of vehicle, customer, warranty, sales, and service information stored in DB2 Universal Database. Says Director of IS, Jerry Rode, "DB2 Universal Database has demonstrated incredible scalability and reliability as the data management solution for our IRIS system." Lotus Domino, residing in another logical partition on the AS/400 server, is the middleware that mediates between the back-end applications and the front-end Web interface. For example, if a customer walks in and asks for a black model

9-3 Saab with a tan leather interior, a sales associate logs into the IRIS menu created by Domino and initiates a search. Domino queries DB2 by location, model, and color and puts the results of the query into an HTML form for the dealer. Upon locating the customer's vehicle, that dealer clicks to another vehicle distribution application and orders the car to be brought on site.[15]

   a. Use this case to describe how Saab went from vision to infrastructure.

   b. What criteria did Saab use in selecting its infrastructure?

CASE STUDY 6-1

HASBRO

Hasbro, the global producer of games and toys, wanted to build an application to help market a new version of their popular Monopoly game, Monopoly Here and Now: World Edition. The application would allow individuals from around the world to vote for their city to be included in the game.

Hasbro's IT organization decided to work with a third party, Digitaria, to create an application that utilized Amazon Web Services (AWS) and open source software to produce the infrastructure that backed up a Web site for the marketing campaign. A director for the project explained, "In a traditional (environment), Hasbro would have had to commit to spending a large sum of money on infrastructure and would only be guaranteed a finite amount of capacity. Also, the Web site probably would have gone down during major traffic spikes. AWS enabled us to adjust to the fluctuating traffic caused by the worldwide press exposure without investing in more hardware. When our monitoring software started . . . to notify us that the load was increasing, we were able to log in and (increase capacity) within minutes."

The IT costs were very low for this application. A manager explained, "If the system is architected properly, using these services, one can launch a campaign or application on a shoe-string budget and scale the application as needed without requiring a large support team."

Discussion Questions

1. What are the key components of the infrastructure Hasbro used for this project?

2. Why do you think Hasbro used a third party, Digitaria, to help them create this project? What resources would they need internally to do this themselves?

3. What are the advantages and disadvantages to Hasbro of using Web services?

Source: Adapted from www.amazon.com/AWS-home-page-Money/b/ref = sv_hp_4?ie = UTF8&node = 3435361 on July 31, 2008.

---

[15] IBM, "Saab Rolls Out Dealer Intranet to Improve Customer Service," available at http://www3.ibm.com/software/success/cssdb.nsf/CS/NAVO-4LJQ8N?OpenDocument&Site = software (accessed June 25, 2002).

CASE STUDY 6-2

JOHNSON & JOHNSON'S ENTERPRISE ARCHITECTURE

In 1995, Johnson & Johnson (J&J), a large pharmaceutical, health-care, and medical devices firm, wanted to offer its key customers a single point of contact. This was a real challenge for the decentralized company with 150 companies that generated operating revenues of $15 billion. Internal and external analysts attributed the company's previous success to an autonomous management structure that held managers accountable for the financial results of their independent operating companies. The focus of these managers was on making their operating companies run as efficiently as possible, and not on making the customer's life easier. J&J's customers had to take it upon themselves to deal with multiple invoices, multiple sales calls, and multiple contracts with the operating companies.

Presenting a single face to the customer translated into massive IT changes. The IT support had been developed around the decentralized operating units. To change IT's focus from the operating unit to the global customer entailed major technology changes. It also meant that everyone in the firm now needed to think about IT in terms of the corporate level as well as the operating level.

J&J realized that it needed to realign IT with its new corporate strategy. J&J began by training its IT staff about the need for integrated systems and common standards. The early groups who went for training found this thinking quite foreign to the operating company environment to which they had become accustomed. The later groups, though, needed little convincing about the value of standards, which became obvious with the implementation of a single global network and desktop configuration.

Before 1995, IT initiatives had been funded by the operating units. However, with the new one-face-to-the-customer strategy, J&J found it necessary to provide corporate funding for the costs of establishing an IT infrastructure to fit its strategy. This funding strategy stimulated standardization and helped management learn how to assess corporatewide IT investments.

J&J has continued to evolve its enterprise architecture. It did not dismantle the operating companies. Rather, its strategic objectives fostered the operating companies while leveraging cross-company IT capabilities where appropriate. J&J created committees to establish and monitor necessary technical standards. New formal organizational units called sectors were created to link operating companies with shared customers and markets. Some sectors sponsored information system development to support the exchange of data across their operating companies. Thus, over time, J&J has aligned its business strategy, IT infrastructure, and technology management practices.

Discussion Questions

1. Discuss Johnson & Johnson's approach to providing an IT infrastructure to support its one-face-to-the-customer strategy.

2. What are the strengths and weaknesses of this approach?

Source: Adapted from Jeanne Ross, "Creating a Strategic IT Enterprise Architecture Competency: Learning in Stages," *MISQ Executive* 2:1 (March 2003), pp. 31–43.

CHAPTER 7

INFORMATION SYSTEMS SOURCING

When JP Morgan (now JP Morgan Chase) signed a 7-year mega-outsourcing contract with IBM in December 2002, it did it with much fanfare. The arrangement included support for running data centers, help desks, distributed computing, and data and voice networks. JP Morgan's vice chairman, Thomas B. Ketchum, declared in a company press release about the contract, "We view technology as a key competitive advantage. . . . Our agreement with IBM will create capacity for efficient growth and accelerate our pace of innovation while reducing costs, increasing quality and providing exciting career opportunities for our employees."[1] The move was designed to improve the group's technology infrastructure and resulted in a cash infusion when IBM purchased some of JP Morgan's hardware. Clearly JP Morgan considered a number of factors in making this major decision.

When JP Morgan terminated its contract and brought information systems (IS) operations back in house only 21 months into a 7-year mega-contract, it did so with equal fanfare. Its costs for doing so were estimated to be in the millions, not to mention the enormous losses in productivity and employee morale. The CIO of JP Morgan, Austin Adams, stated at that time, "We believe managing our own technology infrastructure is best for the long-term growth and success of our company, as well as our shareholders. Our new capabilities will give us competitive advantages, accelerate innovation, and enable us to become more streamlined and efficient."[2]

A number of factors appear to have played a role in the decision to bring the IS operations back in house. As stated in the press release, outsourcing appeared to stagnate information technology (IT) at JP Morgan under the outsourcing arrangement. A JP Morgan systems engineer observed, "Once they signed the contract, we didn't move at all beyond that date as far as picking up new technologies that would give us a competitive advantage. Technology was not

---

[1] Stephanie Overby, "Outsourcing—and Backsourcing—at JP Morgan Chase," *CIO* (2005), http://www.cio.com/article/print/10524 (accessed July 23, 2008).

[2] Ibid.

refreshed, and new projects were not rolled out."[3] What the press release didn't say was that JP Morgan had undergone a major change with its July 2004 merger with Bank One, which had gained a reputation for consolidating data centers and eliminating thousands of computer applications. And the man who had played a big role in the consolidation was Bank One's CIO Austin Adams. Adams, in his new role at JP Morgan Chase, managed the switch from IBM to self-sufficiency by taking advantage of the cost-cutting know-how he had gained at Bank One. The underperforming JP Morgan Chase learned much from the efficient Bank One.[4]

The JP Morgan Chase example demonstrates the series of decisions that it made in relation to outsourcing. Both the decision to outsource, and then the decision to bring IS operations back in-house, were based on a series of factors. These factors are similar to those used by many companies in the sourcing decisions.

The global outsourcing market has been growing steadily from revenues of U.S. \$9 billion in 1990[5] to U.S. \$256 billion in 2008.[6] Companies of all sizes pursue outsourcing arrangements, and many multimillion deals have been widely publicized. As more companies adopt outsourcing as a means of controlling IT costs and acquiring "best of breed" capabilities, managing these supplier relationships becomes increasingly important. IS must maximize the benefit of these relationships to the enterprise and preempt problems that might occur. Failure in this regard could result in deteriorating quality of service, loss of competitive advantage, costly contract disputes, low morale, and loss of key personnel.

This chapter looks at the sourcing cycle to consider the full range of decisions related to who should perform the information systems work of an organization. The cycle begins with a decision to make or buy information services and products. If the decision is to buy, a series of questions must be answered about where and how these services should be delivered or products developed. The discussion is built around the Sourcing Decision Cycle Framework discussed in the next section. Next we discuss types of sourcing: insourcing, outsourcing, outsourcing abroad, and backsourcing. We conclude the chapter with a discussion of various outsourcing models. This discussion focuses on what should be outsourced and how it can be outsourced.

---

[3] Ibid.

[4] Paul Strassmann, "Why JP Morgan Chase Really Dropped IBM," *Baseline Magazine*, 2005-01-13, http://www.baselinemag.com/c/a/Projects-Management/Why-JP-Morgan-Chase-Really-Dropped-IBM/.

[5] Mary C. Lacity and Leslie P. Willcocks, "Relationships in IT Outsourcing: A Stakeholder's Perspective," in *Framing the Domains of IT Management: Projecting the Future... Through the Past*, ed. Robert W. Zmud, 355–384 (Cincinnati: Pinnaflex Education Resources, Inc., 2000).

[6] Dean Blackmore, Robert De Souza, Allie Young, Eric Goodness, and Ron Silliman, "Forecast: IT Outsourcing, Worldwide, 2002–2008 (Update)," *Gartner Report* (March 2005).

► SOURCING DECISION CYCLE FRAMEWORK

Sourcing doesn't really just involve one decision. It involves many decisions. As demonstrated in Figure 7.1, the first sourcing decision is the original make-or-buy decision. In cases where the "buy" option is selected and the company outsources, the client company must decide whether to work with an outsourcing provider in its own country or offshore. If the company decides to go offshore because labor is cheaper or needed skills are more readily available, the client company is faced with another decision: It must decide if it wants the work done in a country that is relatively nearby or in a country that is quite distant. Finally, the client company settles on an outsourcing provider (or decides to do its own IS work). After a while, it faces another decision. It periodically must evaluate the arrangement and see whether a change is in order. If the in-house work is unsatisfactory or if other opportunities have become available that are preferable to the current arrangement, then the company may turn to outsourcing. If, on the other hand, the outsourcing arrangement is unsatisfactory, the client company has several options to consider: correct any existing problems and continue outsourcing with its current provider, outsource with another provider, or backsource. If the company decides to make a change in its sourcing arrangements at this point, the sourcing decision cycle starts over again.

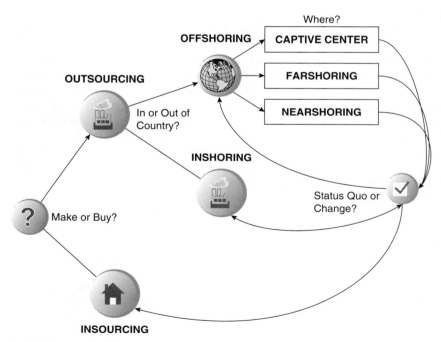

FIGURE 7.1 Sourcing Decision Cycle Framework.

▶ INSOURCING

The most traditional approach to sourcing is **insourcing**, or the situation in which a firm provides IS services or develops IS in its own in-house IS organization. The decision to insource is really the same as the "make" decision. Several drivers favor the decision to insource. Probably the most common is to keep core competencies in house. It is argued that if a company outsources a core competency, it can lose control over that competency or lose contact with suppliers who can help it remain innovative in relation to that competency. Failing to control the competency or stay innovative is a sure way to forfeit the company's competitive advantage. Further, by outsourcing commodity work, a firm can concentrate on its core competencies. Other factors that weigh in favor of insourcing are having an IS service or product that requires considerable security or confidentiality or that requires resources that are not adequately available in house (i.e., qualified personnel or IT professionals with the needed skills). Challenges for insourcing include gaining the respect and support from top management that is needed to acquire needed resources and get the job done. A second challenge is finding a reliable, competent outsourcing provider that is likely to stay in business for the long term—or at least the duration of the contract. The drivers and challenges of insourcing are listed in Figure 7.2.

▶ OUTSOURCING

Beginning in the 1970s, some IT managers turned to outsourcing as an important weapon in the battle to control costs. **Outsourcing** means the purchase of a good or service that was previously provided internally or that could be provided internally. With IT outsourcing, an outside vendor provides IT services traditionally provided by the internal MIS department. Over the years, however, motives for outsourcing broadened. This section examines outsourcing's drivers and challenges, as well as ways of avoiding pitfalls.

Insourcing Drivers	Insourcing Challenges
Good for core competencies	Dealing with inadequate support from top management to acquire needed resources
Good for confidential or sensitive IS services or software development	
Time available in house to complete software development projects	Finding a reliable, competent outsourcing provider that is likely to stay in business
In-house IT professionals have adequate training, experience, or skills to provide service or develop software	

FIGURE 7.2 Insourcing drivers and challenges.

Outsourcing Drivers

What factors drive companies to decide to outsource? One of the most common is the need to reduce costs. Outsourcing providers derive savings from economies of scale. They realize these economies through centralized (often "greener") data centers, preferential contracts with suppliers, and large pools of technical expertise. Most often, enterprises lack such resources on a sufficient scale within their own IS departments. A single company may need only 5,000 PCs, but an outsourcing provider can negotiate a contract for 50,000 and achieve a much lower unit cost.

A second common factor driving companies to outsource is to help a company transition to new technologies. Outsourcing providers generally offer access to larger pools of talent and more current knowledge of advancing technologies. For example, many outsourcing providers gain vast experience solving business intelligence problems, whereas IS staff within a single company only have limited experience, if any. The provider's experienced consultants are more readily available to the marketplace than any comparably trained and experienced IT professionals who might be recruitable for in-house employment. Many companies turn to outsourcing providers to help them implement such technologies as Web 2.0 tools and ERP systems.

Third, by bringing in outside expertise, management often can focus less attention on IS operations and more on core activities. IS department personnel manage the relationships with outsourcing providers and are ultimately still responsible for IS services. Using outsourcing providers, which are separate businesses rather than internal departments, frees up managers to devote their energies to areas that reflect core competencies for the business.

Fourth, to the extent that outsourcing providers specialize in IS services, they are likely to understand how to hire, manage, and retain IS staff effectively. An outsourcing provider often can offer IS personnel a professional environment that a typical company cannot afford to build. For example, a Web designer would have responsibility for one Web site within a company, but for multiple sites at an outsourcing provider. It becomes the outsourcing provider's responsibility to find, train, and retain highly marketable IT talent. An outsourcing provider often opens greater opportunity for training and advancement in IT than can a single IS organization. Outsourcing relieves a client of costly investments in continuous training so that IS staff can keep current with marketplace technologies and the headaches of hiring and retaining a staff that easily can change jobs with more pay or other lures.

Fifth, as long as contract terms effectively address contingencies, the larger resources of an outsourcing provider make available greater capacity on demand. For instance, at year-end, outsourcing providers potentially can allocate additional mainframe capacity to ensure timely completion of nightly processing in a manner that would be impossible for an enterprise running its own bare-bones data center.

Finally, an outsourcing provider may help a company overcome inertia to consolidate data centers that could not be consolidated by an internal group or following a merger or acquisition. Outsourcing may also offer an infusion of cash as a company sells its equipment to the outsourcing vendor. These drivers are summarized in Figure 7.3.

Outsourcing Challenges

Opponents of outsourcing cite a number of challenges (see Figure 7.3). A manager should consider each of these before making a decision about outsourcing. Each can be mitigated with effective planning and ongoing management.

First, outsourcing requires that a company surrender a degree of control over critical aspects of the enterprise. The potential loss of control could extend to several areas: control of the project, scope creep, the technologies, the costs, and their company's IT direction. By turning over data center operations, for example, a company puts itself at the mercy of an outsourcing provider's ability to manage this function effectively. A manager must choose an outsourcing provider carefully and negotiate terms that will support an effective working relationship.

Second, outsourcing clients may not adequately anticipate new technological capabilities when negotiating outsourcing contracts. Outsourcing providers may not recommend so-called bleeding-edge technologies for fear of losing money in the process of implementation and support, even if implementation would best serve the client. Thus, poorly planned outsourcing risks a loss in IT flexibility. For example, some outsourcing providers were slow to adopt Web technologies for their clients because they feared the benefits would not be as tangible as the costs of entering the market. This reluctance impinged on clients' ability to realize business strategies involving e-business. To avoid this problem, outsourcing clients should have a chief technology officer (CTO) or technology group that is charged with learning about and assessing emerging technologies for their ability to support their company's business strategy.

Outsourcing Drivers	Outsourcing Challenges
Offers costs savings	Maintaining an adequate level of control
Eases transition to new technologies	Maintaining ability to respond to techno-logical innovation
Offers opportunity for better strategic focus	Avoiding a loss of strategic advantage
Provides better management of IS staff	Avoiding overreliance on outsourcing provider
Offers better ability to handle peaks	Mitigating outsourcing risks
Makes it easier to consolidate data centers	Ensuring cost savings while protecting quality
Provides a cash infusion	Working effectively with suppliers (especially multiple suppliers at the same time)

FIGURE 7.3 Outsourcing drivers and challenges.

Third, by surrendering IT functions, a company gives up any real potential to develop them for competitive advantage—unless, of course, the outsourcing agreement is sophisticated enough to comprehend developing such advantage in tandem with the outsourcing company. However, even these partnerships potentially compromise the advantage when ownership is shared with the outsourcing provider, and the advantage may become available to the outsourcing provider's other clients. Under many circumstances, the outsourcing provider becomes the primary owner of any technological solutions developed, which allows the outsourcing provider to leverage the knowledge to benefit other clients, possibly even competitors of the initial client.

Fourth, contract terms may leave clients highly dependent on their outsourcing provider, with little recourse in terms of terminating troublesome vendor relationships. Outsourcing providers should avoid entering relationships in which they might face summary dismissal. On the other hand, clients must ensure that contract terms allow them the flexibility they require to manage and, if necessary, sever supplier relationships. The 10-year contracts that were so popular in the early 1990s are being replaced with shorter-duration contracts lasting 3 to 5 years. The contracts are being tightened by adding clauses describing actions to be taken in the event of a deterioration in quality of service or noncompliance to service-level agreements. Service levels, baseline period measurements, growth rates, and service volume fluctuations are specified to reduce opportunistic behavior on the part of the outsourcing vendor. Research demonstrates that tighter contracts tend to lead to more successful outsourcing arrangements.[7] Unfortunately, a tight contract does not provide much solace to an outsourcing client when an outsourcing provider goes out of business.

Fifth, when a company turns to an outsourcing provider, it must realize that its competitive secrets are likely to be harder to keep. Its databases are no longer kept in house, and the outsourcing provider's other customers may have easier access to sensitive information. This is a major risk that needs to be mitigated or at least thought through carefully. Other risks include business, legal, political, infrastructure, workforce, social, and logistical risks. As the size of projects entrusted to the offshore outsourcing providers or captives grows, so does the risk. DHL Worldwide Express recently entrusted 90 percent of its IT development and maintenance projects to a large Indian-based company, Infosys. "There's a lot of money wrapped up in a contract this size, so it's not something you take lightly or hurry with," said Ron Kifer, DHL's Vice President of Program Solutions and Management.[8] Clearly DHL is facing considerable risk in offshoring with Infosys.

---

[7] See, for example, C. Saunders, M. Gebelt, and Q. Hu, "Achieving Success in Information Systems Outsourcing," *California Management Review* 39, no. 2 (1997), 63–79; and M. Lacity and R. Hirschheim, *Information Systems Outsourcing: Myths, Metaphors and Realities* (Hoboken, NJ: John Wiley & Sons, 1995).

[8] Stephanie Overby, "The Hidden Costs of Offshore Outsourcing," *CIO Magazine* (September 1, 2003), Page 7 retrieved from http://www.swqual.com/newsletter/vol2/no8/Hidden%20Costs.PDF (on September 27, 2008).

Sixth, although many companies turn to outsourcing because of perceived cost savings, these savings may never be realized. Typically, the cost savings are premised on activities that were performed by the company. However, implementation of new technologies may fail to generate any savings because the old processes on which they were premised are no longer performed. Further, the outsourcing client is, to some extent, at the mercy of the outsourcing provider. Increased volumes due to unspecified growth, software upgrades, or new technologies not anticipated in the contract may end up costing a firm considerably more than it anticipated when it signed the contract. Also, some savings, although real, may be hard to measure.

Finally, there may be specific challenges for working with outsourcing providers that have not been addressed already, such as the challenges of dealing with multiple vendors. Following are some suggestions for dealing with these challenges.

Avoiding Outsourcing Pitfalls

Outsourcing decisions must be made with adequate care and deliberation. The steps outlined in Figure 7.4 are recommended when considering this option.

What is the future of outsourcing? Every enterprise faces different competitive pressures. These factors shape how it will view IT and how it will decide to leverage IT for the future. Most will need to outsource at least some IT functions. How each enterprise chooses to manage its outsourced functions will be crucial to its success.

- Do not negotiate solely on price.
- Craft full life-cycle service contracts that occur in stages.
- Establish short-term supplier contracts.
- Use multiple, best-of-breed suppliers.
- Develop skills in contract management.
- Carefully evaluate your company's own capabilities.
- Thoroughly evaluate outsourcing providers' capabilities.
- Choose an outsourcing provider whose capabilities complement yours.
- Base a choice on cultural fit as well as technical expertise.
- Determine whether a particular outsourcing relationship produces a net benefit for your company.
- Plan transition to offshoring.
- Use SOAs to increase agility.

FIGURE 7.4 Steps to avoid pitfalls.

▶ OUTSOURCING ABROAD

As the outsourcing phenomenon has matured, the marketplace has differentiated across different types of outsourcing abroad. The most general term for outsourcing abroad is offshoring. Offshoring can be either relatively proximate (nearshoring) or in a distant land (farshoring). An alternative to offshoring is a captive center. Each of these is described in more detail below.

Offshoring

Offshoring (which is short for outsourcing offshore) is when the management information systems (MIS) organization uses contractor services, or even builds its own data center in a distant land. The functions sent offshore range from routine IT transactions to increasingly higher-end, knowledge-based business processes.

Programmer salaries can be a fraction of those in the home country in part because the cost of living and the standard of living in the distant country are much lower. Depending on the type of work that is outsourced and the skill level it requires, labor savings alone can range from 40 to 70 percent.[9] However, these savings come at a price because other costs increase. Additional technology, telecommunications, travel, process changes, and management overhead are required to relocate and supervise operations overseas. For example, during the transition period, which can be rather lengthy, offshore workers must often be brought to the U.S. headquarters for extended periods to become familiar with the company's operations and technology. Because of the long transition period, it may often take several years for offshoring's labor savings to be fully realized. And even if they are realized, they may never reflect the true cost to a country. Many argue, especially those who have lost their jobs to offshore workers, that offshoring cuts into the very fiber of the society in the origin country where companies are laying off workers.

Even though the labor savings are often very attractive, companies sometimes turn to offshoring for other reasons. The employees in many offshore companies are typically well educated (often holding master's degrees) and proud to work for an international company. The offshore service providers are often "profit centers" that have established Six Sigma, ISO 9001, or another certification program. They usually are more willing to "throw more brainpower at a problem" to meet their performance goals than many companies in the United States or Western Europe. In offshore economies, technology know-how is a relatively cheap commodity in ample supply.[10] USAA CEO Bob Davis cited the superiority of offshore IT talent

---

[9] Aditya Bhasin, Vinay Couto, Chris Disher, and Gil Irwin, "Business Process Offshoring: Making the Right Decision," *CIO Magazine* (January 29, 2004), available at http://www2.cio.com/consultant/report2161.html (accessed August 14, 2005).

[10] Ibid.

that his company uses extensively when he proffered this reason for offshoring: " . . . because it helps us get our projects done, and because of the level of expertise of this technology, these technology companies and individuals is incredible."[11]

Selecting Offshoring Destinations

A difficult decision that many companies face is selecting an offshoring destination. Approximately 100 countries are now exporting software services and products. For various reasons, some countries are more attractive than others as hosts of offshoring business because of the firm's geographic orientation. With English as the predominant language of outsourcing countries (i.e., U.S. and UK), countries with a high English proficiency are more attractive than those where different languages prevail. Geopolitical risk is another factor that affects the use of offshore firms in a country. Countries on the verge of war, countries with high rates of crime, and countries without friendly relationships with the home country are typically not suitable candidates for this business. Regulatory restrictions, trade issues, data security, and intellectual property also affect the attractiveness of a country for an offshoring arrangement. The level of technical infrastructure available in some countries also can add to or detract from the attractiveness of a country. Although a company may decide that a certain country is attractive overall for offshoring, it still must assess city differences when selecting an offshore outsourcing provider or creating wholly owned subsidiaries ("captives"). For example, Chennai is a better location in India for finance and accounting, but Delhi has better call-center capabilities.[12]

Some countries make an entire industry of offshoring. India, for example, took an early mover advantage in the industry. With a large, low-cost English-speaking labor pool, many entrepreneurs set up programming factories that produce high-quality software to meet even the toughest standards. One measure of the level of proficiency of the development process within an IS organization is the Software Engineering Institute's Capability Maturity Model (CMM). Level 1 means that the software development processes are immature, bordering on chaotic. Few processes are formally defined, and output is highly inconsistent. At the other end of the model is level 5, where processes are predictable, repeatable, highly refined, and consistently innovating, growing, and incorporating feedback. The software factories in many Indian enterprises are well known for their CMM level 5 software development processes, making them extremely reliable, and, thus, desirable as vendors.

A very important factor in selecting an offshore destination is the level of development of the country, which will often subsume a variety of other factors. For example in the highest tier, the countries have an advanced technological

---

[11] Ben Worthen and Stephanie Overby, "USAA IT Chief Exits," *CIO Magazine* (June 15, 2004), available at http://www.cio.com/archive/061504/tl_management.html (accessed August 14, 2005).
[12] Ibid.

foundation and a broad base of institutions of higher learning. Carmel and Tjia suggest that there are three tiers of software exporting nations:[13]

- *Tier 1.* Mature Software Exporting Nations—These include such highly industrialized nations as United Kingdom, United States, Japan, Germany, France, Canada, the Netherlands, Sweden, and Finland. It also includes the 3 "I's" (i.e., India, Ireland, and Israel) that became very prominent software exporters in the 1990s, as well as China and Russia, which entered the tier in the 2000s.

- *Tier 2.* Emerging Software Exporting Nations—These nations are the up-and-comers. They tend to have small population bases or unfavorable conditions such as political instability or an immature state of economic development. Countries in this tier include Brazil, Costa Rica, South Korea, and many Eastern European countries.

- *Tier 3.* Infant Stage Software Exporting Nations—These nations have not significantly affected the global software market, and their software industry is mostly a "cottage industry" with smaller, isolated firms. Some Tier 3 countries are Cuba, Vietnam, Jordan, and 15 to 25 others.

The tiers were determined on the basis of industrial maturity, the extent of clustering of some critical mass of software enterprises, and export revenues.

Cultural Differences

Often misunderstandings arise because of differences in culture and, sometimes, language. For example, GE Real Estate's CIO quickly learned that American programmers have a greater tendency to speak up and offer suggestions, whereas Indian programmers might think something does not make sense, but they go ahead and do what they were asked, assuming that this is what the client wants.[14] Thus, a project that is common sense for a U.S. worker—like creating an automation system for consumer credit cards—may be harder to understand and take longer when undertaken by an offshore worker. The end result may be a more expensive system that responds poorly to situations unanticipated by its offshore developers. It is important to be aware of and to manage the risks due to cultural differences.

Sometimes cultural and other differences are so great that companies take back in-house operations that were previously outsourced offshore. Carmel and Tjia outlined some examples of communication failures with Indian developers due to differences in language, culture and perceptions about time:[15]

- Indians are less likely than Westerners, especially the British, to engage in small talk.

---

[13] Erran Carmel and Paul Tjia, *Offshoring Information Technology* (Cambridge, UK: University Press, 2005).

[14] Stephanie Overby, "The Hidden Costs of Offshore Outsourcing".

[15] Ibid. Carmel and Tjia, Offshoring Information Technology.

- Indians often are not concerned with deadlines. When they are, they are likely to be overly optimistic about their ability to meet the deadlines of a project. One cultural trainer was heard to say, "When an Indian programmer says the work will be finished tomorrow, it only means it will not be ready today."[16]
- Indians, like Malaysians and other cultures, are hesitant about saying "no." Questions where one option for response is "no" are extremely difficult to interpret.
- What is funny in one culture is not necessarily funny in another culture.

Offshoring Best Practices

Offshoring raises the fundamental question of what you send offshore, and what you keep within your enterprise IS organization. Will CIOs be losing some important learning opportunities if they outsource, and ultimately offshore, basic programming processes? Because communications are made difficult by differences in culture, time zones, and possibly language, outsourced tasks are usually those that can be well specified. They typically, but not always, are basic noncore transactional systems that require little in-depth knowledge of the users or customers. In contrast, early-stage prototypes and pilot development are often kept in house because this work is very dynamic and needs familiarity with business processes. Keeping the work at home allows CIOs to offer learning opportunities to in-house staff. In summary, the costs savings that lure many companies to turn to offshoring need to be assessed in relation to the increased risks in working with offshore workers and relying on them to handle major projects.

A recent survey of companies involved with offshoring suggests the top 20 practices with offshore sourcing. These are displayed in Figure 7.5. Also in the figure is a comparison of offshoring practices with inshoring (domestic) practices. Some practices such as creating a program management office, selecting locations, projects, suppliers, and managers to leverage in-house sourcing expertise, using pilot projects, developing meaningful career paths for staff, and creating balanced scorecard metrics are used by both. Most are used by both but are more important for offshoring. Still others, including some related to CMM processes, are unique to offshoring.

Government Involvement with Offshoring

Government actions to support offshoring   Politicians in countries around the world are trying to create an environment so that their country can become "the next India." India invested in a substantial infrastructure, and other hopefuls will have to do the same. Part of that infrastructure is in human capital, telecommunications, and technology parks. Most important, a groundwork must be laid in science and technology education, especially IT education. Offshoring will only be possible

---

[16] Ibid., 181.

Sourcing Challenge	Practices to Overcome the Challenge	Equally Important for Both Domestic & Offshore	More Important For Offshore	Unique to Offshore
How can we swiftly move through the learning curve?	1. Create a centralized program management office to consolidate management	X		
	2. Hire an intermediary consulting firm to serve as a broker and guide		X	
	3. Select locations, projects, suppliers, and managers to leverage in-house sourcing expertise	X		
How can we mitigate risks?	4. Use pilot projects to mitigate business risks	X		
	5. Give customers a choice of sourcing location to mitigate business risks			X
	6. Hire a legal expert to mitigate legal risks		X	
	7. Openly communicate the sourcing strategy to all stakeholders to mitigate political risks		X	
	8. Use secure information links or redundant lines to mitigate infrastructure risks		X	
	9. Use fixed-price contracts to mitigate workforce risks		X	
How can we effectively work with suppliers?	10. Elevate your own organization's CMM certification to close the process gap between you and your supplier			X
	11. Negotiate the CMM processes you will and will not pay for to avoid wasting money			X
	12. Cross-examine or replace the supplier's employees to overcome cultural communication barriers		X	
	13. Let the project team members meet face-to-face to foster camaraderie		X	
	14. Consider innovative techniques, such as real-time dashboards, to improve workflow verification, synchronization, and management		X	
	15. Manage bottlenecks to relieve the substantial time zone differences			X
How can we ensure cost savings while protecting quality?	16. Consider both transaction and production costs to calculate overall savings realistically		X	
	17. Size projects large enough to receive total cost savings		X	
	18. Establish the ideal in-house/onsite/offshore ratio only after the relationship has stabilized			X
	19. Develop meaningful career paths for subject matter experts, project managers, governance experts, and technical experts to help ensure quality	X		
	20. Create balance scorecard metrics	X		

FIGURE 7.5 Sourcing best practices.
Source: J. Rottman and M. C. Lacity, "Twenty Practices for Offshore Sourcing," *MIS Quarterly Executive* 3, no. 3 (September 2004), 119, Table 1.

if its key resource, the country's potential job pool, consists of highly skilled workers. Other actions that governments can take to make their countries more appealing to outsourcing clients are to give marketing assistance to offshore vendors, assist firms in attaining recognized standards of quality in the global marketplace, and promote collaborative efforts between the government, software companies, financial institutions, and universities.[17] Governments can also offer

[17] Carmel and Tjia, *Offshoring Information Technology*.

specific incentives to companies that are considering their country as an offshoring destination. They can, for example reduce/eliminate various taxes or ease the bureaucratic process required for the company.[18]

One other obvious step that governments need to take is to ensure political stability for their country. In 2002, both India and Pakistan were amassing troops on their common border, and rumors were rampant that the nuclear war heads were being prepared to see service. Not surprisingly, offshoring companies headquartered in India saw the hostilities as threatening to the viability of their businesses. Says N. Krishnakumar, president of MindTree, a leading Indian knowledge outsourcing firm in Bangalore, "What we explained to our government, through the Confederation of Indian Industry, is that providing a stable, predictable operating environment is now the key to India's development."[19] Apparently the elderly leaders in New Delhi saw the confrontation in a new light after the Confederation members explained that the confrontation was very bad for Indian business and the Indian economy. Shortly thereafter, the Indian prime minister toned down the rhetoric and averted a nuclear war.

Government actions to protect against offshoring Some claim that offshoring has resulted in a high number of lost information technology jobs in the United States and Western Europe. Forrester Research estimated that 500,000 U.S. jobs moved offshore in 2004 and that this number will grow to 3.4 million in 2015.[20] A follow-up report estimated that the UK would lose 750,000 jobs to offshoring by 2015, and a fifth of them would be IT jobs.[21] Deloitte consulting predicted that two million jobs in the financial sector would be lost globally to offshoring.[22] These job losses have sparked considerable controversy.[23] On the one hand, critics argue that these job losses are harmful to American citizens in the short run. In addition, they see an ultimate decrease in the subjective quality of the new jobs or lowered pay scales in the long run. They point to the necessity of government funding for education and training, health-care insurance and pension portability, and unemployment-compensation programs for the displaced workers—funding that unfortunately is unlikely during this time of growing federal budget deficits. To stem the outflow of lost jobs, the U.S. Congress proposed more

---

[18] Ibid.

[19] Friedman, Thomas *The World Is Flat* (New York: Farrar, Straus and Giroux, 2005), 436.

[20] Metrics, "Offspring to Steadily Increase Through 2015," CIO.com (May 21, 2004), available at http://www2.cio.com/metrics/2004/metric697.html (accessed August 14, 2005).

[21] Carmel and Tjia, *Offshoring Information Technology.*

[22] Deloitte Research, *Making the Off-shore Call: The Road Map for Communications Operators.* Research Report, (2004).

[23] Analysis of the Bureau of Labor Statistics Mass Layoff Statistics and European Restructuring Monitor in 2005 did not find support for the idea that large numbers of IT jobs are being offshored. Raymond Panko, "IT Employment Prospects: Beyond the Dotcom Bubble," *European Journal of Information Systems* (2008).

than 20 federal law proposals ("bills") to restrict offshoring.[24] In addition, state legislatures in Connecticut, Maryland, Missouri, New Jersey, Rhode Island, and Washington proposed laws to restrain offshoring by more heavily regulating the "privatization" of state services, and 30 other states discussed some kind of legislation. Because the number of contracts offered by state governments is limited, these "privatization" bills, if enacted into law, probably would have little impact on offshoring. Nonetheless, lobbying efforts and public pressure to legislate against offshoring and for making the business dealings of publicly owned firms that engage in offshoring more transparent are likely to continue.

On the other hand, offshoring is argued to benefit both the origin (frequently the United States, Western Europe, and Australia) as well as the destination country through free trade. A recent study of manufactured components outsourced by U.S. computer and telecommunications companies in the 1990s found that outsourcing reduced the prices of computers and communications equipment by 10 to 30 percent and fueled the rapid expansion of IT jobs. Offshoring of IT services may similarly create high-level jobs for U.S. workers to design, tailor, and implement IT packages for a range of industries and companies.[25] Forrester Research's dire prediction about job losses from offshoring only studied job losses from offshored work and not gains from work that American companies export. Other studies show that the United States has enjoyed a growing surplus in IT services, which suggests that inshoring may be more important than offshoring for the U.S. labor force. Clearly, not all offshoring goes from high-wage countries to low-wage countries. For example, the UK purchases four times as much computer service from Germany than it does from India. Surprisingly, India ranks sixth—behind the United States, the United Kingdom, Germany, France, and the Netherlands—as a top recipient of global offshoring pacts based on an International Monetary Fund Study.

Nearshoring

Nearshoring is "sourcing service work to a foreign, lower-wage country that is relatively close in distance or time zone (or both)."[26] Nearshoring was first presented as an alternative to "farshoring." With nearshoring, the client company hopes to benefit from one or more ways of being close: geographically, temporally, culturally, linguistically, economically, politically, or from historical linkages. Nearshoring basically challenges the assumption on which offshoring is premised: Distance doesn't matter. With nearshoring, distance matters! The advocates of nearshoring argue that by being closer on one or more of the dimensions listed, the client company will face less challenges in terms of communication, control, supervision, coordination, or bonding socially.

---

[24] Carmel and Tjia, *Offshoring Information Technology*.

[25] Laura D'Andrea Tyson, "Outsourcing: Who's Safe Anymore?" *Executive Viewpoint* (February 23, 2004).

[26] Erran Carmel and Pamela Abbott "Why 'Nearshore' Means that Distance Matters," *Communications of the ACM* 50, no. 10 (October 2007), 40–46. The quote is from page 44.

A recent analysis of the nearshoring literature found three major global clusters of countries focused on building a reputation as a home for nearshoring: a cluster of 20 nations around the United States and Canada, a cluster of 27 countries around Western Europe, and a smaller cluster of three countries in East Asia. This smaller cluster contains China, Malaysia, and Korea.[27] The ways, or dimensions, of being close clearly extend beyond distance and time zone. For example, language makes a difference in nearshoring. That is why Latin American nearshoring destinations are appealing to Texas or Florida, where there is a large Spanish-speaking population and why French-speaking North African nations are appealing to France. These dimensions likely play a key role when companies are trying to decide between a nearshore or a farshore destination (particularly India). Ironically, India, which exports roughly five times the software of the strictly nearshoring nations, is responding to the competitive threat that these nations pose by offering clients nearshoring options. For example, India-based Tata Consulting Services (TCS) offers its British clients services that are nearshore (Budapest, Hungary), farshore (India), or inshore (London, UK). It is likely that the differentiation based on "distance" is likely to continue to be important in the outsourcing arena.

Captive Centers

An alternative to offshoring or nearshoring is a captive center. A **captive center** is an overseas subsidiary that is set up to serve the parent company. Companies set up captive centers as an alternative to offshoring. Although many companies first set them up in the 1990s to do software maintenance and customer service, these same companies are adopting other strategies. A recent study found four major strategies that are being employed:[28]

- Hybrid Captive—captive center that performs core business processes for parent company but outsources noncore work to an offshore provider. That is, the captive center performs the more expensive, higher-profile work and outsources the more commoditized work that is more cheaply provided by the offshore vendor.

- Shared Captive—captive center that performs work for both a parent company and external customers. By increasing the volume of work that is performed, the shared captive can become more efficient in terms of processes, equipment, and costs.

- Divest captive—captive center that has a large enough scale and scope that it is well positioned to be sold for a profit by the parent company.

- Terminated Captive—captive center that has been shut down, usually because its inferior service was hurting the parent company's reputation.

---

[27] Ibid.

[28] I. Oshri, J. Kotalarsky, and C.-M. Liew "What to Do with Your Captive Center: Four Strategic Options," *Wall Street Journal*, (May 12, 2008).

When a center is terminated, the parent company minimizes its losses by outsourcing the noncore work and bringing the core components back in house where they can be managed more effectively.

In determining which captive strategy to adopt, the parent company should consider its goal for the center (i.e., cost savings vs. growth) and the extent to which the offshore market is developed (i.e., developed vs. underdeveloped), as well as the offshoring considerations discussed earlier.

▶ BACKSOURCING

Backsourcing is a business practice in which a company takes back in-house assets, activities, and skills that are part of its information systems operations and were previously outsourced to one or more outside IS providers.[29] It may be partial or complete reversal of an outsourcing contract. A growing number of companies around the globe have brought their outsourced IS functions back in house after terminating, renegotiating or letting their contracts expire. Some companies, such as Continental Airlines, Cable and Wireless, Halifax Bank of Scotland, Sears, Bank One, and Xerox, have backsourced contracts worth over a billion dollars or more. The biggest backsourcing of a contract to date was the one that JP Morgan had signed with IBM for $5 billion dollars and that was described at the start of the chapter.

It isn't only large companies that are backsourcing. A recent study by Deloitte Consulting reports that 70 percent of outsourcing clients have had negative experiences with outsourcing and 25 percent of outsourcing clients have backsourced.[30] An even more recent Compass poll of 70 North American companies found that only 4 percent would not consider backsourcing when their current outsourcing contracts expired.[31] Given the size and number of the current outsourcing contracts and the difficulties of delivering high-quality information services and products, backsourcing is likely to remain an important option to be considered by many client companies.

Ironically, the reasons given for backsourcing often mirror the reasons for outsourcing in the first place. That is, companies often claim that they backsource to reduce costs and become more efficient. Based on reports in the popular press, the most common reasons given for backsourcing are a change in the way the IS is

---

[29] Rudy Hirschheim, "Backsourcing: An Emerging Trend," *Outsourcing Journal*, 1998; Mary C. Lacity and Leslie P. Willcocks, "Relationships in IT Outsourcing: A Stakeholder's Perspective," in *Framing the Domains of IT Management. Projecting the Future... Through the Past*, ed. Robert W. Zmud, 355–384 (Cincinnati: Pinnaflex Education Resources, Inc., 2000).

[30] Daniel Mucisko and Evonne Lum, "Outsourcing Falling from Favor with World's Largest Organizations, Deloitte Consulting Study Reveals," *Deloitte Consulting LLP Report* (April 2005).

[31] Bill Fowler and Geraldine Fox, "Bringing IT Back Home: Repatriation Emerges as a Viable Sourcing Option," *Compass Report* (October 2006), http://www.compassmc.com/pdf/Insourcing.pdf.

perceived by the organization, the need to regain control over critical activities that had been outsourced, a change in the executive team (where the new executives favored backsourcing), higher than expected costs, and poor service. The study found that backsourcing wasn't always due to problems. Sometime companies saw opportunities, such as mergers, acquisition, or new roles for IS, that required backsourcing to be realized.[32]

Outsourcing decisions can be difficult and expensive to reverse because outsourcing requires the enterprise to acquire the necessary infrastructure and staff. Unless experienced IT staff can contribute elsewhere in the firm, outsourcing major IT functions means staff will be lost either to the outsourcing provider or to other companies. When IT staff get news that their company is considering outsourcing, they often seek work elsewhere. Even when staff are hired by the outsourcing provider to handle the account, they may be transferred to other accounts, taking with them critical knowledge. Backsourcing represents the final decision in one sourcing decision cycle. However, it is invariably followed by another cycle of decisions as the company seeks to respond to its dynamic environment.

▶ OUTSOURCING MODELS

The classic outsourcing model dictates that an enterprise should outsource only those functions that do not give it a competitive advantage. For instance, mainframe computer maintenance and monitoring are not often considered core competencies of an enterprise and therefore are often farmed to vendors such as Computer Sciences Corporation or Electronic Data Systems. In the early days of outsourcing, such contracts ran long term—often for 10 years or more. Frequently, outsourcing providers took over entire IS departments, including people, equipment, and management responsibility. This classic approach prevailed through most of the 1970s and 1980s, but then experienced a decline in popularity.

In 1989, Eastman Kodak Company's multivendor approach to meeting its IS needs created the "Kodak effect." Kodak outsourced its data center operations to IBM, its network to Digital Equipment Company, and its desktop supply

---

[32] N. Veltri, C. Saunders, and C. B. Kavan, "Information Systems Backsourcing: Correcting Problems and Responding to Opportunities." *California Management Review* (2008). These economic and relationship issues are similar to the three empirical studies to date that have performed backsourcing research: Bandula Jayatilaka, "IS Sourcing a Dynamic Phenomena: Forming an Institutional Theory Perspective," in *Information Systems Outsourcing: Enduring Themes, New Perspectives and Global Challenges*, ed. Rudy Hirschheim, Armin Heinzl, and Jens Dibbern, 103–134 (Berlin: Springer-Verlag, 2006); R. Hirschheim and M. C. Lacity, "Four stories of information systems sourcing," in *Information Systems Outsourcing: Enduring Themes, New Perspectives and Global Challenges*, ed. R. Hirschheim and J. Dibbern, 303–346 (Berlin: Springer, 2006); and Dwayne Whitten and Dorothy Leidner, "Bringing IT Back: An Analysis of the Decision to Backsource or Switch Vendors," *Decision Sciences* 37, no. 4 (2006): 605–621.

and support operations to Businessland.[33] Kodak managed these relationships through strategic alliances.[34] Kodak retained IS staff to act on behalf of its business personnel with outsource vendors. Vendor contracts created incentives for new investment in technology and provided enough flexibility to encourage quick problem resolution. Vendors made fair profits and received additional business if they performed well. Within a couple of years, Kodak's capital expenditures attributable to computing dropped by 90 percent.[35] Its approach to supplier management became a model emulated by Continental Bank, General Dynamics, Continental Airlines, and National Car Rental.[36]

Kodak's watershed outsourcing arrangement ushered in changes to outsourcing practices in the 1990s that put all IS activities up for grabs, including aspects that provide competitive advantage. As relationships with outsourcing providers become more sophisticated, companies realize that even such essential functions as customer service are sometimes better managed by experts on the outside. Sometimes these experts may be offshore. In addition, the ubiquity of the Internet has spawned a series of new application service providers (ASPs) who perform similar services using Web-based applications and, more recently, wireless application service providers (WASP).

Application Service Provider Model

An **application service provider (ASP)** is a company that "rents" the use of an application to the customer. In return, the ASP provides not only the software, but also the infrastructure, people, and maintenance to run it in a customized fashion for a client. It is different from the traditional outsourcing relationship in which an entire IS shop is run by an outside organization. With an ASP, the outsourcing occurs application by application. The goal is to provide trouble-free operation for the customer. This model is particularly useful for the IS that are necessary, but not core, to the business. Companies may also use ASPs to free up IT staff, combine data resources, rapidly deploy new applications, control a widely distributed user base, develop a non-IT-based application, implement new technologies, and in many other ways. Because the ASP is typically responsible for security and maintenance of the systems, they make systems easier to scale and manage. Finally, they provide the infrastructure and applications necessary to get the business up and running. A variation to ASP is the multi-tenant software-as-a-service (SaaS). Companies may host SaaS software so that clients can save not only their software costs, but also their hardware costs.

---

[33] L. Applegate and R. Montealegre, "Eastman Kodak Co.: Managing Information Systems Through Strategic Alliances," Harvard Business School case 192030 (September 1995).

[34] Anthony DiRomualdo and Vijay Gurbaxani, "Strategic Intent for IT Outsourcing," *Sloan Management Review* (June 22, 1998).

[35] Steven L. Alter, *Information Systems: A Manager's Perspective* (San Francisco: Benjamin Cummings, 1996).

[36] Mary C. Lacity, Leslie P. Willcocks, and David F. Feeny, "The Value of Selective IT Sourcing," *Sloan Management Review* (March 22, 1996).

Crowdsourcing

Crowdsourcing is the act of taking a task traditionally performed by an employee or contractor and outsourcing it to an undefined, generally large group of people, in the form of an open call. Typically the people performing the work do so either for small amounts of money or because they think it will be fun or give them some desired experience. The content is produced by crowds of people (outside the company) using their collective intelligence. It has international appeal because for some people in third-world countries, even a small reimbursement can go a long way.

Large corporations and businesses of all sizes are issuing open calls as a way of increasing productivity, lowering production cost, and filling skill gaps. Crowdsourcing can be used for a variety of tasks including manufacturing, photography, software development, and scientific research. However, with this approach, corporations do not have control over the people performing the work and often have little say in how or when the work will be performed. In some cases, crowdsourcing has cost a business more than it would have cost using a straightforward, traditional outsourcing approach.

Some well-known crowdsourcing sites are Innocentive (for solving pharmaceutical problems), Cambrian House and Rent-a-Coder (for software development), and iStockPhoto for professional-looking images.[37] A very recent open call was issued by a Finnish Internet community called "eCars—Now!" The community wants to shake up the automotive industry by developing electric cars, with the first rollout due by the end of 2008.[38]

Full versus Selective Outsourcing Models

Once a company decides to outsource, despite possible challenges, it must decide whether to pursue it fully or selectively. As the term **full outsourcing** implies, an enterprise can outsource all its IT functions from desktop services to software development. An enterprise would outsource everything if it does not view IT as a strategic advantage that it needs to cultivate internally. Full outsourcing can free resources to be employed in areas that add greater value. It can also reduce overall cost per transaction due to size and economies of scale.[39] Many companies outsource IT simply to allow their managers to focus attention on other business issues. Others outsource to accommodate growth and respond to their business environment. Palm Inc. had no choice but to outsource when it split off from parent 3Com Corp. It was a $3 billion company with a 100 percent annual growth rate that had to build its internal capabilities quickly.[40]

[37] Top 10 Crowdsourcing Companies (August 2006). http://innovationzen.com/blog/2006/08/01/top-10-crowdsourcing-companies/ (accessed July 23, 2008).

[38] Reuters, "Crowd Sourcing the Electric Car," *BaseLine* (July 23, 2008), http://www.baselinemag.com/c/a/Automotive/CrowdSourcing-the-Electric-Car/?kc=BLBLBEMNL07242008STR1 (accessed July 23, 2008).

[39] Tom Field, "An Outsourcing Buyer's Guide: Caveat Emptor," *CIO Magazine* (April 1, 1997).

[40] Lorraine Cosgrove Ware, "Adventures in Outsourcing," *CIO Magazine* (May 3, 2002), available at http://www2.cio.com/research/surveyreport.cfm?id=78 (accessed June 22, 2002).

With **selective outsourcing**, an enterprise chooses which IT capabilities to retain in house and which to give to an outsider. A "best-of-breed" approach is taken in which suppliers are chosen for their expertise in specific technology areas. Areas include Web site hosting, Web 2.0 applications, business process application development, help desk support, networking and communications, and data center operations. Although an enterprise can acquire top-level skills and experience through such relationships, the effort required to manage them grows tremendously with each new provider. Still, selective outsourcing gives greater flexibility and often better service due to the competitive market.[41] To illustrate, an enterprise might retain a firm to develop virtual world applications and at the same time select a large outsourcing provider, such as Perot Systems, to assume mainframe maintenance. Such firms as GM and Southland Corporation have adopted this approach, also called "strategic sourcing."

To illustrate the ins and outs of selective and full outsourcing, consider the case of a company that pursued both approaches. British Petroleum (BP) selected only a few outsourcing providers with short-term contracts to meet its IT needs.[42] BP awarded Sema Group management of its data center, Science Applications International Corporation, its European IT facility management and companywide applications support, and Syncordia, its telecommunications and telex networks. This arrangement was selective in that BP chose each company for its particular expertise, but full in that BP turned over a significant percentage of its IT to outsourcing providers. Thus, it gained the benefits of best of breed and competitive pricing along with fewer contract management worries and the ability to develop long-term relationships. BP encouraged the outsourcing providers to work together to provide high-quality services.

What were the results of BP's approach? The company saw its IT costs fall from $360 million in 1989 to $132 million in 1994. At the same time, it gained more flexible IT systems and higher-quality service. BP saw its IT staff shrink by 80 percent. The remaining staff became internal consultants throughout the company. In fact, BP is considering outsourcing its internal consultants to other companies. Not all outsourcing arrangements are so successful, but BP illustrates the best-case scenario.

Single versus Multiple Vendors

Kodak ushered in the practice of multiple vendors when it contracted IBM, Digital Equipment Company, and Businessland to perform work for which they each were considered to be leaders in the industry. Multiple vendors allows client companies to distribute work to the "best in breed." It comes with its downsides, though. More vendors means more coordination than with working with a single outsourcing provider. Further, when a major problem occurs, there may be a tendency to

---

[41] Tom Field, "An Outsourcing Buyer's Guide: Caveat Emptor," *CIO Magazine* (April 1, 1997).

[42] J. Cross, "IT Outsourcing: British Petroleum," *Harvard Business Review* (May–June 1995), 94–102.

"finger-point." That is, each vendor may claim that the problem is caused by, or can only be corrected by, another vendor.

With time the various outsourcing models blossom and then wane in popularity. For example, the ASP model, which was hyped around the turn of the millennium, is now much less popular than crowdsourcing. And crowdsourcing, which capitalizes on Web 2.0 tools, surely will be supplanted by other sourcing models as new technologies enter the scene. Further, as companies take steps to become more flexible, they will enact their preference for shorter and more selective outsourcing contracts.

▶ FOOD FOR THOUGHT: OUTSOURCING AND STRATEGIC NETWORKS

Typically outsourcing relationships are couched in terms of a provider and a client. The client must decide whether to develop the system or provide a service in house or to turn to a provider for the service. That is, many of today's corporations turn to the two traditional ways to organize economic activity: make (i.e., also called insourcing or vertical integration) or buy (i.e., also called outsourcing or subcontracting). Both forms have their advantages and disadvantages, which were discussed earlier in the chapter. In the extreme, outsourcing may lead to a situation in which a company transfers so much of its competitive advantage to an outsourcing provider that the provider becomes a competitor or the client company's strategic knowledge is diffused to its competitors who also use the same provider.[43] Unfortunately, the outsourcing client may become distanced from both its customers and sources of innovation. The worse fear for a company is that it becomes a "hollow" corporation that merely shuffles product components from one supplier to another and that eventually loses its core competencies. Jarillo persuasively describes a third approach for organizing economic activity: the strategic network.[44]

A strategic network is a long-term, purposeful "arrangement by which companies set up a web of close relationships that form a veritable system geared to providing product or services in a coordinated way."[45] It becomes a hub and its suppliers, including its outsourcing providers, are part of its network. The advantage of the strategic network is that it lowers the costs of working with others in its network. In doing so, the company can become more efficient than its competitors, as well as flexible enough to respond to its rapidly changing environment. Perhaps the strategic network is the best way to think about outsourcing arrangements in today's world.

An example of a strategic network is the keiretsu. Japanese *keiretsu* is similar to a strategic network in that it has a hub company, a policy that encourages

---

[43] J. C. Jarillo, *Strategic Networks: Creating the Borderless Organization* (Oxford, UK: Butterworth-Heinemann, 1993).

[44] Ibid.

[45] Ibid., 7.

specialization within the network, and investments (financial and otherwise) in long-term relationships.[46] The Japanese companies manage their outsourcing activities based on the types of inputs from different types of suppliers.[47] The strategic suppliers (kankei kaisa) fall into the keiretsu category, whereas independent suppliers (dokuritsu kaisha) do not. Japanese companies work very closely with companies in the keiretsu. Foreign multinationals, especially the Japanese, have capitalized on having different types of outsourcing arrangements (i.e., strategic partnerships and arm's-length arrangements) to achieve both effectiveness and efficiency.

► SUMMARY

- Firms typically face a range of sourcing decisions. The Sourcing Decision Cycle Framework highlights decisions about where the work will be performed. Decisions include insourcing versus outsourcing, inshoring versus offshoring, and selecting among offshoring options (nearshoring versus farshoring versus captive centers). The cycle involves an assessment of the adequacy of the IS service/product delivery. The assessment can trigger a new cycle.

- Cost savings or filling the gaps in the organization's IT skills are powerful drivers for outsourcing. Other drivers include the ability for the company to adopt a more strategic focus, manage IS staff better, better handle peaks, consolidate data centers, or benefit from a cash infusion, The numerous risks involved in outsourcing arrangements must be carefully assessed by IS and general managers alike.

- Offshoring may be performed in a country that is proximate along one or a number of dimensions (nearshoring) or that is distant (farshoring). Offshoring must be managed carefully and take into consideration functional differences.

- Different ways of outsourcing include application service providers (ASPs) and crowdsourcing.

- Full or selective outsourcing offers organizations an alternative to keeping top-performing IS services in-house. Firms can meet their outsourcing needs by using a single-vendor or multiple-vendor models.

► KEY TERMS

application service
  provider (ASP) (p. 208)
backsourcing (p. 206)
captive center (p. 205)

crowdsourcing (p. 209)
full outsourcing (p. 209)
insourcing (p. 193)
nearshoring (p. 204)

offshoring (p. 198)
outsourcing (p. 193)
selective outsourcing
  (p. 210)

---

[46] Ibid., 122.

[47] Masaaki Kotabe and Janet Y. Murray, "Global Sourcing Strategy and Sustainable Competitive Advantage," *Industrial Marketing Management* 33 (2004), 7–14.

► DISCUSSION QUESTIONS

1. The make-versus-buy decision is important every time a new application is requested of the IS group. What, in your opinion, are the key reasons an IS organization should make its own systems? What are the key reasons it should buy an application?

2. Is offshoring a problem to your country? To the global economy? Please explain.

3. Premiere Technologies, Inc., a fast-growing supplier of communication services in more than 30 countries, provides an example of successful use of an ASP. Premiere began to implement an enterprise resource planning (ERP) system and found that whenever there was a problem or call to work on a "revenue producing" information system, all resources were diverted from the implementation of the ERP.

Premiere decided to outsource the ERP applications. The ASP not only came in to help plan how to best make the ERP system successful, but it also bought and maintained the servers on which the ERP runs, installed and configured the ERP software, and staffed the help desk to make the deployment smooth. When Premiere acquires a new company, something they do regularly, the ASP takes care of incorporating the new acquisition into the ERP. By one estimate, Premiere saved about $3 million over five years by using the ASP instead of doing it themselves.[48]

    a. Discuss the advantages an ASP offers Premiere Technologies, Inc.

    b. What possible risks are associated with Premiere's use of an ASP?

    c. What would determine which application(s) to give to an ASP versus the ones to keep in house?

    d. Premiere Technologies was seven years old when it turned to using ASPs. When would it make sense to use an ASP for start-up companies?

4. When does using crowdsourcing make sense for a large corporation that already has an IS organization? Give an example of when crowdsourcing might make sense for a start-up company?

CASE STUDY 7-1

SODEXHO ASIA PACIFIC

Sodexho Asia Pacific, a major subsidiary of one of the world's largest food and support services, Sodexho Alliance, provides a wide range of catering, food and management services, and facilities management. Sodexho Asia Pacific employs 20,000 employees in nine countries. It has used a decentralized business model, which gave its managers considerable autonomy to adapt their operations to meet local customer needs. However, the autonomy came with a price, and Sodexho Asia Pacific found that over time information silos were created that made it difficult to communicate across national boundaries. Its processes were

[48] Adapted from Cynthia Morgan, "ASPs Speak the Corporate Language," *Computerworld* (October 25, 1999), 74–77.

adapted to accommodate the information systems and back-office processes of the many different service providers in each country. Further adaptation was required following a series of mergers and acquisitions in the early 2000's. When Sodexho absorbed these many organizations, it had to design additional systems and middleware to integrate each legacy system with the others.

As a result of the decentralization, mergers, and acquisitions, Sodexho Asia Pacific's processes were extremely complex, its information systems were fragmented, and communication across systems was difficult. Even though Sodexho Asia Pacific was very large, it could not leverage the company's overall purchasing power. Nor could its managers respond quickly enough to take advantage of opportunities or make timely decisions. In an industry challenged by its low profit margins, expenditures ballooned as a result of processing inefficiencies and multiple procurement systems. The company knew it needed to take dramatic action. It determined an organizationwide integrated system was required to improve information sharing and leverage its purchasing power.

"We have about 250 contracts with customers in Australia alone," noted Sodexho Asia Pacific's Director of Finance and IS Garen Azoyan in 2004. "We needed to get more information out of our SAP system about the profitability of each contract, and about how well we are meeting the needs of our customers."

In 2004 Sodexho Asia Pacific awarded IBM Global Business Services in Australia a two-phase, multi-million-dollar, five-year outsourcing contract. The first phase provided application system support for remodeling and integrating accounting and financial processes into an existing Australian SAP system. It was developed and delivered using offshore resources in India working in concert with the Sodexho Asia Pacific personnel. The revamped SAP system replaced six different systems in 17 of Sodexho's companies in six Asia Pacific countries. The adoption of the revamped system meant Sodexho Asia Pacific could centralize all its finance efforts. This allows better organization and retrieval of the available information and the management of the finance operations from a single site in Sydney, Australia.

Azoyan explained the reasons for the outsourcing arrangement: "Sodexho has invested in IBM's consulting and e-business hosting expertise to improve the efficiency of its operations and to maximize its bottom line. We will realize significant financial benefits as well as utilizing better finance and accounting processes. This will improve our ability to respond quickly to changing business conditions, to focus on our clients needs, and to continue improving the quality of daily life of our customers."

In the second phase of the agreement IBM migrated Sodexho Asia Pacific's SAP infrastructure to an e-business hosting environment that is managed and supported by IBM Global Services. The expanded system was transitioned to IBM's eServer pSeries servers. IBM's hosted solution is on a pay-per-user basis that is consistent with Sodexho's contract-based model. That is, it allows Sodexho Asia Pacific to shift its fixed IT costs to variable costs, just as Sodexho tends to do with its customers.

Because it is now able to leverage its buying power, Sodexho realized a 3 percent increase in profits within two years. It has also reduced its infrastructure costs by 25 percent, increased its operational efficiency, and improved organizational decision making. Since undertaking the project Sodexho has reported improvements in the speed of financial and accounting performance. With less focus required on these processes, the company is better able to address the needs of its consumers by shifting their efforts to areas of competencies of its core business skills, enhancing client services, and executing better cost management.

Outsourcing has traditionally been associated with the loss of jobs at the source company; however, in the case of Sodexho, not a single job has been lost due to the outsourcing to IBM. The people that were working in the company's finance section have shifted into analytical roles, allowing better business decisions rather than solely processing, as had been the case prior to the outsourcing exercise.

For all the successes that have been realized by Sodexho's outsourcing, the implementation has not been without hiccups. Outsourcing presents a large cultural change for any organization; getting the support from employees is paramount for the implementation's success. It was found that the most effective way to gain the support of the employees was to involve them throughout the process. Even now, after the implementation is complete, the company holds two meetings a week to ensure support and maintenance is of the highest quality.

Discussion Questions

1. How were jobs actually saved by Sodexho's decision to outsource?
2. What are the important factors to consider when deciding whether to outsource a particular part of a business?
3. Describe five advantages that are commonly attributed to outsourcing. Demonstrate how the Sodexho Asia Pacific case illustrates (or does not illustrate) each of these advantages.
4. Sodexho used offshore resources in India working in concert with the Sodexho Asia Pacific personnel. Why do you think Sodexho decided to offshore to an Indian provider? What do you anticipate were some of the challenges experienced in offshoring to an Indian provider?
5. What steps did Sodexho take to make the outsourcing arrangement a success?

Source: Excerpted from minicase by Chad Elliott and "Sodexho Asia Pacific." *IBM Global Financing*, (October 16, 2007), http://www-01.ibm.com/software/success/cssdb.nsf/cs/BTHD-778TLM? OpenDocument&Site=igf&cty=en_us; Sodexho Selects IBM for business process and application support work, http://www.physorg.com/news839.html, (August 16, 2004); and Sodexho Asia Pacific, http://www.qubix-au.com/Qubix%20Case%20Studies%20-%20Sodexho.pdf.

CASE STUDY 7-2

OVERSEAS OUTSOURCING OF MEDICAL TRANSCRIBING

The following is a discussion between Chris Boss, CEO of Good Hospital and M.D. Noitall, the Medical Director at the same hospital in Brisbane, Australia. Chris met M.D. in the hallway early one Monday morning.

CHRIS: Good morning, M.D. I read a report in the *Financial Times* this morning that many hospitals and doctors are now sending medical files overseas to be typed up. The article says that it is cheaper. But I see a number of problems. I am especially concerned about privacy issues. How can medical histories remain confidential if they are being sent halfway around the globe? And what about the language barrier? Can we guarantee that exact detail is being translated by people who do not normally speak English? Have you heard of this?

M.D.:   Good morning, Chris. Yes, I've heard of this. I mean, we know that many things are now done in a global network. So whether it is reading the X-ray reports or recording bank transactions or transcribing medical transactions, it is certainly going on.

CHRIS: How many hospitals are sending records overseas to be typed up?

M.D.:   Well, I really don't know the numbers. I would imagine that it is a pretty large number of hospitals. And the reason for that is, they are trying to downsize the medical administration within the hospitals.

CHRIS: But if we were to do this, how could we be absolutely sure that what one of our doctors says in a report is actually being translated correctly?

M.D.:   Well I mean, the same errors in transcription would occur whether the transcriber sits here or sits in India or sits . . .

CHRIS: No. This is going overseas to Malaysia. Surely the risks are increased unbelievably.

M.D.:   Well, the risks will be based on the quality of the recording, the quality of the decoding at the other end, and the person at the other end who is doing the transcribing. But that comes back to basics. If you're sending work out, you've got to be assured wherever you're sending it to be transcribed, that it is a secure environment and that confidentiality is maintained. And when it comes back to you, you have got to check it. And, of course, we've got to have a secure environment on our end.

I do not think that will have the whole three inches of somebody's medical file going to and fro on the Internet. We'll only have recordings of a conversation, which needs to be transcribed as a letter or recordings of findings. Nonetheless, it has got to be confidential. We would have to make sure that confidentiality is maintained throughout this whole process.

CHRIS: You don't have a problem with this, then?

M.D.:   I have a problem if it is not done in a confidential way designed to maintain patients' privacy or if the transcribing is not checked. We also need to make sure that the IT environment that we have actually allows us to share that information and send the reports securely over the Internet.

CHRIS: How much cheaper is it?

M.D.:   The cost of doing this electronically, compared to having somebody here, would obviously vary on the size of the job. But obviously, there are cost savings; otherwise it wouldn't be done. And I suppose there may be some efficiencies in time. Because if you finish your work at 6 p.m. here, you can send it to somewhere else in the world where it is several hours earlier. Then when you go back to work the next morning, it is done! And besides, it is hard to find people in Brisbane who even want to do medical transcribing.

CHRIS: So, do you think we should look into medical transcribing here at Good Hospital?

Discussion Questions

1. Are Chris and M.D. talking about outsourcing? Is it an example of offshoring? Is it an example of nearshoring? Explain.
2. What challenges do you see in sending the medical transcription work to Malaysia? What would you do to reduce those challenges?
3. How would you respond to Chris's question?

Source: Based heavily on "Overseas Outsourcing of Medical Transcribing—2GB," interview by Luke Bona reporting the conversation between Bona and Dr. Haikerwal, *AMA Media Transcript*, (April 19, 2007) http://www.ama.com.au/web.nsf/doc/WEEN-72E7QP (accessed July 25, 2008).

CHAPTER 8

GOVERNANCE OF THE INFORMATION SYSTEMS ORGANIZATION[1]

When 3M's CEO James McNerney came on board, he handed the chief information officer (CIO) David Drew a big surprise. Prior to McNerney's arrival, the Information Systems Steering Committee (ISSC) had met six times a year to provide direction for the information technology (IT) group, endorse IT projects of more that $1million, and prioritize IT resources. The board included 3M's heavy hitters, including all six business division chiefs, top functional leaders, and the CIO. But to Drew's chagrin, the CEO broke up the group. A disappointed Drew stated, "The corporate IT prioritization process was moved back to IT, and I would really rather have it at the highest business level."[2]

Now 3M's IT governance structure starts at the business process level. Its six divisions each must document the productivity of their IT projects. Business unit leaders select and champion their IT projects, while IT plays a supporting role. Each project is reviewed to make sure that it is in line with the division's quarterly cost-reduction dollar target. If it isn't, the business unit leadership is accountable to the top executives. Thus, the business units are motivated to devote the resources necessary to help the IT staff successfully complete the IT projects. Of course, Drew is also accountable for making sure that his staff are well managed and have the resources that they need. Projects that could conceivably benefit more than one business unit get elevated to corporate-level sponsorship.[3]

Drew decided, "You can't solve everything with committees. . . . You have to figure out the most practical way to interrelate with senior management on

---

[1] The authors wish to acknowledge and thank David M. Zahn, MBA 1999, for his help in researching and writing early drafts of this chapter.

[2] Christopher Koch, "IT Governance Strategies from State Street, 3M and Others," *CIO*, (September 15, 2002), www.cio.com/article/print/31330.

[3] Understanding IT Governance, *Public CIO Magazine*, (May 2005), http://209.85.215.104/search?q= cache:Z1CM3KbCY44J:tgb.iowa.gov/images/pdf/Understanding%2520IT%2520Governance%2520 Article.doc+IT+governance+3m&hl=en&ct=clnk&cd=2&gl=us (accessed July 23, 2008).

IT issues and be prepared to change the way you do it. There's no standard model for that."[4]

The CIO at 3M recognizes that it is important to get the buy-in of business leaders for information systems (IS) projects. The higher the level of support, the better it is for the IS projects. That is why the CIO was disappointed when the high-level ISSC was disbanded. In its place, however, is a governance structure to help both his IS organization and the business units work toward achieving corporate goals. Although each IS organization is unique in many ways, all have elements in common. The focus of this chapter is to introduce managers to the typical activities of an IS organization to facilitate interaction with management information systems (MIS) professionals. Managers will be more effective consumers of services from MIS professionals in their organization if they understand, in general, what these professionals do. This chapter examines the roles, tasks and governance of the IS organization.

▶ UNDERSTANDING THE IS ORGANIZATION

Consider an analogy of a ship to help explain the purpose of an IS organization and how it functions. A ship transports people and cargo to a particular destination in much the same way that an IS organization directs itself toward the strategic goals set by the larger enterprise. Sometimes the IS organization must navigate perilous waters or storms to reach port. For both the IS organization and the ship, the key is to perform more capably than any competitors. It means using the right resources to propel the enterprise through the rough waters of business. Each of these resources is discussed in the following sections.

Chief Information Officer

If an IS organization is like a ship, then the **chief information officer (CIO)** is at the helm. The CIO is an executive who manages IT resources to implement enterprise strategy. The Gartner Group defines a CIO as one who "provides technology vision and leadership for developing and implementing IT initiatives that create and maintain leadership for the enterprise in a constantly changing and intensely competitive marketplace."[5] We would add that the CIO's role is also to provide expertise in the strategy formulation processes along with the executive team.

This definition may seem clear, but to understand what the CIO does, we should explore the historical origins of this position. The CIO function is a relatively new position when compared to the more established chief executive officer (CEO) or chief financial officer (CFO), which have existed in the corporate structure for decades. In fact, the CIO position did not really emerge until the early 1980s, when top management perceived a need for an executive-level manager to focus

---

[4] Koch, "IT Governance Strategies."

[5] Available at http://www.cio.com/forums/executive/gartner_description.html.

on cutting the ever-increasing costs of IT. Cost-cutting measures typically took the form of outsourcing arrangements, which are addressed later in this chapter and in Chapter 7.

The evolution of the CIO's role closely follows the evolution of technology in business. Throughout the late 1980s and into the 1990s, technology grew from an expensive necessity to a strategic enabler. As technology's role increased in importance, so did that of the CIO. As the Internet became a core component in the business environment, the CIO's role became a critical component of the strategy formulation process. In fact, many organizations include the CIO as an integral member of the executive-level decision-making team.

CIOs are a unique breed. They have a strong understanding of the business and of the technology. In many organizations they take on roles that span both of these areas. More often than not, CIOs are asked to play strategic roles at some part of their day and operations roles at other times, rather than spending all their time on one or the other. It appears that the scope and depth of the CIO are expanding. Now, 12 main responsibilities often define the CIO role:

1. *Championing the organization.* Promoting IT within the enterprise as a strategic tool for growth and innovation

2. *Architecture management.* Setting organizational direction and priorities

3. *Business strategy consultant.* Participating in executive-level decision making

4. *Business technology planning.* Bridging business and technology groups for purposes of collaborating in planning and execution

5. *Applications development.* Overseeing legacy and emerging enterprise initiatives, as well as broader strategic business unit (SBU) and divisional initiatives

6. *IT infrastructure management (e.g., computers, printers, and networks).* Maintaining current technologies and investing in future technologies

7. *Sourcing.* Developing and implementing a strategy for outsourcing (versus retaining in-house) IT services and/or people

8. *Partnership developer.* Negotiating relationships with key suppliers of IT expertise and services and making sure everyone is working toward mutual goals

9. *Technology transfer agent.* Providing technologies that enable the enterprise to work better with suppliers and customers—both internal and external—and consequently, increase shareholder value

10. *Customer satisfaction management.* Understanding and communicating with both internal and external customers to ensure that customer satisfaction goals are met

11. *Training.* Providing training to IT users, as well as senior executives who must understand how IT fits with enterprise strategy

12. *Business discontinuity/disaster recovery planning.* Planning and implementing strategies to limit the impact of natural and human-made disasters on information technology and, consequently, the conduct of business

CIOs must work effectively not only within the technical arena, but also in overall business management. This means that they need the technical ability to conceive, build, and implement multiple IT projects on time and within budget. Their technical skills must be balanced against business skills such as the ability to realize the benefits and manage the costs and risks associated with IT, to articulate and advocate for a management vision of IT, and to mesh well with the existing management structure. Further, CIOs must have both the technical and business skills to bridge the technology and business gaps between available technologies and business needs, including nontechnical internal clients. They must see the business vision and understand how the IT function can contribute to realizing this vision.

Where the CIO fits within an enterprise is often a source of controversy. In the early days of the CIO position, when the CIO was predominantly responsible for controlling costs, the CIO reported to the chief financial officer (CFO). Because the CIO was rarely involved in enterprise governance, this reporting structure worked. However, as IT burgeoned into a source for competitive advantage in the marketplace, reporting to the CFO proved too limiting. Conflicts arose because the CFO misunderstood the vision for IT or saw only the costs of technology, or because management still saw the CIO's primary responsibility as controlling costs. More recently, CIOs report directly to the CEO, president, or other executive manager.

Confusion often occurs regarding whether the CIO is more of a strategist or an operational manager. He or she is often asked to be both. Because the CIO is the top IS professional in the hierarchy, it is imperative that this person also be a strategist. The title CIO signals to both the organization and to outside observers that this executive is a strategic IS thinker and is responsible for linking IS strategy with the business strategy. With the increasing importance of the Internet to every business, the CIO is increasingly asked to assist, advise, and participate in discussions in which business strategy is set. However, just as the CFO is somewhat involved in operational management of the financial activities of the organization, the CIO is involved with operational issues related to IS. These include activities such as identifying and managing the introduction of new technologies into the firm, setting purchasing and vendor policies, and managing the overall IT budget. Actual day-to-day management of the data center, the vendor portfolio, and other operational issues is typically not handled directly by the CIO, but by one of the managers in the IS organization.

What, then, does a CIO do? Although there is no such thing as an average day in the life of a CIO, the following examples give a picture of how varied the role is across organizations. Several years ago, the longtime CIO for Northrop Gumman Corp., Tom Shelman, was asked to transform the role so that it would be more "strategic" and "transformational." The result was Shelman overseeing a project that subsequently led to a $500 municipal contract. The implementation of a wireless network at one of Northrop's shipyards in Pascagoula, Mississippi, was a stepping-stone to a contract for a citywide wireless network for a number of New York City's departments. H–P's CIO Randy Mott now spends less time on tech support and more on meeting with customers to describe to them how to use the company's products in a major way. Louie Ehrlich, the CIO of one of Chevron Corp.'s business units, used to spend much of his time integrating the company's far-flung IT operations. Now that he has been given the additional title of vice president of strategy and services, he only spends about 10% of his time supervising IT. "The CIO title is misused," he claims adding if the CIO only oversees IT, "they should be named a tech manager. A CIO should be enabling a business to grow."[6]

Some organizations choose not to have a CIO. These organizations do not believe that the CIO should have decision-making authority to lead strategic IT initiatives. Rather, they typically hire an individual to be responsible for running the computer systems and possibly to manage many of the activities described later in this chapter. But they signal that this person is not a strategist by giving them the title of data processing manager or director of information systems or some other reference that clearly differentiates this person from other top officers in the company. Using the words *chief* and *officer* usually implies a strategic focus, and some organizations do not see the value of having an IS person on their executive team.

Chief Technology Officer, Chief Privacy Officer, and Other Similar Roles

Although the CIO's role is to guide the enterprise toward the future, this responsibility is frequently too great to accomplish alone. Many organizations recognize that certain strategic areas of the IS organization require more focused guidance. This recognition led to the creation of new positions, such as the chief knowledge officer (CKO), chief technology officer (CTO), chief telecommunications officer (also CTO), chief network officer (CNO), chief information security officer (CISO), chief privacy officer (CPO), and chief resource officer (CRO). See Figure 8.1 for a list of their different responsibilities. Each of these positions typically subordinates to the CIO, with the occasional exception of the chief technology officer. Together, they form a management team that leads the IT organization.

The **chief technology officer (CTO)** is an especially critical role. The CTO, or the enterprise's top technology architect, often works alongside the CIO. The CTO must have enough business savvy and communication skills to create an organizational vision for new technologies, as well as to oversee and manage the firm's technological operations and infrastructure. The new position is often created because one person isn't qualified to fill the broadly defined CIO role.

---

[6] Pui-Wing Tam "CIO Jobs Morph from Tech Support into Strategy," *Wall Street Journal*, (March 22, 2007), http://online.wsj.com/public/article/SB117193647410313201-fqJsAOxwVGloj_OngdVIS_bjVI_20070322.html?mod=tff_article.

Title	Responsibility
Chief technology officer (CTO)	Track emerging technologies Advise on technology adoption Design and manage IT architecture to ensure consistency and compliance
Chief knowledge officer (CKO)	Create knowledge management infra-structure Build a knowledge culture Make corporate knowledge pay off
Chief telecommunications officer (CTO)	Manage phones, networks, and other communications technology across entire enterprise
Chief network officer (CNO)	Build and maintain internal and external networks
Chief resource officer (CRO)	Manage outsourcing relationships
Chief information security officer (CISO)	Ensure information management practices are consistent with security requirements
Chief privacy officer (CPO)	Responsible for processes and practices that ensure privacy concerns of customers, employees, and vendors are met

FIGURE 8.1 The CIO's lieutenants.

New "chief" roles spring up almost daily as enterprises try to share the complex and growing responsibilities of managing IT. Giving someone the title of "chief" is one way to signal that this individual is ultimately responsible for decisions in their area, even though he or she does not report directly to the CEO of the enterprise. This individual is recognized as the most senior person in the organization charged with responsibility for that functional area. For example, Earthlink, one of the largest U.S. information service providers (ISPs), created the office of chief privacy officer (CPO) to interface with the FBI and privacy advocates about the mandated use of Carnivore, a controversial e-mail surveillance tool. The CPOs at AllAdvantage.com, AT&T, and Excite@home represent customers' privacy interests in negotiations with business developers, top management, and technology executives.[7] Other firms eliminated the CIO altogether in favor of some configuration of the typically subordinate positions. These enterprises hope that flatter organizations will prove more effective.

---

[7] Steve Ulfleder, "OhNo, Not Another O," *CIO Magazine* (January 15, 2001), http://www.cio.com/archive/011501/ohno_content.html (accessed June 21, 2002).

Many large corporations take the concept of CIO one step further and identify a business unit CIO. This is someone who has similar responsibilities to a corporate CIO, but the scope is the business unit. Typically the business unit CIO has dual reporting responsibility to both the corporate CIO and the president of the business unit. General Motors established divisional CIO positions that report to the corporate CIO.[8]

► WHAT A MANAGER CAN EXPECT FROM THE IS ORGANIZATION

This chapter explores the roles and processes performed by a typical IS organization (i.e., IS department). We now turn to the customer of the IS organization, the general manager or "user" of the systems. What can a manager expect from the IS organization?

Managers must learn what to expect from the IS organization so they can plan and implement business strategy accordingly. A manager typically can expect 13 core activities: (1) anticipating new technologies, (2) participating in setting and implementing strategic goals, (3) innovating current processes, (4) developing and maintaining information systems, (5) managing supplier relationships, (6) establishing architecture platforms and standards, (7) promoting enterprise security, (8) planning for business discontinuities, (9) managing data, information, and knowledge, (10) managing Internet and network services, (11) managing human resources, (12) operating the data center, and (13) providing general support.[9]

Anticipating New Technologies

Given the breakneck speeds at which technology moves, the IS organization must keep an eye toward the horizon in order for an enterprise to leverage state-of-the art tools. The chief technology officer (CTO) or IS staff members in a new technology group assess the costs and benefits of new technologies for the enterprise. The CTO or new technology group works closely with business groups to determine which technologies can provide the greatest benefit, how the technologies might affect the organization, and when they should be implemented. They are the watchdogs who ensure that the enterprise does not invest heavily in new technologies that quickly become obsolete or incompatible with other enterprise standards. To correctly assess the enterprise's needs, business and IS staff must work closely to evaluate which technologies can best advance the business strategy and capitalize on new cost savings or sources of revenue. It is the job of the IS organization to scout new technology trends and help the business integrate them into planning and operations.

---

[8] Lauren Gibbons Paul, "A Separate Piece," *CIO Magazine* (October 15, 1998).

[9] Eight activities are described by John F. Rockart, Michael J. Earl, and Jeanne W. Ross, "Eight Imperatives for the New IT Organization," *Sloan Management Review* (Fall 1996), 52–53. Five activities have been added to their eight imperatives.

Participating in Setting Strategic Direction

Ideally, IS staff enable business managers to achieve strategic goals by acting as consultants or by teaching them about developing technologies. As consultants, IS staff can advise managers on best practices within IT and work with them to develop IT-enhanced solutions to business problems. IS personnel also educate managers about current technologies as well as IT trends. Sharing business and technical knowledge between groups encourages better, more informed decisions across the enterprise. No longer anonymous techies, IS staff are partners in moving the enterprise forward. They must initiate, foster, and grow strong partnerships with their business colleagues. For instance, over 2,000 UPS technicians are now commissioned to provide on-site support at Mail Boxes, Etc (a 2001 UPS acquisition) in the United States.[10] This tighter relationship improves integration between systems and business and helps in using IT to meet the customers' needs.

Innovating Current Processes

IS staff, especially IS managers, business analysts, and developers, work with managers to innovate processes that can benefit from technological solutions. Such solutions can range from installing voice mail to networking personal computers or automating general ledger transactions. Over the last decade such solutions include ERP implementations (see Chapter 5 for more discussion about ERPs). Business process reviews usually begin with a survey of best practices. Information technology becomes an integral component of new processes designed for the enterprise. Thus, IS personnel can play a crucial role by designing systems that facilitate these new ways of doing business.

When systems are incorrectly designed, or when IS processes do not function correctly, the IS organization can become a "disabler" of innovation. In some cases, the lack of flexibility in existing systems, and the reluctance to discard technology before the investment return is realized, block business managers from implementing decisions they would otherwise choose to make.

Developing and Maintaining Systems

The primary processes performed by most IS organizations are that of building systems or buying software packages to meet business needs. Systems development itself is discussed in more detail in Chapter 11, the chapter on project management. In this core IS organization activity, business analysts and systems developers work together in analyzing needs, designing the software, writing or coding the software, and testing to make sure the software works and meets the business objectives. Other systems development activities identify, acquire, and install outside software packages to fill a need for individuals in the organizations. As more companies move to software-as-a-service (see Chapter 6 for more on SaaS), developing systems is

---

[10] "UPS Governance: The Key to Aligning Technology Initiatives with Business Direction," http://www.pressroom.ups.com/mediakits/factsheet/0,2305,1043,00.html (accessed July 23, 2008).

done by using Web services and tinkering together services available on the Internet. Once systems are implemented or installed, many people work toward their continued maintenance. For instance, once a general ledger system is installed, support personnel or DBAs monitor the daily processing of transactions and reports. Developers and business personnel address postimplementation needs, such as writing additional reports, correcting system errors, or enhancing the system to respond to changing business environments and governmental regulations.

Managing Supplier Relationships

As more companies adopt outsourcing as a means of controlling IT costs and acquiring "best-of-breed" capabilities, managing these supplier relationships becomes increasingly important. IS must maximize the benefit of these relationships to the enterprise and preempt problems that might occur. Failure in this regard could result in deteriorating quality of service, loss of competitive advantage, costly contract disputes, low morale, and loss of key personnel. Managing the sourcing relationships is so important that we have devoted Chapter 7 to issues related to sourcing.

Establishing Architecture Platforms and Standards

Given the complex nature of IT in the enterprise, the role of the IS organization in developing, maintaining, and communicating standards is critical. Failure could mean increased maintenance costs due to incompatibilities between platforms, redundant or incorrect data, and slow processing. For example, precise naming standards are crucial in implementing a new data warehouse or accounts payable system. Even small variations in invoice entries—the difference between showing a payment to "IBM," "I.B.M.," or "International Business Machines"—could yield incomplete information when business managers query the data warehouse to understand how much was paid to the vendor in a given period. Inconsistent data undermines the integrity of a data warehouse.

Promoting Enterprise Security

Information security is generally seen as very technical and only dealing with the internal operations of the IS organization. However, this process is actually one of importance to all general managers because it involves maintaining the integrity of the organizational infrastructure. IS security is much more than a technical problem. Rather, it is a social and organizational problem because the technical systems are operated and used by people. In Chapter 9 we discuss the governance that must be put in place to ensure that a structure for dealing with technical, social, and organizational problems is in place.

Because general managers typically look to the IS organization to handle security, the IS organization identifies and prioritizes threats to the company's information assets. It develops and implements security policies and technical controls to address each threat. Because many security breaches are the result of human negligence enabled by weak operational practices, the IS organization works with the business units to make their operational practices more secure and to train employees about security risks and the importance of security to their work. The IS organization typically is also responsible for implementing an awareness program that keeps security on employees' minds as they deal with information on a daily basis.

Planning for Business Continuity

Hurricane Katrina in 2005 and the events of September 11, 2001, presented disaster impacts that few organizations ever face. *Disaster* is broadly defined here as a sudden, unplanned calamitous event that makes it difficult for the firm to provide critical business functions for some period of time and results in great damage or loss. To counter terrorist attacks, hurricanes, tornadoes, floods, or countless other disasters, firms are realizing more than ever the importance of business continuity planning (BCP). In the face of such man-made and natural disasters, businesses not only must recover, but they must also survive. The chances of surviving can be improved with BCP. Further, BCP allows a company to respond to events that may hurt its business without the company directly experiencing a disaster. For example, the BCP should outline how the company would bill its customers if the U.S. Postal Service were to be shut down, or how the company would respond in a situation where its primary and redundant Internet backbone cables were simultaneously cut because they run together over the same interstate overpass.

A **business continuity plan (BCP)** is an approved set of preparations and sufficient procedures for responding to a variety of disaster events. It requires careful and thoughtful preparation. The Disaster Recovery Institute International (DRII) defines three major stages of BCP: preplanning, planning, and postplanning.[11] In the *preplanning stage*, management's responsibility is defined, possible risks are evaluated, and a business impact analysis is performed. In the *planning stage*, alternative business recovery operating strategies are determined. Business recovery operating strategies deal with how to recover business and IT within the recovery time objective while still maintaining the company's critical functions. The IS organization must be involved in preparing off-site storage and alternate recovery sites or in selecting business continuity vendors. An important part of the BCP planning stage is to develop emergency response procedures designed to prevent or limit injury to personnel on site, damage to structures and equipment, and the degradation of vital business functions. These procedures must be kept up-to-date. The final activity in the planning stage is to implement the plan by publishing it and gaining top-management approval for the plan. The *postplanning stage* of BCP familiarizes employees with the plan through awareness and training programs. Regular exercises to test and evaluate the plan should be conducted.

---

[11] "Business Continuity Planning Review," DRI International Professional Development Program DRP 501.

Companies are increasingly using the virtual world, Second Life, to conduct simulations, often under the aegis of the IS organization. With the simulations, the companies can quickly assess the plan, make any adjustments needed, and perform a second simulation with almost no additional costs. Also in this third stage, the BCP should be discussed with public authorities, and public relations and crisis communications should be mapped out.

BCP is designed to respond to threats. In preparing a BCP, it is important to remember that the biggest threat may come not from terrorist attacks or natural disasters, but from disgruntled or dishonest employees. Companies need to screen their employees carefully, create a culture of loyalty to inhibit the internal threats, and develop systems that help promote security.

The tremendous loss of human capital in the collapse of the World Trade Center in New York City on 9/11 highlighted the problem of keeping all of a company's talent in one location. Decentralizing operations, flextime, and telecommuting are ways of dispersing a company's human assets. Similarly, critical technology systems, proprietary computer codes, and other core business assets may need to be distributed. Because the information resources are so integral to business operations, the IS organization is typically in charge of planning for possible scenarios leading to business discontinuity and taking steps to avoid them or alleviate their impact. Clearly firms do not have enough resources to develop a response for every conceivable risky scenario. Thus, each firm needs to determine which detrimental scenarios are likely to occur and/or which are more like to have the greatest impact. These are the risky scenarios that the firm has to devote the most attention to avoiding or mitigating.

Managing Data, Information, and Knowledge

Managing information and knowledge in the enterprise is of particular concern to the IS organization. This text devotes an entire chapter to knowledge management (Chapter 12). Then again, the management of the data itself, or database administration, is an activity that requires the unique expertise of the IS organization. Database administration includes the activities of collecting and storing the actual data created, developed, or discovered by the enterprise. For example, deciding on the format, location, and indexing of stored data are database administration tasks.

Managing Internet and Network Services

Such technologies as intranets, extranets, Web pages, and e-mail are becoming essential in most business environments. General managers must interact with the Web master, Web designers, and Web developers who develop and maintain Internet capabilities. Further, the IS organization typically includes a network group that manages private networks. For example, when problems connecting to the local area network (LAN) arise or when a new user needs to set up new PCs for a department, the networking group eventually processes the request. Networking groups design network architecture. They also build and maintain the network infrastructure. Certain networking systems, along with telephone systems, access to the Internet, and new wireless technologies fall under the rubric of telecommunications. General managers should concern themselves with telecommunications because the quality of service provided affects the daily operations of the business. Moreover, telecommunications costs are typically charged back to the business area cost center.

Managing Human Resources

The IS organization must manage its own resources. Doing so means providing sufficient business and technical training so that staff can perform effectively and retain their value to the enterprise. Additional human resource activities include hiring and firing; training; tracking time; and managing budgets, operations, and projects. These activities often affect one another. For example, some companies seek to fill positions that require "hot" skills, or technology skills that are in high demand, by hiring IS staff who have acquired and used the needed skills at other organizations. Other companies turn to offshoring for immediate fulfillment of hot skills needs. Still other companies adopt a policy of growing their own. They attempt to hire and retain their employees for the employees' entire work careers. To make sure that these employees have hot skills when needed, they maintain a skills inventory and train employees according to a plan that reflects anticipated technical needs. Because most IS organizations lack their own human resource (HR) departments, individual managers bear these responsibilities. It is often wise for them to work with company HR personnel, who may be familiar with interviewing approaches, personnel laws, regulations, and trends. For example, HR personnel may be aware of professional issues related to the retirement of baby boomers that IS managers may not tend to consider.

Operating Data Center

The data center typically houses large mainframe computers or rows of servers on which the company's data and business applications reside. General managers rarely have direct contact with data center personnel unless they experience processing problems. Even then, they may only communicate electronically with data center staff to get their problems solved. Many organizations outsource data center operations. Chapter 6 discusses this approach in the discussion on cloud computing.

Providing General Support

Processes in place to support day-to-day business operations vary, depending on the size of the enterprise and the levels of support required. Typically, support requests are centralized so they can be tracked for quality control purposes and handled more efficiently. Often IS organizations maintain the first client contact through a centralized help desk even for such diverse services as networking and telecommunications. The help desk serves as the primary, easily identifiable point of contact for technical questions and problem reporting.

Help desks are not usually manned by people who solve the problem. Help desk personnel collect pertinent information, record it, determine its priority, contact the appropriate support personnel, and follow up with the business contacts with updates or resolution information. For help beyond daily support, most organizations also maintain a customer service request (CSR) process. A paper or electronic form is used to allow a businessperson to describe the nature of the request, its priority, the contact point, and the appropriate cost center. CSRs initiate much of the work in IS organizations.

The IS organization can be expected to be responsible for most, if not all, of the activities just described. However, instead of actually performing the activities, increasingly the IS organization supervises the outsourcing vendors who do execute them. More traditional activities such as data center operations and system development and maintenance (including application design, development, and maintenance) have been performed by vendors for decades. More recently, enterprises are turning to vendors—even offshore vendors—to perform more newly acquired IT activities such as process innovation (alternatively called business process outsourcing). Figure 8.2 provides a framework for traditional and newer IS activities that are considered the responsibility of the IS organization and suggests alternate ways of executing them.

▶ WHAT THE IS ORGANIZATION DOES NOT DO

This chapter presented typical roles and processes for IS organizations. Although most IS professionals are asked to perform a wide range of tasks for their organization, in reality the IS organization should not do a number of specific tasks. Clearly, the IS organization does not directly do other core business functions such

Traditional IT Activities (often supplied through alliances with vendors)	The New IT Activities (often supplied by MIS organization)	User's Activities (supplied by IS person on payroll in end user department)
• Data Center Management • Network Management • Application Design, Development and Maintenance • Desktop Hardware Procurement, Installation, and Maintenance	• Architecture, Standards and Technology Planning • IT Strategic Planning • Process Innovation • Supplier Management • Training and Internal Consulting • Business Continuity Planning • Security	• Technology scanning and development • Applications Strategy • Choose and maintain Desktop, Laptop, Personal Digital Assistant or other Personal Devices • Implementation

FIGURE 8.2 User management activities.
Source: Adapted from J. Ownes, "Transforming the Informations Systems Organization," CISR Endicott House XXIX presentation, December 2–3, 1993.

as selling, manufacturing, and accounting. Sometimes, however, managers of these functions inadvertently delegate key operational decisions to the IS organization. When general managers ask the IS professional to build an information system for their organization and do not become active partners in the design of that system, they are in effect turning over control of their business operations. Likewise, asking an IS professional to implement a software package without partnering with that professional to ensure the package not only meets current needs, but future needs as well, is ceding control. The IS organization does not design business processes.

As discussed in Chapter 2, when using IS for strategic advantage, the general manager, not the IS professional, sets business strategy. However, in many organizations, the general manager delegates critical technology decisions to the CIO, which in turn may limit the strategic options available to the firm. The role for the IS professional in the discussion of strategy centers on suggesting technologies and applications that enable strategy, identifying limits to the technologies and applications under consideration, and consulting with all those involved with setting strategic direction to make sure they properly consider the role and impact of IS on the decisions they make. The IS organization does not set business strategy.

▶ IT GOVERNANCE

Expectations (or more specifically, what managers should and should not expect from the IS organization) are at the heart of IT governance. **Governance** in the context of business enterprises is all about making "decisions that define expectations, grant power, or verify performance."[12] In other words, governance is about aligning behavior with business goals through empowerment and monitoring. Empowerment comes from granting the right to make decisions, and monitoring comes from evaluating performance. As noted in Chapter 3, a decision right is an important organizational design variable.

A traditional perspective of IT governance focuses on how decision rights can be distributed differently to facilitate centralized, decentralized, or hybrid modes of decision making. In this view of governance, the organization structure plays a major role.

Centralized versus Decentralized Organizational Structures

Organizational structures for IS evolved in a cyclic manner. At one end of the spectrum, **centralized IS organizations** bring together all staff, hardware, software, data, and processing into a single location. **Decentralized IS organizations** scatter these components in different locations to address local business needs. Companies' organizational strategies exist along a continuum from centralization to decentralization, with a combination of the two, called federalism, found in the middle (see Figure 8.3). Enterprises of all shapes and sizes can be found at any

---

[12] Wikipedia definition for governance: http://en.wikipedia.org/wiki/Governance.

FIGURE 8.3 Organizational continuum.

point along the continuum. Over time, however, each enterprise may gravitate toward one end of the continuum or the other, and often a reorganization is in reality a change from one end to the other.

To illustrate these tendencies, consider the different approaches taken to organize IS in the five eras of information usage. (See Figure 2.1.) In the 1960s, mainframes dictated a centralized approach to IS because the mainframe resided in one physical location. Centralized decision making, purchasing, maintenance, and staff kept these early computing behemoths running.[13] The 1970s remained centralized due in part to the constraints of mainframe computing, although the minicomputer began to create a rationale to decentralize. The 1980s saw the advent of the personal computer (PC). PCs allowed computing power to spread beyond the raised-floor, super-cooled rooms of mainframes. This phenomenon gave rise to decentralization, a trend that exploded with the advent of LANs and client/server technology. The Web, with its ubiquitous presence and fast network speeds, shifted some back to a more centralized approach. However, the increasingly global nature of many businesses makes complete centralization impossible. What are the most important considerations in deciding how much to centralize or decentralize? Figure 8.4 shows some of the advantages and disadvantages of each approach.

The centralized and decentralized approaches amalgamated in the 1990s. Companies began to adopt a strategy based on lessons learned from earlier years of centralization and decentralization. Most companies would like to achieve the advantages derived from both organizational paradigms. This desire leads to federalism.[14] **Federalism** is a structuring approach that distributes power, hardware, software, data, and personnel between a central IS group and IS in business units. Many companies adopt a form of federal IT, yet still count themselves as either decentralized or centralized, depending on their position on the continuum. For example, Inditex, a multinational clothing retailer and manufacturer, uses a centralized approach to IT. Zara, the company that we talked about in Chapters 2, 3 and 5, is the largest of Inditex's chain of stores. The head of IT, who is not a CIO, reports directly to the deputy general manager, who is two levels below the CEO.[15] This way of structuring the IT department is consistent

---

[13] Bill Laberis, "Recentralization: Breaking the News," *Computerworld* (June 29, 1998), p. 1.

[14] John F. Rockart, Michael J. Earl, and Jeanne W. Ross, "Eight Imperatives for the New IT Organization," *Sloan Management Review* (Fall 1996), 52–53.

[15] Andrew McAfee, Vincent Dessain, Anders Sjman, "Zara: IT for Fast Fashion," Harvard Business School Case 9-604-081, revised September 6, 2007.

Approach	Advantages	Disadvantages	Companies Adopting
Centralized	• Global standards and common data • "One voice" when negotiating supplier contracts • Greater leverage in deploying strategic IT initiatives • Economies of scale and a shared cost structure • Access to large capacity • Better recruitment and training of IT professionals • Consistent with centralized enterprise structure	• Technology may not meet local needs • Slow support for strategic initiatives • Schism between business and IT organization • Us versus them mentality when technology problems occur • Lack of business unit control over overhead costs	Inditex
Decentralized	• Technology customized to local business needs • Closer partnership between IT and business units • Greater flexibility • Reduced tele-communication costs • Consistency with decentralized enterprise structure • Business unit control over overhead costs	• Difficulty maintaining global standards and consistent data • Higher infrastructure costs • Difficulty negotiating preferential supplier agreements • Loss of control • Duplication of staff and data	VeriFone

FIGURE 8.4 Advantages and disadvantages of organizational approaches.

with the organization's predominately centralized structure. It is also well suited to organizational processing where most administrative decisions are made in the headquarters at LaCoruña, Spain. The users do not require a lot of hand-holding with regard to the rather primitive POS systems in the stores. For these reasons, a centralized approach seems to be a good fit for Inditex. The store managers, however, do retain decision rights about which products to send to the stores. Thus, Inditext is not totally at the end of the centralization continuum. Other companies, such as Home Depot, recognize the advantages of a more hybrid approach and

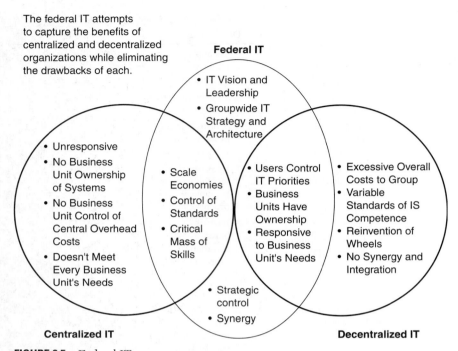

The federal IT attempts to capture the benefits of centralized and decentralized organizations while eliminating the drawbacks of each.

Federal IT

- IT Vision and Leadership
- Groupwide IT Strategy and Architecture

- Unresponsive
- No Business Unit Ownership of Systems
- No Business Unit Control of Central Overhead Costs
- Doesn't Meet Every Business Unit's Needs

- Scale Economies
- Control of Standards
- Critical Mass of Skills

- Users Control IT Priorities
- Business Units Have Ownership
- Responsive to Business Unit's Needs

- Excessive Overall Costs to Group
- Variable Standards of IS Competence
- Reinvention of Wheels
- No Synergy and Integration

- Strategic control
- Synergy

Centralized IT   **Decentralized IT**

FIGURE 8.5   Federal IT.
Source: John F. Rockart, Michael J. Earl, and Jeanne W. Ross, "Eight Imperatives for the New IT Organization," *Sloan Management Review* (Fall 1996) 52–53.

actively seek to benefit from adopting a federal structure. Figure 8.5 shows how these approaches interrelate.

Another Perspective on IT Governance

Sometimes the centralized/decentralized/federal approaches to governance are not fine-tuned enough to help managers deal with the many contingencies facing today's organizations. Thus we turn to a framework developed by Peter Weill and his colleagues.[16] They define **IT governance** as "specifying the decision rights and accountability framework to encourage desirable behavior in using IT." IT governance is not about what decisions are actually made but rather about who is making the decisions (i.e., who holds the decision rights) and how the decision makers are held accountable for them. That is, good IT governance provides a structure to make good decisions. IT governance has two major components:

---

[16] Peter Weill and Jeanne W. Ross, *IT Governance: How Top Performers Manage IT Decision Rights for Superior Results* (Cambridge, MA: Harvard Business School Press, 2004). Also, Peter Weill, "Don't Just Lead, Govern: How Top-Performing Firms Govern IT," *MIS Quarterly Executive*,3, no. 1(2004), 1-17. The quote is on page 3.

(1) the assignment of decision-making authority and responsibility, and (2) the decision-making mechanisms (e.g., steering committees, review boards, policies). When it comes specifically to IT governance, Weill and his colleagues proposed five generally applicable categories of IT decisions: IT principles, IT architecture, IT infrastructure strategies, business application needs, and IT investment and prioritization. A description of these decision categories with an example of major IS activities affected by them is provided in Figure 8.6.

Weill and Ross's study of 256 enterprises shows that a defining trait of high-performing companies is the use of proper decision right allocation patterns for each of the five major categories of IT decisions. They use six political archetypes (business monarchy, IT monarchy, feudal, federal, IT duopoly, and anarchy) to label the combinations of people who either input information or have decision rights for the key IT decisions. An **archetype** is a pattern from decision rights allocation. Decisions can be made at several levels in the organization: enterprisewide, by business unit, and by region or group within a business unit.

Category	Description	Examples of Affected IS Activities
IT Principles	High-level statements about how IT is used in the business	Participating in setting strategic direction
IT Architecture	An integrated set of technical choices to guide the organization in satisfying business needs. The architecture is a set of policies and rules for the use of IT and plots a migration path to the way business will be done	Establishing architecture and standards
IT Infrastructure Strategies	Strategies for the base foundation of budgeted-for IT capability (both technical and human) shared throughout the firm as reliable services and centrally coordinated	Managing Internet and network services; providing general support; managing data; managing human resources
Business Application Needs	Specification of the business need for purchased or internally developed IT applications	Developing and maintaining information systems
IT Investment and Prioritization	Decision about how much and where to invest in IT including project approvals and justification techniques	Anticipating new technologies

FIGURE 8.6 Five major categories of IT decisions.
Source: Adapted from P. Weill, "Don't Just Lead, Govern: How Top Performing Firms Govern IT," *MIS Quarterly Executive* 3, no. 1 (2004), 4, Figure 2.

Decision rights or inputs rights for a particular IT decision are held by:		CxO Level Execs	Corp. IT and/or Business Unit IT	Business Unit Leaders or Process Owners
Business Monarchy	A group of, or individual, business executives (i.e., CxOs). Includes committees comprised of senior business executives (may include CIO). Excludes IT executives acting independently.	✓		
IT Monarchy	Individuals or groups of IT executives.		✓	
Feudal	Business unit leaders, key process owners or their delegates.			✓
Federal	C level executives and at least one other business group (e.g., CxO and BU leaders)—IT executives may be an additional participant. Equivalent to a country and its states working together.	✓	✓	✓
		✓		✓
IT Duopoly	IT executives and one other group (e.g., CxO or BU leaders).	✓	✓	
			✓	✓
Anarchy	Each individual user			

© MIT Sloan Center for Information Systems Research 2003 - Weill

FIGURE 8.7   IT governance archetypes.
Source: P. Weill, "Don't Just Lead, Govern: How Top Performing Firms Govern IT," *MIS Quarterly Executive* 3, no. 1 (2004): 5, Figure 3.

Figure 8.7 summarizes the level and function for the allocation of decision rights in each archetype.

For each decision category, the organization adopts an archetype as the means to obtain inputs for decisions and to assign responsibility for them. Although there is little variation in the selection of archetypes regarding who provides information for decision making, there is significant variation across organizations in terms of archetypes selected for decision right allocation. For instance, the duopoly is used by the largest portion (36%) of organizations for IT principles decisions, whereas the IT monarchy is the most popular for IT architecture and infrastructure decisions (i.e., 73% and 59%, respectively)[17].

There is no one best arrangement for the allocation of decision rights. Rather, the most appropriate arrangement depends on a number of factors, including the type of performance indicator. Some common performance indicators are asset utilization, profit, or growth Figure 8.8 displays the three most effective

[17] Weill and Ross, *IT Governance: How Top Performers Manage IT Decision Rights for Superior Results.*

	IT Principles	IT Architecture	IT Infrastructure	Business Application Needs	IT Investment & Prioritization
Business Monarchy	△3	△3	△3		② △3
IT Monarchy		☆ ②	☆ ②		
Feudal					
Federal				△3 ☆1	
Duopoly	☆1 ②			②	☆1
Anarchy					

Key: Most popular ☆1   Second most popular ②   Third most popular △3

FIGURE 8.8 Top three overall IT governance performers.
Source: Adapted from P. Weill, "Don't Just Lead, Govern: How Top Performing Firms Govern IT," *MIS Quarterly Executive* 3, no. 1 (2004): 13, Figure 6.

arrangements as measured by IT governance performance. There is considerable overlap in the top two, with both of these arrangements using a duopoly for IT principles and an IT monarchy for both IT architecture and infrastructure. Thus, the IS organization is responsible for the most technical decisions, but both the IS organization and business managers are involved in the remaining three decisions.

The Weill framework for decision rights allocation can be used to understand governance of a variety of organizational decisions. In Chapter 9, governance patterns that are suitable for important information security decisions are identified and discussed.

Decision-Making Mechanisms

Many different types of mechanisms can be created to ensure good IT governance. Policies are useful for defining the process of making a decision under certain situations. However, often the environment is so complex that policies are too rigid. Another mechanism that is used very frequently for IT decisions is the **steering committee**. Steering committees work especially well with the federal archetypes, which calls for joint participation of IT and business leaders in the decision-making process. Steering committees can be geared toward different levels of decision making.

At the highest level, the steering committee, also called the IT Governance Council, reports to the board of the directors or the CEO. The steering committee at this level is comprised of top-level executives and the CIO. It provides strategic direction and funding authority for major IT projects. It ensures that adequate

238 ► Chapter 8 Governance of the Information Systems Organization

resources be allocated to the IS organization for achieving strategic goals. Committees with lower-level players typically are involved with allocating scarce resources effectively and efficiently. Lower-level steering committees provide a forum for business leaders to present their IT needs and to offer input and direction about the support they receive from IT operations. Either level may have working groups to help the steering committee to be effective. Further, either level is concerned with performance measurement of the IS organization, though the assessment of performance is more detailed for the lower-level committee. For example, the lower-level committee would focus on the progress of the various projects and adherence to the budget. The higher-level committee would focus on the performance of the CIO and the ability of the IS organization to contribute to the company's achievement of its strategic goals.

Although an organization may have both levels of steering committees, it is more likely to have one or the other. If the IS organization is viewed as being critical for the organization to achieve its strategic goals, the C-level executives are likely to be on the committee. Otherwise, the steering committee will tend to be larger to have widespread representation from the various business units. In this case, the steering committee is an excellent mechanism for helping the business units realize the competing benefits of proposed IT projects and develop an approach for allocating among the project requests. In the case described at the beginning of this chapter, the CIO was disappointed because the disbanding of the ISSC suggested that the new CEO did not think the IS organization was as strategic as it had been viewed in the past. The new governance structure, however, did play an important role in resource allocation and project oversight.

Managing the Global Considerations

How does the management of IT differ when the scope of the organization is global, rather than just within one country? Typically, large global MIS organizations face many of the same organizational issues as any other global department. Managers must figure out how to manage when employees are in different time zones, speak different languages, have different customs and holidays, and come from different cultures. In the case of information management, various issues arise that put the business at risk beyond the typical global considerations. Figure 8.9 summarizes how a global IT perspective affects six information management issues.

Research by The Concours Group in 2007 found that four drivers are shaping the IT organization:

- Growth and innovation agenda of many corporations
- Demand for horizontal integration to facilitate the sharing of best practices across the enterprise
- Changing workforce demographics that indicate the demand for IT professionals is not keeping up with supply
- Expanding options of technology supply such as software-as-a-service, cloud computing, and capacity on demand

Issue	Global IT Perspective	Example
Political Stability	Investments in IT in a country with an unstable government should be carefully considered: How much do you invest? How risky is the investment?	Much offshoring is done with companies in India, a country that is facing an atomic war in its conflict with Pakistan.
Transparency	Domestically, an IT network can be end-to-end with little effort compared to global networks, which makes it difficult for these two types of systems to have the same look and feel, or, sometimes, to get to the data.	SAP-R3 is used to support production processes. When it is not installed in one country, managers cannot monitor the processes in that country the same way.
Business Continuity Planning	When crossing borders, it is important to make sure that contingency plans are in place and working.	After 9/11, many businesses are considering placing backup data centers in remote locations, but the concern when crossing borders is whether that data center will be available when/if needed.
Cultural Differences	Different countries have different cultures; some things are acceptable one place but not another. IT systems must not offend or insult those of a different culture	Using images or artifacts from one culture may be insulting to another culture. For example, DitchWitch could not use its logo globally because a witch is offensive in some countries.
Sourcing	Getting the IT hardware within every country of operation may be difficult. Some technologies cannot be exported from the United States, and other technologies cannot be imported into specific countries. Vendors do not always have the same technologies available in every country.	Some technology is considered a potential threat to national security, such as encryption technologies, so exporting it to some countries, especially those that are not political allies of the United States, is not possible.
Data Flow Across Borders	Data, especially private or personal data, are not allowed to cross some borders.	Brazil refused to let data come across its borders from other countries, making it difficult for businesses to integrate their Brazilian operations into the corporate operations.

FIGURE 8.9   Global considerations for the MIS organization.

Some, if not all, of these drivers are pushing toward greater globalization. For example, many companies are looking to other parts of the globe to grow their companies. In our increasingly flat world, many companies are successfully drawing from labor supplies in other parts of the world to compensate for gaps in skills.

► FOOD FOR THOUGHT: CIO LEADERSHIP PROFILES

As information technology increases its role in business, the work of the IT organization in general and of the CIO in particular has grown in scope and complexity. More often, the CIO is asked to take on additional roles such as chief innovation officer, supply chain officer, or even chief operating officer. CIO Insight's research in 2005 on the "role of the CIO" found that one-third of CIOs manage an additional corporate function; three-quarters of the CIOs report to the CEO, president, or COO; and over one-half listed corporate strategy as one of their top responsibilities.[18] What better leader to take on these roles than the CIO because it is the information systems organization that often has the best cross-functional view of the organization. The information flows are the lifeblood of most organizations, and the CIO has the unique opportunity to understand just how those flows work from the vantage point of managing the IT services that support them.

A recent study presents four profiles that characterize the CIO's leadership role (and their percentage occurrence in the survey).[19]

- IT Orchestrator (32%)—an effective IS leader who has the ear of top management and is involved in strategic decision making.
- IT Advisor (18%)—a CIO who possesses the strategic and business skills to make the IS organization successful, but whose IS organization is not adequately funded to make a strong contribution. The CIO has relatively low decision-making authority.
- IT Laggard (18%)—CIO who has a relatively high level of decision-making authority, but doesn't have the business and strategic skills to capitalize on the top management support. The CIO has a conservative vision for the IS organization.
- IT Mechanic (32%)—CIO who has relatively low levels of strategic effectiveness and decision-making authority; has the lowest level of business skills. Fewer of them report to the CEO than CIOs in the other three profiles.

The survey findings link the contribution of the IS organization to the profiles. In particular, the Orchestrator's IS organization makes the most contribution to the company, followed in order by the Advisor, Laggard, and Mechanic. To change

---

[18] Allan Alter "The Changing Role of the CIO" CIO Insight, April 5, 2005, www.cioinsight.com.
[19] D. Preston, D. Leidner, and D. Chen "CIO Leadership Profiles: Implications of Matching CIO Authority and Leadership Capability on IT impact," *MISQ Executive* 7, no. 2 (June 2008), 57–69.

profiles and, ultimately, develop a more effective IS organization, the authors suggest that the Laggard and Mechanic gain more skills, especially strategic skills. They advise the Advisor to implement strategies to gain more funding for the IS organization.

► SUMMARY

- The chief information officer (CIO) is a high-level IS officer who performs many important organizational functions, including championing the organization, managing the IT architecture and infrastructure, participating in the development of business and IT strategy, planning for technology, overseeing application development, sourcing, overseeing training, advising on emerging technologies, interfacing with internal and external customers, and planning for business discontinuities.

- IS organizations can be expected to anticipate new technologies, participate in setting and implementing strategic goals, innovate current processes, develop and maintain information systems, manage supplier relationships, establish architecture platforms and standards, promote enterprise security, plan for business discontinuities, manage data/information/knowledge, manage Internet and network services, manage human resources, operate the data center, and provide general support. It does not perform core business functions or independently develop business strategy.

- Because each organization differs depending on the nature of the enterprise, a business manager must know the particular needs of his or her organization—just as the IS manager must educate him or her on the IT available. If neither seeks the other out, then a schism can develop between business and IS. The enterprise will suffer due to missed opportunities and expensive mistakes

- In addition to understanding the structure of an IS organization, a manager should work with IT leaders to develop a lean, competitive enterprise in which IT acts as a strategic enabler. Working as a team, business and IS managers can fruitfully address crucial organizational issues such as outsourcing, centralization, and globalization. Such collaboration is essential if the enterprise is to remain afloat amid the difficult waters of business competition.

- IT governance specifies how to allocate decision rights in such a way as to encourage desirable behavior in the use of IT. The allocation of decision rights can be broken down into six archetypes (business monarchy, IT monarchy, feudal, federal, IT duopoly, and anarchy). High-performing companies use the proper decision rights allocation patterns for each of the five major categories of IT decisions.

- Alternative structuring approaches are possible. Centralized IS organizations place IT staff, hardware, software, and data in one location to promote control and efficiency. At the other end of the continuum, decentralized IS organizations with distributed resources can best meet the needs of local users. Federalism is in the middle of the centralized/decentralized continuum.

- Global MIS organizations face a host of issues that domestic departments avoid. Geopolitical risk, language and cultural barriers, business continuity planning, and transborder data flow issues must be reexamined in a global organization, and each country's laws and policies considered in the architectural design.

▶ KEY TERMS

archetype (p. 235)
business continuity plan
  (BCP) (p. 227)
centralized IS
  organizations (p. 231)

chief information officer
  (CIO) (p. 219)
chief technology officer
  (CTO) (p. 222)
decentralized IS
  organizations (p. 231)

federalism (p. 232)
governance (p. 231)
IT governance (p. 234)
steering committee
  (p. 237)

▶ DISCUSSION QUESTIONS

1. Using an organization with which you are familiar, describe the role of the most senior IS professional. Is that person a strategist or an operationalist?

2. What advantages does a CIO bring to a business? What might be the disadvantages of having a CIO?

3. The debate about centralization and decentralization is heating up again with the advent of network computing and the increasing use of the Internet. Why does the Internet make this debate topical?

4. Why is the concept of decision rights important?

5. Why can an IT governance archetype be good for one type of IS decision but not for another?

CASE STUDY 8-1

IT GOVERNANCE AT UPS

UPS has long been concerned about how to keep its IT initiatives aligned with its business direction. One of its earliest governance mechanisms was an executive steering committee made up of four cross-functional, senior-level executives. The steering committee was charged with setting a strategic direction for IT and establishing priorities and funding levels. The steering committee met regularly in the late 1980s and early 1990s when UPS's IT capability was being built. In 2001, the executive steering committee refocused to an overseer role that provided input on UPS's long-term IT strategy. It now establishes IT principles, such as UPS's commitment to standardization and scalability in any system used by its 60,000 drivers. The executive steering committee is a team of three senior executives, including the CIO.

Because the executive steering committee had became less active in IT governance related to the short-term matters, it was replaced with the Information and Technology Strategy Committee (ITSC). ITSC's members includes 15 senior managers from all functional areas within UPS and is headed by the CIO. Its charter was repositioned to study the impacts and application of new technology and to provide a short-term technology direction.

Consider governance for one type of decision—a standards decision. The chief IT architect, a CIO direct report and member of the ITSC, heads the standards committee that handles most of the daily negotiations related to standards. However, the standards committee escalates decisions up to the ITSC when its members think that a standards decision has implications beyond the immediate application in question. Similarly, the CIO escalates a standards decision up to the executive steering committee if the ITSC thinks that a standards decision has long-term strategic implications for UPS.

Discussion Questions

1. Describe the IT governance mechanisms used at UPS.
2. What does the representation of UPS's executive steering committee suggest to you? Do you think that IT plays a strategic role at UPS? Why or why not?
3. What types of skills do you think are important for UPS's CIO? Explain your answer.
4. Why can decisions about standards be important?

Source: Excerpted from Jeanne Ross and Peter Weill, "Recipe for God Governance," *CIO*, June 15, 2004, www.cio.com/article/print/29162 (accessed July 23, 2008); and UPS, *UPS IT Governance: The Key to Aligning Technology Initiatives with Business Direction*, http://www.pressroom.ups.com/mediakits/factsheet/0,2305,1043,00.html (accessed July 23, 2008).

CASE STUDY 8-2

THE BIG FIX AT TOYOTA MOTOR SALES (TMS)

When Barbra Cooper joined Toyota Motor Sales as CIO in late 1996, her reception was lukewarm. She was an outsider in a company that prizes employee loyalty. Cooper was surprised to find that IS was relatively isolated and primitive. "I would describe it as almost 1970s-like," she says. Business units were buying their own IT systems because in-house IT couldn't deliver. There were no PCs or network management. And basic IT disciplines such as business relationship management and financial management were largely absent. "No one understood the cost of delivering IT," she says. Unfortunately IS personnel were more like "order takers" than "business partners." Worse, business execs cut deals with their go-to guys in IS for project approval and funding, with no thought to architecture standards, systems integration, or business benefits.

Before Cooper could rectify the situation, she found herself and her staff buried under the Big Six technology projects. The Big Six were expensive enterprisewide projects that included a new extranet for Toyota dealers and the PeopleSoft ERP rollout, as well as four new systems for order management, parts forecasting, advanced warranty, and financial document management. Feeling besieged, the IS group made the mistake of not explaining to the business all the things it was doing and how much it all cost.

Starting in 2001, Japanese executives were feeling squeezed because of a tanking domestic Japanese market and lukewarm results from its global units. Toyota Motor Sales USA, though, had increasing sales and market share. Japan relied more on its American division's profits, and from across the Pacific, the parent company looked more closely at U.S. spending habits.

Both Japanese and U.S. management wanted to know more about IS's runaway costs, which had doubled after Cooper's arrival and, at its peak, tripled. And Toyota Motor Sales President and CEO Yuki Funo wanted Cooper to tell him where the ceiling of IS's spend was.

At the same time Cooper was feeling the pressure to explain about runaway costs from Japan, she also needed to respond to local grumbling that IS had become an unresponsive, bureaucratic machine. In late 2002, Cooper hired an outside consultancy to interview TMS's top 20 executives. She wanted their honest opinions of how IS was doing. The results didn't provide all the answers to IS's ailments, but she certainly saw the hot spots. "Parts of [the survey results] were stinging," Cooper says. "But you can't be a CIO and not face that."

Cooper spent many introspective weeks in 2003 formulating her vision for a new IT department. What she developed was a strategy for a decentralized and transparent IS organization that focused all its energy on the major business segments. In summer 2003, she called her senior IS staffers into her conference room and presented her vision on her whiteboard.

The first thing Cooper did was set up the Toyota Value Action Program, a team of eight staffers responsible for translating her vision into actionable items for the department and her direct reports. Using the executive's survey results and Cooper's direction, the team winnowed the list down to 18 initiatives, including increasing employee training and development, gaining cost savings, making process improvements, ridding IS inefficiencies, and implementing a metrics program. Each initiative got a project owner, a team, and a mechanism to check the team's success.

The most significant initiative called for improved alignment with the business side. At the heart of this new effort was a revamped office of the CIO structure with new roles, reporting lines, and responsibilities.

As part of the rehaul, top-flight senior personnel were embedded as divisional information officers, or DIOs, in all the business units. These DIOs are accountable for IT strategy, development, and services, and they sit on the management committees headed by top business executives. Further, rotating high-potential IT staff into the business units primes them for a broader understanding of the company and trains them for a leadership position in the IT department. The DIOs' goal is to forge relationships with and gain the respect of high-level business executives. "I still believe in managing IT centrally, but it was incumbent on us to physically distribute IT into the businesses," says Cooper. "They could provide more local attention while keeping the enterprise vision alive."

The difference between the previous relationship managers and the new DIOs is that DIOs have complete accountability and responsibility for the vertical area they serve. For instance, Ken Goltara (Corporate Manager of Business Systems) now heads up a smaller group of internal customers—which includes Toyota, Lexus, and Scion—as well as all of the vehicle-ordering systems, logistics, and dealer portals. "I now have more vertical responsibility, and my responsibilities are deeper, from cradle to grave," Goltara says. "From Toyota to Lexus to Scion, I'm it."

Cooper changed the jobs of 50% of her staffers within six months, yet no one left or was let go. Some took on new responsibilities; others took on expanded or completely new roles. Cooper says some mid- and upper-level staffers were initially uncomfortable with their new roles, but she says she spent a lot of time early on fostering a new attitude about the change. Now she spends approximately 30% of her time mentoring and coaching, and she encourages her senior management team to also be involved in coaching.

To further strengthen the IS–business bond, Cooper chartered the executive steering committee, or ESC, to approve all major IT projects. The committee consists of Cooper; Cooper's boss, Senior Vice President and Planning and Administrative Officer Dave Illingworth; Senior Vice President and Treasurer Mikihiro Mori; and Senior Vice President and Coordinating Officer Masanao Tomozoe. By exposing IT's inner workings to the business side at Toyota Motor Sales, Cooper hoped that this new transparency would lessen IS's role on IT project vetting and monitoring and increase business's responsibility.

The executive steering committee now controls all project funds in one pool of cash, and it releases funds for each project as each phase of the project's goals are achieved. Everyone in the company can look at which dollars were (and were not) going to be spent, the pool's administrators can sweep unused funds out, and other projects can go after those funds. And there are no more spending swings; projects are regularly paced throughout the year.

Initially, many business executives didn't want to participate in the new approval process that required them to seek funding through the ESC. Instead, those executives tapped lower-level business sponsors who worked with IS on business case development and implementation. But then, if a project ran into trouble, those high-level "executives would scatter like cockroaches," says Goltara. No senior-level business execs were willing to take IS project responsibility. After about six months of this, Cooper demanded that a higher-level business executive—a corporate manager, VP-level or above—back each IS proposal. Now, the ESC won't approve a project unless that support is there. "There's equal skin in the game now," says Goltara. The ESC members now grill the business executive, and not the IT executive, to see whether he or she can support the business benefits.

Discussion Questions

1. Describe the advantages of TMS's new decentralized IS structure. What are its disadvantages?

2. What problems was Cooper trying to solve with the new IS structure? How successful do you think the new structure will be in solving these problems?

3. Describe the role of the Executive Steering Committee at TMS. Do you think the Executive Steering Committee is a good idea? Why or why not?

Source: Excerpted from Thomas Wailgum, "The Big Fix," *CIO Magazine* (April 15, 2005), http://www.cio.com/archive/041505/toyota.html (accessed August 15, 2005). Updated with excerpts from Michael Fitzgerald, "How to Develop the Next Generation of IT Leaders," *CIO Magazine* (May 2, 2008), http://www.cio.com/article/print/341067 (accessed July 23, 2008).

CHAPTER 9

USING INFORMATION ETHICALLY[1]

When TJX Co. found the largest data security breach of its computer systems in the history of retailing, it faced a serious ethical dilemma not faced by many companies. It originally estimated that the credit card accounts of 45.6 million customers worldwide were affected (though that number has been updated to 94 million). Given the extent of the breach, multiple state, federal, and foreign jurisdictions dictated how and when it must inform affected customers and what corrective steps it must take. Most jurisdictions allowed 45 days for it to act following the determination of the breach. Any extension beyond 45 days would incur heavy fines. However, on the ethical side it became an even more pressing issue. Should TJX inform the affected customers immediately or wait till the breach was secured and all remedial steps were undertaken, which may take weeks?

As a socially responsible company, TJX takes its obligations to customers seriously. If it informed the customers immediately, the customers could start taking preventive steps to protect themselves from the identity theft and avoid any resulting financial and psychological losses. However, this means the breach would become public knowledge before the remedial steps were taken. More hackers would learn about it and may exploit the weakness in its IT infrastructure. Additionally, the financial markets would lose confidence in the company and severely punish shareholders. Such loss of image would also affect its ability to attract and retain high-quality employees in the long run. On the other hand, if it waited for 45 days, financial stability of many customers would be compromised through misuse of their credit card and other private records. This could result in a major class-action litigation, which might permanently affect the company.

As in the case of TJX, information collected in the course of business is important for the conduct of business and can even create valuable competitive advantage. But ethical questions concerning just how that information will be used and by whom, whether they arise inside or outside the organization, can

[1] The authors wish to acknowledge and thank Arthur J. Ebersole, MBA 1999, for his help in researching and writing early drafts of this chapter.

have powerful effects on the company's ability to carry out its plans.[2] As computer networks and their products come to touch every aspect of people's lives, and as the power, speed, and capabilities of computers increase, managers are increasingly challenged to govern their use in an ethical manner. No longer can managers afford to view information systems (IS) as discrete entities within the corporate structure. In many cases, IS are coming to comprise much of the corporation itself.

In such an environment, managers are called on to manage the information generated and contained within those systems for the benefit not only of the corporation, but also of society as a whole. The predominant issue, which arises due to the omnipresence of corporate IS, concerns the just and ethical use of the information companies collect in the course of everyday operations. Without official guidelines and codes of conduct, who decides how to use this information? More and more, this challenge falls on corporate managers. Managers need to understand societal needs and expectations to determine what they ethically can and cannot do in their quest to learn about their customers, suppliers, and employees, and to provide greater service.

Before managers can deal effectively with issues related to the ethical and moral governance of IS, they need to know what these issues are. Unfortunately, as with many emerging fields, well-accepted guidelines do not exist. Thus, managers bear even greater responsibility as they try to run their businesses and simultaneously develop control methods that meet both corporate imperatives and the needs of society at large. If this challenge appears to be a matter of drafting operating manuals, nothing could be further from the truth.

In a society whose legal standards are continually challenged, managers must serve as guardians of the public and private interest, although many may have no formal legal training and, thus, no firm basis for judgment. This chapter addresses many such concerns. It begins by expanding on the definition of ethical behavior and introduces several heuristics that managers can employ to help them make better decisions. Next this chapter elaborates on the most important issues behind the ethical treatment of information. This is followed by a discussion of some newly emerging controversies that will surely test society's resolve concerning the increasing presence of IS in every aspect of life. It concludes with a discussion of IT governance, security, and accountability.

This chapter takes a high-level view of ethical issues facing managers in today's environment. It focuses primarily on providing a set of frameworks the manager can apply to a wide variety of ethical issues. Omitted is a specific focus on several important issues such as social justice (the impact of computer technology on the poor or "have-nots," racial minorities, and third world nations), nor is there a discussion of social concerns that arise out of artificial intelligence, neural networks, and expert systems. Although these are interesting and important areas for concern, in this chapter the objective is to provide managers with a way to

---

[2] J. Hasnas and J. Smith, "Ethics and Information Systems: The Corporate Domain," Working paper, 1998, p. 2.

think about the issues of ethics, privacy, security, and governance. The interested reader may wish to seek out one of a number of sources for dozens of articles and books on this area of IS management.

▶ NORMATIVE THEORIES OF BUSINESS ETHICS

The landscape changes daily as advances in technology are incorporated into existing organizational structures. IS are becoming omnipresent as companies look to decrease costs, increase efficiency, and build strategic competitive advantages. Increasingly, however, these advances come about in a business domain lacking ethical clarity. Because of its newness, this area of IT often lacks accepted norms of behavior. Companies encounter daily quandaries as they try to use their IS to create and exploit competitive advantages.

Managers must assess current information initiatives with particular attention to possible ethical issues. Because so many managers have been educated in the current corporate world, they are used to the overriding ethical norms present in their traditional businesses. As Conger and Loch observed, "People who have been trained in engineering, computer science, and MIS frequently have little training in ethics, philosophy, and moral reasoning. Without a vocabulary with which to think and talk about what constitutes an ethical computing issue, it is difficult to have the necessary discussions to develop social norms."[3]

Managers in the information age need to translate their current ethical norms into terms meaningful for the new electronic corporation. To suggest a workable framework for this process, consider three theories of ethical behavior in the corporate environment that managers can develop and apply to the particular challenges they face. These normative theories of business ethics—stockholder theory, stakeholder theory, and social contract theory—are widely applied in traditional business situations. They are "normative" in that they attempt to derive what might be called "intermediate-level" ethical principles: principles expressed in language accessible to the ordinary businessperson, which can be applied to the concrete moral quandaries of the business domain.[4] Following is a definition of each theory accompanied by an illustration of its application using the TJX example outlined at the beginning of this chapter.

Stockholder Theory

According to **stockholder theory**, stockholders advance capital to corporate managers, who act as agents in furthering their ends. The nature of this contract binds managers to act in the interest of the shareholders (i.e., to maximize shareholder value). As Milton Friedman wrote, "There is one and only one social responsibility of business: to use its resources and engage in activities designed to

---

[3] S. Conger and K. D. Loch, "Ethics and Computer Use," *Communications of the ACM* 38, no. 12 (December 1995), 31, 32.

[4] Hasnas and Smith, "Ethics and Information Systems," 5.

increase its profits so long as it stays within the rules of the game, which is to say, engages in open and free competition, without deception or fraud."[5]

Stockholder theory qualifies the manager's duty in two salient ways. First, managers are bound to employ legal, nonfraudulent means. Second, managers must take the long-term view of shareholder interest (i.e., they are obliged to forgo short-term gains if doing so will maximize value over the long term).

Managers should bear in mind that stockholder theory itself provides a limited framework for moral argument because it assumes the ability of the free market to fully promote the interests of society at large. Yet the singular pursuit of profit on the part of individuals or corporations cannot be said to maximize social welfare. Free markets can foster the creation of monopolies and other circumstances that limit the ability of members of a society to secure the common good. A proponent of stockholder theory might insist that, as agents of stockholders, managers must not use stockholders' money to accomplish goals that do not directly serve the interests of those same stockholders. A critic of stockholder theory would argue that such spending would be just if the money went to further the public interest.

The stipulation under stockholder theory that the pursuit of profits must be legal and nonfraudulent would not limit TJX from waiting to announce the security breach until it had taken corrective action. The delay allowed by law might also have a positive impact on TJX's stock price. The delay would satisfy the test of maximizing shareholder value because it would help keep the price of its stock from dropping. Further, a recent survey has shown that customers are reluctant to shop in stores once data breaches have been announced, so delaying may be important for maintaining a steady stream of revenues for as long as possible. On the other hand, disgruntled customers would definitely stop shopping at its stores if TJX waited too long.[6]

Any lost revenues would weigh against managers' success in meeting the ethical obligation to work toward maximizing value.

Stakeholder Theory

Stakeholder theory holds that managers, although bound by their relation to stockholders, are entrusted also with a responsibility, fiduciary or otherwise, to all those who hold a stake in or a claim on the firm.[7] The term "stakeholder" is currently taken to mean any group that vitally affects the survival and success of the corporation or whose interests the corporation vitally affects. Such groups normally include stockholders, customers, employees, suppliers, and the local community, though other groups may also be considered stakeholders, depending on the circumstances. At its most basic level, stakeholder theory states that management

---

[5] M. Friedman, *Capitalism and Freedom* (Chicago: University of Chicago Press, 1962), 133.

[6] There is an interesting presentation of a similar breach with commentaries from the CIOs of ChoicePoint, Motorola, Visa International, and Theft Resource Center in Eric McNulty's "Boss I Think Someone Stole Our Customer Data," *Harvard Business Review* (September 2007), 37–50.

[7] Hasnas and Smith, "Ethics and Information Systems," 8.

must enact and follow policies that balance the rights of all stakeholders without impinging on the rights of any one particular stakeholder.

Stakeholder theory diverges most consequentially from stockholder theory in affirming that the interests of parties other than the stockholders also play a legitimate role in the governance and management of the firm. As a practical matter, due to the high transaction costs entailed in canvassing all these disparate groups, managers must act as their agents in deriving business solutions that optimally serve their respective interests. Thus, in most cases, stakeholders' only real recourse is to stop participating in the corporation: Customers can stop buying the company's products, stockholders can sell their stock, and so forth.

Some stakeholders are not in a position to stop participating in the corporation. In particular, employees may need to continue working for the corporation, even though they dislike practices of their employers, or experience considerable stress due to their jobs. The use of monitoring and surveillance software can create levels of control that the employees resent. As employees become aware of these activities, their productivity and morale may fall. Ethically, managers are obliged to consider the welfare of workers. If, as they create employment opportunities and write job descriptions, managers set out to limit individuality, enforce conformity, and increase demands, they violate their ethical responsibilities.

Viewed in light of stakeholder theory, the ethical issue facing TJX presents a more complex dilemma. John Philip Coghlan, CEO of Visa USA noted, "A data breach can put an executive in an exceedingly complex situation, where he must negotiate the often divergent interests of multiple stakeholders."[8] TJX's shareholders stand to gain in the short term, but what would be the effects on other stakeholders? One stakeholder group, the customers, definitely could benefit from knowing about the breach as soon as possible because they could take steps to protect themselves. Customers could be informed of the severity of the breach and protective actions that they could take through a special Web page, toll-free information hotlines, or Webcasts. TJX could also offer them free credit-monitoring service and compensate those who are injured. Research has shown that customers who receive adequate compensation after making a complaint are actually more loyal than those without complaints.[9] On the other hand, if the breach were not announced, fewer hackers might attempt to break into the systems. Nonetheless, it probably could be shown that the costs to customers outweighed the benefits within the larger stakeholder group.

Social Contract Theory

Social contract theory derives the social responsibilities of corporate managers by considering the needs of a society with no corporations or other complex business arrangements. Social contract theorists ask what conditions would have to be met for the members of such a society to agree to allow a corporation to

---

[8] McNulty, "Boss I Think Someone Stole Our Customer Data."
[9] McNulty, "Boss I Think Someone Stole Our Customer Data."

be formed. Thus, society bestows legal recognition on a corporation to allow it to employ social resources toward given ends. This contract generally is taken to mean that, in allowing a corporation to exist, society demands at a minimum that it creates more value to the society than it consumes. Thus, society charges the corporation to enhance its welfare by satisfying particular interests of consumers and workers in exploiting the advantages of the corporate form. The corporation must conduct its activities while observing the canons of justice.[10]

The social contract comprises two distinct components: the social welfare term and the justice term. The former arises from the belief that corporations must provide greater benefits than their associated costs, or society would not allow their creation. Thus, the social contract obliges managers to pursue profits in ways that are compatible with the well-being of society as a whole. Similarly, the justice term holds that corporations must pursue profits legally, without fraud or deception, and avoid activities that injure society.

Social contract theory meets criticism because no mechanism exists to actuate it. In the absence of a real contract whose terms subordinate profit maximization to social welfare, most critics find it hard to imagine corporations losing profitability in the name of altruism. Yet, the strength of the theory lies in its broad assessment of the moral foundations of business activity.

Applied to the TJX case, social contract theory would demand that the manager ask whether the delay in notifying customers about the security breach could compromise fundamental tenets of fairness or social justice. If customers were not apprised of the delay as soon as possible, TJX's actions could be seen as unethical because it would not seem fair to delay notifying them. If, on the other hand, the time prior to notification were used to take corrective action with the consequence of limiting not only hackers from stealing confidential customer information but also of forestalling future attacks that would impact society as a whole, the delay conceivably could be considered ethical.

Although these three normative theories of business ethics possess distinct characteristics, they are not completely incompatible. All offer useful metrics for defining ethical behavior in profit-seeking enterprises under free market conditions. They provide managers with an independent standard by which to judge the ethical nature of superiors' orders as well as their firms' policies and codes of conduct. Upon inspection, the three theories appear to represent concentric circles, with stockholder theory at the center and social contract theory at the outer ring. Stockholder theory is narrowest in scope, stakeholder theory encompasses and expands on it, and social contract theory covers the broadest area. Figure 9.1 summarizes these three theories.

What, ultimately, did TJX do? TJX disclosed the breach in January 2007, but didn't release a comprehensive executive summary of the attack until March 2007, when it made a regulatory filing. TJX had actually noticed suspicious software the preceding December, at which point it hired IBM and General Dynamics to

---

[10] Hasnas and Smith, "Ethics and Information Systems," 10.

Theory	Definition	Metrics
Stockholder	Maximize stockholder wealth, in legal and non-fraudulent manners.	Will this action maximize long-term stockholder value? Can goals be accomplished without compromising company standards and without breaking laws?
Stakeholder	Maximize benefits to all stakeholders while weighing costs to competing interests.	Does the proposed action maximize collective benefits to the company? Does this action treat one or more of the corporate stakeholders unfairly?
Social contract	Create value for society in a manner that is just and nondiscriminatory.	Does this action create a "net" benefit for society? Does the proposed action discriminate against any group in particular, and is its implementation socially just?

FIGURE 9.1   Three normative theories of business ethics.

investigate. Three days later, these investigators determined that TJX's systems had been compromised and that the attacker still had access. That means it took TJX 17 months to find out that their computer systems had been breached on numerous occasions on a colossal scale.[11] It was over a year later, on February 29, 2008, when the President and CEO, Carol Meyrowitz, wrote a letter to "valued customers" about the breach that had been announced on January 2007. The TJX retail chain agreed to pay $24 and $41 million in restitution to MasterCard and Visa issuing lenders, respectively, who were affected by the breach. TJX brokered a separate agreement with a coalition of Massachusetts-based banks who had sued it. The only settlement to date to actual cardholders by TJX has been an offer of free credit monitoring for cardholders and a $30 store voucher.[12] Based on the newspaper accounts, one could surmise that TJX's overriding approach was more consistent with the stockholder theory than social contract theory. At least one stakeholder group, the customers, were not well served.

A number of other cases demonstrate different ethical issues associated with the handling of information as a result of business transactions. One such case arose when DoubleClick, a leading Internet advertisement company, announced its plans to merge its vast database of user navigational history with that of users' offline spending habits. DoubleClick provides the sites of members of its DoubleClick Network with advertisements. It then monitors the viewing of these advertisements through cookies. From cookies, DoubleClick obtains "clickstream

[11] Kevin Murphy, "TJX Hack Is Biggest Ever," *Computer Business Review* (March 30, 2007), http://www.cbronline.com/article_news.asp?guid = 0EFDDC37-4EA7-4A78-9726-E6F63C86234D.
[12] Martin Bosworth, "TJX to Pay Mastercard $24 Million for Data Breach," consumeraffaris.com (April 6, 2008), http://www.consumeraffairs.com/news04/2008/04/tjx_mc.html (accessed July 29, 2008).

data" about the sites visited by a user, the time spent at these sites, and any purchases made by the user at the sites. DoubleClick has extensive Internet navigational histories for identified users. With its purchase of Abacus Direct Corporation in November 1999, it acquired a database with information about the spending habits of more than 88 million people derived from more than two billion offline purchases. Even though it was a complete reversal of its previously stated privacy policies, DoubleClick was going to merge these two powerful databases. A suit filed by Electronic Privacy Information with the Federal Trade Commission, coupled with a public uproar, caused DoubleClick to back down from its proposed merger.[13] DoubleClick has since sold Abacus. However, it has now teamed up with an even more data rich-company than Abacus. It was acquired by Google, a company known for its huge database and innovative search technologies

Living.com, a furniture retailer on the Internet, made a very public decision not to sell its customer information. When it ceased doing business and filed for bankruptcy, the question arose as to whether their customer data was an asset that could be sold to help pay off their debts. Managers at Living.com and the U.S. government officials working with them reached an agreement that their customer information was private and it would be inappropriate to sell it for use by someone other than Living.com.

▶ CONTROL OF INFORMATION

In an economy that is rapidly becoming dominated by knowledge workers, the value of information is tantamount. Those who possess the "best" information and know how to use it, win. The recent trend in computer prices has meant that high levels of computational power can be purchased for relatively small amounts of money. Although this trend means that computer-generated or stored information now falls within the reach of an ever-larger percentage of the populace, it also means that collecting and storing information is becoming easier and more cost effective. Although this circumstance certainly affects businesses and individuals for the better, it also can affect them substantially for the worse. Consider several areas in which the control of information is crucial. Richard O. Mason[14] identified four such areas, which can be summarized by the acronym PAPA: privacy, accuracy, property, and accessibility (see Figure 9.2).

Privacy

Many consider privacy to be the most important area in which their interests need to be safeguarded. **Privacy** has long been considered "the right to be left

---

[13] Jones, Day, Reavis, and Pogue, "DoubleClick and the Privacy Wars," 1, no. 1 (May 2001), available at http://www1.jonesday.com/files/tbl_s31Publications%5CFileUpload137%5C139%5CDouble_Click_Privacy.pdf (accessed June 28, 2002).

[14] Richard O. Mason, "Four Ethical Issues of the Information Age," *MIS Quarterly* 10, no. 1 (March 1986).

Area	Critical Question
Privacy	What information must a person reveal to others? Can the information that the person provides be used to identify his/her personal preferences or history when he/she doesn't want those preferences to be known? Can the information that the person provides be used for purposes other than those for which the person was told that it would be used?
Accuracy	Who is responsible for the reliability and accuracy of information? Who will be accountable for errors?
Property	Who owns information? Who owns the channels of distribution, and how should they be regulated?
Accessibility	What information does a person or organization have a right to obtain, under what conditions, and with what safeguards? Who can access personal information in the files? Does the person accessing personal information "need to know" the information that is being accessed?

FIGURE 9.2 Mason's areas of managerial control.

alone"[15] In today's information-oriented world, it has been defined as "the ability of the individual to personally control information about one's self."[16] It pertains to the authorized collection and use of personal information and is based on what information individuals choose to disclose about themselves. Individuals may be concerned about their privacy when extensive amounts of data that can personally identify them are being collected and stored in databases. They may also be concerned that information is collected for one purpose, but used for another purpose without their authorization.

Employers can monitor their employees' e-mail and computer utilization while they are at work, even though they have not historically monitored telephone calls. Every time someone logs onto one of the main search engines, a "cookie" is placed in their hard drive so that these companies can track their surfing habits. A **cookie** is a message given to a Web browser by a Web server. The browser stores the message with user identification codes in a text file that is sent back to the server each time the browser requests a page from the server.[17] Currently this information is used only to target advertising, but its future use depends on the discretion of managers. Their view is formed in part by how much competitive advantage this knowledge can create. Do customers have a right to privacy while searching the Internet? Courts have decided that the

---

[15] Samuel D. Warren and Louis D. Brandeis, "The Right to Privacy," *Harvard Law Review* 4, no. 5 (December 1890): 193–200.

[16] E. F. Stone, D. G. Gardner, H. G. Gueutal, and S. McClure, "A Field Experiment Comparing Information-Privacy Values, Beliefs, and Attitudes Across Several Types of Organizations," *Journal of Applied Psychology* 68, no. 3 (August 1983): 459–468.

[17] Webopedia, http://www.webopedia.com/TERM/c/cookie.html (accessed June 28, 2002).

answer is no, but as society moves ahead, the right to monitor customer habits will be affected by how managers decide to use the information that they have collected.

Governments around the world are grappling with privacy legislation. Not surprisingly, they are using different approaches for ensuring the privacy of their citizens. The U.S.'s sectoral approach relies on a mix of legislation, regulation, and self-regulation. Examples of the U.S.'s relatively limited privacy legislation include the 1974 Privacy Act that regulates the U.S. government's collection and use of personal information and the 1998 Children's Online Privacy Protection Act that regulates the online collection and use of children's personal information. Much of the privacy legislation in the United States is industry based. For example, the Gramm-Leach-Bliley Act of 1999 followed in the wake of banks selling sensitive information, including account information, Social Security numbers, credit card purchase histories, and so forth to telemarketing companies. This U.S. law somewhat mitigates the sharing of sensitive financial and personal information by allowing customers of financial institutions the limited right to "opt-out" of the information sharing by these institutions with nonaffiliated third parties. The Health Insurance Portability and Accountability Act (HIPAA) of 1996 is designed to safeguard the electronic exchange privacy and security of information in the health-care industry. Its Privacy Rule ensures that patients' health information is properly protected while allowing its necessary flow for providing and promoting health care. HIPAA's Security Rule specifies national standards for protecting electronic health information from unauthorized access, alteration, deletion, and transmission.

In contrast to the U.S.'s sectoral approach combined with strong encouragement of self-regulation by industry, the European Union relies on comprehensive legislation that requires creation of government data protection agencies, registration of databases with those agencies, and in some cases prior approval before processing personal data. Because of pronounced differences in governmental approaches, many U.S. companies were concerned that they would be unable to meet the European "adequacy" standard for privacy protection specified in the European Commission's Directive on Data Protection that went into effect in 1998. This directive prohibits the transfer of personal data to non–European Union nations that do not meet the European privacy standards. Many U.S. companies believed that this directive would significantly hamper their ability to engage in many trans-Atlantic transactions. However, the U.S. Department of Commerce (DOC), in consultation with the European Commission, developed a "safe harbor" framework in 2000 that allows U.S. companies to be placed on a list maintained by the DOC. The U.S. companies must demonstrate through a self-certification process that they are enforcing privacy at a level practiced in the European Union.[18]

---

[18] U.S. Department of Commerce, "Safe Harbor Overview," available at http://www.export.gov/ safeharbor/sh_overview.html (accessed July 15, 2002).

Accuracy

The **accuracy**, or the correctness, of information assumes real importance for society as computers come to dominate in corporate record-keeping activities. When records are inputted incorrectly, who is to blame? In a case in Florida, a family whose bank had recently changed from a paper bookkeeping system to a computer-based system found that a mortgage payment that had been made was not credited. As the family attempted to pay the mortgage in subsequent months, the system rejected the payments because the mortgage was listed as past due. After a year of "missing" payments, the bank foreclosed on the house.[19] Although this incident may highlight the need for better controls over the bank's internal processes, it also demonstrates the risks that can be attributed to inaccurate information retained in corporate systems. In this case, the bank was responsible for the error, but it paid little—compared to the family—for its mistake. Although they cannot expect to eliminate all mistakes from the online environment, managers must establish controls to ensure that situations such as this one do not happen with any frequency.

Over time it becomes increasingly difficult to maintain the accuracy of some types of information. Although a person's birth date does not typically change (my grandmother's change of her birth year notwithstanding), addresses and phone numbers often change as people relocate, and even their names may change with marriage, divorce, and adoption. The European Union Directive on Data Protection requires accurate and up-to-date data and tries to make sure that data is kept no longer than necessary to fulfill its stated purpose. Keeping data only as long as it is necessary to fulfill its stated purpose is a challenge many companies don't even attempt to meet.

Property

The increase in monitoring leads to the question of **property**, or who owns the data. Now that organizations have the ability to collect vast amounts of data on their clients, do they have a right to share data with others to create a more accurate profile of an individual? And if they do create such consolidated profiles, who owns that information, which in many cases was not divulged willingly for that purpose? Who owns images that are posted in cyberspace? With ever more sophisticated methods of computer animation, can companies use newly "created" images or characters building on models in other media without paying royalties? Mason summarizes the issues,

> Any individual item of information can be extremely costly to produce in the first instance. Yet once it is produced, that information has the illusive quality of being easy to reproduce and to share with others. Moreover, this replication can take place without destroying the original. This makes information hard to

[19] Richard O. Mason, "Four Ethical Issues of the Information Age," *MIS Quarterly* 10, no. 1 (March 1986).

safeguard since, unlike tangible property, it becomes communicable and hard to keep it to one's self. It is even difficult to secure appropriate reimbursements when somebody else uses your information.[20]

Accessibility

In the age of the information worker, **accessibility**, or the ability to obtain the data, becomes increasingly important. Would-be users of information must first gain the physical ability to access online information resources, which broadly means they must access computational systems. Recent trends in computer hardware prices have greatly lowered the barriers to entry on this account. Second and more important, the user must gain access to information itself. In this sense, the issue of access is closely linked to that of property. Although major corporations have benefited greatly from the drop in computer prices, the same benefit only now is beginning to filter through the rest of society. Looking forward, the major issue facing managers is how to create and maintain access to information for society at large. As our society moves toward a service- or knowledge-based economy, managers whose organizations control vast quantities of information will have to weigh the benefits of information control against societal needs to upgrade the knowledge bases of individuals or knowledge workers.

Today's managers must ensure that information about their employees and customers is accessible only to those who have a right to see and use it. They should take active measures to see that adequate security and control measures are in place in their companies. It is becoming increasingly clear that they also must ensure that adequate safeguards are working in the companies of their key trading partners. The managers at MasterCard International were no doubt embarrassed when they reported to 68,000 of its cardholders that their accounts were at risk of fraud because one of its card processors, CardSystems Solutions, had violated long-established standards to handle MasterCards' transactions. MasterCard had spent millions of dollars to upgrade its own computer systems with sophisticated fraud-detection software and had sent out teams to processor and merchant sites to make sure that they were in compliance with these standards. Yet, it was only recently that MasterCard detected a rogue computer program that CardSystems Solutions had installed to extract data for unauthorized research purposes. Unfortunately, this extracted data was accessed by data thieves.[21] Accessibility clearly is an issue that extended beyond MasterCard's internal systems.

Accessibility is becoming increasingly important with the surge in **identity theft**, or "the taking of the victim's identity to obtain credit, credit cards from banks and retailers, steal money from the victim's existing accounts, apply for loans, establish accounts with utility companies, rent an apartment, file bankruptcy or obtain a job using the victim's name."[22] In short, identity theft is a crime in which

[20] Ibid.

[21] Eric Dash, "CEO Hacked Card Process Broke Rules," *Orlando Sentinel* (June 18, 2005), p. A12.

[22] Identity Theft Organization, http://www.identitytheft/.org.

the thief uses the victim's personal information (such as driver's license number or Social Security number) to impersonate the victim. In TJX's case, the security breach made its customers vulnerable to identity theft.

According to subject matter experts, identity theft is categorized in two ways: true name and account takeover. True name identity theft means that the thief uses personal information to open new accounts. The thief might open a new credit card account, establish cellular phone service, or open a new checking account to obtain blank checks. Account takeover identity theft means the imposter uses personal information to gain access to the person's existing accounts. Typically, the thief will change the mailing address on an account and run up a huge bill before the person whose identity has been stolen realizes there is a problem.

Identity theft is a problem for both individuals and businesses. The U.S. government keeps statistics on reported cases of identity theft.[23] The incidence of identity theft had been growing at an amazing rate during the early part of this century. Though the number of cases in 2006 was down from the previous year, there were still over 240,000 reported cases of identity theft.[24] A total of 8.4 million Americans experienced losses to the tune of $49.3 billion. The most victimized tend to be college students and young adults who have not learned to use security software or shred documents.[25]

Although some cases of individual identity theft can be traced to carelessness on the part of victims, some may also be credited to the failure of businesses to limit accessibility to their databases. Businesses are also subject to significant losses due to identity theft. Illegitimate e-mail messages that solicit personal information for the thief can ruin a business's hard-won reputation. Purchases made by the thief must be paid for, and often that loss is covered by the business. The U.S. Federal Trade Commission (FTC) maintains a Web site to help both individuals and businesses manage identity theft (http://www.ftc.gov/bcp/edu/microsites/idtheft/).

PAPA and Managers

Managers must work to implement controls over information highlighted by the PAPA principles. Not only should they deter identity theft by limiting inappropriate access to customer information, but they should also respect their customers' privacy. Internet purchasers surveyed believed Internet retailers should post their policies about how they will use private information. Mary Culnan noted in *CIO* magazine that the ease with which consumer information is collected over the Internet makes purchasers increasingly uneasy. "People are balking at giving their

[23] http://www.consumer.gov/sentinel/pubs/Top10Fraud2004.pdf (accessed on August 4, 2005)

[24] Consumer Sentinel, "Executive Summary Consumer Fraud and Identity Theft Complaint Data," (January–December 2006), http://www.consumer.gov/sentinel/Sentinel_CY_2006/executive%20summary.pdf (accessed April 13, 2008).

[25] Allen Alter, "Identity Theft Losses are Falling," *Research Central* (February 2, 2007), http://blog.eweek.com/blogs/research_central/archive/2007/02/02/Identity_Theft_Losses_Are_Falling.aspx (accessed April 13, 2008).

information on the Web in a lot of cases because the organization has not made a good case for why they should," Culnan wrote. "If there are no benefits or if they aren't told why the information is being collected or how it's being used, a lot of people say 'Forget it.' "[26] As customers increasingly appreciate the power new technologies put in the hands of retailers, they become skeptical about the wisdom of providing personal information in transacting business online.

Recently the FTC made strides toward requiring Web retailers to more fully disclose how they will use customers' private information. The FTC's efforts to foster fair information practices for Internet commerce mesh with Mason's PAPA framework. To protect the integrity of information collected about them, federal regulators have recommended allowing consumers limited access to corporate information databases. Consumers thus could update their information and correct errors. Many consumer advocacy groups are arguing for requirement that retailers cannot use personal information unless the customer "opts-in," or specifically gives the retailer permission to use the information. The default practice now is "opting-out," or using the information unless the customer specifically tells the retailer that his or her personal information cannot be used or distributed. For example, the Gramm-Leach-Bliley Act (1999) gave customers of financial institutions the ability to opt-out of information sharing by those institutions. More recent, federal legislation requires states to allow registrants to "opt-in" their driver license information.

Information privacy guidelines must come from above: from the CEO, CIO, and general management. Employees must learn about these issues early in their tenure with a firm to avoid incurring serious problems with FTC oversight.

► SECURITY AND CONTROLS

It should be clear from the earlier discussion that the PAPA principles work hand-in-hand with security and controls. Unfortunately, organizations more often than not may rely on luck rather than proven information systems controls, at least according to a recent Ernst & Young survey. [27] More than half of the high-level executives responding to the survey reported that hardware, telecommunications, and software failures, as well as major viruses, Trojan horses, or Internet worms, had resulted in unexpected or unscheduled outages of their critical business systems. The survey confirmed that companies turn to technical responses to deal with these and other threats. In particular considerable emphasis is placed on using technology (i.e., antivirus countermeasures, spam-filtering software, intrusion detection systems) to protect organizational data from unauthorized hackers and undesirable viruses. Managers go to great lengths to make sure their computers are secure from outsider access, such as a hacker who seeks to enter a computer

---

[26] "Saving Private Data," *CIO Magazine* (October 1, 1998).

[27] Ernst & Young, Global Information Survey, 2004.

for sport or for malicious intent. They also try to safeguard against other external threats such as telecommunications failure, service provider failure, spamming, or distributed denial of service (DDoS) attacks.

Technologies have been devised to manage the security and control problems. Figure 9.3 summarizes three types of tools, such as firewalls, passwords, and

Hardware system security and control	Firewalls	A computer set up with both an internal network card and an external network card. This computer is set up to control access to the internal network and only lets authorized traffic pass the barrier.
	Encryption and decryption	Cryptography or secure writing ensures that information is transformed into unintelligible forms before transmission and intelligible forms when it arrives at its destination.
Network and software security controls	Network operating system software	The core set of programs that manage the resources of the computer or network often have functionality such as authentication, access control, and cryptology.
	Security information management	A management scheme to synchronize all mechanisms and protocols built into network and computer operating systems and protect the systems from authorized access.
	Server and browser software security	Mechanisms to ensure that errors in programming do not create holes and trapdoors that can compromise Web sites.
Broadcast medium security and controls	Labeling and rating software	The software industry incorporates Platform for Internet Content Selection (PICS) technology, a mechanism of labeling Web pages based on content. These labels can be used by filtering software to manage access.
	Filtering/blocking software	Software that rates documents and Web sites that have been rated and contain content on a designated filter's "black list" and keeps them from being displayed on the user's computer.

FIGURE 9.3   Security and control tools.

Source: Adapted from J. Berleur, P. Duquenoy, and D. Whitehouse, "Ethics and the Governance of the Internet," IFIP-SIG9.2.2, White paper, September 1999.

authentication routines, that restrict access to information on a computer by preventing access to the server on the network. They provide warning for early discovery of security breaches, limit losses suffered in case of security breaches, analyze and react to security breaches (and try to prevent them from reoccurring), and recover whatever has been lost from security breaches.[28]

Future technological approaches to security and privacy may include a combination of software and hardware. Some of today's laptop computers have built-in fingerprint identification pads to prevent unauthorized use. Biometrics are also being considered for security purposes at national levels. For example, in the United Kingdom, a debate is underway about making compulsory a national identity card that would contain 49 different types of information, including name, birth date and place, current and past addresses, a head and shoulders photograph, fingerprints, an iris scan and other biometric information, personal reference information, and registration and record histories. The British government is arguing that the card would give people a convenient way of proving their identity and preventing identity theft. It would also offer a secure way of identifying people for national security, detect crime, aid in enforcing immigration controls, prevent illegal workers, and assist in providing public services. Opponents fear the card will create a "Big Brother" world.

RFID tags with passport information and digital pictures of the owners have been included in new passports from Ireland, Japan, Pakistan, Norway, Malaysia, New Zealand, Belgium, the Netherlands, Germany, the United Kingdom, and the United States. However, security concerns were raised after it was clearly demonstrated that special equipment could read test passports from 10 meters (33 feet) away and not from a distance of 10 cm (4 in), as originally claimed. Consequently, U.S. passports were redesigned to incorporate a thin metal lining and a Basic Access Control to make it more difficult for unauthorized readers to "skim" information when the passport is closed. Nonetheless, the Center for Democracy and Technology has issued warnings that significant security weaknesses still exist.[29]

Although the focus on technological security controls just discussed has been primarily on dealing with external threats, managers must also guard against typically more lethal threats—internal threats that originate from within the company. Internal threats include operational errors (i.e., loading the wrong software) and former or current employee misconduct involving information systems, as well as hardware or software failure. Managers from the highest echelons down must champion the human aspect of protecting information. This means that they must be supportive of efforts to develop employees into the company's strongest layer of defense. These efforts include training and awareness programs to alert employees to risks, to make them aware of countermeasures

[28] J. Berleur, P. Duquenoy, and D. Whitehouse, "Ethics and the Governance of the Internet," IFIP SIG 9.2.2, White paper, September 1999.

[29] http://en.wikipedia.org/wiki/RFID#Passports (accessed on April, 23, 2008).

that exist to mitigate these risks, and to drill into them the importance of security, as well as awareness programs. Buttressing the technological controls, training, and awareness programs with security procedures and policies and an overall information security strategy can help round out a company's security efforts.

▶ IT GOVERNANCE AND SECURITY

The Weill and Ross Framework for IT governance introduced in Chapter 8 offers security professionals a new perspective for assigning responsibility for key security decisions.[30] Using the same archetypes described in Chapter 8, their framework is expanded to illustrate appropriate roles of business managers and IT managers in making a company's security decisions. As an example, the framework can be applied to five critical decisions about information security that are frequently discussed in the security literature.[31] A governance pattern that is appropriate for each decision is discussed next and displayed in Figure 9.4.

1. *Information Security Strategy.* A company's information security strategy is based on such IT principles as protecting the confidentiality of customer information, strict compliance with regulations, and maintaining a security baseline that is above the industry benchmark. Security strategy is not a technical decision. Rather, it should reflect the company's mission, overall strategy, business model, and business environment. Deciding on the security strategy requires decision makers who are knowledgeable about the company's strategy and management systems. In contrast, decision makers do not need to be well versed in information security implementation. Thus, a *business monarchy* is a good match for such situations in which the top business executives, including the CIO, set the tone for the company's security. The IT function may need to provide the required technical input for supporting the decision.

2. *Information Security Policies.* Security policies encourage standardization and integration. Following best practices, they broadly define the scope of and overall expectations for the company's information security program. From these security policies, lower-level policies are developed to control specific security areas (e.g., Internet use, access control) and/or individual applications (e.g., payroll systems, telecom systems). Policies must reflect the tenuous balance between the enhanced information security gained from adhering to them versus productivity losses and user inconvenience. As security attacks become more sophisticated, obeying security measures to deflect those attacks places increased cognitive demands on users

[30] P. Weill, and J. W. Ross, *IT Governance: How Top Performers Manage IT Decision Rights for Superior Results* (Boston: Harvard Business School Press, 2004).

[31] Andy Wu, "What Color Is Your Archetype? Governance Patterns for Information Security," PH.D, Dissertation, University of Central Florida, 2007.

Information Security Decision	Recommended Archetype	Rationale
Information Security Strategy	Business monarchy	Business leaders have the knowledge of the company's strategies, on which security strategy should be based. No detailed technical knowledge is required.
Information Security Policies	IT duopoly	Technical and security implications of behaviors and processes need to be analyzed and trade-offs between security and productivity need to be made. Need to know the particularities of company's IT infrastructure.
Information Security Infrastructure	IT monarchy	In-depth technical knowledge and expertise is needed.
Information Security Education/Training/ Awareness	IT duopoly	Business buy-in and understanding are needed. Technical expertise and knowledge of critical security issues is needed in building programs.
Information Security Investments	IT duopoly	Requires financial (quantitative) and qualitative evaluation of business impacts of security investments. Business case has to be presented for rivaling projects.

FIGURE 9.4   Matching information security decisions and archetypes.
Adapted from Andy Wu, "What Color Is Your Archetype? Governance Patterns for Information Security," PH.D, Dissertation, University of Central Florida, 2007.

(e.g., long passwords with special characters for system logon) and sacrifices productivity (e.g., the daily chore of scanning e-mails to spot phishing attempts). Not surprisingly, both IT and business perspectives are important in setting policies. Business users express what they want from the information security program and how they expect the security function to support their business activities. On the other hand, IT leaders should be consulted for two reasons: (1) their judgment prevents unrealistic goals for standardization and integration, and (2) policy decisions require the ability to analyze the technical and security implications of user behaviors and business processes. Thus, for high-level security architecture decisions, *IT duopoly* is a good fit.

3. *Information Security Infrastructure.* The information security infrastructure provides protection by arranging security mechanisms according to the IS architecture specifications. Firewalls, intrusion detection systems (IDSs), and encryption devices are the most popular examples of information security infrastructure, but other security and control tools are listed in Figure 9.3. Infrastructure decisions deal with technology selection

and configuration. Common objectives are to achieve consistency in protection, economies of scale, and synergy among the components. For these reasons, corporate IT typically is responsible for managing the dedicated security mechanisms. Also, general IT infrastructure, such as enterprise network devices, often is centrally controlled by corporate IT. Thus, fitting governance patterns for these decisions is *IT monarchy*, where corporate IT takes the lead.

4. *Information Security Education/Training/Awareness.* An important aspect of information security is making business users aware of security policies and practices. Training and awareness programs build a security-conscious culture. To promote effectiveness and posttraining retention, training and awareness programs must be linked to the unique requirements of individual business processes. User participation in planning and implementing training and awareness programs helps gain acceptance of security initiatives. However, IT security personnel are in the best position to know critical issues. Thus, an *IT duopoly* would be effective for combining the business and technical perspectives.

5. *Information Security Investments.* The "FUD factor" (fear, uncertainty, and doubt) used to be all that was needed to get top management to invest in information security. As information security becomes a routine concern in daily operations, security managers increasingly must justify their budget requests financially. Of course, qualitative cost-benefit assessments often supplement, or even substitute for, more quantitative financial analytical methods. As when determining business needs, different units within the company may have rival or conflicting "wish lists" for information security-related purchases that benefit their unique needs. The IT function also should have a significant say in these decisions, as it is in the best position to assess whether and how the investments may fit with the company's current IT infrastructure and application portfolio. Thus, an appropriate governance pattern for investment and prioritization decisions is IT duopoly. The most typical governance mechanism for this archetype is executive committees/councils composed of business and IT executives, such as the IT steering committee and budget committee, with the CIO having overlapping memberships in both. These committees are where IT and business leaders make business cases for their proposed investments and debate the merit and priorities of the investments. Decisions then are made with the company's best interest in mind.

These critical decision-archetype matches described are by no means etched in stone. Organizational and environmental factors may suggest other governance patterns. For instance, it is easy to imagine that business monarchy governs security investments decisions if a company emphasizes stringent budget review and control from a pure business/financial perspective. In enterprises with many relatively independent business units, a federal archetype that involves the corporate center, business unit leaders, and IT leaders may be the proper archetype for business requirement decisions.

The archetypes clearly define the responsibilities of the major players in the company—business executives, business unit leaders, corporate IT, business unit IT, and so forth. By matching appropriate archetypes to the key security decisions, the board of directors in effect puts the decisions in the hands of those who are in the most appropriate positions for making quality decisions. In addition, decision makers are truly empowered when they hold the authority to make decisions that (1) are suitable for their positions, (2) make the best use of their expertise and knowledge, and (3) cater to the needs and specialization of the organization units to which they belong.

▶ SARBANES–OXLEY ACT OF 2002

In response to rogue accounting activity by major global corporations such as Enron, Worldcom, and their accounting firms, such as Arthur Andersen, the **Sarbanes–Oxley Act (SoX)** was enacted in the United States in 2002 to increase regulatory visibility and accountability of public companies and their financial health. The U.S. federal government wanted to assure the investing public that financial markets could be relied on to deliver valid performance data and accurate stock valuation. All corporations that fall under the jurisdiction of the U.S. Securities and Exchange Commissions are subject to SoX requirements. This includes not only U.S. and foreign companies that are traded on U.S. exchanges, but also those that make up a significant part of a U.S. company's financial reporting. All told, 15,000 U.S. companies, 1,200 non-U.S.-based companies and over 1,400 accounting firms in 76 countries have been affected by SoX.[32]

According to SoX, CFOs and CEOs must personally certify and be accountable for their firms' financial records and accounting (Section 302), auditors must certify the underlying controls and processes that are used to compile the financial results of a company (Section 404), and companies must provide real-time disclosures of any events that may affect a firm's stock price or financial performance within a 48-hour period (Section 409). Penalties for failing to comply range from fines to a 20-year jail term.

Although SoX was not originally aimed at IT departments, it soon became clear that IT played a major role in ensuring the accuracy of financial data. Consequently, in 2004 and 2005, there was a flurry of activity as IT managers identified controls, determined design effectiveness, and validated operation of controls through testing. Five IT control weaknesses repeatedly were uncovered by auditors:[33]

---

[32] These figures were derived from the Public Company Accounting Oversight Board (PCAOB) as were reported in Ashley Braganza and Arnoud Franken's "SOX, Compliance, and Power Relationships," *Communications of the ACM* 50, no. 9 (September 2007): 97–102.

[33] Ben Worthen, *The Top Five I.T. Control Weaknesses* (July 1, 2005), available at http://www.cio.com/archive/070105/sox_sidebar_two.html.

1. Failure to segregate duties within applications, and failure to set up new accounts and terminate old ones in a timely manner.

2. Lack of proper oversight for making application changes, including appointing a person to make a change and another to perform quality assurance on it.

3. Inadequate review of audit logs to ensure that not only were systems running smoothly but also that there was an audit log of the audit log.

4. Failure to identify abnormal transactions in a timely manner.

5. Lack of understanding of key system configurations.

Although SoX's focus is on financial controls, many auditors encouraged (forced) IT managers to extend their focus to organizational controls and risks in business processes. This means that IT managers must assess the level of controls needed to mitigate potential risks in organizational business processes. As companies move beyond SoX certification into compliance, IT managers now must be involved in ongoing and consistent risk identification, actively recognize and monitor changes to the IT organization and environment that may affect SoX compliance, and continuously improve IT process maturity. It is likely that they will turn to software to automate many of the needed controls.

Frameworks for Implementing SoX

COSO

The recent Enron and Worldcom major financial scandals were not the first. In the wake of financial scandals in the mid 1980s the Treadway Commission (or National Commission on Fraudulent Financial Reporting) was created. Its head, James Treadway, had previously served as commissioner of the SEC. The members of the Treadway Commission came from five highly esteemed accounting organizations: Financial Executives International (FEI), the American Accounting Association (AAA), the American Institute of Certified Public Accountants (AICPA), the Institute of Internal Auditors (IIA), and the Institute of Management Accountants (IMA). These organizations became known as the Committee of Sponsoring Organizations of the Treadway Commission (COSO). Together they created three control objectives for management and auditors that focused on dealing with risks to internal control. These control objectives deal with:

- Operations—to help the company maintain and improve its operating effectiveness and protect the assets of shareholders.

- Compliance—to ensure that the company is in compliance with relevant laws and regulations.

- Financial reporting—to ensure that the company's financial statements are produced in accordance with Generally Accepted Accounting Principles (GAAP). *SoX is focused on this control objective.*

To make sure a company is meeting its control objectives, COSO established five essential control components for managers and auditors. These control components are (1) control environment, which addresses the overall culture of the company; (2) risk assessment of the most critical risks to internal controls; (3) control processes that outline important processes and guidelines; (4) information and communication of the procedures; and (5) monitoring by management of the internal controls. The Sabanes–Oxley Act requires public companies to define their control framework, and it specifically recommends COSO as that business framework for general accounting controls. It is not IT specific.

COBIT

COBIT (Control Objectives for Information and Related Technology) is an IT governance framework that is consistent with COSO controls. It is a governance tool that focuses on making sure that IT provides the systematic rigor needed for the strong internal controls and Sarbanes–Oxley compliance. It provides a framework for linking IT processes, IT resources, and IT information to a company's strategies and objectives. As a governance framework, it provides guidelines about who in the organization should be making decisions about the IT processes, resources, and information.

Information Systems Audit & Control Association (ISACA) issued COBIT in 1996. COBIT consists of several overlapping sets of guidance with multiple components, which almost form a cascade of process goals, metrics, and practices. At the highest level, key areas of risks are defined in four major domains (planning and organization, acquisition and implementation, delivery and support, and monitoring). When implementing a COBIT framework, the company determines the processes that are the most susceptible to the risks that it judiciously chooses to manage. There are far too many risks for a company to try to manage all of them.

Once the company identifies processes that it is going to manage, it sets up a control objective and then more specific key goal indicators. As with any control system, metrics need to be established to ensure that the goals are being met. These specific metrics are called key performance indicators. Then, activities to achieve the key goal indicators are selected. These activities, or critical success factors, are the steps that need to be followed to successfully provide controls for a selected process. When a company wants to compare itself with other organizations, it uses a well-defined maturity model. The components of COBIT and examples of each component are provided in Figure 9.5.

One advantage of COBIT is that it is well suited to organizations focused on risk management and mitigation. Another advantage is that it is very detailed. Unfortunately, this high level of detail can serve as a disadvantage in the sense that it makes COBIT very costly and time consuming to implement. Yet, despite the costs, companies are starting to realize benefits from implementing COBIT. As a governance framework, it designates clear ownership and responsibility for key organizational processes in such a way that is understood by all organizational

Component	Description	Example
Domain	One of four major areas of risk (plan and organize, acquire and implement, deliver and support, and monitor and evaluate); each domain consists of multiple processes	Delivery and support
Control Objective	Focuses on control of a process associated with risk; there are 34 processes	DS (delivery and support) 11—Manage data: ensures delivery of complete, accurate, and valid data to the business
Key Goal Indicator	Specific measures of the extent to which the goals of the system in regard to a control objective have been met	"A measured reduction in the data preparation process and tasks"
Key Performance Indicator	Actual, highly specific measures for measuring accomplishment of a goal	"Percent of data input errors" (Note: the percentage should decrease over specified periods of time)
Critical Success Factor	Describes the steps that a company must take to accomplish a control objective; there are 318 critical success factors	"Data entry requirements are clearly stated, enforced, and supported by automated techniques at all levels, including database and file interfaces"
Maturity Model	A uniquely defined six-point ranking of a company's readiness for each control objective made in comparison with other companies in the industry	"0—Data is not recognized as a corporate resource and asset. There is no assigned data ownership or individual accountability for data integrity and reliability; data quality and security is poor or nonexistent"

FIGURE 9.5 Components of COBIT and their examples.
Adapted from Hugh Taylor, *The Joy of SOX* (Indianapolis, IN: Wiley Publishing Inc, 2006).

stakeholders. Consistent with the Information Systems Strategy Triangle discussed in Chapter 1, COBIT provides a formal framework for aligning IT strategy with the business strategy. It does so by recognizing who is responsible for important control decisions using a governance framework. (See Chapter 8 for a discussion of governance.) And, it promotes a focus on risks of internal control and associated processes. Finally, it makes possible the fulfillment of the COSO requirements for the IT control environment that is encouraged by the Sarbanes–Oxley Act.

IT and the Implementation of Sarbanes–Oxley Act Compliance

Because of the level of detail, the involvement of the IT department and the CIO in implementing SoX, most notably Section 404, which deals with management's assessment of internal controls, is considerable. The CIO needs to work with auditors, the CFO, and the CEO in ensuring an appropriate response.[34] Although the IT department typically plays a major role in SoX compliance, it often is without any formal authority. Thus, the CIO needs to tread carefully when working with auditors, the CFO, the CEO, and business leaders. Braganza and Franken provide six tactics that CIOs can use in working effectively in these relationships.[35] These strategies include knowledge building, knowledge deployment, innovation directive mobilization, standardization, and subsidy. A definition for each of these tactics, along with examples of activities to enact these tactics, is provided in Figure 9.6.

The extent to which a CIO could use these various tactics depends on the power that he or she holds relating to the SoX implementation. Those few CIOs who are given a carte blanche by their CEOs to implement SoX compliance can employ more directive activities. That is, they can use subsidy, standardization, and innovative directives tactics. For example, they can establish standards and enforce their compliance; They can create an overarching corporate compliance architecture and use mandate compliance to various controls. They can direct the SoX implementation from top down and put 404 implementation drivers in place. If, on the other hand, the CEO does not vest the CIO with the considerable power to employ such tactics, the CIO may need to take more of a persuasive stance and be more involved in training programs and building an electronic knowledge database of SoX documents. In this case, it is especially important to sell the CIO and CFO on the importance of complying with prescribed procedures and methods. In either situation, the CIO needs to acquire and manage the considerable IT resources to make SoX compliance a reality.

Other Control Frameworks

Although COBIT is the most common set of IT control guidelines for SoX, it is by no means the only control framework. Others include those provided by the International Standards Organization (ISO), as well as **Information Technology Infrastructure Library (ITIL)**. ITIL is a set of concepts and techniques for managing information technology infrastructure, development, and operations that was developed in the United Kingdom. ITIL offers eight sets of management procedures in eight books: service delivery, service support, service management, ICT infrastructure management, software asset management, business perspective, security management, and application management. ITIL is a widely recognized framework for IT service management and operations management that has been adopted around the globe.

---

[34] Braganza and Franken, "SOX, Compliance, and Power Relationships."
[35] Ibid.

Tactic	Definition	Examples of Activities
Knowledge Building	Establishing a knowledge base to implement SoX	Acquiring technical knowledge about SoX and 404
Knowledge Deployment	Disseminating knowledge about SoX and developing an understanding of this knowledge among management and other organizational members	Moving IT staff with knowledge of 404 to parts of the organization that are less knowledgeable; creating a central repository of 404 knowledge; absorbing 404 requirements from external bodies; conducting training programs to spread an understanding of SoX
Innovation Directive	Organizing for implementing SoX and announcing the approach	Issuing instructions that encourage the adoption of 404 compliance practices; publishing progress reports of each subsidiary's progress toward 404 implementation; putting drivers for 404 implementation in place; directing 404 implementation from top down and/or bottom up
Mobilization	Persuading decentralized players and subsidiaries to participate in SoX implementation	Creating a positive impression of SoX (and 404) implementation; conducting promotional and awareness campaigns
Standardization	Negotiating agreements between organizational members to facilitate the SoX implementation	Using mandatory controls, often embedded within the technology, to which users must comply; indicating formal levels of compliance or variance from prescribed controls; establishing standards of control throughout the organization; creating an overarching corporate compliance architecture
Subsidy	Funding implementors' costs during the SoX implementation and users' costs during its deployment and use	Centralizing template development; developing Web-based resources; investing in developing the skills of IT staff to implementing 404; funding short-term skill gaps; investing in tracking implementation; managing funds during implementation to achieve specific IT-related 404 goals.

FIGURE 9.6 CIO Tactics for implementing SoX compliance.

▶ FOOD FOR THOUGHT: GREEN COMPUTING

Gartner Inc. recently put green computing at the top of its list of upcoming strategic technologies, signaling that more and more companies are becoming socially responsible.[36] **Green computing** is concerned with using computing resources efficiently. The need for green computing is becoming more obvious as the amount of power needed to drive the world's PCs, servers, routers, switches, and data centers continues to grow rapidly. Consider, for example, the computing power consumed by the five largest search companies. The five companies currently use about 2 million servers that need approximately 2.4 gigawatts to run. By comparison, the massive Hoover Dam at a maximum only generates about 2 gigawatts. The situation is complicated by the cooling systems that companies need to add to combat the heat that the highest-performing systems generate.[37]

Companies are working in a number of ways to adopt more socially responsible approaches to energy consumption. In particular they are replacing older systems with more energy-efficient ones, moving workloads based on energy efficiency, using the most power-inefficient servers only at times of peak usage, improving air flows in data centers, and turning to virtualization. **Virtualization** lets a computer run multiple operating systems or several versions of the same operating system at the same time. Further, some technologies to improve the temperature interface are being developed to support green computing. For example, localized temperature sensors are being designed to adjust the airflow from distributed fans to optimize cooling for the components of a system that are generating the most heat. Another technology is nanocarpets, which are carbon nanotubes that are configured like a Velcro carpet and are designed to conduct heat away from the chips to which they are attached.

An especially creative green approach is the one contemplated by Google to cool the computers that power its search engine. Google's management is considering placing the computers in a fleet of barges anchored approximately seven miles (11km) offshore. This would allow Google to turn tidal power, a continuous uninterruptible power source, into electricity. The sea could also be used to power a cooling pump to carry away the considerable heat generated by its computers[38].

Green programs can be considered to have a triple bottom line (TBL): economic, environmental, and social. They represent an expanded spectrum of values and criteria for measuring organizational and societal success. The triple bottom line is also known as "3BL," or "People, Planet, Profit".[39]

Green computing can be considered from the social contract theory perspective: Managers benefit society by conserving global resources when they make green, energy-related decisions about their computer operations. These are the "people" and "planet" motivations. However, their actions may also be evaluated

---

[36] P. Thibodeau, "Gartner's Top 10 Strategic Technologies for 2008," *Computerworld* (October 9, 2007), http://www.networkworld.com/news/2007/100907-10-strategic-technologies-gartner.html (accessed April 23, 2008).

[37] G. Lawton, "Powering Down the Computing Infrastructure," *Computer* (February 2007), 16–19.

[38] J. Mick, "Google Looks at Floating Data Centers for Energy," *Daily Tech*, September 16, 2008, http://www.dailytech.com/Google+Looks+to+Floating+Data+Centers+for+Energy/article12966 .htm (accessed October 1, 2008).

[39] Wikipedia. (2008, June 17). Green Computing. Retrieved June 17, 2008, from Wikipedia: http://en .wikipedia.org/wiki/Green_computing.

from the stockholder theory perspective. Energy-efficient computers reduce not only the direct costs of running the computing-related infrastructure, but also the costs of complementary utilities, such as cooling systems for the infrastructure components. This creates a huge "profit" motivation for companies to turn "green." The companies can become more environmentally friendly and reduce their energy costs at the same time.

▶ SUMMARY

- Due to the asymmetry of power relationships, managers tend to frame ethical concerns in terms of refraining from doing harm, mitigating injury, and paying attention to dependent and vulnerable parties. As a practical matter, ethics is about maintaining one's own, independent perspective about the propriety of business practices. Managers must make systematic, reasoned judgments about right and wrong and take responsibility for them. Ethics is about decisive action rooted in principles that express what is right and important and about action that is publicly defensible and personally supportable.
- Three important normative theories describing business ethics are (1) stockholder theory (maximizing stockholder wealth), (2) stakeholder theory (maximizing the benefits to all stakeholders while weighing costs to competing interests), and (3) social contract theory (creating value for society that is just and nondiscriminatory).
- PAPA is an acronym for the four areas in which control of information is crucial: privacy, accuracy, property, and accessibility.
- Issues related to the ethical governance of information systems are emerging in terms of the outward transactions of business that may impinge on the privacy of customers and electronic surveillance and other internally oriented personnel issues.
- Security looms as a major threat to Internet growth. Businesses are bolstering security with hardware, software, and communication devices.
- Security may best be enacted using a framework that assigns responsibility for security-related decision making based on governance archetypes.
- The Sarbanes–Oxley Act (2002) was enacted to improve internal controls. COBIT is an IT governance framework that can be used to promote IT-related internal controls and Sarbanes–Oxley compliance.

▶ KEY TERMS

accessibility (p. 257)
accuracy (p. 256)
cookie (p. 254)
COBIT (Control Objectives for Information and Related Technology) (p. 267)
green computing (p. 271)
identity theft (p. 257)

ITIL (Information Technology Infrastructure Library) (p. 269)
privacy (p. 253)
property (p. 256)
Sarbanes–Oxley Act (SoX) (p. 265)

social contract theory (p. 250)
stakeholder theory (p. 249)
stockholder theory (p. 248)
virtualization (p. 271)

▶ DISCUSSION QUESTIONS

1. Private corporate data is often encrypted using a key, which is needed to decrypt the information. Who within the corporation should be responsible for maintaining the "keys" to private information collected about consumers? Is that the same person who should have the "keys" to employee data?

2. Lotus Development Corporation launched its Marketplace product in 1990. The product was a marketing database of 120 million U.S. consumers, with demographic information based on publicly available information. Each consumer had personal information, such as name and mailing address. But the value proposition for the product was in the fact that it combined several publicly available databases, and the result was a database that made assumptions about lifestyle, income, family and marital status, and several other demographic categories. It was intended to give companies a comprehensive database of individual spending habits for direct-mail marketing using otherwise unthreatening databases. A grassroots outcry on the Internet resulted in over 30,000 letters and phone calls from individuals who wanted their names deleted from the product. The negative press Lotus received, combined with the flood of letters from consumers who were concerned about invasion of privacy, caused Lotus to cancel the project. In this case, the resulting database showed patterns of spending and placed consumers into categories that reflected personal data the consumers felt was private. But many organizations these days collect individual information, including your credit card provider, your bank, your creditors, and virtually any retail store in which you use a credit card or other identifying customer number. Who owns the information that is collected? Do you, the person who initially provided information to the collector? Or the collecting organization that spent the resources to save the information in the first place?

3. Consider arrest records, which are mostly computerized and stored locally by law enforcement agencies. They have an accuracy rate of about 50 percent—about half of them are inaccurate, incomplete, or ambiguous. These records often are used by others than just law enforcement. Approximately 90 percent of all criminal histories in the United States are available to public and private employers. Use the three normative theories of business ethics to analyze the ethical issues surrounding this situation. How might hiring decisions be influenced inappropriately by this information?

4. The European Community's Directive on Data Protection that was put into effect in 1998 strictly limits how database information is used and who has access to it. Some of the restrictions include registering all databases containing personal information with the countries in which they are operating, collecting data only with the consent of the subjects, and telling subjects of the database the intended and actual use of the databases. What effect might these restrictions have on global companies? In your opinion, should these types of restrictions be made into law? Why or why not? Should the United States bring its laws into agreement with the EU directive?

5. Should there be a global Internet privacy policy?

6. Is anonymous clickstream tracking and profiling objectionable? Is sending targeted advertising information to a computer using cookie ID numbers objectionable?

7. What is your opinion of the English ID card discussed in this chapter?

CASE STUDY 9-1

ETHICAL DECISION MAKING

Situation 1

The secretarial pool is part of the group assigned to Doug Smith, the manager of office automation. The pool has produced very low quality work for the past several months. Smith has access to the passwords for each of the pool members' computer accounts. He instructs the pool supervisor to go into each hard drive after hours and obtain a sample document to check for quality control for each pool member.

Discussion Questions

1. If you were the supervisor, what would you do?
2. What, if any, ethical propositions have been violated by this situation?
3. If poor quality were found, could the information be used for disciplinary purposes? For training purposes?
4. Apply PAPA to this situation.

Situation 2

Kate Essex is the supervisor of the customer service representative group for Enovelty.com, a manufacturer of novelty items. This group spends its workday answering calls, and sometimes placing calls, to customers to assist in solving a variety of issues about orders previously placed with the company. The company has a rule that personal phone calls are only allowed during breaks. Essex is assigned to monitor each representative on the phone for 15 minutes a day, as part of her regular job tasks. The representatives are aware that Essex will be monitoring them, and customers are immediately informed when they begin their calls. Essex begins to monitor James Olsen, and finds that he is on a personal call regarding his sick child. Olsen is not on break.

Discussion Questions

1. What should Essex do?
2. What, if any, ethical principles help guide decision making in this situation?
3. What management practices should be in place to ensure proper behavior without violating individual "rights"?
4. Apply the normative theories of business ethics to this situation.

Situation 3

Jane Mark was the newest hire in the IS group at We_Sell_More.com, a business on the Internet. The company takes in $30 million in revenue quarterly from Web business. Jane reports to Sam Brady, the VP of IS. Jane is assigned to a project to build a new capability into the company Web page that facilitates linking products ordered with future offerings of the company. After weeks of analysis, Jane concluded that the best way to incorporate that capability is to buy a software package from a small start-up company in Silicon Valley, California. She convinces Brady of her decision and is authorized to lease the software. The vendor e-mails Jane the software in a ZIP file and instructs her on how to install it. At the initial installation, Jane is asked to acknowledge and electronically sign the license agreement. The installed system does not ask Jane if she wants to make a backup copy of the software on diskettes, so as a precaution, Jane takes it on herself and copies the ZIP files sent to her onto a set of floppies. She stores these floppies in her desk drawer.

A year later the vendor is bought by another company, and the software is removed from the marketplace. The new owner believes this software will provide them with a competitive advantage they want to reserve for themselves. The new vendor terminates all lease agreements and revokes all licenses on their expiration. But Jane still has the floppies she made as backup.

Discussion Questions

1. Is Jane obligated to stop using her backup copy? Why or why not?
2. If We_Sell_More.com wants to continue to use the system, can they? Why or why not?
3. Does it change your opinion if the software is a critical system for We_Sell_More.com? If it is a noncritical system? Explain.

Situation 4

Some of the Internet's biggest companies (i.e., Google, Microsoft, Yahoo, IBM, and Verisign) are working on a new "single sign-on" system that would make it easier to surf the Web. As corporate members of the OpenID Foundation, they are supporting the development of a system that would make it easier for users to sign on to a number of sites without having to remember multiple user IDs, passwords, and registration information. Under OpenID, the companies would share the sign-on information for any Web user who agrees to participate. They would also share personal information such as credit card data, billing addresses, and personal preferences.

Discussion Questions

1. Discuss any threats to privacy in this situation.
2. Who would own the data? Explain.
3. Who do you think should have access to the data? How should that access be controlled?

Situation 5

SpectorSoft markets eBlaster as a way to keep track of what your spouse or children are doing online. Operating in stealth mode, eBlaster tracks every single keystroke entered into a computer, from instant messages to passwords. It also records every e-mail sent and received and every Web site visited by the unsuspecting computer user. The data is sent anonymously to an IP address of the person who installed eBlaster. eBlaster could also be installed onto a business's computers.

Discussion Questions

1. Do you think it would be ethical for a business to install eBlaster to ensure that its employees are engaged only in work-related activities? If so, under what conditions would it be appropriate? If not, why not?
2. Apply the normative theories of business ethics to this situation.

Situation 6

Red-light camera systems are used by government agencies internationally to catch drivers passing through intersections with a red light showing on the traffic signal. The systems continuously monitor the traffic signal, and the camera is triggered by any vehicle entering the intersection following a specified time after the signal has turned red. Cameras record the date, time of day, time elapsed since the beginning of the red signal, vehicle speed, and license plate.

The Insurance Institute for Highway Safety has concluded that cameras reduce red light violations by 40% to 50% and reduce injury crashes by 25% to 30%. However, critics of such programs argue that the decrease in side-impact collisions has been accompanied by an increase in rear-end collisions as drivers slam on their brakes to avoid running a red light.

Some agencies that have implemented the systems have benefited from revenues generated by fines that exceed their costs (i.e., the costs of installing the system and the charges of the private contractors who operate the programs). Some criticize the fines and revenue-sharing arrangement with the technology providers, arguing that cameras are placed to optimize revenues rather than to promote the most safety. Consequently, some red-light camera technology providers have negotiated flat-fee, rather than revenue-based, contracts.

Discussion Questions

1. Do you see any ethical issues involved in the use of red-light camera systems? Why or why not?
2. Should cities allow outsourcing of the operation of the systems? Why or why not?
3. Apply the normative theories of business ethics to the use of red-light camera systems.

Sources: Situations 1 to 4 adapted from short cases suggested by Professor Kay Nelson, University of Utah. The names of people, places, and companies have been made up for these stories. Any similarity to real people, places, or companies is purely coincidental. Situation 6 was based on a minicase by Chad Hutyra and adapted from Jonathan Miller, "With Cameras on the Corner, Your Ticket Is in the Mail," *New York Times*, (January 6, 2005), http://www.nytimes.com/2005/01/06/technology/circuits/06came.html?ei=5090&en=8bc6df38e1042a40&ex=1262667600&partner=techdirt&pagewanted=all&position= (accessed March 30, 2008); and Jonathan Silverstein, "Do Red-Light Traffic Cameras Help?" abcnews.com, (February 19, 2005), http://abcnews.go.com/US/story?id=292547&page=1 (accessed March 30, 2008).

CASE STUDY 9-2

MIDWEST FAMILY MUTUAL GOES GREEN

Midwest Family Mutual Insurance Co. ($70 million in annual premiums) has declared itself "operationally green." Through a variety of initiatives it has reduced its annual energy, natural gas, and paper consumption by 63%, 76%, and 65%, respectively. Ron Boyd, the carrier's CEO, attributes most of the improvements in energy usage to creating a virtual "work from home" office environment. As a result of implementing a series of electronic processes and applications, including imaging and workflow technology, networking technology, and a VoIP network, all but two of Midwest Family Mutual's 65 employees can now work from home. In addition to the energy savings that Midwest Family Mutual has directly experienced, Boyd estimates that the company's telecommuting policy has resulted in fuel savings of at least 25,000 gallons.

Though green computing was a commendable goal in itself, Midwest Family Mutual's bottom line also has benefitted from the company's socially responsible approach. "In the past five years the company has decreased its expense ratio from 33.5% to 29.9% of every dollar," Boyd states. "Being environmentally green can equate to financial green."

Green computing grew out of Midwest Family Mutual's IT successes, according to Boyd. "As we saw the effectiveness of our imaging and workflow in establishing a truly paperless environment, we started thinking about work-from-home [arrangements]. It became obvious that many of our jobs could be done wherever a high-speed connection existed . . . VOIP completed the technology requirements for all [employees] to work from home."

Boyd summarizes: "We became green as a side benefit of saving resources and cost." The company continued its green policy with its decision to sell its 24,000-square-foot office building in Minnetonka, Minnesota. After the sale of the property, it moved to a more energy-efficient rental property in Plymouth, which conforms to the Environmental Protection Agency's Energy Star standards.

Discussion Questions

1. Do you think that the economic benefits that Midwest Family Mutual realized as a result of green computing are unusual? Do you think most companies can see similar types of economic gains? Explain.
2. What are some possible disadvantages the employees of Midwest Family Mutual may be experiencing as a result of their new virtual "work from home" office environment?
3. Apply the normative theories of business ethics to this situation.

Source: Adapted from Anthony O'Donnell, "Plymouth, Minnesota-based Midwest Family Mutual's Move to a Paperless, Work-at-Home Operational Paradigm Has Yielded Both Environmental and Bottom-Line Benefits," *Insurance & Technology* (February 24, 2008), http://www.insurancetech .com/resources/fss/showArticle.jhtml;jsessionid=AYMVWDKZBGIFIQSNDLOSKHSCJUNN2JVN? articleID=206801556 (accessed April 23, 2008).

10

FUNDING IT

The CIO of Avon Products, Inc., in New York relies heavily on hard-dollar metrics such as net present value (NPV) and internal rate of return (IRR) to demonstrate the business value resulting from information technology (IT) investments. Although these are not the typical IT metrics, they are the language of business. Funding IT becomes a matter of speaking the language of business. "We apply all of the analytical rigor and financial ROI tools against each of our IT projects as well as other business projects," the CIO (Chief information officer) of Avon Products remarked. Avon uses payback, NPV, IRR, and risk analyses for every investment. Further, each IT project is monitored using a green-/yellow-/red-coded dashboard to convey the status as "on target," "warning," or "having serious problems." Monthly reports to the senior management team inform them about the status of major projects. Other business tools, such as investment-tracking databases and monitors on capital spending, assist the CIO's office in managing the funds allocated to the IT group.[1]

The business side of IT is similar to the business itself. Projects are funded through budget allocations or a multitude of other sources, and managing those funds is done with prudent business practices. As Avon's CIO's comments indicate, the basic tools of finance and accounting are the basic tools for the financial management of IT and, further, for determining and communicating the value received from IT investments.

In this chapter we explore issues related to the financial side of IT. We begin by looking at ways of funding the IT department, then continue with an exploration of several ways to calculate the cost of IT investments, including total cost of ownership and activity-based costing, and ways of monitoring IT investments once they are made, including portfolio management. These topics are critical for the IT manager to understand, but a general manager must also understand how the business of IT works to successfully propose, plan, manage, and use IT systems.

▶ FUNDING IT RESOURCES

Who pays for IT? The users? The IT department? The corporate function? Certain costs are associated with designing, developing, delivering, and maintaining the

---

[1] Adapted from Thomas Hoffman, "How Will You Prove IT Value?" *Computerworld* (January 6, 2003).

IT systems. How are these costs recovered? The three main funding methods are chargeback, allocation, and corporate budget. Both chargeback and allocation methods distribute the costs back to the businesses, departments, or individuals within the company. This distribution of costs is used for management reasons, so that managers can understand the costs associated with running their organization, or for tax reasons, where the costs associated with each business must be paid for by the appropriate business unit. Corporate budgeting, on the other hand, is a completely different funding method in which IT costs are not linked directly with any specific user or business unit; costs are recovered using corporate coffers.

Chargeback

With a **chargeback funding method**, IT costs are recovered by charging individuals, departments, or business units based on actual usage and cost. The IT department collects usage data on each system it runs. Rates for usage are calculated based on the actual cost to the IT group to run the system and billed out on a regular basis. For example, a desktop PC might be billed out at $100/month, which includes the cost of maintaining the system, any software license fees for the standard desktop configuration, e-mail, network access, a usage fee for the help desk, and other related services. Each department receives a bill showing the number of desktop computers they have and the charge per desktop, the number of printers they have and the charge per printer, the number of servers they have and the charge per server, the amount of mainframe time they have used and the cost per second of that time, and so on. When the IT department wants to recover administrative and overhead costs using a chargeback system, these costs are built into rates charged for each of the services.

Chargeback systems are popular because they are viewed as the most equitable way to recover IT costs. Costs are distributed based on usage or consumption of resources, ensuring that the largest portion of the costs is paid for by the group or individual who consumes the most. Chargeback systems can also provide managers with the most options for managing and controlling their IT costs. For example, a manager may decide to use desktop systems rather than laptop systems because the unit charge is less expensive. The chargeback system gives managers the details they need to understand both what IT resources they use and how to account for IT consumption in the cost of their products and services. Because the departments get a regular bill, they know exactly what their costs are.

Creating and managing a chargeback system, however, is a costly endeavor itself. IT departments must build systems to collect details that might not be needed for anything other than the bills they generate. For example, if PCs are the basis for charging for network time, then the network connect time per PC must be collected, stored, and analyzed each billing cycle. The data collection quickly becomes large and complex, which often results in complicated, difficult-to-understand bills. In addition, picking the charging criteria is more of an art than a science. For example, it is relatively easy to count the number of PCs located in a particular business unit, but is that number a good measure of the network resources used? It might be more accurate to charge based on units of network time used, but how would that be captured and calculated?

Chargeback methods are most appropriate when there is a wide variation in usage among users or when actual costs need to be accounted for by the business units.

Allocation

To simplify the cost recovery process compared to the chargeback method, an allocation system can be used. An **allocation funding method** recovers costs based on something other than usage, such as revenues, login accounts, or number of employees. For example, suppose the total spending for IT for a year is $1 million for a company with 10,000 employees. A business unit with 1,000 employees might be responsible for 10%, or $100,000, of the total IT costs. Of course, with this type of allocation system, it does not matter whether these employees even use the IT; the department is still charged the same amount.

The allocation mechanism is simpler to implement and apply each month. Actual usage does not need to be captured. The rate charged is often fixed at the beginning of the year. It offers two main advantages. First, the level of detail required to calculate the allocations is much less, and for many organizations that aspect saves expense. Second, the charges from the IT department are predictable. Unlike the chargeback mechanism, where each bill opens up an opportunity for discussion about the charges incurred, the allocation mechanism seems to generate far less frequent arguments from the business units. Often, quite a bit of discussion takes place at the beginning of the year, when rates and allocation bases are set, but less discussion occurs each month because the managers understand and expect the bill.

Two major complaints are made about allocation systems. First is the free-rider problem: A large user of IT services pays the same amount as a small user when the charges are not based on usage. Second, deciding the basis for allocating the costs is an issue. Choosing the number of employees over the number of desktops or other basis is a management decision, and whichever basis is chosen, someone will pay more than their actual usage would imply. Allocation mechanisms work well when a corporate directive requires use of this method and when the units agree on the basis for dividing up the costs.

Often when an allocation process is used, a follow-up process is needed at the end of the fiscal year, in which total IT expenses are compared to total IT funds recovered from the business units, and any extra funds are given back to the business. Sometimes this process is called a "true-up" process because true expenses are balanced against payments made. In some cases, additional funds are needed; however, IT managers try to avoid asking for funds to make up for shortfalls in their budget. The true-up process is needed because the actual cost of the information system is difficult to predict at the beginning of the year. Cost changes over the year because hardware, software, or support costs fluctuate in the marketplace and because IT managers, like all managers, work constantly on improving efficiency and productivity, resulting in lower costs. In an allocation process, where the rate charged for each service is fixed for the year, a true-up process allows IT managers to pass along any additional savings to their business counterparts. Business managers often prefer the predictability of their monthly IT bills along with a true-up process over the relative unpredictability of being charged actual costs each month.

Corporate Budget

An entirely different way to pay for IT costs is to simply consider them all to be corporate overhead and pay for them directly out of the corporate budget. With the **corporate budget funding method**, the costs fall to the corporate bottom line, rather than levying charges on specific users or business units.

Corporate budgeting is a relatively simple method for funding IT costs. It requires no calculation of prices of the IT systems. And because bills are not generated on a regular cycle to the businesses, concerns are raised less often by the business managers. IT managers control the entire budget, giving them control of the use of those funds and, ultimately, more input into what systems are created, how they are managed, and when they are retired. This funding method also encourages the use of new technologies because learners are not charged for exploration and inefficient system use.

As with the other methods, certain drawbacks come with using the corporate budget. First, all IT expenditures are subjected to the same process as all other corporate expenditures, namely, the budgeting process. In many companies, this process is one of the most stressful events of the year: Everyone has projects to be done, and everyone is competing for scarce funds. If the business units do not get billed in some way for their usage, many companies find that they do not control their usage. Getting a bill for services motivates the individual business manager to reconsider his or her usage of those services. Finally, if the business units are not footing the bill, the IT group may feel less accountable to them, which may result in an IT department that is less end-user or customer oriented.

Figure 10.1 summarizes the advantages and disadvantages of these methods.

▶ HOW MUCH DOES IT COST?

The three major IT funding approaches in the preceding discussion are designed to recover the costs of building and maintaining the information systems in an enterprise. The goal is to simply cover the costs, not to generate a profit (although some MIS organizations are actually profit centers for their corporation). The most basic method for calculating the costs of a system is to add the costs of all the components, including hardware, software, network, and the people involved. Many management information systems (MIS) organizations calculate the initial costs and ongoing maintenance costs in just this way.

Funding Method	Description	Why Do It?	Why Not Do It?
Chargeback	Charges are calculated based on actual usage.	Fairest method for recovering costs because it is based on actual usage. IT users can see exactly what their usage costs.	IT department must collect details on usage, which can be expensive and difficult. IT must be prepared to defend the charges, which takes time and resources.
Allocation	Total expected IT expenditures are divided by nonusage basis such as number of login IDs, employees, or desktops.	Less bookkeeping for IT because rate is set once per fiscal year, and basis is well understood. Predictable monthly costs.	IT department must defend allocation rates; may charge low-usage department more than their usage would indicate is fair.
Corporate Budget	Corporate allocates funds to IT at annual budget session.	No billing to the businesses. IT exercises more control over what projects are done. Good for encouraging use of new technologies.	Competes with all other budgeted items for funds.

FIGURE 10.1 Comparison of IT funding methods.

Activity-Based Costing

Another method for calculating costs is known as **activity-based costing (ABC)**. Traditional accounting methods account for direct and indirect costs. Direct costs are those costs that can be clearly linked to a particular process or product, such as the components used to manufacture the product and the assembler's wages for time spent building the product. Indirect costs are the overhead costs, which include everything from the electric bill, the salary of administrative managers, and the expenses of administrative function, to the wages of the supervisor overseeing the assembler, the cost of running the factory, and the maintenance of machinery used for multiple products. Further, depending on the funding method used by the organization, indirect costs are allocated or absorbed elsewhere in the pricing model. The allocation process can be cumbersome and complex and often is a source of trouble for many organizations. The alternative is ABC.

Activity-based costing counts the actual activities that go into making a specific product or delivering a specific service. *Activities* are processes, functions, or tasks that occur over time and produce recognized results. They consume assigned resources to produce products and services. Activities are useful in costing because they are the common denominator between business process improvement and information improvement across departments.

Rather than allocate the total indirect cost of a system across a range of services according to an allocation formula, ABC calculates the amount of time that system was spent supporting a particular activity and allocates only that cost to that activity. For example, an accountant would look at the ERP (enterprise resource planning system) and divide its cost over the activities it supports by calculating how much of the system is used by each activity. Product A might take up one-twelfth of an ERP system's capacity to control the manufacturing activities needed to make it, so it would be allocated one-twelfth of the system's costs. The help desk might take up a whole server, so the entire server's cost would be allocated to that activity. In the end, the costs are put in buckets that reflect the products and services of the business, rather than the organization structure or the processes of any given department. In effect, ABC is the process of charging all costs to "profit centers" instead of to "cost centers."

Total Cost of Ownership

When a system is proposed and a business case is created to justify the investment, summing up the initial outlay and the maintenance cost does not provide an entirely accurate total system cost. In fact, if only the initial and maintenance cost are considered, the decision is often made on incomplete information. Other costs are involved, and a time value of money affects the total cost. One technique used to calculate a more accurate cost is **total cost of ownership (TCO)**. It is fast becoming the industry standard. Gartner Group introduced TCO in the late 1980s when PC-based IT infrastructures began gaining popularity.[2] Other IT experts have since modified the concept, and this section synthesizes the latest and best thinking about TCO.

TCO looks beyond initial capital investments to include costs associated with technical support, administration, training, and system retirement. Often, the initial cost is an inadequate predictor of the additional costs necessary to successfully implement the system. TCO techniques estimate annual costs per user for each potential infrastructure choice; these costs are then totaled. Careful estimates of TCO provide the best investment numbers to compare with financial return numbers when analyzing the net returns on various IT options. The alternative, an analysis without TCO, can result in an "apples and oranges" comparison. Consider a decision about printers. The initial cost of one printer may be much less than a second choice. However, the cost and longevity of the ink cartridges necessary to run each printer may vary significantly. Likewise, a laser printer may be more expensive initially, but when considering the expected lifetime of the

---

[2] M. Gartenberg, "Beyond the Numbers: Common TCO Myths Revealed," GartnerGroup Research Note: Technology (March 2, 1998).

printer, compared to an inexpensive alternative, the total cost of ownership may be much less. A similar analysis of a larger IT system clarifies similar alternatives and comparisons.

A major IT investment is for infrastructure. Figure 10.2 uses the hardware, software, network, and data categories to organize the TCO components the manager needs to evaluate for each infrastructure option. This table allows the manager to assess infrastructure components at a medium level of detail and categorically to allocate "softer" costs like administration and support. More or less detail can be used as needed by the business environment. The manager can adapt this framework for use with varying IT infrastructures.

TCO Component Breakdown

To clarify how the TCO framework is used, this section examines the hardware category in greater detail. As used in Figure 10.2, hardware means computing platforms and peripherals. The components listed are somewhat arbitrary, and an organization in which every user possesses every component would be highly unusual. For shared components, such as servers and printers, TCO estimates should be computed per component and then divided among all users who access them.

For more complex situations, such as when only certain groups of users possess certain components, it is wise to segment the hardware analysis by platform. For example, in an organization in which every employee possesses a desktop that accesses a server and half the employees also possess stand-alone laptops that do not access a server, one TCO table could be built for desktop and server hardware and another for laptop hardware. Each table would include software, network, and data costs associated only with its specific platforms.

Soft costs, such as technical support, administration, and training, are easier to estimate than they may first appear. To simplify, these calculations can be broken down further using a table such as Figure 10.3.

The final soft cost, informal support, may be harder to pin down, but it is important nonetheless. Informal support comprises the sometimes highly complex networks that develop among coworkers through which many problems are fixed and much training takes place without the involvement of any official support staff. In many circumstances, these activities can prove more efficient and effective than working through official channels. Still, managers want to analyze the costs of informal support for two reasons:

1. The costs—both in salary and in opportunity—of a nonsupport employee providing informal support may prove significantly higher than analogous costs for a formal support employee. For example, it costs much more in both dollars per hour and foregone management activity for a midlevel manager to help a line employee troubleshoot an e-mail problem than it would for a formal support employee to provide the same service.

2. The quantity of informal support activity in an organization provides an indirect measure of the efficiency of its IT support organization. The

Category	Infrastructure Component	Cost per end user of Option 1	Cost per end user of Option 2
Hardware	Desktops		
	Servers		
	Mobile platforms		
	Printers		
	Archival storage		
	Technical support		
	Administration		
	Training		
	Informal support		
	Retirement		
	Total Hardware Cost		
Software	OS		
	Office Suite		
	Database		
	Proprietary		
	Technical support		
	Administration		
	Training		
	Informal support		
	Total Software Cost		
Network	LAN		
	WAN		
	Dial-in lines/modems		
	Technical support		
	Administration		
	Total Network Cost		
Data	Removable media		
	Onsite backup storage		
	Offsite backup storage		
	Total Data Cost		

FIGURE 10.2 TCO component evaluation.

Category	Component	Responsible party	Annual hours	Cost/ hour	Total cost
Technical support	Hardware phone support	Call center			
	In-person hardware troubleshooting	IT operations			
	Hardware hot swaps	IT operations			
	Physical hardware repair	IT operations			
	Total cost of technical support				
Administration	Hardware setup	System administrator			
	Hardware upgrades/ modifications	System administrator			
	New hardware evaluation	IT operations			
	Total cost of administration				
Training	New employee training	IT operations			
	Ongoing administrator training	Hardware vendor			
	Total cost of training				
	Total soft costs for hardware				

FIGURE 10.3   Soft costs considerations.

formal support organization should respond with sufficient promptness and thoroughness to discourage all but the briefest informal support transactions.

Various IT infrastructure options affect informal support activities differently. For example, a more user-friendly systems interface may alleviate the need for much informal support, justifying a slightly higher software expenditure. Similarly, an investment in support management software may be justified if it reduces the need for informal support. Web-based applications change the equation even further. Those companies who use a vendor-supplied Web-based application may find support activities are provided by the vendor, or the applications are written in such as way as to minimize or eliminate support entirely.

Although putting dollar values on informal support may be a challenge, managers want to gauge the relative potential of each component option to affect the need for informal support.

TCO as a Management Tool

This discussion focused on TCO as a tool for evaluating which infrastructure components to choose, but TCO also can help managers understand how infrastructure costs break down. Gartner Group research consistently shows that the labor costs associated with an IT infrastructure far outweigh the actual capital investment costs.[3] TCO provides the fullest picture of where managers spend their IT dollars. Like other benchmarks, TCO results can be evaluated over time against industry standards (much TCO target data for various IT infrastructure choices are available from industry research firms). Even without comparison data, the numbers that emerge from TCO studies assist in decisions about budgeting, resource allocation, and organizational structure.

However, like the ABC approach, the cost of implementing TCO can be a detriment to the program's overall success. Both ABC and TCO are complex approaches that may require significant effort to determine the costs to use in the calculations. Managers must weigh the benefits of using these approaches with the costs of obtaining reliable data necessary to make their use successful.

▶ BUILDING A BUSINESS CASE

To gain support and a "go-ahead" decision on an IT investment (or any business investment, for that matter), a manager must often create a business case. Similar to a legal case, a **business case** is a structured document that lays out all the relevant information needed to make a go/no-go decision. The business case for an IT project is also a way to establish priorities for investing in different projects, an opportunity to identify how IT and the business will deliver new benefits, gain commitment from business managers, and create a basis for monitoring the investment.[4]

The components of a business case vary from corporation to corporation, depending on the priorities and decision-making environment. However, there are several primary elements of any business case. They are listed in Figure 10.4. Critical to the business case is the identification of both costs and benefits, both in financial and nonfinancial terms.

Building the business case is more an art than a science. Of particular note is how is a description of the benefits to be gained with the acceptance of the project being sold in the business case. Ward, Daniel, and Peppard[5] have suggested framework for identifying and describing both financial and nonfinancial benefits, shown in Figure 10.5. The first step in this framework is to identify each benefit as innovation, or allowing the organization to do new things; improvement, or allowing the organization to do things better; or cessation, stopping things. Then

---

[3] W. Kirwin, "TCO: The Emerging Manageable Desktop," GartnerGroup Top VIEW (September 24, 1996).

[4] John Ward, Elizabeth Daniel, and Joe Peppard, "Building Better Business Cases for IT Investments" *MISQE* 7, no. 1 (March 2008), 1–15.

[5] Ibid.

Section or Component	Description
Executive Summary	One- or two-page description of the overall business case document.
Overview and Introduction	Includes a brief business background, the current business situation, a clear statement of the business problem or opportunity, and a recommended solution at a high level.
Assumptions and Rationale	Includes issues driving the proposal (could be operational, human resource, environmental, competitive, industry or market trends, financial or otherwise).
Program Summary	Includes high-level and then detailed description of the project, well-defined scope, objectives, contacts, resource plan, key metrics (financial and otherwise), implementation plan (high-level discussion and potential impacts) and key components to make this a success.
Financial Discussion and Analysis	Starts with financial summary. Then includes details such as projected costs/revenues/benefits, financial metrics, financial model, cash flow statement, and assumptions that went into creating financial statements. Total Cost of Ownership (TCO) calculations analysis would go in this section.
Benefits and Business Impacts	Starts with business impacts summary. Then includes details on all nonfinancial outcomes such as new business, transformation, innovations, competitive responses, organizational, supply chain, and human resource impacts.
Schedule and Milestones	Outlines the entire schedule for the project, highlights milestones and details of expected metrics at each stage (what makes the go/no-go decision at each stage). If appropriate, this section can also include a marketing plan and schedule (sometimes this is a separate section).
Risk and Contingency Analysis	Includes details on risks, risk analysis, and contingencies to manage those risks. Includes sensitivity analysis on the scenario(s) proposed and contingencies to manage anticipated consequences. Includes interdependencies and impact they will have on potential outcomes.
Conclusion and Recommendation	Reiterates primary recommendation and draws any necessary conclusions
Appendices	Can include any backup materials that were not directly included in the body of the document such as detailed financial investment analysis, marketing materials, and competitors' literature.

FIGURE 10.4 Components of a business case.

		Type of Business Change		
		Innovation (Do new things)	Improvement (Do things better)	Cessation (Stop doing things)
High	Financial Benefits	Financial value can be calculated by applying a cost/price or other valid financial formula to a quantifiable benefit		
	Quantifiable Benefits	There is sufficient evidence to forecast how much improvement/benefit should result from the changes.		
degree of explicitness	Measurable Benefits	Although this aspect of performance is currently measured, or an approximate measure could be implemented, it is not possible to estimate how much performance will improve when changes are implemented.		
Low	Observable Benefits	By using agreed criteria, specific individuals or groups will use their experience or judgment to decide the extent the benefit will be realized.		

FIGURE 10.5 Classification framework for benefits in a business case.
Source: Adapted from John Ward, Elizabeth Daniel, and Joe Peppard, "Building Better Business Cases for IT Investments," *MISQE* 7, no. 1 (March 2008): 1–15.

the benefits can be classified by degree of explicitness or the ability to assign a value to the benefit. As shown in Figure 10.5, benefits fall into one of these categories:

- Observable—can only be measured by opinion or judgment. These are the subjective, intangible, soft, or qualitative benefits.
- Measurable—There is already a well-accepted way to measure for the benefit (but it may not be a quantifiable measure). Using existing measures to ensure alignment with the business strategy.
- Quantifiable—There is a way to measure the size or magnitude of the benefit. Most business cases revolve around quantifiable benefits, so ensuring that as many benefits as possible have a quantifiable metric is important.
- Financial—There is a way to express the benefit in financial terms. These are the metrics that are most easily used to judge the go-no go decision because financial terms are universal across all business decisions.

Consider this example of a UK-based mobile telephone company. The company's strategy was to differentiate itself with excellent customer service, and it identified a project to upgrade the call centers as a potential opportunity. Figure 10.6 contains a sample of the cost-risk-benefit analysis for this business case. Note that in this example, costs were described in terms of six categories: purchases, implementation technical consultants, development, infrastructure, business change, and training costs. Risks were categorized as financial risks, technical risks, and organizational risks.[6]

---

[6] Ibid.

Objective Type	Doing New Things	Doing Things Better	Stop Doing Things
Financial		**Benefit:** Increased customer retention due to improved service provision **Measure:** Reduction in customer defections. Avoided defections due to service failure = 1,750 pa Cost per defection = £500—saving of £875,000 pa **Benefit Owner:** Customer accounts manager **Benefit:** 20% reduction in call servicing costs **Measure:** Cost per service call. Number of calls pa = 5.6 million, total servicing costs = £1.2 million—savings of £240,000 pa **Benefit Owner:** Telechannel sales manager	**Benefit:** Stop call-backs to customers after failed service calls **Measure:** Number of call-backs. Number in previous years = 1.5 million. Cost per call-back = £0.46—savings of £690,000 pa **Benefit Owner:** Call center operations manager
Quantifiable			**Benefit:** Eliminate call waiting times over 2 minutes for customers **Measure:** Number of calls currently waiting over 2 minutes = 1.1 million **Benefit Owner:** Call center operations manager
Measurable	**Benefit:** Call center staff able to undertake sales calls/promote new services **Measure:** Number of sales calls per staff member or sales per staff member. Current value = 0 (call center currently purely inbound) **Benefit Owner:** Telechannel sales manager	**Benefit:** Customers not switching to competitors' products and services **Measure:** Number of defections to competitors. Current number of customers switching = 5,500 pa **Benefit Owner:** Customer accounts manager	
Observable	**Benefit:** Call center staff motivated by being trained about newer services **Measure:** Increased call center motivation **Benefit Owner:** Call center staff manager	**Benefit:** Ability to develop future services based on customer data **Measure:** Quantity and quality of customer profile data **Benefit Owner:** New service development manager	**Benefit:** Stop customers becoming frustrated/rude because of service failure **Measure:** Call center staff opinion **Benefit Owner:** Call center staff manager

Investment Costs	
Purchase of new call center hardware and software:	£250,000
Cost of implementation technical consultants:	£120,000
Internal systems development costs (for configuration):	£150,000
Infrastructure upgrade costs:	£75,000
Business change costs:	£270,000
Training costs:	£80,000
Total:	**£945,000**
Net increase in annual systems support and license costs:	£80,000

FIGURE 10.6 Cost-risk-benefit analysis for a business case.

Risk Analysis	
Technical Risks:	Complexity of the systems functionality
	Number of system interfaces and systems being replaced
Financial Risks:	Confidence in some investment costs—especially business change
	Confidence in the evidence for some of the benefits
	Business criticality of areas affected by the system
Organizational Risks:	The extent of changes to call center processes and practice
	Limited existing change management capability
	Call center staff capability to promote more technical services
	Customer willingness to share information for profiling purposes

FIGURE 10.6 (continued)   Cost-risk-benefit analysis for a business case.
Source: Adapted from John Ward, Elizabeth Daniel, and Joe Peppard, "Building Better Business Cases for IT Investments," *MISQE* 7, no. 1 (March 2008): 1–15.

▶ IT PORTFOLIO MANAGEMENT

Managing the set of systems and programs in an IT organization is similar to managing resources in a financial organization. There are different types of IT investments, and together they form the business's IT portfolio. **IT portfolio management** refers to the process of evaluating and approving IT investments as they relate to other current and potential IT investments. It often involves deciding on the right mix of investments from funding, management, and staffing perspectives. The overall goal of IT portfolio management is for the company to fund and invest in the most valuable initiatives that, taken together as a whole, generate maximum benefits to the business.

Professor Peter Weill and colleagues at MIT's Center for Information Systems Research (CISR) describe four asset classes of IT investments that typically make up the company's IT portfolio:

- Transactional Systems—systems that streamline or cut costs on the way business is done
- Informational Systems—systems that provide information used to control, manage, communicate, analyze, or collaborate
- Strategic Systems—Systems used to gain competitive advantage in the marketplace
- Infrastructure Systems—the base foundation of shared IT services used for multiple applications such as servers, networks, databases, or laptops

In analyzing the composition of any single company's IT portfolio, one can come up with a profile of the relative investment made in each asset class. Weill's study found that the average firm allocates 46% of its total IT investment each year to infrastructure and only 25% of its total IT investment in transactional systems.

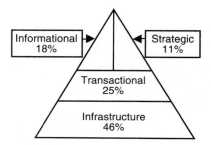

FIGURE 10.7 Average company's IT portfolio profile.
Source: ©Massachusetts Institute of Technology, 2007. This work was created by MIT's Sloan Center for Systems Research (CISR).

Figure 10.7 summarizes a typical IT portfolio. At a more detailed level, different industries allocate their IT resources differently. For example, Weill found that services companies (such as IT Services and professional services) on average, allocate more to infrastructure systems (about 47%), transactional systems (about 27%), and strategic systems (about 13%) but less to informational systems (about 18%).

Managers use a portfolio view of IT investments to manage resources. Decision makers use the portfolio to analyze risk, assess fit with business strategy, and identify opportunities for reducing IT spending. Just like an individual or company's investment portfolio is aligned with the individual or company's objectives, the IT portfolio must be aligned with the business strategy. Weill's work suggests that a different balance between IT investments is needed for a cost-focused strategy compared to an agility-focused strategy. A company with a cost-focused strategy would seek an IT portfolio that helps lower costs as the primary business objective. In that case, Weill's work suggest that on average 27% of the IT investments are made in transactional investments, suggesting higher use of applications that automate processes which and typically lower operational costs. On the other hand, a company with an agility focus would be more likely to invest a higher percent of their IT portfolio in infrastructure, and less in transactional systems. The infrastructure investment would create a platform that would likely be used to more quickly and nimbly create solutions needed by the business, whereas the transactional systems might lock in the current processes and take more effort and time to change. Figure 10.8 summarizes the differences.

▶ VALUING IT INVESTMENTS

Monetary costs and benefits are important but not the only considerations in making IT investments. Soft benefits, such as the ability to make future decisions, are often part of the business case for IT investments, making it difficult to measure the payback of the investment.

Several unique factors of the IT function increase the difficulty of assessing value from IT investments. First, in many enterprises, IT is a significant part of the annual budget. Hence it comes under close scrutiny. Second, the systems

	Infrastructure investments	Transactional investments	Informational investments	Strategic investments
Average Firm	46%	25%	18%	11%
Cost Focus	44%	27%	18%	11%
Agility Focus	51%	24%	15%	10%

FIGURE 10.8 Comparative IT portfolios for different business strategies.
Source: ©Massachusetts Institute of Technology, 2007. This work was created by MIT's Sloan Center for Systems Research (CISR).

themselves are complex, and as already discussed, calculating the costs is an art, not a science. Third, because many IT investments are for infrastructure, the payback period is much longer than other types of capital investments. Fourth, many times the payback cannot be calculated because the investment is a necessity rather than a choice, without any tangible payback. For example, upgrading to a newer version of software or buying a new design of hardware may be required because the older models are broken or simply not supported any longer. Many managers do not want to be placed in the position of having to upgrade simply because the vendor thinks an upgrade is necessary. Instead, managers may resist IT spending on the grounds that the investment adds no incremental value. These factors and more fuel a long-running debate about the value of IT investments.

For example, because of the large expense of preparing for the year 2000, the Y2K crisis strained IT budgets.[7] Y2K compliance was a business necessity addressed only by implementing new systems or upgrading existing ones. Limited financial resources caused management executives to examine more closely the expected return on other IT investments. A 1998 survey by *Information Week* found that "more than 80% of the 150 IS executives at U.S. companies surveyed say their organizations require them to demonstrate the potential revenue, payback, or budget impact of their IT projects."[8]

Thus, a clear need exists to understand the true return on an IT project. Measuring this return is difficult, however. To illustrate, consider the relative ease

---

[7] The Y2K crisis, otherwise known as the Millennium Bug, refers to software that was unable to distinguish between years beginning with the "20" from years beginning with "19". Some programs were not set up to distinguish between "1919" and "2019" for example. The fear was that programs would crash, or act in abnormal ways, when the century turned over. The amount of systems affected by this problem was enormous. Most government and corporations were busy in the latter half of the 1990's addressing this problem. In reality, however, most of the problems were fixed before the century started, and very few entities experienced the anticipated problems.

[8] Bob Violino, "ROI In the Real World," *Information Week* (April 27, 1998), p. 2.

with which a manager might analyze whether the enterprise should build a new plant. The first step would be to estimate the costs of construction. The plant capacity dictates project production levels. Demand varies, and construction costs frequently overrun, but the manager can find sufficient information to make a decision about whether to build.

Most of the time, the benefits of investing in IT are less tangible than those of building a plant. Such benefits might include tighter systems integration, faster response time, more accurate data, better leverage to adopt future technologies, among others. How can a manager quantify these intangibles? He or she should also consider many indirect, or downstream, benefits and costs, such as changes in how people behave, where staff report, and how tasks are assigned. In fact, it may be impossible to pinpoint who will benefit from an IT investment when making the decision.[9]

Despite the difficulty, the task of evaluating IT investments is necessary. Knowing which approaches to use and when to use them are important first steps. A number of approaches are summarized in Figure 10.9. Managers should choose based on the attributes of the project. For example, **return on investment (ROI)** or payback analysis can be used when detailed analysis is not required, such as when a project is short-lived and its costs and benefits are clear. When the project lasts long enough that the time value of money becomes a factor, **net present value (NPV)** and **economic value added (EVA)** are better approaches. EVA is particularly appropriate for capital-intensive projects.

An IT manager may encounter a number of pitfalls when analyzing return on investment. First, not every situation calls for in-depth analysis. Some decisions—such as whether to invest in a new operating system to become compatible with a client operating system—are easy to make. The costs are unlikely to be prohibitively high, and the benefits are clear.

Second, not every evaluation method works in every case. Depending on the assets employed, the duration of the project, and any uncertainty about implementation, one method may work better than another.

Third, circumstances may alter the way a particular valuation method is best used. For instance, in a software implementation, estimates of labor hours required often fall short of actual hours spent. Accordingly, some managers use an "adjusting" factor in their estimates.

Fourth, managers can fall into "analysis paralysis." Reaching a precise valuation may take longer than is reasonable to make an investment decision. Because a single right valuation may not exist, "close enough" usually suffices. Experience and an eye to the risks of an incorrect valuation help decide when to stop analyzing.

Finally, even when the numbers say a project is not worthwhile, the investment may be necessary to remain competitive. For example, UPS faced little choice but to invest heavily in IT. At the time, FedEx made IT a competitive advantage and was winning the overnight delivery war.

---

[9] John C. Ford, "Evaluating Investment in IT," *Australian Accountant* (December 1994), p. 3.

Valuation Method	Description
Return on investment (ROI)	Percentage rate that measures the relationship between the amount the business gets back from an investment and the amount invested using the formula: ROI = (Revenue-Investment)/Investment. Although popular and easy to use and understand, ROI lacks sophistication in assessing intangible benefits and costs.
Net present value (NPV)	Finance departments typically use NPV because it accounts for the time value of money. After discounting and then adding the dollar inflows and outflows, a positive NPV indicates a project should be undertaken, as long as other IT investments do not have higher values. It is calculated by discounting the costs and benefits for each year of the system's lifetime using the present value factor calculated each year as $1/(1+ \text{discount rate})^{\text{year}}$.
Economic value added (EVA)	EVA accounts for opportunity costs of capital to measure true economic profit and revalues historical costs to give an accurate picture of the true market value of assets.[a] EVA is sufficiently complex that consultants typically are required to implement it. It provides no hard and fast rules for intangibles. Calculating EVA is simple: EVA = Net operating profit after taxes − [(Capital)(Cost of capital)].[a]
Payback analysis	Simple, popular method that determines the payback period, or how much time will lapse before accrued benefits overtake accrued and continuing costs.
Internal rate of return (IRR)	Calculation is made to determine the return that the IT investment would have, and then it is compared to the corporate policy on rate of return. If IT investment's rate of return is higher than the corporate policy, the project is considered a good investment.
Weighted scoring methods	Costs and revenues/savings are weighted based on their strategic importance, level of accuracy or confidence, and comparable investment opportunities.
Prototyping	A scaled-down version of a system is tested for its costs and benefits. This approach is useful when the impact of the IT investment seems unclear.
Game theory or role-playing	These approaches may reveal behavioral changes or new tasks attributable to a new system. They are less expensive than prototyping.
Simulation	A model is used to test the impact of a new system or series of tasks. This low-cost method surfaces problems and allows system sensitivities to be analyzed.

[a] http://www.sternstewart.com.

FIGURE 10.9 Valuation methods.

▶ MONITORING IT INVESTMENTS

An old adage says: "If you can't measure it, you can't manage it." Management's role is to ensure that the money spent on IT results in benefits for the organization. Therefore, common, accepted set of metrics must be created, and those metrics must be monitored and communicated to senior management and customers of the IT department. These metrics are often financial in nature (i.e., ROI, NPV). But financial measures are only one category of measures used to manage IT investments. Other MIS metrics include logs of errors encountered by users, end-user surveys, user turnaround time, logs of computer and communication up-/downtime, system response time, and percentage of projects completed on time and/or within budget. Additional, business-focused metrics might include measures such as the number of contacts with external customers, sales revenue accrued from web channels, and new business leads generated.

The Balanced Scorecard

Deciding on appropriate measures is half of the equation for effective MIS organizations. The other half of the equation is ensuring that those measures are accurately communicated to the business. Two methods for communicating these metrics are the scorecards and dashboards.

Financial measures may be the language of stockholders, but managers understand that they can be misleading if used as the sole means of making management decisions. One methodology used to solve this problem, created by Robert Kaplan and David Norton, and first described in the *Harvard Business Review* in 1992, is the **balanced scorecard**, which focuses attention on the organization's value drivers (which include, but are not limited to, financial performance).[10] Companies use it to assess the full impact of their corporate strategies on their customers and workforce, as well as their financial performance.

This methodology allows managers to look at the business from four perspectives: customer, internal business, innovation/learning, and financial. For each perspective, the goals and measures are designed to answer these basic questions:

- How do customers see us? (Customer perspective)
- At what must we excel? (Internal business perspective)
- Can we continue to improve and create value? (Innovation and learning perspective)
- How do we look to shareholders? (Financial perspective)

Figure 10.10 graphically shows the relationship of these perspectives.

Since the introduction of the Balanced Scorecard, many have modified it or adapted it to apply to their particular organization. Managers of information

---

[10] For more detail, see R. Kaplan and D. Norton, "The Balanced Scorecard—Measures That Drive Performance," *Harvard Business Review* (January–February 1992).

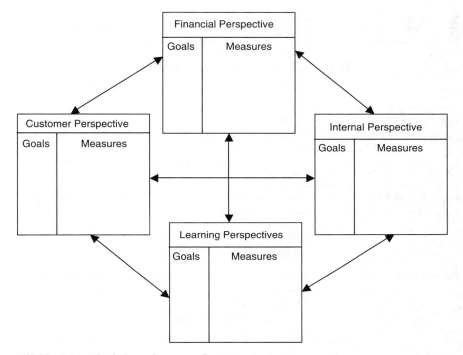

FIGURE 10.10 The balanced scorecard perspectives.
Source: Adapted from Kaplan and Norton, "The Balanced Scorecard—Measures That Drive Performance," *Harvard Business Review* (January–February 1992): 72.

technology found the concept of a scorecard useful in managing and communicating the value of the IT department. For example, US West used this methodology when it undertook an e-commerce project. The manager of this project described its use:

> The Balanced Scorecard approach defined goals in areas beyond the technical, e-commerce platform. It helped us look at internal processes, employee impact and finances. It meant getting the associated computer systems Y2K compliant in the internal processes category, implementing an IT career structure in the employee learning category and meeting overall budget commitments in the financial category. The Balanced Scorecard helped us organize our thoughts, and it was then used for all of our IT planning.[11]

Applying the categories of the balanced scorecard to IT might mean interpreting them more broadly than originally conceived by Kaplan and Norton. For example, the original scorecard speaks of the customer perspective, but for the MIS scorecard, the customer might be a user within the company, not the external

[11] Adapted from Robin Robinson, "Balanced Scorecard," *Computerworld* (January 24, 2000).

Dimension	Description	Example IT Measures
Customer perspective	*How do customers see us?* Measures that reflect factors that really matter to customers	Impact of IT projects on users, impact of IT's reputation among users, and user-defined operational metrics
Internal business perspective	*What must we excel at?* Measures of what the company must do internally to meet customer expectations	IT process metrics, project completion rates, and system operational performance metrics
Innovating and learning perspective	*Can we continue to improve and create value?* Measures of the company's ability to innovate, improve, and learn	IT R&D, new technology introduction success rate, training metrics
Financial perspective	*How do we look to shareholders?* Measures to indicate contribution of activities to the bottom line	IT project ROI, NPV, IRR, cost/benefit, TCO, ABC

FIGURE 10.11 Balanced scorecard applied to IT departments.

customer of the company. The questions asked when using this methodology within the IT department are summarized in Figure 10.11.

David Norton commented, "[D]on't start with an emphasis on metrics—start with your strategy and use metrics to make it understandable and measurable (that is, to communicate it to those expected to make it happen and to manage it)."[12] He found the balanced scorecard to be the most effective management framework for achieving organizational alignment and strategic success.

FirstEnergy, a multibillion-dollar utility company, provides a good example of how the MIS scorecard can be used. The company set a strategic goal of creating "raving fans" among its customers. In addition, they identified three other business value drivers: reliability, finance, and winning culture. The MIS group interpreted "raving fans" to mean satisfied internal customers. They used three metrics to measure their performance along this dimension:[13]

- Percentage of projects completed on time and on budget

[12] "Ask the Source: Interview with David Norton," *CIO Magazine* (July 25, 2002), available at www.cio.com (accessed February 22, 2003).

[13] Adapted from Eric Berkman, "How to Use the Balanced Scorecard," *CIO Magazine* (May 15, 2002).

- Percentage of projects released to the customer by agreed-on delivery date
- Client satisfaction recorded on customer surveys done at the end of a project

A scorecard used within the IT department helps senior IS managers understand their organization's performance and measure it in a way that supports its business strategy. The IT scorecard is linked to the corporate scorecard and ensures that the measures used by IT are those that support the corporate goals. At DuPont Engineering, the balanced scorecard methodology forces every action to be linked to a corporate goal, which helps promote alignment and eliminate projects with little potential impact. The conversations between IT and the business focus on strategic goals and impact rather than on technology and capabilities.[14]

IT Dashboards

Scorecards provide summary information gathered over a period of time. Another common MIS management monitoring tool is the IT **dashboard**, which provides a snapshot of metrics at any given point in time. Much like the dashboard of an automobile or airplane, the IT dashboard summarizes key metrics for senior managers in a manner that provides quick identification of the status of the organization. Like scorecards, dashboards are useful outside the IT department and are often found in executive offices as a tool for keeping current on critical measures of the organization. For this section, we focus on the use of these tools within the IT department.

Dashboards provide frequently updated information on areas of interest within the IT department. Depending on who is actually using the dashboard, the data tend to focus on project status or operational systems status. For example, a dashboard used by GM North America's IT leadership team contains a metric designed to monitor project status.[15] Because senior managers question the overall health of a project rather than the details, the dashboard they designed provides red, yellow, or green highlights for rapid comprehension. A green highlight means that the project is progressing as planned. A yellow highlight means at least one key target has been missed. A red highlight means the project is significantly behind and needs some attention or resources to get back on track.

At GM, each project is tracked and rated monthly. GM uses four dashboard criteria: (1) performance to budget, (2) performance to schedule, (3) delivery of business results, and (4) risk. At the beginning of a project, these metrics are defined and acceptable levels set. The project manager assigns a color status monthly, based on the defined criteria, and the results are reported in a spreadsheet. When managers look at the dashboard, they can immediately tell whether projects are on schedule based on the amount of green, yellow, or red on the dashboard. They can then drill into yellow or red metrics to get the projects back on track.

---

[14] Ibid.

[15] Adapted from Tracy Mayor, "Red Light, Green Light," *CIO Magazine* (October 1, 2001).

The dashboard provides an easy way to identify where their attention should be focused. The director of IT operations explains, "Red means I need more money, people or better business buy-in.... The dashboard provides an early warning system that allows IT managers to identify and correct problems before they become big enough to derail a project."[16]

Dashboards are useful for projects, but they have additional applications within the IT department. A number of organizations also use a similar dashboard to track operations to measure network performance, system availability, help desk satisfaction, and a number of other key performance data. Green means the metric is within acceptable limits; yellow means the metric has slipped once or twice; and red means the metric is consistently outside the acceptable range.

At Intel, the MIS department uses a "CIO dashboard" that condenses about 100 separate pieces of paper into one unified set of indicators in a matrix format.[17] Each key topic area is represented by a trend indicator as well as a status indicator. The Intel dashboard also uses green-yellow-red, as well as an arrow to indicate up, down, or sideways movement of a trend. All Intel employees, including IT staff, can scan the dashboard, which is electronically stored and updated, on the Intel intranet. In this way, issues can be identified and handled without waiting for the monthly CIO meeting, and dashboard statistics are monitored frequently to enable proactive behavior. In Intel's case, the dashboard improved both the reporting process, as well as team communication, because it made information available in real time in an easy-to-read manner.

Dashboards are built on the information contained in the other applications, databases, and analytical systems of the organization (see Chapter 12 for a more complete discussion of business intelligence and business analytics). Figure 10.12 contains the architecture of a sample dashboard for Western Digital, a $3 billion global designer and manufacturer of high-performance hard drives for PCs, networks, storage devices, and entertainment systems.[18]

▶ OPTIONS PRICING

Options pricing has long been used on financial assets as a method of locking in a price to be paid in the future. For example, you may have been able to purchase an option to buy 500 shares of Cisco stock at $50 per share on January 1, 2005, for a price (i.e., $600). The concept of options can be extended to evaluating IT investments. In this case, an IT project is viewed as an option to exchange the cost of the project for its benefits down the road. In particular, investing in one phase

---

[16] Ibid.

[17] Adapted from Johanna Ambrosio, "Walking the Walls No More," *Computerworld* (July 6, 2001).

[18] Robert Houghton, O. A. El Sawy, P. Gray, C. Donegan, and A. Joshi, "Vigilant Information Systems for Managing Enterprises in Dynamic Supply Chains: Real-Time Dashboards at Western Digital," *MISQE* 3, no. 1 (March 2004), 19–35.

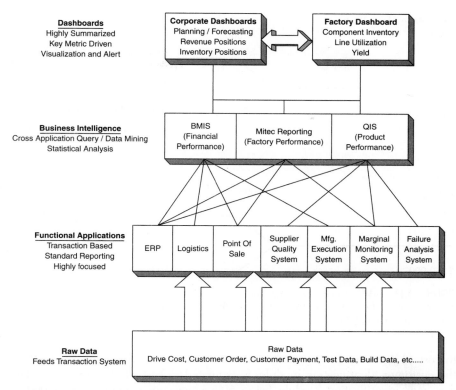

FIGURE 10.12 Example Architecture of a Dashboard.
Source: Houghton, Robert, et al. "Vigilant Information Systems For Managing Enterprises in Dynamic Supply Chains: Real-Time Dashboards at Western Digital," MISQE, Vol. 3 No. 1, March 2004.

of an IT project may result in an option to invest in the next phase, as long as the project is not terminated before then.

The reason that options pricing is so appealing is that it offers management the opportunity to take some future action (such as abandoning, deferring, or expanding the scale of a project) in response to uncertainty about changes in the business and its environment. **Options pricing** offers a risk-hedging strategy to minimize the negative impact of risk when uncertainty can be resolved by waiting to see what happens. To be applied, managers need to have a project that can be divided into investment stages and be armed with estimates of costs of the project at each stage, the projected revenues or savings, and the probability of these costs and revenues/savings being realized.

Figure 10.13 offers a simple example of how options pricing would work for a new CRM system that has two major components: a customer identification module and a customer tracking module. (*Note:* In this model all costs and revenues reflect discounting.) The customer identification module is projected

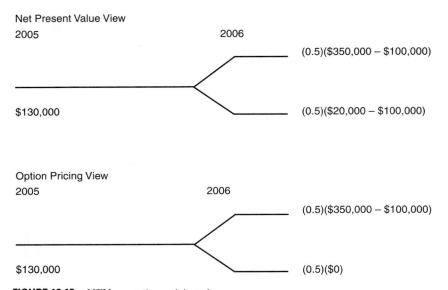

Net Present Value View

2005   2006

                                                           (0.5)($350,000 − $100,000)

$130,000   (0.5)($20,000 − $100,000)

Option Pricing View

2005   2006

                                                           (0.5)($350,000 − $100,000)

$130,000   (0.5)($0)

FIGURE 10.13   NPV vs. option pricing view.
Source: Adapted from Ram Kumar, "Managing Risks in IT Projects: An Options Perspective," *Information & Management* 40 (2002): 63–74.

to cost $130,000 in 2005, and the customer tracking module, which is built on the customer identification module, is estimated to cost $100,000 in 2006. The customer identification module has a 50% chance of generating $350,000 in additional revenues in 2006 if conditions are favorable. If they are unfavorable, revenues are projected to be only $20,000. The net present value (NPV) view would assume a 50% chance of positive net revenue of $250,000 (i.e., $350,000 − $100,000) in 2006, and a 50% chance of loss of $80,000 (i.e., $20,000 − $100,000) in 2006. Options pricing views this investment opportunity a little differently. With options pricing there is a 50% chance of net revenue of $250,000 and a 50% chance of net revenue of $0 a year later because the option to invest $100,000 in the customer tracking module need not be exercised if conditions are unfavorable.

Conceptualizing risk hedging in terms of options can help managers better understand and manage IT investment decisions. It offers an analysis approach that matches the way many senior managers think about the risk in making investments. Sometimes it may result in investment decisions that would be rejected based on NPV or cost-benefit analysis. For example, IT infrastructure investments often fare poorly on NPV analysis because the immediate expectation of payback is limited. However, from an options pricing perspective these investments provide the business with opportunities that would not be possible without the IT investment. Ideally, the investment yields applications with measurable revenue.

Option pricing is especially applicable in the following situations:[19]

- *When an investment decision can be deferred.* When considerable uncertainty surrounds a major project, dividing it into "chunks" allows managers to monitor their investment over time.

- *In helping managers strike a balance between waiting to obtain valuable information and forgoing revenues or strategic benefits from an implemented project.* For example, Yankee 24 could have used options pricing when deciding to offer a POS debit card network to its member institutions. Yankee 24 was established in 1984 to provide electronic banking network services, such as ATMs, to more than 200 member institutions. As early as 1987, Yankee's president, Richard Yanak, realized the potential for a POS network. If customer acceptance were as slow as it had been in California a decade earlier, revenues would be low and could not offset the heavy investment required for network infrastructure. The question that options pricing could have resolved was how long should Yankee wait before investing in this infrastructure and POS technology without giving its competitor, the New York Cash Exchange, a first mover advantage.

- *For emerging technology investments.* For example, IBM OS/2-based computing infrastructures became less attractive as Microsoft Windows NT gained a large installed base in the world of client/server computing. Thus, the use of IT projects with a phased rollout of an OS/2 platform, or of applications depending on OS/2 for critical support, would have been negatively affected over time using an options pricing model.

- *For prototyping investments.* When managers are uncertain about whether an application can "do the job," a prototype provides value in the options that it offers the firm for future actions.

- *For technology-as-product investments.* When the technology is at the core of a product, issues of level of commitment, timing, rollout, deferment, and abandonment can be considered more fully.

Like all the evaluation approaches, options pricing has a downside.[20] Option value calculations are sensitive to certain parameters, especially volatility. Having multiple stakeholders involved in estimation and calculating for a range of parameter values are two strategies that can help lessen this sensitivity. Options pricing may be attractive for infrastructure investments that open the door to possible applications in the future, but a number of assumptions must be made about those

---

[19] M. Benaroch and R. J. Kauffman, "A Case for Using Real Options Pricing Analysis to Evaluate Information Technology Project Investments," *Information Systems Research* 10:1 (1999), pp. 70–86.
[20] Ram Kumar, "Managing Risks in IT Projects: An Options Perspective," *Information & Management* 40 (2002), pp. 63–74.

opportunities for the options model to work. However, the probability of all the assumptions coming true is small.

► FOOD FOR THOUGHT: WHO PAYS FOR THE INTERNET?

There are over 1.4 billion users of the Internet, an estimated 21.9% of the world's population,[21] and not one of them pays a bill to the Internet. Although everyone uses the Internet, the question arises, "Who pays for the Internet?" Most of us use the Internet every day, and although the ads we may be forced to watch on the pages we seek are annoying, they do not pay for the Internet. Individuals pay a service provider, such as a telephone company or cable provider, to access the Internet, but the service provider is like a gatekeeper. That company lets you into the Internet. Likewise, many of the content providers fund their own Web sites and applications either through standard business practices, such as marketing budgets or allocation methods to sponsoring departments. But that doesn't pay for the Internet either.

There is no "Internet Incorporated" who runs and pays for the Internet. There are a number of organizations who have responsibilities for portions of the management. For example, the Internet Society (ISOC), a nonprofit, nongovernment organization with thousands of members from all over the world make up ISOC member organizations and address issues of how to generate progress and growth. The Internet Engineering Task Force (IETF), a large open international community of network designers, vendors, and researchers, is concerned with the evolution of the Internet architecture and operation. The Internet Corporation for Assigned Names and Number (ICANN) coordinates the technical elements of the Domain Name System (DNS) and works with numerous private companies who help users get their own domain name. There are numerous other organizations in this mix who oversee standards, domain names, and architecture.

So who pays for the Internet? The U.S. federal government, through the National Science Foundation (NSF), subsidizes a portion of the Internet to provide a communications and collaboration backbone for science, engineering, and education. Academic institutions and commercial businesses bear some of the cost by making a connection available to employees, students, and customers. Service providers pay for computers and networks that are linked together over backbone networks. When commercial ventures pay for the computers that house their Web sites, they are paying for the Internet. Users pay their access fees to service providers, so in a sense, part of the cost is passed on to the actual users themselves.

So the Internet is actually paid for by everyone who uses it. It is the ultimate peer-to-peer network. Costs are covered by those who pay for the computers that

---

[21] www.internetworldstats.com/stats.htm (accessed on August 8, 2008).

host the applications, by provider charges for network usage, and through taxes that then in turn fund the NSF. It's interesting to note that although most think that the Internet is free, it's actually not free. But the costs are covered in various innovative ways.

► SUMMARY

- IT is funded using one of three methods: chargeback, allocation, or corporate budget.
- Chargeback systems are viewed as the most equitable method of IT cost recovery because costs are distributed based on usage. Creating an accounting system to record the information necessary to do a chargeback system can be expensive and time consuming and usually has no other useful application.
- Allocation systems provide a simpler method to recover costs, because they do not involve recording system usage to allocate costs. However, allocation systems can sometimes penalize groups with low usage.
- Corporate budgeting systems do not allocate costs at all. Instead, the CIO seeks and receives a budget from the corporate overhead account. This method of funding IT does not require any usage recordkeeping, but is also most likely to be abused if the users perceive "it is free."
- Total cost of ownership is a technique to understand all the costs, beyond the initial investment costs, associated with owning and operating an information system. It is most useful as a tool to help evaluate which infrastructure components to choose and to help understand how infrastructure costs occur.
- Activity-based costing is another technique to group costs into a meaningful bucket. Costs are accounted for based on the activity, or product or service, they support. ABC is useful for allocating large overhead expenses.
- The portfolio of IT investments must be carefully evaluated and managed.
- ROI is difficult, at best, to calculate for IT investments because the benefits are often not tangible. The benefits might be difficult to quantify, difficult to observe, or long range in scope.
- Popular metrics for IT investments measure quality of information outputs, IT contributions to a firm's financial performance, operational efficiency, management/user attitudes, and the adequacy of systems development practices.
- A business case is a tool used to support a decision or a proposal of a new investment. It is a document containing a project description, financial analysis, marketing analysis, and all other relevant documentation to assist managers in making a go/no-go decision.
- Benefits articulated in a business case can be categorized as observable, measurable, quantifiable, and financial. These benefits are often for innovations, improvements, or cessation.
- Monitoring and communicating the status and benefits of IT is often done through the use of balanced scorecards and IT dashboards.
- Options pricing offers a risk-hedging strategy to minimize the negative impact of risk when resolving uncertainty by waiting to see what happens.

▶ KEY TERMS

activity-based costing
(ABC) (p. 282)
allocation funding method
(p. 280)
business case (p. 287)
balanced scorecard
(p. 296)
chargeback funding
method (p. 279)

corporate budget funding
method (p. 281)
dashboard (p. 299)
economic value added
(EVA) (p. 294)
IT portfolio management
(p. 291)
net present value (NPV)
(p. 294)

options pricing (p. 301)
return on investment
(ROI) (p. 294)
total cost of ownership
(TCO) (p. 283)

▶ DISCUSSION QUESTIONS

1. Under what conditions would you recommend using each of these funding methods: allocation, chargeback, and corporate budgeting?

2. Describe the conditions under which ROI, payback period, NPV, and EVA are most appropriately applied.

3. A new inventory management system for ABC Company could be developed at a cost of $250,000. The estimated net operating costs and estimated net benefits over six years of operation would be:

Year	Estimated Net Operating Costs	Estimated Net Benefits
0	$250,000	$ 0
1	7,000	52,000
2	9,400	68,000
3	11,000	82,000
4	14,000	115,000
5	15,000	120,000
6	16,000	120,000

    a. What would the payback period be for this investment? Would it be a good or bad investment? Why?

    b. What is the ROI for this investment?

    c. Assuming a 15% discount rate, what is this investment's NPV?

4. Would you suggest using options pricing on the investment described in Question 3? Why or why not?

5. Compare and contrast the IT scorecard and dashboard approaches.

6. TCO is one way to account for costs associated with a specific infrastructure. This method does not include additional costs such as disposal costs—the cost to get rid of the system when it is no longer of use. What other additional costs might be of importance in making total cost calculations?

CASE STUDY 10-1

TROON GOLF

Troon Golf, headquartered in Scottsdale, Arizona, is one of the world's leading luxury-brand golf management and marketing firm with 197 golf courses worldwide in its portfolio. When it saw its IT expenses spiraling out of control, Cary Westmark, its vice president for technology decided to introduce the concept of total cost of ownership. Like most companies, managers had viewed hardware as one-time expense and had failed to recognize the hidden cost of operating and maintaining the hardware. Often support costs increased over the projected life of IT, contributing to unexpected rise in IT expenses. For better planning of IT costs and to develop a funding mechanism for IT projects throughout their planned lives, managers created a strategic replacement program. Under the program, managers calculated total cost by including cost of technical support, user productivity loss, downtime loss, and any associated data quality loss. This allowed Troon management to refresh its aging hardware at the optimal cost level. As a result, its support costs reduced from $800 per month to $300, saving roughly over $50,000.

Discussion Questions

1. Why does the TCO approach allow Troon management to refresh its hardware at the optimal cost level?
2. Why, in your opinion, were IT expenses spiraling out of control before the TCO system? What are examples of the hidden costs of operating and maintaining the hardware?
3. If you were the head of marketing for Troon, what benefit would you receive from Mr. Westmark's decision to implement TCO?

Source: Adapted from "Slicing Through IT Costs," *Baseline Magazine*, March 31, 2008.

CASE STUDY 10-2

VALUING IT

In May 2003, writer Nick Carr lobbed a hand grenade into the IT world. He published an article in *Harvard Business Review* titled "IT Doesn't Matter." In that article, Carr asserted that as information technology's power and ubiquity grows, its strategic importance diminishes. The influence of infrastructure investments in technology is not felt at the individual company level, but rather in the macroeconomic level, he continued. He compared IT to railroads, viewing it as simply a transport mechanism carrying digital information, just as railroads carried goods. "Like any transport mechanism, it is far more valuable when shared than when used in isolation.... For most business applications today, the benefits of customization would be overwhelmed by the costs of isolation," Carr suggested. There are few opportunities to gain a competitive advantage from IT, Carr suggests. He described a number of companies such as Dell Computer, American Airlines, and Federal Express, who were at the proverbial right place at the right time and who were able to get a competitive edge by strategic IT applications. But the window for such advantage is closing, and perhaps was only open briefly. Carr continued,

> The opportunities for gaining IT based advantage are already dwindling. Best Practices are now quickly built into software or otherwise replicated. And as for IT-spurred industry transformations, most of the ones that are going to happen have likely already happened or are in the process of happening. Industries and markets will continue to evolve, of course, and some will undergo fundamental changes—the future of the music business, for example, continues to be in doubt. But history shows that the power of an infrastructural technology to transform industries always diminishes as its build out nears completion.

Carr believes that companies should no longer seek competitive advantage from IT investments. "The key to success, for the vast majority of companies, is no longer to seek advantage aggressively but to manage costs and risks meticulously," he concluded.

Discussion Questions

1. Do you agree with Carr that as information technology's power and ubiquity grows, its strategic importance diminishes? Why or why not?
2. Where do you think the next IT-based strategic advantage may occur? Give an example.
3. Consider the IT portfolio management triangle presented in this chapter. Would Carr's arguments hold for all types of IT investments or just for infrastructure investments? Explain.
4. The original article in *Harvard Business Review* raised a number of questions by senior business managers about their IT investment. As an IT manager, what questions would you anticipate you would have to respond to, and what would be your response?

Source: Adapted from Nicholas Carr, "IT Doesn't Matter," *Harvard Business Review* (May 2003): 41–49.

CHAPTER 11

PROJECT MANAGEMENT[1]

The Rural Payments Agency (RPA), an agency responsible for administering agricultural subsidies to UK farmers, blamed poor planning and lack of testing of their IT system for delays in paying out £1.5bn of EU subsidies. The UK government developed a complex system for administering the Single Payment Scheme, which maps farmers' land to a database. By the end of 2006, only 15% of the subsidies had been paid to farmers.

An independent watchdog group investigated the situation and learned that the implementation of the system began before final specifications and regulations were agreed on by the European Commission. The RPA then had to make many substantial changes in the system after implementation. Further, the investigation found that testing did not take into account the real environment, leading to unanticipated work to populate the database in the first place.

Where was the project manager for the project? Despite receiving three "red" warnings from the Office of Government Commerce during reviews, the implementation continued. Time was not built into the schedule for testing the whole system as well as the individual components. The components were not compatible with the business processes they were supposed to support. The cost so far of the project was £122m, which was £46.5m more than estimated. As of the writing of this case the system was still not stable.[2]

This example highlights the possible financial and social consequences of a failed information systems (IS) project. Such failures occur at an astonishing rate. The Standish Group, a technology research firm, found that 67% of all software projects are challenged—that is, delivered late or over budget or simply fail to meet their performance criteria.[3] Business projects increasingly rely on IS to attain their objectives, especially with the increased focus to do business on the Internet. Thus, managing a business project means managing, often to a large degree, an

---

[1] The authors wish to acknowledge and thank W. Thomas Cannon, MBA 1999, for his help in researching and writing early drafts of this chapter.

[2] Adapted from http://www.silicon.com/publicsector/0,3800010403,39168359,00.htm (accessed on July 28 2008).

[3] The information from the Standish Group CHAOS Report for 2006 was quoted in C. Sauer, A. Gemino, and B. H. Reich, "The Impact of Size and Volatility on IT Project Performance," *Communications of the ACM* 50, no. 11 (November 2007), 79–84.

information systems project. To succeed, a general manager must be a project manager and must learn how to manage this type of risk.

In the current business environment, the quality that differentiates firms in the marketplace—and destines them for success or failure—is often the ability to adapt existing business processes and systems to new, innovative ideas faster than the competition. The process of continual adaptation to the changing marketplace drives the need for business change and thus for successful project management. Typical adaptation projects include the following elements:

- Rightsizing the organization
- Reengineering business processes
- Adopting more comprehensive, integrative processes

Projects comprise a set of one-time activities that can transform the current situation into the desired new one. Firms seek to compete through new products and processes, but the work of initially building or radically changing them falls outside the scope of normal business operations. That is where projects come in. When work can only be accomplished through methods that fundamentally differ from those employed to run daily operations, the skilled project manager plays a crucial role.

Successful business strategy requires executive management to decide which objectives can be met through normal daily operations and which require specialized project management. Virtually all projects involve both information technology (IT) and information flow components Many projects involve the Internet, using Web applications in the systems design. Rapidly changing business situations make it difficult to keep the IT elements aligned with business strategy. Furthermore, the complexity of IT-intensive projects has increased over the years, magnifying the risk that the finished product or process will no longer satisfy the needs of the business originally targeted to benefit from the project in the first place. Thus, learning to manage projects successfully, especially the IT component of the projects, is a crucial competency for every manager. Executive management no longer has an option but to consider skilled IT project management as fundamental to business success.

This chapter provides an overview of what a project is and how to manage one. It begins with a more general discussion of project management, then continues with aspects of IT-intensive projects that make them uniquely challenging. Finally, it identifies the issues that shape the role of the general manager in such projects and help them to manage risk.

▶ WHAT DEFINES A PROJECT?

In varying degrees, organizations combine two types of work—projects and operations—to transform resources into profits. Both types require people and a flow of resources. The flight of an airplane from its point of departure to its destination is an operation that requires a pilot and crew, the use of an airplane,

Characteristics	Operations	Projects
Labor skills	Low	High
Training time	Low	High
Worker autonomy	Low	High
Compensation system	Hourly or weekly wage	Lump sum for project
Material input requirements	High degree of certainty	Uncertain
Supplier ties	Longer duration	Shorter duration
	More formal	Less formal
Raw materials inventory	Large	Small
Scheduling complexity	Lower	Higher
Quality control	Formal	Informal
Information flows	Less important	Very important
Worker-mgmt communication	Less important	Very important
Duration	On-going	Temporary
Product or service	Repetitive	Unique

FIGURE 11.1   Characteristics of operational and project work.

and fuel. The operation is repetitive: After the plane is refueled, it takes new passengers to another destination. The continuous operation the plane creates is a transportation service. However, developing the design for such a plane is a project that may require years of work by many people. When the design is completed, the work ends. Figure 11.1 compares characteristics of both project and operational work. The last two characteristics are distinctive and form the basis for the following formal definition:

> [A] **project** is a temporary endeavor undertaken to create a unique product or service. Temporary means that every project has a definite beginning and a definite end. Unique means that the product or service is different in some distinguishing way from all similar products or services.[4]

To organize the work facing a project team, the project manager may break a project into subprojects. He or she then organizes these subprojects around distinct activities, such as quality control testing. This organizing method allows the project manager to contract certain kinds of work externally to limit costs or other drains on crucial project resources. At the macro level, a general manager may choose to organize various projects as elements of a larger program, if doing so creates efficiencies. Such programs then provide a framework from which to manage competing resource requirements and shifting priorities among a set of projects.

---

[4] Project Management Institute Standards Committee, *A Guide to the Project Management Body of Knowledge* (Project Management Institute, 1996).

▶ WHAT IS PROJECT MANAGEMENT?

Project management is the "application of knowledge, skills, tools, and techniques to project activities in order to meet or exceed stakeholder needs and expectation from a project."[5] Project management always involves continual trade-offs, and it is the manager's job to manage them. Even the tragic sinking of the *Titanic* has been attributed, in part, to project trade-offs. The company that built the *Titanic*, Harland and Wolff of Belfast, Northern Ireland, had difficulty finding the millions of rivets it needed for the three ships it was building at the same time. Under time and cost pressures to build these ships, the company managers decided to sacrifice quality by purchasing low-grade rivets that were used on some parts of the *Titanic*. When making the trade-offs, it was unlikely that the company's management knew that they were purchasing something so substandard that their ship would sink if it hit an iceberg. Nonetheless, the trade-off proved disastrous.[6]

Trade-offs can be subsumed in the project triangle (see Figure 11.2), which highlights the importance of balancing scope, time, and cost. *Scope* may be divided into product scope (the detailed description of the product's quality, features, and functions), and project scope (the work required to deliver a product or service with the intended product scope). *Time* refers to the time required to complete the project, whereas *cost* encompasses all the resources required to carry out the project. In the tragic case of the *Titanic*, the managers were willing to trade off *quality* for lower-*cost* rivets that allowed them to build all three ships (*scope*) in a more timely fashion (*time*). In contrast, a successful balance of scope, time, and cost yields a high-quality project—one in which the needs and expectations of the users are met. The tricky part of project management is successfully juggling these three elements while on a high wire, which amounts to shifting the triangle's base to keep it in balance. Changes in any one of the sides of the triangle affect one or both of the other sides. For example, if the project scope increases, more time and/or more resources (cost) are needed to do the additional work. This increase in scope after a project has begun is aptly called *scope creep*. In most projects only

Time   Cost

QUALITY

Scope

FIGURE 11.2   Project triangle.

[5] Ibid.

[6] This research was described in J. H. McCarty and T. Foecke, *What Really Sank the Titanic*, 2007 and is based on J. H. McCarty's dissertation.

two of these elements can be optimized, and the third must be adjusted to maintain balance. For example, a project with a fixed budget and fixed deadline may need to restrict scope. Likewise, a project that must be completed in a short period of time, with a large scope, may need flexibility in budget to obtain the resources necessary to meet the goal. It is important that the project stakeholders decide on the overriding "key success factor" (i.e., time, cost, or scope), though the project manager has the important responsibility of demonstrating to the stakeholders the impact on the project of selecting any of these. In the RPA case at the beginning of this chapter, scope was the key success factor, which failed to be managed appropriately, ultimately resulting in a much longer time and much higher cost.

But the key success factor is only one metric to use when managing a project. Stakeholders are concerned about all facets of the project. Measuring and tracking progress is often done by tracking time (How are we doing compared to the schedule?), cost (How are we doing compared to the budget?), scope (Does the scope continue to be reasonable?), as well as resources (How much of our resources have we consumed so far?), quality (Is the quality of the output/deliverables at the level required for success?), and risks (How are we doing managing the risk associated with this project?).

The project manager's role is to effectively and efficiently manage the activities necessary to complete the project juggling competing demands. Typical activities include the following:

- Ensuring progress of the project according to defined metrics
- Identifying risks and assessing their probability of occurrence
- Ensuring progress toward deliverables within constraints of time and resources
- Running coordination meetings of the project team
- Negotiating for resources on behalf of the project in light of its scope

When a general manager oversees more than one project, his or her role can vary on each project. For example, the manager may be the customer for any given project, as well as the source of its resources. These dual roles can make it easier for the general manager to ensure attention to both a project's risks and its business value.

Business projects are often initiated because of a successful business case. A successful project begins with a well-written business case that spells out the components of the project. The business case clearly articulates the details of the project and argues for resources for the project, For example, UPS prioritizes projects on the strength of their business cases and financial metrics. They also make nonfinancial considerations such as weighing international projects more heavily to spur the company's growth. The components of a business case and the financial metrics are discussed in Chapter 10.[7]

---

[7] UPS IT Governance: The Key to Aligning Technology Initiatives with Business Direction, http://www.pressroom.ups.com (accessed July 22, 2008).

The process used to develop the business case sets the foundation for the project itself. Therefore detailed planning, along with contingency planning, is an important part of project management. It is often in the planning phase that implementation issues, areas of concern, and gaps are first identified. Further, a strong business plan gives all the project team a reference document to help guide decisions and activities.

Project management software is often used to manage projects and keep track of key metrics. Programs such as Microsoft Project, Intuit Quickbase, and many others keep track of team members, deliverables, schedules, budgets, priorities, tasks, and other resources. Many of these programs provide a dashboard of key metrics to help project managers quickly identify areas of concern or potentially critical issues that need attention.

▶ PROJECT ELEMENTS

Project work requires in-depth situational analyses and the organization of complex activities into often coincident sequences of discrete tasks. The outcomes of each activity must be tested and integrated into the larger process to produce the desired result. The number of variables affecting the performance of such work is potentially enormous.

Four elements essential for any project include (1) a common project vocabulary, (2) teamwork, (3) a project cycle plan, and (4) project management. A common project vocabulary allows all those involved with the project to understand the project and communicate effectively. Teamwork ensures that all parts of the project come together correctly and efficiently. The plan represents the methodology and schedule to be used by the team to execute the project. Finally, management is necessary to make sure the entire project is executed appropriately and coordinated properly. As a result of good project management, the project scope can be realistically defined, and the project can be completed on time and within budget.

It is essential to understand the interrelationships among these elements and with the project itself. Both a commitment to teamwork and a common project vocabulary must permeate the management of a project throughout its life. The project plan consists of the sequential steps of organizing and tracking the work of the team. Finally, project management itself comprises a set of tools to balance competing demands for resources and ensure the completion of work at each step and as situational elements evolve through the project plan.

Common Project Vocabulary

The typical project teams include a variety of members from different backgrounds and different parts of the organization. Often the team is made up of consultants who are new to the organization, a growing number of technical specialists, and business members. Each area of expertise represented by team members uses a different technical vocabulary. When used together in the team context, these different vocabularies make it difficult to carry on conversations, meetings, and correspondence. For example, a market research analyst and software analyst may use words unique to their specialty or attach different meanings to the same words. To avoid misunderstandings, project team members should commit to a consistent meaning for terms used on their project. After agreeing on definitions and common meanings, the project team should record and explain the terms in its own common project vocabulary. The common project vocabulary includes many terms and meanings that are unfamiliar to the general manager and the team's other business members. To improve their communications with general managers, users, and other nontechnical people, technical people should limit their use of acronyms and cryptic words and should strive to place only the most critical ones in the common project vocabulary.

Teamwork

Business teams often fail because members don't understand the nature of the work required to make their team effective. Teamwork begins by clearly defining the team's objectives and each member's role in achieving these objectives. Teams need to have a common standard of conduct, shared rewards, a shared understanding of roles, and team spirit. Project managers should leverage team member skills, knowledge, experiences, and capabilities when assigning the team members to complete specific activities on an as-needed basis. In addition to their completing team activities, team members also represent their departments and transmit information about their department to other team members. Such information sharing constitutes the first step toward building consensus on critical project issues that affect the entire organization. Thus, effective project managers use teamwork both to organize and apply human resources and to collect and share information throughout the organization.

Project Cycle Plan

The project cycle plan organizes discrete project activities and sequences them in steps along a timeline so that the project delivers according to the requirements of customers and stakeholders. It identifies critical beginning and end dates and breaks the work spanning these dates into phases. Using the plan, the time and resources needed to complete the work based on the project's scope are identified, and tasks are assigned to team members. The general manager tracks the phases to coordinate the eventual transition from project to operational status, a process that culminates on the "go live" date. The project manager uses the phases to control the progress of work. He or she may establish control gates at various points along the way to verify that project work to date has met key requirements regarding cost, quality, and features. If it has not met these requirements, he or she can make corrections to the project plan and adjust the cycle as necessary.

The project cycle plan can be developed using various approaches and software tools. The three most common approaches are the project evaluation and review technique (PERT), critical path method (CPM), and Gantt chart. PERT identifies the tasks within the project, orders the tasks in a time sequence, identifies their interdependencies, and estimates the time required to complete the task. Tasks that must be performed individually and that, together, account for the total elapsed time of the project are considered to be critical tasks. Noncritical tasks are those for which some slack time can be built into the schedules without affecting the duration of the entire project. A PERT chart is shown in Figure 11.3.

CPM is a project planning and scheduling tool that is similar to PERT. Unlike PERT, CPM incorporates a capability for identifying relationships between costs and the completion date of a project, as well as the amount and value of resources that must be applied in alternative situations. The two approaches differ in terms of time estimates. PERT builds on broad estimates about the time needed to complete project tasks. It calculates the optimistic, most probable, and pessimistic time estimates for each task. In contrast, CPM assumes that all time requirements for completion of individual tasks are relatively predictable. Because of these differences, CPM tends to be used on projects for which direct relationships can be established between time and resources (costs).

Gantt charts are a commonly used visual tool for displaying time relationships of project tasks and for monitoring the progress toward project completion. Gantt charts list project tasks. For each task, a bar indicates the relative amount of time expected to complete the task. Milestones (i.e., due dates) are noted with diamonds. At the start of the project, Gantt charts are useful for planning purposes. As the project progresses, the chart is modified to reflect the extent to which each task is completed at the time the project is monitored. A Gantt chart is displayed in Figure 11.4.

Figure 11.5 compares a generic project cycle plan with one for a typical high-tech commercial business and with one for an investigative task force. Notice that although each of these plans has unique phases, all can loosely be described by three periods (shown at the top of the diagram): requirements period, development period, and production/distribution period.

Elements of Project Management

The nine elements described in this section represent management skills that can be organized into a toolbox of sorts. Each element addresses a specific factor that affects a project's chances of success. The challenge facing a project manager is to learn and apply the techniques properly in the situations that require them. The elements include (1) identification of requirements, (2) organizational integration, (3) team management, (4) risk and opportunity management, (5) project control, (6) project visibility, (7) project status, (8) corrective action, and (9) project leadership. Figure 11.6 summarizes these elements, the rationale behind the element, and how a project manager would attend to that element.

The leadership of a project guides the other eight elements. Lack of leadership can result in unmotivated people doing the wrong things and ultimately derailing the project. Strong project leaders skillfully manage team composition, reward systems, and other techniques to focus, align, and motivate team members. Figure 11.7 reflects the inverse relationship between the magnitude of the project leader's role

FIGURE 11.3 PERT chart.

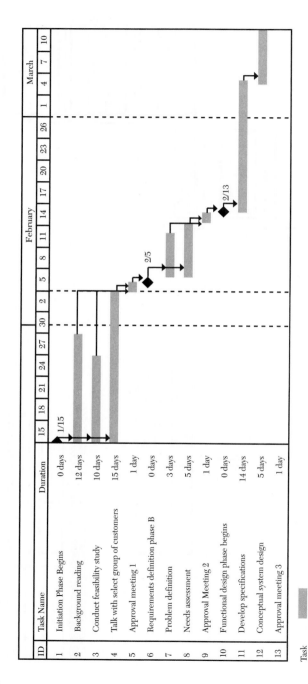

ID	Task Name	Duration
1	Initiation Phase Begins	0 days
2	Background reading	12 days
3	Conduct feasibility study	10 days
4	Talk with select group of customers	15 days
5	Approval meeting 1	1 day
6	Requirements definition phase B	0 days
7	Problem definition	3 days
8	Needs assessment	5 days
9	Approval Meeting 2	1 day
10	Functional design phase begins	0 days
11	Develop specifications	14 days
12	Conceptual system design	5 days
13	Approval meeting 3	1 day

Task
Split
Progress
Milestone

FIGURE 11.4 Gantt chart.

Requirements Definition Period			Production Period				Deployment/ Dissemination Period	
Investigation Task Force								
User requirement definition	Research concept definition	Information use specification	Collection planning phase	Collection and analysis phase	Draft report phase	Publication phase		Distribution phase
Typical High Tech Commercial Business								
Product requirements phase	Product definition phase	Product proposal	Product develop-ment phase	Engineer model phase	Internal test phase	External test phase	Production phase	Manufacturing sales & support phase
Generic Project Cycle Template								
User require-ment definition phase	Concept definition phase	System specifi-cation phase	Acqui-sition planning phase	Source selection phase	Development phase	Verification phase	Deploy-ment or produc-tion phase	Operations/ maintenance or sales/ support phase	Deacti-vate phase

FIGURE 11.5 Project cycle template.
Source: Adapted from K. Forsberg, H. Mooz, and H. Cotterman, *Visualizing Project Management* (Hoboken, NJ: John Wiley & Sons, 1996). Used with permission.

and the experience and commitment of the team. In organizations with strong processes for project management and professionals trained for this activity, the need for aggressive project leadership is reduced. However, strong project leaders are needed to help the organization develop project competency to begin with.

▶ IT PROJECTS

IT projects are a specific type of business project. Much research has been done to observe, understand, and help managers increase chances of success of IT projects. One of the sayings in the industry is that there is no such thing as an IT project; all projects are really business projects involving varying degrees of IT. Sometimes, managing the IT component of a project is referred to separately as an IT project, not only for simplicity, but also because the business world perceives that managing an IT project is somehow different from managing any other type of project. However, projects done by the IT department typically include an associated business case; and even though the project owner may be an IT person, mounting evidence indicates that IT projects are just business projects involving significant amounts of technology. The more complex the IT aspect of the project, the higher is the risk of failure of the project.

IT projects are difficult to estimate, despite the increasing amount of attention given to mastering this task. Like the case of the RPA's Single Payment Scheme most software projects fail to meet their schedules and budgets. Managers attribute

Element	Description	Rationale	Major Focus
Identification of Requirements	The items to be delivered by the project.	Mismanagement of requirements and scope is a primary cause of failure.	Formulative
Organizational Integration	The structure of the team, including reporting relationships and reward systems.	Structure around key activities, people, and resources helps manage the process.	Formulative
Team Management	The team assigned to work on the project.	Teams are often newly formed around projects and can include contractors and vendors.	Formulative
Risk and Opportunity Management	The potentially derailing events, the probability of occurrence, and the potential impact.	Planning provides road map and contingencies to guide project process.	Proactive
Project Control	The systems used to measure the project's status, outcomes, and exceptions.	Controls identify whether project is proceeding appropriately.	Proactive
Project Visibility	The techniques used to manage communication among team members and with other stakeholders.	Communication keeps all stakeholders informed.	Proactive
Project Status	The measure of the project's performance against the plan to identify needed adjustments.	Hard metrics, measures and variances provide support for managerial intuition of project's progress.	Variance Control
Corrective Action	The activities to place the project back on track after a variation from the plan is detected.	Innovative actions may be needed to get project back on track.	Reactive
Project Leadership	The management quality that binds the other elements together.	Management creates team energy and incentive to complete project plan.	Motivate

FIGURE 11.6 Elements of project management.
Source: K. Forsberg, H. Mooz, and H. Cotterman, *Visualizing Project Management* (Hoboken, NJ: John Wiley & Sons, 1996). Used with permission.

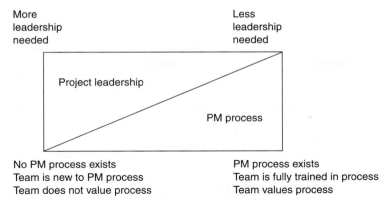

More leadership needed   Less leadership needed

Project leadership

PM process

No PM process exists
Team is new to PM process
Team does not value process

PM process exists
Team is fully trained in process
Team values process

FIGURE 11.7   Project leadership vs. project management (PM) process.

that failure to poor estimating techniques, poorly monitored progress protocols, and the idea that schedule slippage can be solved by simply adding additional people.[8] Not only does this assume that people and months are interchangeable, but also if the project is off schedule, it may be that the project was incorrectly designed in the first place, and putting additional people on the project just hastens the process to an inappropriate end.

Many projects are measured in "man-months," the most common unit for discussing the size of a project. For example, a project that takes 100 man-months means that it will take one person 100 months to do the work, or 100 people can do it in a month. A recent study found that managing projects using the man-months metric was linked to more underperforming projects than managing projects using any other metric of size (i.e., budget, duration, team size).[9] Man-months may be a poor metric for project management because some projects cannot be sped up with additional people. An analogy is that of pregnancy. It takes one woman nine months to carry a baby, and putting nine people on the job for one month cannot speed up the process. Software systems often involve highly interactive, complex sets of tasks that rely on each other to make a completed system. In some cases additional people can speed up the process, but most projects cannot be made more efficient simply by adding labor. Often, adding people to a late project only makes the project later.[10]

Measuring how well the system meets specifications and business requirements laid out in the project scope is more complex. Metrics for functionality are typically divided along lines of business functionality and system functionality. The first set of measures are those derived specifically from the requirements and business needs

---

[8] Frederick Brooks, *The Mythical Man-Month: Essays on Software Engineering* (Reading, MA: Addison-Wesley, 1982).

[9] Sauer et al., "The Impact of Size and Volatility on IT Project Performance."

[10] Brooks, *The Mythical Man-Month.*

that generated the project, such as automating the order entry process or building a knowledge management system for product design. In examples such as these, a set of metrics can be derived to measure whether the system meets expectations. However, other aspects of functionality, related to the system itself, are also important to measure. An example is usability, or how well individuals can and do use the system. Sample measures might be the number of users who use the system, their satisfaction with the system, the time it takes them to learn the system, the speed of performance, and the rate of errors made by users. Another common metric is system reliability. For example, one might measure the amount of time the system is up (or running) and the amount of time the system is down (or not running).

▶ IT PROJECT DEVELOPMENT METHODOLOGIES

The choice of development methodologies and managerial influences also distinguish IT projects from other projects. The general manager needs to understand the issues specific to the IT aspects of projects to select the right management tools for the particular challenges presented in such projects. Traditionally IT professionals use four main methodologies to manage the technology projects. Of those methods, **systems development life cycle (SDLC)** is a popular method for developing information systems. Other traditional methods are prototyping, rapid applications development (RAD), and joint applications development (JAD).

Systems Development Life Cycle

Systems development is the set of activities used to create an IS. The SDLC typically refers to the process of designing and delivering the entire system. Although the system includes the hardware, software, networking, and data (as discussed in Chapter 6), the SDLC generally is used in one of two distinct ways. On the one hand, SDLC is the general project plan of all the activities that must take place for the entire system to be put into operation, including the analysis and feasibility study, the development or acquisition of components, the implementation activities, the maintenance activities, and the retirement activities. In the context of an information system, however, SDLC can refer to a highly structured, disciplined, and formal process for design and development of system software. In either view, the SDLC is grounded on the systems approach and allows the developer to focus on system goals and trade-offs.

SDLC refers to a process in which the phases of the project are well documented, milestones are clearly identified, and all individuals involved in the project fully understand what exactly the project consists of and when deliverables are to be made. This approach is much more structured than other development approaches, such as prototyping, RAD, or JAD. However, despite being a highly structured approach, no single well-accepted SDLC process exists.

For any specific organization, and for a specific project, the actual tasks under each phase may vary. In addition, the checkpoints, metrics, and documentation may vary somewhat. SDLC typically consists of seven phases (see Figure 11.8).

Phase	Description	Sample Activities
Initiation and feasibility	Project is begun with a formal initiation and overall project is understood by IS and user/customers.	Document project objectives, scope, benefits, assumptions, constraints, estimated costs and schedule, and user commitment mechanisms.
Requirements definition	The system specifications are identified and documented.	Define business functionality; review existing systems; identify current problems and issues; identify and prioritize user requirements; identify potential solutions; develop user acceptance plan, user documentation needs, and user training strategy.
Functional design	The system is designed.	Complete a detailed analysis of new system including entity-relationship diagrams, data-flow diagrams, and functional design diagrams; define security needs; revise system architecture; identify standards, define systems acceptance criteria; define test scenarios; revise implementation strategy; freeze design.
Technical design and construction	The system is built.	Finalize architecture, technical issues, standards and data needs; complete technical definition of data access, programming flows, interfaces, special needs, inter-system processing, conversion strategy, and test plans; construct system; revise schedule, plan, and costs, as necessary.
Verification	The system is reviewed to make sure it meets specifications and requirements.	Finalize verification testing, stress testing, user testing, security testing, error handling procedures designed, end-user training, documentation and support.
Implementation	The system is brought up for use.	Put system into production environment; establish security procedures; deliver user documentation; execute training and complete monitoring of system.
Maintenance and review	The system is maintained and repaired as needed throughout its lifetime.	Conduct user review and evaluation, and internal review and evaluation; check metrics to ensure usability, reliability, utility, cost, satisfaction, business value, etc.

FIGURE 11.8 Systems development life cycle (SDLC) phases.

Each phase is carefully planned and documented. The first phase, project initiation, is where it is first considered and scoped. Approval is acquired before proceeding to the second phase, after it is determined that the project is technically, operationally, and financially feasible. The second phase is the requirements definition phase, where the problem is defined and needs and prerequisites are assessed and documented. Often the requirements are determined by studying the existing systems. Again, approval is obtained before proceeding. The third phase involves the functional design, at which point the specifications are discussed and documented.

The system is designed in conceptual terms. Approval is obtained on the functional specifications before technical design is begun. At phase four, functional specifications are translated into a technical design, and construction takes place. Here the system is actually built. If the system is acquired, it is at this point customized as needed for the business environment. Following construction is the verification phase, where the system is tested to ensure usability, security, operability, and that it meets the specifications for which it is designed. Multiple levels of testing are performed in this phase: unit testing, pairs testing, system testing, and acceptance testing.

After acceptance testing, project sign-off and approval signal that the system is acceptable to the users, and implementation, the sixth phase, begins. This phase is the "cutover" where the new system is put in operation and all links are established. Cutover may be performed in several ways: The old system may run alongside the new system (**parallel conversion**), the old system may stop running as soon as the new system is installed (**direct cutover**), or the new system may be installed in stages across locations, or in phases. The safest way to convert from an old system to a new system is parallel conversion because if the new system fails, users easily can revert to the old system. The riskiest approach is direct cutover because there is no backup system to turn to in the event of problems with the new system. Usually direct cutover is reserved from smaller, less-critical systems or for systems that were not previously available. Another instance when direct cutover was a good idea was Dagen H (*Högertrafik* day) on September 3, 1967, when Swedish drivers were to change from driving on the left-hand to the right-hand side of the road. On Dagen H, all vehicles on the road had to come to a complete stop at 04:50, then carefully change to the right-hand side of the road and stop again before being allowed to proceed at 05:00.[11]

Finally, the system enters the maintenance and review phase, where an evaluation is conducted to ensure the system continues to meet the needs for which it was designed. The system development project is evaluated using post-project feedback (sometimes called post-implementation audit) from all involved in the project. Feedback can be in the form of a formal survey or interview, a team debrief meeting, or informal solicitation through e-mail or Web-based social networking site. Post-project feedback brings closure to the project by identifying what went

---

[11] Dagen H, wikipedia, http://en.wikipedia.org/wiki/Dagen_H

right and what could be done better next time. Maintenance and enhancements are conducted on the system until it is decided that a new system should be developed and the SDLC begins anew. The maintenance and review phase is typically the longest phase of the life cycle.

Prototyping

Several problems arise with using traditional SDLC methodology for current IT projects. First, many systems projects fail to meet objectives, even with the structure of SDLC. The primary reason is often because the skills needed to estimate costs and schedules are difficult to obtain, and each project is often so unique that previous experience may not provide the skills needed for the current project. Second, even though objectives that were specified for the system were met, those objectives may reflect a scope that is too broad or too narrow. Thus, the problem the system was designed to solve may still exist, or the opportunity that it was to capitalize on may not be appropriately leveraged. Third, organizations need to respond quickly because of the dynamic nature of the business environment. Not enough time is available to adequately do each step of the SDLC for each IT project. Therefore, three other methodologies have become popular: prototyping, RAD, and JAD. These methodologies all use an iterative approach, as shown in Figure 11.9.

Prototyping is a type of evolutionary development, the method of building systems where developers get the general idea of what is needed by the users, and then build a fast, high-level version of the system as the beginning of the project. The idea of prototyping is to quickly get a version of the software in the hands of the users and to jointly evolve the system through a series of iterative cycles of

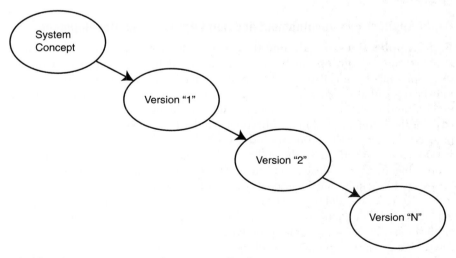

FIGURE 11.9 Iterative approach to systems development.

design. In this way, the system is done either when the users are happy with the design or when the system is proven impossible, too costly, or too complex. Some IS groups use prototyping as a methodology by itself because users are involved in the development much more closely than is possible with the traditional SDLC process. Users see the day-to-day growth of the system and contribute frequently to the development process. Through this iterative process, the system requirements usually are made clear.

The drawbacks to this methodology are, first, documentation may be more difficult to write. Because the system evolves, it takes much more discipline to ensure the documentation is adequate. Second, because users see the prototype develop, they often do not understand that a final prototype may not be scalable to an operational version of the system without additional costs and organizational commitments. Once users see a working model, they assume the work is also almost done, which is not usually the case. An operational version of the system needs to be developed. However, an operational version may be difficult to complete because the user is unwilling to give up a system that is up and running, and they often have unrealistic expectations about the amount of work involved in creating an operational version. This reluctance leads to the fourth drawback. Because it may be nearly impossible to definitively say when the prototype is done, the prototyping development process may be difficult to manage. Fifth, this approach is not suitable for all systems. It is difficult to integrate across a broad range of requirements, which makes this approach suited for "quick-and-dirty" types of systems. Developers should rely on a more structured approach such as the SDLC for extremely large and complex systems. Finally, because of the speed of development, system design flaws may be more prevalent in this approach, and the system may be harder to maintain than when the system is developed using the SDLC.

Rapid Applications Development and Joint Applications Development

Rapid applications development (RAD) is similar to prototyping in that it is an interactive process, in which tools are used to drastically speed up the development process. RAD systems typically have tools for developing the user interface—called the graphical user interface (GUI)—reusable code, code generation, and programming language testing and debugging. These tools make it easy for the developer to build a library of standard sets of code (sometimes called objects) that can easily be used (and reused) in multiple applications. Similarly, RAD systems typically have the ability to allow the developer to simply "drag and drop" objects into the design, and the RAD system automatically writes the code necessary to include that functionality. Finally, the system includes a set of tools to create, test, and debug the programs written in the pure programming language. RAD is commonly used for developing user interfaces and rewriting legacy applications. It may incorporate prototyping to involve users early and actively in the design process. Although RAD is an approach that works well in the increasingly dynamic environment of systems developers, it does have some drawbacks.

Sometimes basic principles of software development (e.g., programming standards, documentation, data-naming standards, backup and recovery) are overlooked in the race to finish the project. Also, the process may be so speedy that requirements are frozen too early.[12]

Joint applications development (JAD) is a version of RAD or prototyping in which users are more integrally involved, as a group, with the entire development process up to and, in some cases, including coding. JAD uses a group approach to elicit requirements in a complete manner. Interviewing groups of users saves interviewing and data collection time, but it can be expensive in terms of the travel and living expenses needed to get the participants together. A summary of the advantages and disadvantages of the SDLC, prototyping, RAD, and JAD are found in Figure 11.10.

Methodology	Advantages	Disadvantages
SDLC	• Structured approach with milestones and approvals for each phase • Uses system approach • Focuses on goals and trade-offs • Emphasizes documentation	• Systems often fail to meet objectives • Needed skills are often difficult to obtain • Scope may be defined too broadly or too narrowly • Very time consuming
Prototyping	• Improved user communications • Users like it • Speeds up development process • Good for eliciting system requirements • Provides a tangible model to serve as basis for production version	• Often underdocumented • Not designed to be an operational version • Often creates unrealistic expectations • Difficult-to-manage development process • Integration often difficult • Design flaws more prevalent than in SDLC • Often hard to maintain
RAD	• Speed of development • Heavy user participation • Use of GUI and other development tools	• Requirements frozen too early • Basic standards often overlooked
JAD	• Saves interviewing and data collection time • Structured process • Highly collaborative with business	• Expensive • Low use of technology

FIGURE 11.10 Comparison of IT project development methodologies.

[12] Joey F. George, "The Origins of Software: Acquiring Systems at the End of the Century," in R. Zmud (ed.), *Framing the Domains of IT Management* (Cincinnati, OH: Pinnaflex Education Resources, 2000).

Other Development Methodologies

One of the dangers that developers face is pretending to follow a predictable development process when they really can't. In response to this challenge, **agile development** methodologies are being championed. These include XP (Extreme Programming), Crystal, Scrum, Feature-Driven Development, and Dynamic System Development Method (DSDM). To deal with unpredictability, agile methodologies tend to be people- rather than process-oriented. They adapt to changing requirements by iteratively developing systems in small stages and then testing the new code extensively. The mantra for agile programming is "Code a little; test a little." Some agile methodologies build on existing methodologies. For example, DSDM is an extension of RAD used in the United Kingdom that draws on the underlying principles of active user interaction, frequent deliveries, and empowered teams. It is based on three types of cycles (i.e., functional model cycle, design and build cycle, and the implementation cycle) that occur (and reoccur) in cycles of between two and six weeks. In contrast is XP, a more prescriptive agile methodology that revolves around 12 practices, including pair programming, test-driven development, simple design, and small releases.[13]

Object-oriented development is becoming increasingly popular as a way to avoid the pitfalls of procedural methodologies. Object-oriented development, unlike more traditional development using the SDLC, builds on the concept of objects. An **object** encapsulates both the data stored about an entity and the operations that manipulate that data. A program developed using an object orientation is basically a collection of objects. The object orientation makes it easier for developers to think in terms of reusable components. Using existing components can save programming time. Such component-based development, however, assumes that the components have been saved in a repository and can be retrieved when needed. It also assumes that the components in the programs in newly developed information systems can communicate with one another.

Many good references are available for systems development, but further detail is beyond the scope of this text. The interested general manager is referred to a more detailed systems development text for a deeper understanding of this critical IS process.

▶ MANAGERIAL INFLUENCES

General managers face a broad range of influences during the development of projects. Many of these technical, organizational, and socioeconomic influences are relatively unique to IT projects.

---

[13] Kent Beck, *Extreme Programming Explained: Embrace Change* (Reading, MA: Addison Wesley Longman, Inc., 1999).

Technical Influences

Complex technical issues potentially command attention that might be better focused on business and budget issues. General managers who are uncomfortable with technology often either ignore the issues, delegating entirely to the IS organization, or focus inappropriate attention on managing the technology to counter their fear. The technical aspects of IT projects do require special attention, but no more than the people, financial, or other resources of the project.

Three software tools used to aid in managing the technical issues are the software development library, an automated audit trail, and software metrics. The *software development library* is a controlled collection of software, documentation, test data, and associated tools. Programs, utilities, and other software modules are kept here for several reasons. First is integrity. With multiple copies of a piece of software floating around an organization, it is difficult to know which copy is the actual one for the project. The software library keeps the copy that other modules can use to ensure that the correct version is available. Second is reuse. A software library is useful for programmers who need code, but do not know where to find it. The library is the storage area where programmers would look for code they want to reuse in their module. Third is control. Not only does the library ensure that the software is the right one, but it can also make sure that only those authorized to work on the code have access to it.

Another tool, an *automated audit trail*, allows the team to track each change made to the code. Each step is recorded in such a way as to capture exactly what was done, making it possible to undo if necessary. The ability to trace each step is important should a problem be found. It allows the troubleshooter to retrace and in some cases to regenerate old code to identify where the problem originates. Further, some quality assurance processes require analysis of the generation process, and the audit trail provides that information.

Software metrics are another tool used to manage the technical aspects of the project. The following list serves to identify some of the key terms that a general manager is likely to encounter.

- *Source lines of code (SLOC):* The number of lines of code in the source file of the software product
- *Source statement:* The number of statements in the source file
- *Function points:* The functional requirements of the software product, which can be estimated earlier than total lines of code
- *Inheritance depth:* The number of levels through which values must be remembered in a software object
- *Schedule slip:* The current scheduled time divided by the original scheduled time
- *Percentage complete:* The progress of a software product measured in terms of days or effort

Taken together, these tools can help the team to manage technical aspects of a project in such a way as to maintain a balance with other business aspects.

Managing Organizational and Socioeconomic Influences

The general manager must understand and anticipate the influences of organizational control systems and culture variables (see Chapter 1 for a discussion of these factors): The control systems used for non-project-based operations usually do not support project management in an efficient manner. For example, financial reporting systems designed for daily transaction-based operations do not fit well with the reporting needs of a project. Knowing daily profit and loss may not be the best metric for managing a project. A better system would link financial and other metrics with the goals of project stakeholders such as project cost or completion progress. A consultant who bills monthly based on the percentage of the project that is complete should be monitored with a financial system that tracks resource costs based on percentage complete. The general manager should strive to align the organizational systems with project goals.

The organizational culture influences the leadership style of the project manager and the communication between team members. When selecting a project manager, cultural factors should be evaluated. For example, a culture that rewards individual achievement over team participation may hinder a project team. Members might hoard information instead of sharing it. A leader who sets the example for the team has the opportunity to either eliminate or reinforce these barriers. Project time and leadership might also be allocated to help the project teamwork through these barriers.

Socioeconomic influences on projects include government and industry standards, globalization, and cultural issues. Trends external to the organization, such as changes in industry standards and regulations, usually affect all projects in varying degrees. An example is the growth of Java as an operating standard for Web-developed applications. This factor greatly affected projects written in other languages. Programmers were increasingly difficult to find, and many of the best and brightest only wanted jobs in the newest language. In certain cases the standards or regulations may not be known, and managing them means including possible scenarios in the risk management program. Globalization trends create the need for projects that span time zones, oceans, and national boundaries, adding to already complex conditions. Cultural influences, such as economic, ethical, and religious factors, affect the relationships between people and between organizations. All these factors need to be considered in the project decisions made by the general manager. These influences should not be underestimated—every management text considers them important enough to warrant extensive coverage.

► MANAGING PROJECT RISK

IT projects are often distinguished from many non-IT projects on the basis of their high levels of risk. Although every manager has an innate understanding of what risk is, there is little consensus as to the definition of risk. Risk is perceived as the possibility of additional cost or loss due to the choice of alternative. Some alternatives have a lower associated risk than others. Risk can be quantified by assigning a probability of occurrence and a financial consequence to each alternative. We consider risk to be a function of complexity, clarity, and size.

Complexity

The first determinant of risk on an IT project is the complexity level, or the extent of difficulty and interdependent components, of the project. Several factors contribute to greater complexity in IT projects. The first is the sheer pace of technological change. The increasing numbers of products and technologies affecting the marketplace cause rapidly changing views of any firm's future business situation. For example, introducing a new programming language such as Java creates significantly different ideas in people's minds about the future direction of Web development. Such uncertainty can make it difficult for project team members to identify and agree on common goals. This fast rate of change also creates new vocabularies to learn as technologies are implemented, which can undermine effective communication.

The development of more complex technologies accelerates the trend toward increased specialization among members of a project team and multiplies the number of interdependencies that must be tracked in project management. Team members must be trained to work on the new technologies. More subprojects must be managed, which, in turn, means developing a corresponding number of interfaces to integrate the pieces (i.e., subprojects) back into a whole.

High complexity played a part in the 2008 failure at Heathrow's Terminal 5.[14] The terminal project involved 180 IT suppliers and over 160 IT systems. There are more than 9,000 devices connected to it along with another 2,100 PCs. The system includes 175 lifts (elevators), 131 escalators, and 18 km of conveyor belts for baggage handling. According to the British Airports authority (BAA), "It has taken 400,000 man-hours of software engineering just to develop the complex system, and coding is set to continue even after installation begins." The British Airways CIO was quoted as saying that "even the construction of T5 involved creating a small town with a full telecommunications network for the construction workers, merely to enable the terminal to be built."[15] But the failure in 2008 resulted in cancelled flights, lost baggage, substantial delays and frustrated customers and employees. According to blogger Michael Krigsman, "the systems incorporated in T5 severely taxed BA's planning, testing and deployment capabilities."[16]

Complexity can be determined once the context of the project has been established. Consider the hypothetical case of a manager given six months and

---

[14] Adapted from Michael Krigsman, blogs.zdnet.com/projectfailures/?p=681 (accessed July 28, 2008).

[15] CIO UK at www.cio.co.uk/concern/change/news/index.cfm?articleid=2487&pn=2.

[16] Michael Krigsman, blogs.zdnet.com/projectfailures/?p=681. August 1, 2008.

$500,000 to build a corporate Web site to sell products directly to customers. Questions that might be used to build context for this case include the following:

- How many products will this Web site sell?
- Will this site support global, national, regional, or local sales?
- How will this sales process interface with the existing customer fulfillment process?
- Does the company possess the technical expertise in-house to build the site?
- What other corporate systems and processes will this project affect?
- How and when will these other systems be coordinated?

Clarity

A project is more risky if it is hard to define. Clarity is concerned with the ability to define the requirements of the system. A project has low clarity if the users cannot easily state their needs or define what they want from the system. The project also has low clarity if user demands for the system or regulations that guide the structure of the system change considerably over the life of a project. A project with high clarity is one in which the systems requirements do not change and can be easily documented. Purchasing a scheduling software package that applies scheduling rules across a broad range of organizations would be an example of a high-clarity project for most firms.

Size

Size also plays a big role in project risk. All other things being equal, big projects are riskier than smaller ones. A project can be considered big if it has the following characteristics:

- Large budget relative to other budgets in the organization
- Large number of team members (and hence reflecting a large number of man-months)
- Large number of organizational units involved in the project
- Large number of programs/components
- Large number of function points or lines of code

It is important to consider the relative size.[17] At a small company with an average project budget of $30,000, $90,000 would be a large project. However, to a major corporation that just spent $2 million implementing an ERP, a $90,000 budget would be peanuts.

---

[17] L. Applegate, F. W. McFarlan, and J. L. McKenney, *Corporate Information Systems Management: Text and Cases*, 5th ed. (Boston: Irwin McGraw-Hill, 1999).

Managing Project Risk Level

The IS project management literature usually views risk management as a two-stage process: first the risk is assessed and then actions are taken to control it.[18] The project's complexity, clarity, and size determine its risk. Varying levels of these three determinants differentially affect the amount of project risk. At one extreme, large, highly complex projects that are low in clarity are extremely risky. In contrast, small projects that are low in complexity and high in clarity are low risk. Everything else is somewhere in between.

The level of risk determines how formal the project management system and detailed the planning should be. When it is difficult to estimate how long or how much a project will cost because it is so complex or what should be done because its clarity is so low, formal management practices or planning is inappropriate. A high level of planning is not only almost impossible in these circumstances because of the uncertainty surrounding the project, but it also makes it difficult to adapt to external changes that are bound to occur. On the other hand, formal planning tools may be useful in low-risk projects because they can help structure the sequence of tasks as well as provide realistic cost and time targets.[19]

Managing the Complexity Aspects of Project Risk

The more complex the project, the greater is the risk. The increasing dependence on IT in all aspects of business means that managing the risk level of an IT project is critical to a general manager's job. Organizations increasingly embed IT deeper into their business processes, raising efficiency but also increasing risk. Many companies now rely entirely on IT for their revenue-generating processes, whether the process uses the Internet or not. For example, airlines are dependent on IT for generating reservations and ultimately sales. If the reservation system goes down, that is, if it fails, agents simply cannot sell tickets. In addition, even though the airplanes technically can fly if the reservation system fails, the airline cannot manage seat assignments, baggage, or passenger loads without the reservation system. In short, the airline would have to stop doing business should its reservation system fail. That type of dependence on IT raises the risk levels associated with adding or changing the system. The manager may adopt several strategies in dealing with complexity, including leveraging the technical skills of the team, relying on consultants to help deal with project complexity, and other internal integration strategies.

Leveraging the Technical Skills of the Team When a project is complex, it is helpful to have a leader with experience in similar situations, or who can translate

---

[18] R. Schmidt, K. Lyytinen, M. Keil, and P. Cule, "Identifying Software Project Risks: An International Delphi Study," *Journal of Management Information Systems* 17:4 (Spring 2001), pp. 5–36.

[19] H. Barki, S. Rivard, and J. Talbot, "An Integrative Contingency Model of Software Project Risk Management," *Journal of Management Information Systems* 17:4 (Spring 2001), pp. 37–69.

experiences in many different situations to this new complex one. For projects high in complexity, it also helps to have team members with significant work experience, especially if it is related.

Relying on Consultants and Vendors   Few organizations develop or maintain the in-house capabilities they need to complete complex IT projects. Risk-averse managers want people who possess crucial IT knowledge and skills. Often that skill set can be attained only from previous experience on similar IT projects. Such people are easier to find at consulting firms because consultants' work is primarily project based. Consulting firms rely on processes that develop the knowledge and experience of their professionals. Thus, managers often choose to "lease" effective IT team skills rather than try to build them within their own people. However, the project manager must balance the benefits achieved from bringing in outsiders with the costs of not developing that skill set in house. When the project is over and the consultants leave, will the organization be able to manage without them? Having too many outsiders on a team also makes alignment more difficult. Outsiders may have different objectives, such as selling more business, or learning new skills, which might conflict with the project manager's goal of completing the project.

Integrating Within the Organization   Highly complex projects require good communication among the team members, which helps them to operate as an integrated unit. Ways of increasing internal integration include holding frequent team meetings, documenting critical project decisions, and conducting regular technical status reviews.[20] These approaches ensure that all team members are "on the same page" and are aware of project requirements and milestones.

Managing Clarity Aspects of Project Risk

When a project has low clarity, project managers need to rely more heavily on the users to define system requirements. It means managing project stakeholders and sustaining commitment to projects.

Managing Project Stakeholders   A project's low clarity may be the result of its multiple stakeholders' conflicting needs and expectations for the system. Stakeholders are individuals and organizations that are actively involved in the project, or whose interests may be positively or negatively affected as a result of project execution or successful project completion.[21] The project manager must balance the goals of the various project stakeholders to achieve desired project outcomes. The project manager may also need to specifically manage stakeholders.

---

[20] Barki et al., "An Integrative Contingency Model of Software Project Risk Management"; and Applegate et al., *Corporate Information Systems Management*.

[21] Project Management Institute Standards Committee, *A Guide to the Project Management Body of Knowledge* (Project Management Institute, 1996), p. 15.

It is not always a simple task to identify project stakeholders. They may be employees, managers, users, other departments, or even customers. However, failure to manage these stakeholders can lead to costly mistakes later in the project if a particular group is not supportive of the project.

Key stakeholders on every project include the following:[22]

- *Project manager:* This individual is responsible for managing the project.

- *Customer:* This individual or organization uses the project product. Multiple layers of customers may be involved. For example, the customers for a new pharmaceutical product may include the doctors who prescribe it, the patients who take it, and the insurers who pay for it.

- *Performing organization:* This enterprise provides the employees who are most directly involved in doing the work of the project.

- *Sponsor:* This individual or group within the performing organization provides the financial resources, in cash or in kind, for the project.

Managing the expectations and needs of these people often involves both the project manager and the general manager. Project sponsors are especially critical for IT projects with organizational change components. Sponsors use their power and influence to remove project barriers by gathering support from various social and political groups both inside and outside the organization. They often prove to be valuable when participating in communication efforts to build the visibility of the project.

Sustaining Commitment to Projects

A key job of the project management team is to gain commitment from stakeholders and to sustain that commitment throughout the life of the project. Research indicates four primary types of determinants of commitment to projects (see Figure 11.11)[23] They include project determinants, psychological determinants, social determinants, and organizational determinants. Project teams often focus on only the project factors, ignoring the other three types because of their complexity. By identifying how these factors are manifested in an organization, however, project managers can use tactics to ensure a sustained commitment. For example, to maintain commitment, a project team might continually remind stakeholders of the benefits to be gained from completion of this project. Likewise, assigning the right project champion the task of selling the project to all levels of the organization can maintain commitment. Other strategies to encourage stakeholder, especially user, buy-in so that they can help clarify project requirements are making a user

[22] Ibid.

[23] See, for example, Mark Keil, "Pulling the Plug: Software Project Management and the Problem of Project Escalation," *MIS Quarterly* 19:4 (December 1995), pp. 421–447; and Michael Newman and Rajiv Sabherwal, "Determinants of Commitment to Information Systems Development: A Longitudinal Investigation," *MIS Quarterly* 20:1 (March 1996), pp. 23–54.

Determinant	Description	Example
Project	Objective attributes of the project such as cost, benefits, expected difficulty, and duration.	Projects are more likely to have higher commitment if they involve a large potential payoff.
Psychological	Factors managers use to convince themselves things are not so bad, such as previous experience, personal responsibility for outcome, and biases.	Projects are more likely to have higher commitment when there is a previous history of success.
Social	Elements of the various groups involved in the process, such as rivalry, norms for consistency, and need for external validation.	Projects are more likely to have higher commitment when external stakeholders have been publicly led to believe the project will be successful.
Organizational	Structural attributes of the organization, such as political support, and alignment with values and goals.	Projects are more likely to have higher commitment when there is strong political support from executive levels.

FIGURE 11.11 Determinants of commitment for IT projects.
Source: Adapted from Mark Keil, "Pulling the Plug: Software Project Management and the Problem of Project Escalation," *MIS Quarterly* (December 1995); and Michael Newman and Rajiv Sabherwal, "Determinants of Commitment to Information Systems Development: A Longitudinal Investigation," *MIS Quarterly* (March 1996).

the project team leader; placing key stakeholders on the project team; placing key stakeholders in charge of the change process, training, or installing the system; and formally involving stakeholders in the specification approval process.

Pulling the Plug

These various risk management strategies are designed to turn potentially troubled projects into successful ones. Often, projects in trouble persist long after they should be abandoned. Research shows that the amount of money already spent on a project biases managers toward continuing to fund the project, even if its prospects for success are questionable.[24] Other factors can also enter in the decision to keep projects too long. For example, when the penalties for failure within an organization are high, project teams are often willing to go to great lengths to ensure that their project persists, even if it means extending resources.

[24] M. Keil, et al, "A Cross-Cultural Study on Escalation of Commitment Behavior in Software Projects," *MIS Quarterly* 24:2 (2000), pp. 299–325.

Also, a propensity for taking risks or an emotional attachment to the project by powerful individuals within the organization can contribute to a troubled project continuing well beyond reasonable time limits.

Gauging Success

How does a manager know when a project has been a success? At the start of the project, the general manager who built the business case would have considered several aspects based on achieving the business goals. Care is needed to prevent forming a set of goals that is too narrow or too broad. It is important that the goals be measurable so that they can be used throughout the project to provide the project manager with real-time feedback.

Four dimensions of success are shown in Figure 11.12. The dimensions are defined as follows:

- *Resource constraints:* Does the project meet the established time and budget criteria? Most projects set some measure of success along this dimension, which is a short-term success metric that is easy to measure.

- *Impact on customers:* How much benefit does the customer receive from this project? Although some IT projects are transparent to the organization's end customer, every project can be measured on the benefit to the immediate customer of the IS. This dimension includes performance and technical specification measurements.

- *Business success:* How high are the profits and how long do they last? Did the project meet its return on investment goals? This dimension must be aligned with the business strategy of the organization.

- *Prepare the future:* Has the project altered the infrastructure of the organization so that in the future business success and customer impact are more likely? Today many companies are building Internet infrastructures in anticipation of future business and customer benefits. Overall success of this strategy will only be measurable in the future, although projects underway now can be evaluated on how well they prepare the business for future opportunities.

What other considerations should be made when defining success? Is it enough just to complete a project? Is it necessary to finish on time and on budget? What other dimensions are important? The type of project can greatly influence how critical each of these dimensions is in determining the overall success of the project. It is the responsibility of the general manager to coordinate the overall business strategy of the company with the project type and the project success measurements. In this way, the necessary organizational changes can be coordinated to support the new information system. After the project is completed, a post-project feedback (post-implementation audit) should be completed to ensure that the system met its requirements and the system development process was a good one.

Success Dimension	Low Tech	Medium Tech	High Tech
	Existing technologies with new features	*Most technologies are new but available before the project*	*New, untested technologies*
Resource Constraint	Important	Overruns acceptable	Overruns most likely
Impact on Customers	Added value	Significantly improved capabilities	Quantum leap in effectiveness
Business Success	Profit; Return on Investment	High profits; Market share	High, but may come much later; Market leader
Prepare the Future	Gain additional capabilities	New market; New service	Leadership-core and future technologies

FIGURE 11.12   Success dimensions for various project types.
Source: Adapted from Aaron Shenhar, Dov Dvir, and Ofer Levy, "Project Success: A Multidimensional Strategic Approach," Technology and Innovation Management Division (1998).

▶ THE PMO

Although managing projects is not a new set of activities for management, it is a struggle for many to bring a project in on time, on budget, and within scope. Some organizations create a **Project Management Office (PMO)** to boost efficiency, gather expertise, and improve project delivery. A PMO is created to bring discipline to the project management activities within the enterprise. The Sarbanes–Oxley Act is also a driver because it forces companies to pay closer attention to project expenses and progress. Although companies may not immediately realize cost savings, the increased efficiencies and project discipline may eventually lead to cost savings.

PMOs can be expected to function in the following seven areas, according to *CIO Magazine*:

- Project support
- Project management process and methodology
- Training
- Project manager home base
- Internal consulting and mentoring
- Project management software tools and support
- Portfolio management (managing multiple projects)

The responsibilities of a PMO range widely, based on the preferences of the CIO under which the PMO typically falls. Sometimes the PMO is simply a clearinghouse for best practices in project management, and other times it is the organization that more formally manages all major projects. At risk management company Assurant Group, for example, a number of project managers work in the PMO under the direction of the COO. Using well-defined software development and project management methodologies, these PMO managers work with business managers to refine their project management efforts—from requirements definition to post-implementation audits. Within four years of the installation of its PMO, 97% of Assurant's projects were delivered on schedule and within budget.[25]

The structure of the PMO may vary, but usually mirrors the organization, culture, and bureaucracy of the CIO's organization. If the culture is rigid and strictly controlled, then the PMO will likely have first-hand and significant oversight of projects. Likewise, if the culture is collaborative and open, then the PMO will likely play a more coordinating role.

▶ FOOD FOR THOUGHT: OPEN SOURCING

Linux, the brainchild of Linus Torvalds, is a world-class operating system created from part-time hacking by several thousand developers scattered all over the planet and connected only by the Internet. This system was built using a development approach called **open sourcing**, or the process of building and improving "free" software by an Internet community. Torvalds managed the development process by releasing early and often, delegating as much as possible, being open to new ideas, and archiving and managing the various versions of the software.

Eric Raymond, the author of *The Cathedral and the Bazaar*, suggests that the Linux community resembles a great bazaar of differing agendas and approaches (with submissions from *anyone*) out of which a coherent and stable system emerged. This development approach is in contrast to cathedrals, in which software is carefully crafted by company employees working in isolation. The most frequently cited example of a cathedral is Microsoft, a company known, if not ridiculed, for espousing a proprietary approach to software development.[26]

Software is **open source software (OSS)** if it is released under a license approved by the Open Source Initiative (OSI). The most widely used OSI license

[25] M. Santosus, "Why You Need a Project Management Office (PMO)," *CIO Magazine*, http://www.cio.com/article/29887/Why_You_Need_a_Project_Management_Office_PMO_/1 (accessed July 15, 2008).
[26] Eric S. Raymond, "The Cathedral and the Bazaar," available at http://www.tuxedo.org/~esr/writings/cathedral-bazaar/ (accessed June 27, 2002).

is the GNU general public license (GPL), which is premised on the concept of free software. *Free software* offers the following freedoms for the software users:[27]

- The freedom to run the program, for any purpose.
- The freedom to study how the program works, and adapt it to your needs. Access to the source code is a precondition for this.
- The freedom to distribute copies so that you can help your neighbor.
- The freedom to improve and release your improvements to the public, so that the whole community benefits. Access to source code is a precondition for this.

A user who modifies the software must observe the rule of *copyleft*, which stipulates that the user cannot add restrictions to deny other people their central freedoms regarding the free software.

Open sourcing is a movement that offers a speedy way to develop software. Further, because it is made available to a whole community, testing is widespread. Finally, its price is always right—it is free. However, a number of managerial issues are associated with its use in a business organization.

- *Preservation of intellectual property.* The software is open to the whole community. It cannot be sold, and its use cannot be restricted. So the community is the "owner" of the code. Yet, how are the contributions of individuals recognized?
- *Updating and maintaining open source code.* A strength of the open source movement is that it is open to the manipulation of members of an entire community. That very strength makes it difficult to channel the updating and maintenance of code.
- *Competitive advantage.* Because the code is available to all, a company would not want to open-source a system that it hopes can give it a competitive advantage.
- *Tech support.* The code may be free, but technical support usually isn't. Users of a system that was open-sourced must still be trained and supported.
- *Standards.* Standards are open. Yet in a technical world that is filled with incompatible standards, open sourcing may be unable to charter a viable strategy for selecting and using standards.

Applications written following the open source standards were initially rejected by corporate IT organizations. Executives wondered how code that was free, open, and available to all could be counted on to support critical business applications. However, a number of case studies recorded by OSI highlight the benefits

---

[27] GNU Project—Free Software Foundation, "The Free Software Definition," available at http://www.gnu.org/philosophy/free-sw.html (accessed April 3, 2002).

of open source code. In addition to Linux, *Mozilla* (a popular Web browser core), *Apache* (Web server), *PERL* (Web scripting language) *OpenOffice* (a Sun Microsystems-originated set of office applications that support the Microsoft Office suite formats), and *PNG* (graphics file format) are all examples of very popular software that is based on open source. In some cases, companies now sponsor OSS projects by directly contributing resources to their development. For example, IBM contributed developers to work on Apache's Web server. In other cases, companies provide commercial support for OSS products, such as RedHat does with Linux. Advances in the applications available on the Internet, particularly many of the Web 2.0 applications that are making their way slowly into the corporate infrastructure, are open sourced.

▶ SUMMARY

- A general manager fulfills an important role in project management. As a participant, the general manager may be called on to select the project manager, to provide resources to the project manager, and to provide direction to the project.
- The business case provides foundation for a well-managed project by specifying the objectives of the project, the required resources, the critical elements, and the stakeholders.
- Project management involves continual trade-offs. The project triangle highlights the need to delicately balance cost, time, and scope to achieve quality in a project.
- Four important project elements are common project vocabulary, teamwork, project cycle plan, and project management.
- Understanding the complexity of the project, the environment in which it is developed, and the dimensions used to measure project success allows the general manager to balance the trade-offs necessary for using resources effectively and to keep the project's direction aligned with the company's business strategy.
- Four popular information technology project development methodologies are the SDLC, prototyping, JAD, and RAD. Each of these methodologies offers both advantages and drawbacks. Other methodologies are emerging.
- In increasingly dynamic environments, it is important to manage project risk. Project risk is a function of project size, clarity, and level of complexity. For low-clarity projects, it is important to interface with users and gain their commitment in the project. Projects that are highly complex require leveraging the technical skills of the team members, bringing in consultants when necessary, and using other strategies to promote internal integration.
- The PMO, Project Management Office, brings focus and efficiency to project management activities. Often the PMO is a formal organization under the CIO.
- Projects are here to stay, and every general manager must be a project manager at some point in his or her career. As a project manager, the general manager is expected to lead the daily activities of the project. This chapter offers insight into the necessary skills, processes, and roles that project management requires.

► KEY TERMS

agile development (p. 328)
direct cutover (p. 324)
joint applications
  development (JAD)
  (p. 327)
object (p. 328)
open sourcing (p. 339)

open source software
  (OSS) (p. 339)
parallel conversion
  (p. 324)
project (p. 311)
project management
  (p. 312)

project management
  office (PMO) (p. 338)
prototyping (p. 325)
rapid applications
  development (RAD)
  (p. 326)
systems development life
  cycle (SDLC) (p. 322)

► DISCUSSION QUESTIONS

1. What are the trade-offs between cost, quality, and time when designing a project plan? What criteria should managers use to manage this trade-off?

2. Why does it often take a long time before troubled projects are abandoned or brought under control?

3. What are the critical success factors for a project manager? What skills should managers look for when hiring someone who would be successful in this job?

4. What determines the level of technical risk associated with a project? What determines the level of organizational risk? How can a general manager assist in minimizing these risk components?

5. Lego's Mindstorms Robotics Invention System was designed for 12-year-olds. But after more than a decade of development at the MIT Media Lab using the latest advances in artificial intelligence, the toy created an enormous buzz among grown-up hackers. Despite its stiff $199 price tag, Mindstorms sold so quickly that store shelves were emptied two weeks before its first Christmas in 1998. In its first year, a staggering 100,000 kits were sold, far beyond the 12,000 units the company had projected. Seventy percent of Mindstorms' early customers were old enough to vote. These customers bought the software with the intention of hacking it. They wanted to make the software more flexible and powerful. They deciphered Mindstorms' proprietary code, posted it on the Internet, began writing new advanced software, and even wrote a new operating system for their robots. To date Lego has done nothing to stop this open source movement, even though thousands of Lego's customers now operate their robots with software the company didn't produce or endorse and can't support. The software may end up damaging the robot's expensive infrared sensors and motors.[28]

    a. What are the advantages of Lego's approach to open sourcing?

    b. What are the disadvantages of Lego's approach to open sourcing?

    c. How should Lego manage the open source movement?

[28] Excerpted from Paul Keegan, "Lego: Intellectual Property Is Not a Toy," *Business 2.0* (October 2001), available at http://www.business2.com/articles/mag/0,1640,16981,FF.html (accessed June 27, 2002).

SABRE HOLDINGS

Sabre Holdings Corp. embarked on a $100-million-plus project to rebuild their air-travel reservation system. The old system was designed when assembly code was the rage; the system was 10 million lines of code. The new system was designed for C++ and Java, using servers and databases that were not even possible when the original system was built. That means the new system was a complete redo. And they brought the system in on time and on budget. How did they do it?

It was no small feat this time around. In 1988, Sabre managers tried to overhaul the system and spent $125 million. The project was well planned and broken into manageable pieces to be built in parallel, as was the prevailing project management advice at the time. After 3 1/2 years of development, it didn't work. Partners like Budget Rent a Car and Hilton and Marriott hotel chains were scheduled to use it. But a few weeks before the due date, the entire project was scrapped.

But this time, managers took a different approach similar to agile programming for this project. First they did the project as a series of small steps, each providing functionality that can be tweaked or redesigned as necessary. Small steps make it possible to change direction or even respond to changes in technology without disrupting the entire project. For example, functions originally targeted for one type of server were rearchitected for a different server. In addition, Linux servers, which did not look viable when the project began, could be used later when they were proven to be appropriate for this environment. Second, the small steps make it possible to go live with each iteration of the system before beginning the next step. This ensures that the system works and meets the users' needs.

Observers noted, "That doesn't sound like a big IT project. Everything we expect from a big IT project is missing: The grand, detailed plan; the divide-at-the-start-and-integrate-at-the-end strategy; the years-before-it-goes-live schedule. That approach has doomed big IT projects for generations. IT had too much risk built into it, requiring too many predictions in the face of too much change, and depending on too much perfection in execution."[29]

Discussion Questions

1. In what ways do you think this project was managed differently than the 1988 overhaul project? What are the advantages of agile programming in this situation?
2. What were the risks Sabre Holdings faced when they decided to redesign their reservation systems? What actions did they take to minimize the risks?
3. How did the Sabre project managers ensure that the system met users' needs?

Source: Adapted from Frank Hayes, "Big IT: Doomed" (June 2004), http://www.computerworld.com/action/article.do?command=viewArticleBasic&articleId=93641&paageNumber=1.

[29] http://www.computerworld.com/managementtopics/management/project/story/0,10801,93641,00.html.

DEALING WITH TRAFFIC JAMS IN LONDON

It's hard to think of traffic in any big city as being good. But London's traffic at the turn of the millennium may have been far worse than that of the average metropolis. When driving in London's downtown area, drivers spent around half their time waiting in traffic, incurring 2.3 minutes of delay for every kilometer they traveled. To get its horrendous traffic jams under control, the city government decided to marry information technology with 699 cameras at 203 sites in the 8 square miles targeted for congestion control. Rather than wait in lines to pay a toll, drivers now pay for a daily toll when they drive their cars in the areas marked by a red C logo painted on signs and streets. To verify their being in toll areas, the cameras daily take over a quarter of a million pictures of the license plates of cars in designated areas. Motorists who don't pay the toll that day are automatically fined about $130. The fines and tolls resulted in a project payback period of about one and a half years. In ten years this will translate into total revenues of $2.2 billion—all of which will be used to improve London's public transportation systems. Further, as of March 2003, traffic in the city's center had fallen by an unexpectedly high 20%, improving journey times by 5% and saving drivers 2 million to 3 million hours of frustration every year.

The project risks were obvious from the outset. The project faced a tight implementation timetable, there was no preexisting model anywhere in the world to follow, and a brand-new transit authority working under a brand-new mayor faced the challenge of integrating new technologies. The narrow, convoluted streets that were hundreds of years old did not lend themselves to collecting tolls. Cameras needed to be situated carefully to achieve sufficiently high levels of number recognition accuracy. For the new mayor, the political risk was huge, as failure of the system would be extremely damaging to his career.

The department implementing the system, Transport for London, recognized its own limitations in terms of experience, IT ability, and management time. Consequently, Transport for London decided to outsource critical elements of the project management first to consultants from PricewaterhouseCooper and then Deloitte & Touche.

Early in the project, project managers identified the critical technical elements and divided the project into five "packages" that could, if required, be bought and managed separately. These included (1) the camera component; (2) the image store component that collected images, converted them into license numbers, and condensed the images (duplicates would occur when one vehicle was photographed by several cameras); (3) the telecommunications links between the cameras and the image store component; (4) the customer services infrastructure, including the ability to pay by phone, Web, and mail; and (5) an extensive network of retail outlet kiosks and gas stations where people could pay the toll.

Even at this early stage, risk aversion played a role. Instead of combining the customer services infrastructure and the retail side into a single customer-facing operation, retail was seen as a big enough challenge to be bought and managed separately. To reduce the risks, the technologies selected for each of the five packages were the best available.

Transport for London requested bids on the project early in 2001. The estimated $116.2 million project was large enough to require listing in the European Union's public-sector register, and tenders were open to companies throughout Europe. Separate bids could be tendered for the camera and communications packages, whereas the remaining three could receive bids on a combined basis or individually. The bid process was managed by Deloitte

& Touche, who narrowed the original 40 bids to 4. Then two of these bidders undertook a three-month technical design study to focus on issues such as data throughput, how the retail channels would work, how to achieve the best number recognition performance, and what payments might be expected through each payment channel. Although both bidders were paid for their technical design, it was decided that the benefits of contracting the two analyses for improving overall project quality would outweigh the cost of paying the losing bidder. The Capita Group, the winning bidder, gained confidence through the process that their technical design, especially for the challenging image store component, was viable.

From the technical point of view, the greatest challenge was the creation and management of the image store. This component had to process a million records each day (picture those 250,000 vehicles moving about the city center all day)—as well as store them for evidentiary purposes for the subsequent prosecution of nonpayers. Meeting the challenge meant carefully evaluating design considerations (such as using the most reliable technology available) and writing software code that would automatically detect which image of a passing vehicle would yield the most accurate number recognition. Simon Pilling, executive director at Capita, who was in charge of the project, stated: "The deadlines were very tight and were politically driven, and it highlighted where the risks were." Capita's contract included clear milestones and damages against the contractor for failure to deliver on time. Deloitte was hired to rigorously monitor Capita's progress in completing the estimated 300 years of effort that would be required to complete the project in the space of a year. The targeted deadline for completion was February 17, 2003.

Capita had successfully bid for the image store, customer payments, and the links to retailers' packages. So that Transport for London could deal with one prime contractor, it awarded Capita the remaining two project packages related to managing the camera and communications. Selecting one company made the task easier. Capita responded by physically locating all people working on the project together in a single building in Coventry, in central England.

The project was delivered on time and on budget, and it has reduced traffic congestion more than originally projected. Its success was attributed to several project management aspects. First, scope creep was vigorously guarded against by limiting changes to the requirements. One of the few changes was an option for motorists to pay tolls through the popular SMS text messaging format. Second, Capita's deliverables were spread out over a manageable time scale, rather than concentrated toward the project's end. And third, there was strong top management support from political leaders.

Discussion Questions

1. Assess the risks of this project. Given your assessment of the project complexity, clarity, and size, what management strategies would you recommend? What, if any, of these strategies were adopted in this project?

2. Describe the development methodology that was applied to this project. Was this the most appropriate approach? Provide a rationale for your response.

3. When a project is outsourced, who should manage the project—the internal group or the outsourcer? Why?

Source: Adapted from Malcolm Wheatley, "How IT Fixed London's Traffic Woes," *CIO Magazine* (July 15, 2003).

CHAPTER 12

MANAGING BUSINESS KNOWLEDGE[1]

Harrah's, the largest gaming company in the world by some measures, found a way to more than double revenues by collecting and then analyzing customer data. According to CEO Gary Loveman, "We've come out top in the casino wars by mining our customer data deeply, running marketing experiments, and using the results to implement finely tuned marketing and service delivery strategies that keep our customers coming back."[2] This is more than just implementing loyalty cards to track customer activity and reward "frequent buyers." In 2000, Harrah's was valued at close to $3 billion. When it was sold 7 years later to a private equity group, it was valued at $17 billion. Much of that increase was credited to the innovative and widespread use of business analytics to turn around the gaming company.

Analytics at Harrah's begins when a customer is issued a Loyalty Card. Similar to the ubiquitous cards used by airlines, grocery stores, and even coffeehouses, the Harrah's card tracks customer usage of the various games offered in their casinos. What differentiates Harrah's is what they do with the information they collect from their loyalty program. Harrah's uses sophisticated analytical tools to understand as much as possible about their customers. For example, they thought their best customers were high rollers. In fact, they found that 82% of revenues came from 26% of customers, and they were not the gold cuff-link-wearing, limousine-riding high rollers, but average, middle-aged, and seniors. The management at Harrah's wanted to know what motivated these customers. They conducted experiments and focus groups, using well-structured experiments designed to gather data and test hypotheses. They found that these customers were motivated by reduced rates on hotel rooms, or if they lived in the area, free chips. Special gifts and expensive rooms were not as effective as incentive. They studied the customer's value over time and identified ways to increase spending on repeat visits. For example, when they looked at the data about their best customers, they learned that these customers wanted service quickly. So Harrah's found ways to reduce the wait at the

---

[1] The authors wish to acknowledge and thank Ben Ballengee, MBA 1993, PhD 2001, for his help in researching and writing early drafts of this chapter.

[2] Gary Loveman, "Diamonds in the Data Mine," *Harvard Business Review* (May 2003): 110.

valet parking lot and at the restaurants. Diamond customers, those that were the very best customers, rarely waited in line at all, providing a very visible "reward" for their business and motivating others to seek Diamond-level status (something they could earn through the loyalty card program). They studied individual behaviors and created a program that was custom tailored to each customer offering specific incentives based on the results of their analytical models. As Loveman described, "If we discovered that a customer who spends $1000 per month with us hadn't visited us in three months, a letter or telephone call would invite him back. If we learned that he lost money during his last visit, we invited him back for a special event."[3] They found ways to keep the small-level gamblers in the casino longer and to lure them back again at very low costs. Analytics drives their business, and the results have turned the company into a model for successfully integrating technical algorithms with marketing techniques.

This chapter provides an overview of some of the ways business manage their collective knowledge. Enterprises have long sought a way to harness the value locked inside the extensive data they collect and store about customers, markets, competitors, products, people, and processes. This chapter will review some of the basic concepts of knowledge management, then look at business intelligence, including business analytics.

▶ KNOWLEDGE MANAGEMENT

Knowledge management includes the processes necessary to generate, capture, codify, and transfer knowledge across the organization to achieve competitive advantage. Individuals are the ultimate source of organizational knowledge. The organization gains only limited benefit from knowledge isolated within individuals or among workgroups; to obtain the full value of knowledge, it must be captured and transferred across the organization. In this chapter, we focus on knowledge management as infrastructure for business applications.

Knowledge management is related to information systems (IS) in three ways. First, information technologies make up the infrastructure for knowledge management systems. Second, knowledge management systems make up the data infrastructure for many IS and applications. The knowledge management system provides the source for information needed to run the business. Third, in the increased use of business analytics like that used at Harrah's in the opening example, knowledge management is often referred to as an application of IS, much like e-mail, word processing, and spreadsheets. It is increasingly being used as a business application itself in such forms as document management, information retrieval, data mining, data warehousing, and data visualization.

Two other terms frequently encountered in discussions of knowledge are *intellectual capital* and *intellectual property*. **Intellectual capital** is defined

---

[3] Loveman, "Diamonds in the Data Mind," 112.

as knowledge that has been identified, captured, and leveraged to produce higher-value goods or services or some other competitive advantage for the firm. Both knowledge management and intellectual capital are often used imprecisely and interchangeably to describe similar concepts. Information technology (IT) provides an infrastructure for capturing and transferring knowledge, but does not create knowledge and cannot guarantee its sharing or use.

Intellectual property allows individuals to own their creativity and innovation in the same way that they can own physical property. Owners can be rewarded for the use of their ideas and can have a say in how their ideas are used. To protect their ideas, owners typically apply for and are granted intellectual property rights, though some protection such as copyright arises automatically, without any registration, as soon as a record is made in some form of what has been created. The four main types of intellectual property are patents for inventions, trademarks for brand identity, designs for product appearance, and copyrights for literary and artistic material, music, films, sound recordings, broadcasts, and software.[4] In 2002, the music sharing Web site Napster raised controversial issues long surrounding the practice of copyright. The Audio Home Recording Act (1992) was passed in the United States to prevent serial copying, but this didn't seem to apply to Napster, who only facilitated sharing. Although the act protected intellectual property, it also confirmed the freedom to copy music for personal use. In 1998, the more stringent Digital Millennium Copyright Act (DCMA) passed by a unanimous vote in the U.S. Senate with the active support of the entertainment industry.[5] The DCMA makes it a crime to circumvent copy protection, even if that copy protection impairs rights established by the Audio Home Recording Act. Furthermore, the Digital Tech Corps Act of 2002, passed in the U.S. House of Representatives, seeks to protect intellectual property by placing a lifetime ban on employees from revealing trade secrets, and imposing a criminal penalty of up to five years in prison and a $50,000 fine.[6] More recently a senior-level position, Coordinator for International Intellectual Property Enforcement in the U.S. Department of Commerce, was created to coordinate the battle against global piracy of intellectual property.

▶ DATA, INFORMATION, AND KNOWLEDGE

The terms *data*, *information*, and *knowledge* are often used interchangeably, but have significant and discrete meanings within the knowledge management domain. As was first presented in the introduction of this textbook, the differences are shown in Figure 12.1. **Data** are specific, objective facts or observations, such as

---

[4] "What Is Intellectual Property or IP?" available at http://www.intellectual-property.gov.uk/std/faq/question1.htm (accessed June 25, 2002).

[5] On March 10, 2004, the European Union passed the EU Copyright Directive, which is similar in many ways to DCMA.

[6] Jason Miller, "House Passes IT Employee Exchange Program," Government Computer News, available at http://www.gcn.com/vol1_no1/regulation/18347-1.html (accessed June 25, 2002).

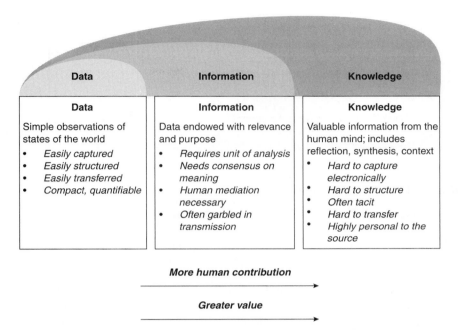

FIGURE 12.1 The relationships between data, information, and knowledge.
Source: Adapted from Thomas H. Davenport, *Information Ecology* (New York: Oxford University Press, 1997), 9.

"inventory contains 45 units." Standing alone, such facts have no intrinsic meaning, but can be easily captured, transmitted, and stored electronically.

Information is defined by Peter Drucker as "data endowed with relevance and purpose."[7] People turn data into information by organizing them into some unit of analysis (e.g., dollars, dates, or customers). Deciding on the appropriate unit of analysis involves interpreting the context of the data and summarizing them into a more condensed form. Consensus must be reached on the unit of analysis.

Knowledge is a mix of contextual information, experiences, rules, and values. It is richer and deeper than information and more valuable because someone has thought deeply about that information and added his or her own unique experience, judgment, and wisdom. One way of thinking about knowledge is to consider the different types of knowing.[8] *Knowing what* often is based on assembling information and eventually applying it. It requires the ability to recognize, describe, and classify concepts and things. The process of applying knowledge helps generate *knowing how* to do something. This kind of knowing

[7] Peter F. Drucker, "The Coming of the New Organization," *Harvard Business Review* (January–February 1988), 45–53.
[8] M. H. Zack, "Managing Codified Knowledge," *Sloan Management Review* 40, no. 4 (1999), 45–58.

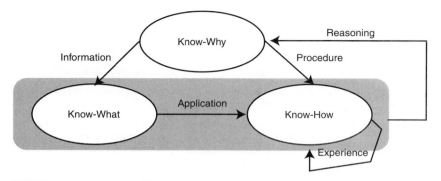

FIGURE 12.2 Taxonomy of knowledge.
Source: H-W. Kim and S. M. Kwak, "Linkage of Knowledge Management to Decision Support: A System Dynamics Approach," presented at the National University of Singapore, July 2002.

requires an understanding of an appropriate sequence of events or the ability to perform a particular set of actions. Sometimes the first inkling of knowing how to do something stems from an understanding of procedures, routines, and rules. Knowing how to do something is fully learned by actually experiencing a situation. Finally knowing how and knowing what can be synthesized through a reasoning process that results in *knowing why*. Knowing why is the causal knowledge of why something occurs. These types of knowing are modeled in Figure 12.2.

Values and beliefs are also a component of knowledge; they determine the interpretation and the organization of knowledge. Tom Davenport and Larry Prusak, experts who have written about this relationship, say, "The power of knowledge to organize, select, learn, and judge comes from values and beliefs as much as and probably more than, from information and logic."[9] Knowledge also involves the synthesis of multiple sources of information over time.[10] The amount of human contribution increases along the continuum from data to information to knowledge. Computers work well for managing data, but are less efficient at managing information. The more complex and ill-defined elements of knowledge (for example, "tacit" knowledge, described later in this chapter) are difficult if not impossible to capture electronically.

Tacit versus Explicit Knowledge

Knowledge can be further classified into two types: tacit and explicit. **Tacit knowledge** was first described by philosopher Michael Polyani in his book, *The Tacit Dimension*, with the classic assertion that "We can know more than we can tell."[11] For example, try writing a memorandum, or even explaining verbally,

---

[9] Thomas H. Davenport and Laurence Prusak, *Working Knowledge* (Boston: Harvard Business School Press, 1998), 12.

[10] Thomas H. Davenport, *Information Ecology* (New York: Oxford University Press, 1997), 9–10.

[11] Michael Polanyi, *The Tacit Dimension*, 1966 ed. (Magnolia, MA: Peter Smith, 1983), 4.

how to swim or ride a bicycle. Tacit knowledge is personal, context-specific, and hard to formalize and communicate. It consists of experiences, beliefs, and skills. Tacit knowledge is entirely subjective and is often acquired through physically practicing a skill or activity.

In 2007, Tom Brady broke the NFL single-season record for the most passing touchdowns with 50. It would be nearly impossible to verbally describe all the factors that Brady had to consider when making those passes, yet he knew who to throw the ball to, where to put the ball, and why to make that throw, all in a matter of seconds. Brady's ability to pass the football incorporates so much of his own personal experience and kinesthetic memory that it is impossible to separate that knowledge from the player himself. His bone structure, muscular development, and the nerves between his arm and his brain all make it possible for him to throw the types of passes he does.

IT has traditionally focused on **explicit knowledge**, that is, knowledge that can be easily collected, organized, and transferred through digital means, such as a memorandum or financial report. Individuals, however, possess both tacit and explicit knowledge. Explicit knowledge, such as the knowledge gained from reading this textbook, is objective, theoretical, and codified for transmission in a formal, systematic method using grammar, syntax, and the printed word. Figure 12.3 summarizes these differences.

▶ FROM MANAGING KNOWLEDGE TO BUSINESS INTELLIGENCE

Managing knowledge is not a new concept,[12] but it has been invigorated and enabled by new technologies for collaborative systems, the emergence of the Internet and intranets, which in themselves act as a large, geographically distributed

Tacit Knowledge	Explicit Knowledge
• Knowing how to identify the key issues necessary to solve a problem	• Procedures listed in a manual
• Applying similar experiences from past situations	• Books and articles
	• News reports and financial statements
• Estimating work required based on intuition and experience	• Information left over from past projects
• Deciding on an appropriate course of action	

FIGURE 12.3   Examples of explicit and tacit knowledge.

---

[12] The cuneiform texts found at the ancient city Ebla (Tall Mardikh) in Syria are, at more than 4,000 years old, some of the earliest known attempts to record and organize information.

knowledge repository, and the well-publicized successes of companies using business analytics, like Harrah's. The discipline draws from many established sources, including anthropology, cognitive psychology, management, sociology, artificial intelligence, IT, and library science. Knowledge management remains, however, an emerging discipline, with few generally accepted standards or definitions of key concepts.

Business intelligence (BI) is the term used to describe the set of technologies and processes that use data to understand and analyze business performance.[13] Although some may argue with this relationship, business intelligence can be considered a component of knowledge management. Knowledge management deals with the processes necessary to capture, codify, and make sense of all types of knowledge as described earlier. Business intelligence is more specifically about extracting knowledge from data. Davenport and Harris suggest that **business analytics** is the term used to refer to the use of quantitative and predictive models and fact-based management to drive decisions. By this definition, business analytics is a subset of BI.

The most profound aspect of knowledge management and business intelligence is that, ultimately, an organization's only sustainable competitive advantage lies in what its employees know and how they apply that knowledge to business problems. Exaggerated promises and heightened expectations, couched in the hyperbole of technology vendors and consultants, may create unrealistic expectations. Knowledge management is not a magic bullet, that is, an appropriate solution for all business problems. While reading this chapter, managers should consider the implications of managing knowledge, but should not believe that knowledge management by itself is the sole answer for managerial success. Knowledge must serve the broader goals of the organization, and analytics alone do not create competitive advantage. How the information is used and how the knowledge is linked back to business processes are important components of knowledge management.

▶ WHY MANAGE KNOWLEDGE?

Although knowledge has always been important to the success of organizations, it was presumed that the natural, informal flow of knowledge was sufficient to meet organizational needs and that no explicit effort had to be made to manage that knowledge. The value chain,[14] discussed in earlier chapters of this text, illustrates the need for knowledge in such diverse areas as raw materials handling, operations, manufacturing, sales and marketing, product distribution, customer service, firm infrastructure, human resources, research and development (R&D), and purchasing. Each element of the chain, for example R&D, also becomes

---

[13] Thomas Davenport and Jeanne Harris, *Competing on Analytics* (Harvard Business School Press, 2007), 7.

[14] Michael E. Porter, *Competitive Advantage: Creating and Sustaining Superior Performance* (New York: Free Press, 1985), 39–43.

knowledge intensive: technological developments, market trends, product design, and customer requirements must all be known and managed. In short, information and knowledge are now the basis for competition. Several trends highlight the need for businesses to manage knowledge for competitive advantage. Figure 12.4 summarizes these trends.

Sharing Best Practices

As the workplace becomes more complex and chaotic, workers and managers seek ways to share knowledge. The familiar scenario is that of an experienced guru within a business, sought by others within the organization who want to learn from the guru's experience. Sharing best practices is the concept of leveraging knowledge gained by a subset of an organization. It is increasingly important for organizations whose livelihood depends on applying expertise, such as accounting firms, consulting firms, training firms, architectural firms, and engineering firms. In these types of environments, it is inefficient to have everyone "reinvent the wheel" themselves. Rather, managers set up knowledge management systems to capture best practices and to disseminate that experience throughout the firm.

Institutionalizing best practices by embedding them in IT makes it more efficient for an organization to handle routine, linear, and predictable situations in stable environments. When major, discontinuous change is involved, the basic

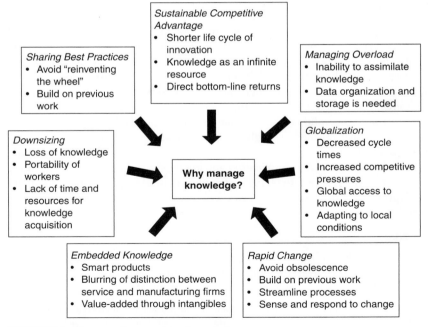

FIGURE 12.4 Reasons for managing knowledge.
Source: Adapted from IBM Global Services. Used with permission.

premises of the best practices stored in organizational knowledge bases must be constantly reevaluated.[15]

Globalization

New computing and telecommunications technologies allow data, information, and knowledge, albeit explicit knowledge, to flow instantly around the world, resulting in the emergence of an interconnected global economy. In the past, land, labor, and capital gave nation-states their comparative economic advantage. As a greater percentage of economic growth arises from the knowledge sector, comparative advantage derives instead from the collective ability to leverage what people know. Knowledge-based businesses seem to grow according to previously unforeseen patterns, creating new markets, and attracting and producing innovations with little need for the traditional requirements of land, labor, and capital.

Peter Drucker described this trend as follows:

> Another implication [of the emerging knowledge society] is that how well an individual, an organization, an industry, a country, does in acquiring and applying knowledge will become the key competitive factor. The knowledge society will inevitably become far more competitive than any society we have yet known—for the simple reason that with knowledge being universally accessible, there will be no excuses for nonperformance...[16]

Rapid Change

Rapid change means that existing knowledge becomes obsolete faster and that employees must learn new skills in less time. New technologies and unexpected forms of competition are announced daily. To keep up, new tools, processes, and strategies must be introduced. Knowledge management provides a way to optimize the use of existing knowledge and streamline the transfer and absorption of new knowledge across the firm. Rather than "reinventing the wheel," firms can customize preexisting solutions for unique customer needs. The combination of knowledge-intensive businesses, highly skilled knowledge workers, and new and relatively inexpensive computing and telecommunications technologies creates the need to organize and transfer information and knowledge in new ways. Firms must be able to sense and respond to changing trends and markets, encourage creativity and innovation, and help knowledge workers to continuously learn and improve their productivity.

Downsizing

Downsizing initiatives tend to eliminate employees and remove knowledge, in the form of experience, from the organization. By firing experienced workers and

---

[15] Yogesh Malhotra, "Knowledge Management in Inquiring Organizations," in *Proceedings of 3rd Americas Conference on Information Systems* (Philosophy of Information Systems Mini-Track), Indianapolis, IN, August 15–17, 1997, 293–295; available at http://www.brint.com/km/km.htm.

[16] Peter F. Drucker, "The Age of Social Transformation," *The Atlantic Monthly* (November 1994).

driving away the talented, important knowledge captured in the heads of former employees is lost. A change in corporate direction can result in the wholesale firing (sometimes incorrectly called a "restructuring") of an entire class of employees with specialized knowledge. As a result, veteran employees with extensive knowledge about an organization and its processes become increasingly rare. New employees, even if educated in the subject matter, need time and experience to develop specialized knowledge unique to the firm.

Downsizing also changes the traditional contract between firms and their employees, creating a more mobile workforce than in the past. The changing contract results in an organizational knowledge base that becomes more volatile with employee transience. As workers change jobs more frequently, retaining knowledge within the organization, rather than in the heads of individuals, becomes more important.

By reducing the number of employees, firms increase the pressure on those remaining to accomplish more with less. Fewer employees are available to maintain and update the organization's knowledge, and less slack time is available for acquiring new knowledge. Concurrently, the speed of innovation is increasing so that knowledge evolves and must be assimilated at a more rapid rate.

Managing Information and Communication Overload

The growth of information resources along with the accelerating rate of techno-logical change produces a mass of information that often exceeds the ability of managers and employees to assimilate and use it productively. Individuals complain of receiving hundreds of e-mail messages, in addition to voice mail messages, faxes, regular telephone calls, and paper mail. As one manager put it, "If I am to keep up with my job I have to spend all of my time, both on and supposedly off the job, communicating. I don't have a life anymore."[17] One research report found that this flood of communication translates into white-collar workers spending a total of two hours each day on e-mail alone, and as many as 10 billion nonspam e-mail messages are received per day.[18] No wonder managers complain of being stressed and overwhelmed as a result.

Knowledge Embedded in Products

Products and services are becoming increasingly complex, giving them a significant information component. Consulting firms, software manufacturers, and research laboratories all sell knowledge. Managing that knowledge is as important to them as managing inventory is to a manufacturing firm. However, other firms not traditionally viewed as knowledge-based are beginning to realize that much of the value in their products lies in the knowledge embedded in those products. Traditional manufacturing firms differentiate themselves from their competitors

[17] Thomas H. Davenport, *Information Ecology* (New York: Oxford University Press, 1997), 48.

[18] T. Davenport and J. C. Beck, *The Attention Economy* (Boston: Harvard Business School Press, 2001), 190–191.

by offering products that embed specialized knowledge. One classic example is the development of an automatic bread-baking machine by the Japanese firm Matsushita. To design the machine, Matsushita sought out a master baker, observed his techniques, and incorporated those techniques into the machine's functionality.[19] The intangibles that add the most value to goods and services are becoming increasingly knowledge based, such as creativity, engineering, design, marketing, customer knowledge, and innovation.

Sustainable Competitive Advantage

Perhaps the best reason for knowledge management is that it can be a source of lasting and sustainable competitive advantage. It has become increasingly difficult to prevent competitors from copying and improving on new products and processes. The mobility of workers, the availability of powerful and relatively inexpensive technology, and reverse engineering make the advantages of new products and efficient processes more difficult to maintain. The life cycle of innovation is growing shorter. Competitors can usually meet or exceed the standards of price and quality developed by the market leader in a short period of time. Before that happens, however, the company managing its knowledge can move to new levels of efficiency, quality, and creativity. Unlike raw material, knowledge is not depleted through use. Shared knowledge enriches the recipient while still remaining with the original source. Knowledge is not governed by the law of diminishing returns; on the contrary, the more knowledge that is shared and used, the more new knowledge that is generated. In an age of increasing competition and unprecedented change, only one sustainable competitive advantage remains: the capacity to learn.

▶ KNOWLEDGE MANAGEMENT PROCESSES

Knowledge management involves four main processes: the generation, capture, codification, and transfer of knowledge. **Knowledge generation** includes all activities that discover "new" knowledge, whether such knowledge is new to the individual, the firm, or the entire discipline. **Knowledge capture** involves continuous processes of scanning, organizing, and packaging knowledge after it has been generated. **Knowledge codification** is the representation of knowledge in a manner that can be easily accessed and transferred. **Knowledge transfer** involves transmitting knowledge from one person or group to another, and the absorption of that knowledge. Without absorption, a transfer of knowledge does not occur. Generation, codification, and transfer all take place constantly without management intervention. Knowledge management seeks to enhance the efficiency and effectiveness of these activities and leverage their value for the firm as well as the individual. Knowledge management is a dynamic and continuously evolving process.

---

[19] Ikujiro Nonaka and Hirotaka Takeuchi, *The Knowledge-Creating Company* (New York: Oxford University Press, 1995), 100.

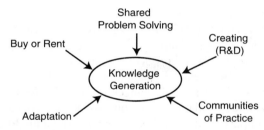

FIGURE 12.5 Knowledge generation strategies.

Knowledge Generation

Knowledge generation concerns the intentional activities of an organization to acquire or create new knowledge. In this context, knowledge does not have to be newly created, only new to the organization. The two primary ways of generating knowledge are knowledge creation (exploration) and knowledge sharing (exploitation).[20] Knowledge creation (exploration) involves experimenting, seeking, and discovering knowledge about alternatives. It generates new knowledge. Knowledge sharing (exploitation) uses and develops available knowledge. It tends to be faster than knowledge creation. Techniques for knowledge generation are summarized in Figure 12.5. Exploration techniques include creation and adaptation to changing circumstances. Exploitation techniques include purchase or rental, shared problem solving, and development through informal networks. Facilitating knowledge generation promotes continuous innovation and growth of knowledge in the firm.

Research and Development

True creation of knowledge is the rarest form of knowledge generation. Besides funding outside research, another way to create knowledge is through use of a dedicated R&D unit. Financial returns on research often take years to develop. Realizing value from R&D depends largely, however, on how effectively the new knowledge is communicated and applied across the rest of the firm.

Knowledge generated by R&D efforts, or by individuals, frequently arises from synthesis. Most new inventions are not based on entirely new ideas, but combine knowledge from different sources in unique ways so that new ideas emerge. For example, the first airplane was an innovative synthesis of three preexisting ideas: the bicycle, the motor, and the airfoil.[21] Synthesis brings disparate pieces of knowledge together, often from extremely diverse sources, then seeks interesting and useful relationships among them.

---

[20] D. A. Levinthal and J. G. March, "The Myopia of Learning," *Strategic Management Journal* 14 (Winter 1993), 95–112.

[21] Rudy Ruggles, "Knowledge Tools: Using Technology to Manage Knowledge Better," Working paper, Ernst & Young Center for Business Innovation (July 28 1997), available at http://www.businessinnovation.ey.com/mko/pdf/TOOLS.PDF.

Adaptation

Firms must often generate knowledge in response to external threats; new products or competitors, changes in economic or social conditions, and government regulation are examples. These outside threats force knowledge generation because if the firm does not change, it will cease to exist.[22] Adaptation is the ability to apply existing resources in new ways when external changes make old ways of doing business prohibitive. A firm's ability to adapt is based on two factors: having sufficient internal resources to accomplish change and being open and willing to change. A firm's *core capabilities* (i.e., competitive advantages built up over time that cannot be easily duplicated) can simultaneously be core rigidities (i.e., the unwillingness to modify tried-and-true business practices).

Buy or Rent

Knowledge may be acquired by purchasing it or by hiring individuals, either as employees or consultants, who possess the desired knowledge. Another technique is to support outside research in exchange for rights to the first commercial use of the results.

One example of this type of purchase is cell-phone manufacturer Nokia Corporation's acquisition of software company Symbian in 2008. The acquisition gave Nokia access to valuable software that created a direct competitor to Google's cellphone-software service.[23] To have built this software would have taken expertise and time, possibly keeping Nokia out of the business at a critical time.

Shared Problem Solving

Also called "fusion," shared problem solving brings together people with different backgrounds and cognitive styles to work on the same problem. Although this practice can cause divisiveness, it also provides opportunities for creative solutions. Even the most intelligent individuals can be bound by prior experience and personal style when attacking a problem.

The creative energy generated by problem-solving groups with diverse backgrounds has been termed *creative abrasion*.[24] The term *diversity*, as used to describe the backgrounds of individuals in the group, should not be equated with race- or gender-based diversity as popularly conceived; rather, the key element of diversity for shared problem solving is a difference in cognitive styles. Creative abrasion does, however, require some common ground among group members, namely, a common vocabulary or shared elements of knowledge about the problem and the organization.

---

[22] Although theoretically related, a discussion of self-organizing, complex adaptive systems is beyond the scope of this chapter. See, generally, Stuart A. Kauffman, *At Home in the Universe: The Search for the Laws of Self-Organization and Complexity* (New York: Oxford University Press, 1995).

[23] Online.wsj.com (accessed July 28, 2008).

[24] Dorothy Leonard, *Wellsprings of Knowledge* (Boston: Harvard Business School Press, 1995), 63.

This overlapping knowledge is sometimes referred to as "knowledge redundancy" and provides a basis for group members to communicate about the problem.[25] Some cultural ideas that can help fusion work more effectively include (1) fostering awareness of the value of the knowledge sought and a willingness to invest in it, (2) emphasizing the creative potential inherent in different styles of thinking and viewing the differences as positive, and (3) clearly specifying the parameters of the problem to focus the group on a common goal.[26]

Communities of Practice

Informal, self-organizing networks within firms are another source of knowledge generation. Known as **communities of practice**, these groups are composed of workers who share common interests and objectives, but who are not necessarily employed in the same organization, same department, or same physical location and who often occupy different roles on the organization chart. Communities of practice are held together by a common sense of purpose and a need to know what other members of the network know. Members' effective collaboration can generate new knowledge.

Managers can nurture knowledge generation by providing sufficient time and incentives for employees to collaborate and exchange ideas. They can also recognize that knowledge generation is an important activity for the firm and encourage employees to engage in knowledge-generating activities. For example, Google promotes a culture of creativity and innovation in all employees by allowing them to spend 20% of their time on a project of their own choosing. "[Since] it is axiomatic that a firm's greatest asset is its knowledge, then the firm that fails to generate new knowledge will probably cease to exist."[27]

Knowledge Codification

Generating knowledge by itself is a pointless task. Aside from concerns about intellectual property and proprietary knowledge, once knowledge has been generated, it must be used or shared to be of value. Codification puts the knowledge in a form that makes it possible to easily find and use. Although data can be compared to a record and information to a message, knowledge resembles an inventory. It accumulates and changes over time. Like inventory, knowledge has a "shelf life" to the extent that it may only add value for a period of time, depending on its purpose and use.

The boundaries of knowledge are difficult to identify because of context sensitivity; one person's crucial fact is another person's irrelevant trivia. Consider, for example, when an instructor imparts his or her knowledge to a class. Each

---

[25] Ikujiro Nonaka and Hirotaka Takeuchi, *The Knowledge-Creating Company* (New York: Oxford University Press, 1995), 86.

[26] Thomas H. Davenport and Laurence Prusak, *Working Knowledge* (Boston: Harvard Business School Press, 1998), 62.

[27] Ibid., 67.

student in the class hears the same information, but acquires different knowledge. The instructor's personal knowledge exists in the world that he or she knows. When that instructor imparts it, it leaves that world and its associated context. The students receive that which was imparted and then map it against that which they know to make it their own knowledge. Because each student's base of knowing is different, each will map the information differently and, thus, will have different knowledge.[28]

In one respect, knowledge capture and codification embody the same idea: although knowledge may be technically "captured" when it resides in a database or on a sheet of paper, that knowledge is unavailable across the firm until it has been codified in a manner that will allow those who need it to find it. Davenport and Prusak identify four basic principles of knowledge codification:[29]

1. Decide what business goals the codified knowledge will serve (define strategic intent).

2. Identify existing knowledge necessary to achieve strategic intent.

3. Evaluate existing knowledge for usefulness and the ability to be codified.

4. Determine the appropriate medium for codification and distribution.

Knowledge Capture

Knowledge capture takes into account the media used in the codification process. The media are used during the three major knowledge capture activities: scanning, organizing, and designing knowledge maps.

Scanning

Scanning typically combines electronic and human approaches as a first step in capturing knowledge after strategic knowledge has been identified. Traditionally, electronic scanning captured relevant information from a particular source (provided the information is available electronically), then filtered out redundant or duplicative information. Human analysts then added the most value to the scanning process by using their own knowledge of what is important to the company to provide context, interpretation, comparison, and condensation. Today, there are tools on the Internet that can do much of this type of scanning. **RSS feeds** for example, make it possible to automatically scan relevant Web sites and filter the way it is displayed.

Humans are also needed to scan and filter the soft, unstructured information available from experts and through rumor. Organizations usually have no formal or centralized scanning process and leave the scanning up to individual employees. However with Web 2.0 sites that aggregate information from various sources, many individuals are able to see just the topics of interest.

---

[28] We are indebted to a reviewer for this example.

[29] Thomas H. Davenport and Laurence Prusak, *Working Knowledge* (Boston: Harvard Business School Press, 1998), 69.

Organizing

This process attempts to take the mass of knowledge accumulated through scanning and structure it into an accessible form. Some structure is necessary to permit rapid access; however, too much structure can effectively hide knowledge from employees whose mental models do not fit those of the organizer. One example would be the index of the Yellow Pages (the real ones, not the knowledge management variety to be discussed later). One person might look under "car sales" and find no entries, while another might look under "auto dealers" and discover a large number of listings. Categorization schemes are always arbitrary and never value-neutral.

The problem of categorizing is especially salient for **folksonomies**, or sites for collaboratively creating and managing tags for annotating and categorizing content. The best known folksonomies include del.icio.us and Flickr. The keywords for tagging are generated by users of the content. The problem with this classification system is that everyone has different perceptions of the content. Thus, user tags tend to be imprecise, irrelevant, and often very messy. Further, folksonomies are ill-organized because they contain many unlinked variants such as plurals, singulars, spelling errors, and typos.

One scheme for categorizing knowledge uses four broad classifications:[30]

- *Process knowledge*. Sometimes referred to as "best practices," this kind of knowledge is useful for increasing efficiency.

- *Factual knowledge*. Basic information about people and things that has been synthesized and placed in context; easy to document.

- *Catalog knowledge*. Individuals who possess catalog knowledge know where things are. These people are like directories of expertise, and while such knowledge can often be codified into a sort of Yellow Pages, the dynamics within organizations change so quickly, some individuals will always be more valuable because they know where to go for the right knowledge.

- *Cultural knowledge*. Knowing how things actually get done in an organization, culturally and politically. The absence of cultural knowledge can reduce efficiency when employees must learn or relearn invisible norms and behaviors.

Another interesting example of a categorization scheme is *Encyclopædia Britannica*'s "Propædia," or "Outline of Knowledge." The Propædia was originally developed as a framework to classify all knowledge for inclusion in the printed encyclopedia. The designers of the search and retrieval system for *Encyclopædia Britannica*'s CD-ROM edition and Web site used the Propædia as a benchmark

---

[30] Rudy Ruggles, "Knowledge Tools: Using Technology to Manage Knowledge Better," Working paper, Ernst & Young Center for Business Innovation (July 28 1997), http://www.businessinnovation.ey.com/mko/pdf/TOOLS.PDF.

to measure the effectiveness of their system. The written Propædia structure told them which articles, from various parts of the encyclopedia, should be retrieved by a given query. The developers used the results to optimize their search algorithms.[31] The search engine developed from the Propædia is now being used at a Web site developed by Britannica called eBLAST.[32] A team of editors and indexers scans and identifies high-quality knowledge resources, which are then concisely described, rated according to consistent standards, and indexed for retrieval using the organizational hierarchy taken from the Propædia. The eBLAST Web navigator uses the Propædia categorization scheme to classify Web sites indexed in the system.

Designing Knowledge Maps

A **knowledge map** (see Figure 12.6) serves as both a guide to where knowledge exists in an organization and an inventory of the knowledge assets available. Although it may be graphically represented, a knowledge map can consist of nothing more than a list of people, documents, and databases telling employees where to go when they need help. A good knowledge map gives access to resources that would otherwise be difficult or impossible to find. Maps may also identify knowledge networks or communities of practice within the organization.

Several different schemes may be used to map knowledge. A common, but fairly ineffective, way to map knowledge is by its physical location within the firm's IS, identifying the databases, file servers, document management systems,

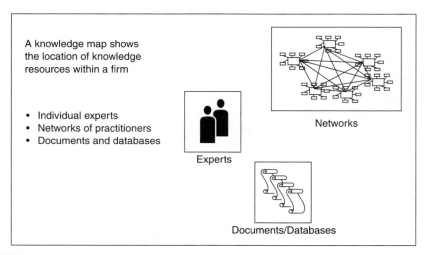

FIGURE 12.6 Contents of knowledge maps.
Source: © IBM Global Services. Used with permission.

[31] James Fallows, "The Java Theory," *The Atlantic Monthly* (March 1996), 113–117.
[32] Available at http://www.eblast.com/.

and groupware locations where it resides. This categorization scheme can help technically astute employees find information quickly because it shows them exactly where to find it. However, *physical mapping* is primarily of use only to those who are interested in learning the IT architecture of the organization.

Qualitative mapping points to information by topic rather than location. Qualitative mapping can be organized around processes, functions, or concepts. *Process mapping* uses a generalized model of how a business functions and maps it to the knowledge contained in the organization. *Functional mapping* is based loosely on the organizational chart and is usually not effective for sharing knowledge across functions, because most workers do not have time to browse through the knowledge assets of other functional areas in hopes of finding something useful. *Conceptual mapping* is the most useful of these methods for organizing knowledge, but harder to design, build, and maintain. Conceptual maps organize information around objects, such as proposals, customers, or employees. These objects or topical areas contain information originally produced in different functional areas, which leads to transfer of knowledge across the organization.[33]

Codifying Tacit Knowledge with Narratives

Mapping the identities of experts in an organization does not guarantee access to those experts' knowledge. An expert must have both the time and the willingness to share the knowledge. If the expert is unavailable or leaves the firm, the value of his or her knowledge is lost. A partial answer to this problem is to transfer as much knowledge as possible through mentoring or apprenticeship programs so that important tacit knowledge is not entirely concentrated in one person. Capturing tacit knowledge through narratives provides another answer.

Research shows that knowledge is communicated most effectively through a good story that, told with feeling, resonates with other people. "War stories" can convey a rich and complex understanding of an event or situation in human context, making them one of the most effective ways to both capture tacit knowledge without losing much of its value and transfer it to the listener. Knowledge is most likely to be absorbed if shared in a context that is understood by the listeners. More firms are beginning to circulate videotapes that tell the story, for example, about how an important sale was closed. These narratives "codify" the expert's tacit knowledge of how to close a sale in a way that conveys much of its underlying meaning.[34] The very act of telling the story shapes the firm's meaning about how expert salespeople should act.

At IDEO, a leading design firm, knowledge is spread through stories and not databases. Typically half the weekly Monday morning meetings are dedicated to

---

[33] Tom Davenport, David DeLong, and Mike Beers, "Building Successful Knowledge Management Projects," Working paper, Ernst & Young Center for Business Innovation (June 6, 1997), available at http://www.businessinnovation.ey.com/mko/pdf/KPROJE.PDF.

[34] Thomas H. Davenport and Laurence Prusak, *Working Knowledge* (Boston: Harvard Business School Press, 1998), 82.

sharing stories about projects or best business practices. "People hold stories in their heads better than other forms of inform," says IDEO president Tim Brown.[35]

Knowledge Transfer

In their book *The Knowledge Creating Company*, Ikujiro Nonaka and Hirotaka Takeuchi describe four different modes of *knowledge conversion*, their term for knowledge transfer (see Figure 12.7). The modes are (1) from tacit knowledge to tacit knowledge, called **socialization**, (2) from tacit knowledge to explicit knowledge, called **externalization**, (3) from explicit knowledge to explicit knowledge, called **combination**, and (4) from explicit knowledge to tacit knowledge, called **internalization**.[36]

Socialization is the process of sharing experiences; it occurs through observation, imitation, and practice. Common examples of socialization are sharing war stories, apprenticeships, conferences, and casual, unstructured discussions in the office or "at the water cooler." When the Web is used as the vehicle for transferring, **mashups**, a Web 2.0 tool, combines data from more than one source to create a distinct, integrated Web service that was not previously available at any of the sources. For example explicit data about real estate sales (i.e., type of

	TO	
	Tacit Knowledge	Explicit Knowledge
FROM — Tacit Knowledge	SOCIALIZATION Transferring tacit knowledge through shared experiences, apprenticeships, mentoring relationships, on-the-job training, "talking at the water cooler"	EXTERNALIZATION Articulating and thereby capturing tacit knowledge through use of metaphors, analogies, and models
FROM — Explicit Knowledge	INTERNALIZATION Converting explicit knowledge into tacit knowledge; learning by doing; studying previously captured explicit knowledge (manuals, documentation) to gain technical know-how	COMBINATION Combining existing explicit knowledge through exchange and synthesis into new explicit knowledge

FIGURE 12.7 The four modes of knowledge conversion.
Source: Ikujiro Nonaka and Hirotaka Takeuchi, *The Knowledge-Creating Company* (New York: Oxford University Press, 1995), 62.

---

[35] Catherine Fredman, "The IDEO Difference," *Hemispheres* (August 2002), 52–57.

[36] Ikujiro Nonaka and Hirotaka Takeuchi, *The Knowledge-Creating Company* (New York: Oxford University Press, 1995), 62–70.

property and sale price) could be mapped to explicit cartographic location data available from Google Maps to create a map of recent sales. Internalization is the process of experiencing knowledge through an explicit source. For example, after viewing the videotape and combining the new knowledge conveyed by the narrative with prior experiences, a salesperson might close a sale he or she would have otherwise lost.

► COMPETING WITH BUSINESS ANALYTICS

In recent years, many companies have found success competing through better use of analytics. Companies such as Harrah's Entertainment, as described at the beginning of this chapter, have turned around an otherwise lackluster business to become a leader in their industry. Capital One has also emerged from a crowded field of financial services firms, to become one of the industry leaders through use of extensive business analytics to continuously create and invent new products and services to reach out to new customers and reinvigorate relationships with existing customers. In their case, the company was founded on the idea that by mining data about individual customers they could create financial service products that addressed what the big players would consider "'niche markets," unattractive to the larger players because of the smaller number of potential customers, but profitable nonetheless. Using the customer database of a small bank, and running numerous analytical tests, they identified characteristics that would create a profitable service. They learned, for example, that the most profitable customers were ones who charged a large amount, but paid their credit cards off slowly. At the time, most credit cards companies didn't differentiate between these and other customers. The innovative idea was to create a product that catered to these customers. Today, Capital One runs hundreds of experiments, identifying new products that target individual customers. Using analytics to simulate and test is a very low cost way to design and develop these products.[37]

Sports teams have propelled themselves to league success through business analytics. The systematic use of factual data in proprietary models is credited with helping the Oakland As and the Boston Red Sox. Billy Beane was one of the first general managers in Major League Baseball to build his organization, the Oakland As, around analytics. Although this industry collected data extensively, it was mostly used to manage the game in process. The Oakland As managed by using data on things that they could measure such as the on-base percentage (the number of times a player gets on-base), instead of softer criteria such as determination or effort the player is willing to put in. They used analytics in their recruiting efforts to predict which young players had the best chances of becoming major league players. Their strategy paid off, consistently carrying them to the playoffs

---

[37] Davenport and Harris, *Competing on Analytics*, 41–42.

despite a budget for player's salaries that was a fraction of what some of their competitors had.

One reason for the rise in companies competing on analytics is that many companies in many industries offer similar products and use comparable technologies. Therefore, business processes are among the last remaining points of differentiation, and analytic competitors are wringing every last drop of value from those processes.[38] Business analytics fuel fact-based decision making. For example, a company may use inventory reports to figure out what products are selling quickly and which are moving slowly, but a company that uses analytics will also know who is buying them, what price each customer pays, how many items the customer will purchase in a lifetime, what motivates each customer to purchase, and which incentives to offer to increase the revenue from each sale.

Davenport and Harris suggest that companies who successfully compete using their business analytics skills have these five capabilities:

- Hard to duplicate: Because successfully using analytics to compete means having a strong culture and organizational support system, as well as business processes that utilize the results of the analytical analyses, copying the capability is difficult, if not impossible. A competitor may have the same tools, but success comes from how they are used.

- Uniqueness: There are many ways to use business analytics to compete. A specific business will choose a path based on their business, their strategy, their market, their competitors, and their industry.

- Adaptability: Successful companies use analytics across boundaries and in creative ways. Workers are not held back from using analytics, and in fact are encouraged to find new and innovative ways to apply their tools. By creating a culture of analytics, virtually everyone in the organization seeks applications for analytics to enhance their business operations.

- Better than competition: Some organizations are better at applying analytics than others. For example, the Oakland As and the Boston Red Sox are well known for their use of analytics in an industry, Major League Baseball, well known for its data collection and statistical analysis.

- Renewability: Agility is an important characteristic of sustainable competitive advantage. Companies who use analytics for competitive advantage are exceptionally adaptable, continuously reinvest, and constantly renew their capabilities.

▶ COMPONENTS OF BUSINESS ANALYTICS

To successfully build business analytics capabilities in the enterprise, companies make a significant investment in their technologies, their people, and their strategic

---

[38] Ibid.

Component	Definition	Example
Data Repository	Servers and software used to store data	Data warehouses
Software Tools	Applications and processes for statistical analysis, forecasting, predictive modeling, and optimization	Data mining process; forecasting software package
Analytics Environment	Organizational environment that creates and sustains the use of analytics tools	Reward system that encourages the use of the analytics tools; willingness to test or experiment
Skilled Workforce	Workforce that has the training, experience, and capability to use the analytics tools	Harrah's and Capital One have such workforces

FIGURE 12.8   Components of business analytics.

decision-making processes. Four components are needed (these four components are summarized in Figure 12.8).

Data Repositories

Data used in the analytical processes must be gathered, codified, and stored. **Data warehouses**, or collections of data designed to support management decision making, sometimes serve as repositories of organizational knowledge. They contain a wide variety of data used to create a coherent picture of business conditions at a single point in time. In fact, the data contained in data warehouses may represent a large part of a company's knowledge, for example, the business's knowledge about its clients and their demographics.

Software Tools

At the core of business analytics are the tools An approach that simulates business intelligence is **data mining**, which is the process of analyzing data warehouses for "gems" that can be used in management decision making. It identifies previously unknown relationships among data. Typically, data mining refers to the process of combing through massive amounts of customer data to understand buying habits and to identify new products, features, and enhancements. The analysis may help a business better understand its customers by answering such questions as: Which customers prefer to contact us via the Web instead through a call center? How are customers in Location X likely to react to the new product that we will introduce next month? How would a proposed change in our sales commission policy likely affect the sales of Product Y? Using data mining to answer such questions helps a business reinforce its successful practices and anticipate future customer preferences.

There are four categories of tools that are typically included under the business analytics umbrella. They include[39]

- Statistical Analysis—answers questions like, "Why is this happening?"
- Forecasting/extrapolation—answers questions like, "What if these trends continue?"
- Predictive Modeling—answers questions like, "What will happen next?"
- Optimization—answers questions like, "What is the best that can happen?"

These tools are used with the data in the data warehouse to gain insights and support decision making.

Analytics Environment

Building an environment that supports and encourages analytics is a critical component. This includes alignment of the corporate culture, the incentive systems, the metrics used to measure success of initiatives, and the processes for using analytics with the objective of building competitive advantage through analytics. For example, one financial services firm encouraged the use of analytics by changing its appraisal system so that demonstration of skills associated applying analytics was made a significant factor in compensation decisions.

Although many companies have some sort of analytical tools in place, most are not used for mainstream decision making, and they certainly do not drive the strategy formulation discussions of the company. To build a competitive advantage from analytics, executives use analytics as an integral component of their business.

Skilled Workforce

It's clear that to be successful with analytics, data and technology must be used. But experts point out that even with the best data and the most sophisticated analytics, people must be involved. Managers must have enough knowledge of analytics to use them in their decision making. Leaders must set examples for the organization by using analytics and requiring that decisions made by others use analytics. Perhaps the most important role is sponsorship. Davenport and Harris point out that it was the CEO-level sponsorship and the corresponding passion for analytics that enabled firms such as Harrah's and Capital One to achieve the success they did.

▶ CAVEATS FOR MANAGING KNOWLEDGE

Following such a broad survey, it seems appropriate to conclude with a few caveats. First, recall that knowledge management and business intelligence are emerging disciplines. Viewing knowledge management as a process rather than an end by itself requires managers to remain flexible and open-minded.

---

[39] Ibid.

Second, the objective of knowledge management is not always to make knowledge more visible or available. Like other assets, it is sometimes in the best interests of the firm to keep knowledge tacit, hidden, and nontransferable. Competitive advantage increasingly depends on knowledge assets that are difficult to reproduce. Retaining knowledge is as much a strategic issue as sharing knowledge.

Third, knowledge can create a shared context for thinking about the future. If the purpose of knowledge management is to help make better decisions, then it should focus on future events. Through the use of multiple scenarios, organizations can create "memories of the future." The goal is not to know the future, but rather to know what projections influence long-term strategy and short-term tactics.[40]

Finally, people lie at the heart of knowledge management. Establishing and nurturing a culture that values learning and sharing of knowledge enables effective and efficient knowledge management. Knowledge sharing—subject, of course, to the second caveat already described—must be valued and practiced by all employees for knowledge management to work. The success of knowledge management ultimately depends on a personal and organizational willingness to learn.

▶ FOOD FOR THOUGHT: BUSINESS EXPERIMENTATION

In his book, *Experimentation Matters*, Professor Stefan Thomke discusses a concept of business experimentation as a means of innovation for organizations.[41] Products and services are created and improved using analytics through a process of experimentation. **Business experimentation** uses controlled, well-designed experiments to innovate and support business strategy. It's more than testing out a new software package or building a new prototype. Companies who excel at business experimentation are able to create new products and services at a fraction of the cost of similar companies who lack this competency.

Capital One is a primary example of a company built around experimentation. Capital One was founded by two individuals who believed that the data collected by a bank, when systematically analyzed, would reveal new, profitable financial services products. As discussed earlier in this chapter, they ran thousands of experiments on their bank's customer database to test their initial hypotheses and develop their first products. Today, Capital One managers run several hundred experiments a day to target individual customers and offer innovative financial service products. For example, through structured testing and analysis of their data repositories, managers found that CD interest rates, rollover incentives, and minimum balances had predictable effects on retention rates and new additional deposits. Through experimentation, they increased the business savings retention by 87% and lowered the cost of acquiring new accounts by 83%.[42]

---

[40] Liam Fahey and Laurence Prusak, "The Eleven Deadliest Sins of Knowledge Management," *California Management Review* 40, no. 3 (1998), 265–276.

[41] Stefan Thomke, *Experientation Matters* (Harvard Business School Press, 2003).

[42] Adapted from Davenport and Harris, *Competing on Analytics*, 42.

The ability to manage uncertainty is fundamental to innovation. Uncertainty can come from many sources. For example, technological uncertainty arises from the concern that the innovation will work as designed. Production uncertainty arises in the unknowns associated with producing the innovation for customers. Market uncertainty arises when the pace of change is so fast that what is a need today may no longer be a need tomorrow, when the innovation gets to market. To resolve uncertainty, managers can turn to experimentation.

At the core of business experimentation is the concept of "test and learn." Companies who regularly experiment manage their projects as experiments. That means they design their projects with a series of rapid iterations through many experiments where they fail early and often then continue to learn. That means building processes, using technologies, and creating a culture that supports experimentation. Although this sounds easy, most business cultures do not support experimentation. Instead, and especially in an era of tight resources, business leaders expect projects to proceed along a well-planned path from idea to successful implementation. The learning is supposed to take place before the project begins. In a business experiment friendly culture, projects begin with a series of experiments that result in learning, and then as the ideas emerge, the project may proceed to concrete idea then implementation.

Capital One and Harrah's are both examples of companies who have built a core competency in business experimentation and analytics. Managers have built processes to support experimentation with analytics. Data is collected in vast quantities knowing that the next innovation, and perhaps the entire strategy of the company, will emerge from systematic analysis of the data.

► SUMMARY

- Knowledge management is related to information systems (IS) in three ways: (1) information technologies make up the infrastructure for knowledge management systems; (2) knowledge management systems make up the data infrastructure for many IS and applications; and (3) knowledge management is often referred to as an application of IS.

- Data, information, and knowledge should not be viewed as interchangeable. Knowledge is more valuable than information, which is more valuable than data because of the human contributions involved.

- The two kinds of knowledge are tacit and explicit. Tacit knowledge is personal, context-specific, and hard to formalize and communicate. Explicit knowledge is easily collected, organized, and transferred through digital means.

- Reasons for managing knowledge include benefits derived from sharing best practices, the need to respond to globalization and rapid change, organizational downsizing, the need to manage information and communication overload, controlling knowledge embedded in products, and leveraging knowledge to gain competitive advantage.

- Knowledge management is a dynamic and continuously evolving process that involves knowledge generation, capture, codification, and transfer.

- Business Intelligence uses data and technologies to understand business performance. Business Analytics is a component of business intelligence referring to the quantitative and predictive models and fact-based management that drive business decisions.
- Successfully competing with business analytics means that the organization have these five capabilities: hard to duplicate, uniqueness, adaptability, better than competition, and renewability
- Business experiments provide a structured, relatively low cost process for systematically innovating and ultimately creating business strategy, often using analytics and simulation.

▶ KEY TERMS

business analytics (p. 352)
business intelligence (p. 352)
business experimentation (p. 369)
combination (p. 364)
communities of practice (p. 359)
data (p. 348)
data mining (p. 367)
data warehouses (p. 367)
explicit knowledge (p. 351)

externalization (p. 364)
folksonomies (p. 361)
information (p. 349)
intellectual capital (p. 347)
intellectual property (p. 348)
internalization (p. 364)
knowledge (p. 349)
knowledge capture (p. 356)
knowledge codification (p. 356)

knowledge generation (p. 356)
knowledge management (p. 347)
knowledge map (p. 362)
knowledge transfer (p. 356)
mashup (p. 364)
RSS feeds (p. 360)
socialization (p. 364)
Tacit knowledge (p. 350)

▶ DISCUSSION QUESTIONS

1. The terms *data*, *information*, and *knowledge* are often used interchangeably. But as this chapter discussed, they can be seen as three points on a continuum. What, in your opinion, comes after knowledge on this continuum?

2. What is the difference between tacit and explicit knowledge? From your own experience, describe an example of each. How might an organization manage tacit knowledge?

3. What does it take to be a successful competitor using business analytics? What is IT's role in helping build this competence for the enterprise?

4. How do knowledge maps aid an organization?

5. Do you think that the Digital Millennium Copyright Act is the type of legislation that should be enacted to protect intellectual property? Why or why not?

6. PricewaterhouseCoopers has an elegant, powerful intranet knowledge management system called Knowledge Curve. Knowledge Curve makes available to its consultants and auditors a compendium of best practices, consulting methodologies, new tax and audit insights, links to external Web sites and news services, online training courses, directories of in-house experts, and other forms of explicit knowledge. Yet, according to one of the

firm's managing partners, "There's a feeling it's underutilized. Everybody goes there sometimes, but when they're looking for expertise, most people go down the hall."[43] Why do you think that Knowledge Curve is underutilized?

7. How do analytics support business experimentation? Give an example of how a company might use business experimentation to create a new product or service.

GSD&M'S VIRTUAL CROWD USES ANALYTICS

Advertising giant GSD&M has always been on the leading edge at its home, Idea City, in Austin, Texas. This time they are using virtual simulation and collaboration to help their clients develop advertising strategies. They have created a "virtual marketplace" to help test messages, media, and audiences. One of their managers, Maury Giles, head of accountability and analytics, describes it this way

> In the same way you can create 'SimCity,' you can create a virtual marketplace. Instead of spending $30 million on a campaign, you're not sure is going to work, you can try it and run it...It's like a simulation of what would happen if we spend this money on this message with this group of people.

The technology lets GSD&M managers set up a simulated population of as many customers as they want. They set up rules, such as what percent likes what products in the market, what city they live in, what their network of friends looks like, what the economy looks like, and what competitors are doing. The system uses its database to simulate customer behavior.

For example, a simulation would help a customer decide if they should use the Web, TV, radio, or some combination to create the results they seek. It's a tool to help make marketing decisions, but managers must still make those decisions. Although it may take four to six months to set up a simulation, the results are compelling. One manager said that the predictions from their system are within 95% of what actually happens.

Discussion Questions

1. What is the benefit to GSD&M and their clients of using a simulation to predict customer behavior?
2. What other scenarios can you think of that might benefit from this type of simulation?
3. Describe the culture necessary to support GSD&M's use of simulation as a means of experimenting with marketing scenarios.

Source: Adapted from Lilly Rockwell, "GSD&M Taps Virtual Crowds to Test Real Ads," *Austin American-Statesman*, April 21, 2008, Section D, p. 1.

---

[43] Thomas Stewart, "The Case Against Knowledge Management," *Business 2.0* (February 2002), p. 81.

THE BRAIN BEHIND THE BIG, BAD BURGER

At a time when most fast-food restaurants were touting nutrition, Hardee's proudly introduced the Monster Thickburger. This burger boasts a phenomenal 1420 calories and 107 grams of fat. It consists of two, one-third-pound charbroiled 100% Angus beef patties, three slices of American cheese, a dollop of mayonnaise, and four crispy strips of bacon on a toasted buttery sesame seed bun. What on earth was CKE Restaurants, the owners of the Hardee's chain, thinking?

Because of its Business Intelligence System (BIS), CKE was confident about introducing the Monster Thickburger across the United States on November 15, 2004. A BIS uses data mining, analytical processing, querying, and reporting to process a business's data and derive insights from it. CKE's BIS, known ironically inside the company as CPR (CKE Performance Reporting) monitored the performance of its Monster Thickburger in test markets to ensure that the burger contributed to increases in sales and profits at restaurants without cannibalizing sales of other more modest burgers. To do so, CKE's BIS studied a variety of factors—such as menu mixes, Monster Thickburger production costs, average unit volumes for the Monster Thickburger compared with other burgers, gross profits and total sales for each of the test stores, and the contribution that each menu item (including the Monster Thickburger) made to total sales. Because the sales of Monster Thickburger exceeded expectations in the test markets, CKE developed a $7 million dollar advertising campaign to launch its nationwide introduction. Monster Thickburger sales exceeded expectations, and Hardee's sales revenues increased immediately. "The Monster Thickburger was directly responsible for a good deal of that increase," says Brad Haley, Hardee's executive vice president of marketing.

CKE, partially because of its reliance on CPR, was rescued from the brink of bankruptcy in 2000. It increased sales at restaurants open more than a year, narrowed its overall losses, and finally turned a profit in 2003. CPR, their proprietary system, consists of a Microsoft SQL server database and uses Microsoft development tools to parse and display analytical information. It uses econometric models to provide context and to explain performance. The company reviews and refines these models each month. The econometric models take into consideration 44 factors, including the weather, holidays, coupon activity, discounting, free giveaways, and new products. With the click of a button, for example, a sales downturn can be explained on a screen that shows that 5% of the 8% decrease was due to torrential rain in the Northeast and 2% was due to free giveaways.

In the competitive restaurant chain industry, companies have to be agile and responsive to the dynamic environment that they face. They must align their BIS initiatives with their business strategies. They use the insights derived from their BISs to improve operations and their bottom lines. BISs assist them in making strategic decisions about menu items and closures of underperforming stores, as well as tactical matters such as renegotiating contracts with food suppliers, monitoring food costs, and identifying opportunities to improve inefficient processes. To derive value from their BISs, many restaurant chains have successfully reduced the three biggest barriers to BIS success: voluminous amounts of irrelevant data, poor data quality, and user resistance.

CKE's CIO and executive vice president of strategic planning, Jeff Chasney, states: "If you're just presenting information that's neat and nice but doesn't evoke a decision or impart important knowledge, then it's noise. You have to focus on what are the really important things going on in your business."

Chasney stresses a BIS should be different from the plain-vanilla standard corporate reporting tools that have been around for decades. Rather a BIS should provide managers with insights, not just mountains of data. "There's nothing worse, in my opinion, than a business intelligence system that reports changes on a weekly basis," he says, "because those systems don't provide any context as to what factors are influencing those changes. Without that context, you don't know whether the data is good or bad; it's just useless." Chasney further noted: "If your business intelligence system is not going to improve your decision making and find problem areas to correct and new directions to take, nobody's going to bother to look at it."

When developing a BIS, Chasney advises companies to first analyze their decision-making processes. They must determine the information that executives need to confidently make decisions in rapidly changing environments, as well as their preferred presentation format for that information (for example, as a report, a chart, online, hard copy). Only then can that information be collected, analyzed, and published in their BISs.

In 2000 when he started building CPR, Chasney asked the CEOs and the chief operating officers (COOs) of CKE's three restaurant chains—Hardee's, Carl's Jr., and La Salsa Fresh Mexican Grill—what information is most important to them in their efforts to run their company. The CEO wanted to know what caused changes in sales. The COOs wanted help in exposing business opportunities, as well as clear indicators of underperforming restaurants. The discussions taught Chasney that a BIS needed to add value by focusing on a company's most important performance indicators: sales and cost of sales; exceptions, such as those areas of the business that are outperforming or underperforming other segments; and historical and forward-looking business trends.

Discussion Questions

1. How does the BIS at CKP add value to the business?
2. What are some tips for developing and using the Business Intelligence System described in this case?
3. Was the introduction of the Monster Thickburger a good idea or an example of information leading to a wrong decision?

Source: Adapted from Meredith Levinson, "The Brain Behind the Big, Bad Burger and Other Tales of Business Intelligence," *CIO Magazine* (March 15, 2005), available at http://www.cio.com/archive/031505/intelligence.html.

Glossary

Administrator: An employee who "takes care of" a computer or a number of computers. Administrator duties typically include backing up data (and restoring it if it is lost), performing routine maintenance, installing software upgrades, troubleshooting problems, and assisting users.

ANSI X12: The name of the standard used by EDI applications to allow a software program on one computer system to relay information back and forth to a software program on another computer system, thus allowing organizations to exchange data pertinent to business transactions.

Application: A software program designed to facilitate a specific practical task, as opposed to control resources. Examples of application programs include Microsoft Word, a word processing application; Lotus 1-2-3, a spreadsheet application; and SAP R/3, an enterprise resource planning application. Contrast to *operating system*.

Archetype: A pattern from decision rights allocation.

ASP (Application Service Provider): An Internet-based company that offers a software application used through their Web site. For example, a company might offer small business applications that a small business owner could use on the Web, rather than buying software to load on their own computers.

Authentication: A security process where proof is obtained to verify that the users are truly who they say they are.

B2B (Business to Business): Using the Internet to conduct business with business customers. (See B2C.)

B2C (Business to Consumer): Using the Internet to conduct business directly with consumers of goods and services. (See B2B.)

Backsourcing: A business practice in which a company takes back in-house assets, activities, and skills that are part of its information systems operations and were previously outsourced to one or more outside IS providers.

Bandwidth: The rate at which data can travel through a given medium. The medium may be a network, an internal connection (say from the CPU to RAM), a phone line, etc. For networks and internal connections, bandwidth is typically measured in terms of megabytes per second (MB/sec) or gigabytes per second (GB/sec).

Bit: A "binary digit"; the smallest unit of data as represented in a computer. A bit can take only the values 0 or 1.

Bricks-and-clicks: The term used to refer to businesses with a strong business model on both the Internet and in the physical world.

Business Analytics: The use of data, analysis, and modeling to arrive at business decisions. Some organizations use business analytics to create new innovations or to support the modification of existing products or services.

Business Diamond: A simple framework for understanding the design of an organization, linking together the business processes, its values and beliefs, its management control systems, and its tasks and structures.

Business Experimentation: A method of studying a business problem that involves the use of a structured process such as the scientific method to learn about the potential success or failure of a product, service, or innovation. Businesses use this method to create new innovations and to study hunches and hypotheses. Often business analytics are used to create frequent, low-cost business experiments.

Business Intelligence: This term refers to the broader practice of using technology, applications, and processes to collect and analyze data to support business decisions.

Byte: 8 bits. A byte can be thought of as a "character" of computer data.

Captive Center: An overseas subsidiary that is set up to serve the parent company. Companies set up captive centers as an alternative to offshoring.

CIO (Chief Information Officer): The senior-most officer responsible for the information systems activities within the organization. The CIO is a strategic thinker, not an operational manager. The CIO is typically a member of the senior management team and is involved in all major business decisions that come before that team, bringing an information systems perspective to the team.

Client/Server: A computing architecture in which one software program (the client) requests and receives data and sometimes instructions from another software program (the server) usually running on a separate computer. In a client/server architecture, the computers running the client program typically require less power and resources (and are therefore less expensive) than the computer running the server program. In many corporate situations, a client/server architecture can be very cost effective.

Client: A software program that requests and receives data and sometimes instructions from another software program, usually running on a separate computer.

Cloud Computing: This is a style of infrastructure where capacity, applications, and services (such as development, maintenance, or security) are provided by a third-party provider over the Internet often on a "fee for use" basis. Customers go to the Web for the services they need.

Coaxial Cable (coax): A kind of copper wire typically used in networking. An inner wire is surrounded by insulation, which is surrounded by another copper wire and more insulation.

Complementor: One of the players in a co-opetitive environment. It is a company whose product or service is used in conjunction with a particular product or service to make a more useful set for the customer. (See Value Net.)

Co-opetition: A business strategy whereby companies cooperate and compete at the same time.

Cost Leadership Strategy: A business strategy where the organization aims to be the lowest-cost producer in the marketplace. (See Differentiation Strategy; Focus Strategy.)

CPU (Central Processing Unit): The computer hardware on which all computation is done.

CRM (Customer Relationship Management): The management activities performed to obtain, enhance, and retain customers. CRM is a coordinated set of activities revolving around the customer.

Crowdsourcing: The act of taking a task traditionally performed by an employee or contractor and outsourcing it to an undefined, generally large group of people, in the form of an open call.

Cycle plan: A project management plan that organizes project activities in relation to time. It identifies critical beginning and end dates and breaks the work spanning these dates into phases. The general manager tracks the phases to coordinate the eventual transition from project to operational status, a process that culminates on the "go live" date.

Data Mining: The process of analyzing databases for "gems" that will be useful in management decision making. Typically, data mining is used to refer to the process of combing through massive amounts of customer data to understand buying habits and to identify new products, features, and enhancements.

Database: A collection of data that is formatted and organized to facilitate ease of access, searching, updating, addition, and deletion. A database is typically so large that it must be stored on disk, but sections may be kept in RAM for quicker access. The software program used to manipulate the data in a database is also often referred to as a "database."

DBA (Database Administrator): The person within the information systems department who manages the data and the database. Typically, this person makes sure that all the data that goes into the database is accurate and appropriate, and that all applications and individuals who need access have it.

Debugging: The process of examining and testing software and hardware to make sure it operates properly under every condition possible. The term is based on calling any problem a "bug"; therefore, eliminating the problem is called "debugging."

Decision Models: Information systems-based model used by managers for scenario planning and evaluation. The information system collects and analyzes the information from automated processes and presents them to the manager to aid in decision making.

Differentiation Strategy: A business strategy where the organization qualifies its product or service in a way that allows it to appear unique in the marketplace. (See Cost Leadership Strategy; Focus Strategy.)

Digital Signature: A digital code applied to an electronically transmitted message used to prove that the sender of a message (e.g., a file or e-mail message) is truly who he or she claims to be.

DSL (Digital Subscriber Line): A technology used for connecting users to the Internet. The connection is typically offered by a telephone company or other independent company to homes and businesses who desire direct, all the time access. DSL subscribers are able to use the Internet without dialing up a server, and the connection is usually of higher speed than dial-up lines.

E-business (Electronic Business): Any business activities done electronically within or between businesses. Many use this term to specifically refer to business activities done over the Internet.

E-commerce (Electronic Commerce): Transacting business electronically, typically over the Internet or directly with an EDI system.

EDI (Electronic Data Interchange): A mechanism for exchanging business data between two computers over some kind of network.

EFT (Electronic Funds Transfer): The business transaction of sending payments directly from a customer's bank account to a vendor's bank account electronically.

E-learning: Using the Internet to enable training, learning, and knowledge transfer. E-learning includes distance learning, computer-based training (CBT), on-demand learning, and Web-based training.

E-mail (electronic mail): A way of transmitting messages over communication networks.

E-marketplaces: A special application of the Internet that brings together different companies to buy and sell goods and services. Sometimes called "net-markets" or "virtual markets."

Encryption: The translation of data into a code or a form that can be read only by the intended receiver. Data is encrypted using a key or alphanumeric code and can be decrypted only by using the same key.

Enterprise 2.0: A term used to describe a company using the technologies and practices resulting from Web 2.0 architectures, applications, and services. Enterprise 2.0 typically means a flat organization with unimpeded information flows between all levels and individuals in the organization. Companies adopting these practices seek to be agile, flexible, user driven, on-demand, and transparent.

Enterprise Architecture: The term used for a "blueprint" for the corporation that includes the business strategy, the IT architecture, the business processes, and the organization structure and how all these components relate to each other. Often this term is IT-centric, specifying the IT architecture and all the interrelationships with the structure and processes.

ERP (Enterprise Resource Planning Software): A large, highly complex software program that integrates many business functions under a single application. ERP software can include modules for inventory management, supply chain management, accounting, customer support, order tracking, human resource management, and so forth. ERP software is typically integrated with a database.

Ethernet: A standard for local area networks. Ethernet specifies software protocols and hardware specifications for creating a LAN to interconnect two or more computers. There are three common versions of Ethernet: 10Base-T, which provides for bandwidths of up to 10 megabits per second; 100Base-T, which provides 100 megabits per second; and Gigabit Ethernet, which provides 1 gigabit per second.

Explicit Knowledge: Objective, theoretical, and codified for transmission in a formal, systematic method using grammar, syntax, and the printed word. (See Tacit Knowledge.)

Extranet: A network based on the Internet standard that connects a business with individuals, customers, suppliers, and other stakeholders outside the organization's boundaries. An extranet typically is similar to the Internet; however, it has limited access to those specifically authorized to be part of it.

Fiber Optic (or optical fiber): A data transmission medium (and technology) that sends data as pulses of light along a glass or plastic wire or "fiber." Fiber-optic technology is capable of far greater bandwidth than copper technologies such as coax.

Firewall: A security measure that blocks out undesirable requests for entrance into a Web site and keeps those on the "inside" from reaching outside.

Focus Strategy: A business strategy where the organization limits its scope to a narrower segment of the market and tailors its offerings to that group of customers. This strategy has two variants: *cost focus*, in which the organization seeks a cost advantage within its segment, and *differentiation focus*, in which it seeks to distinguish its products or services within the segment. This strategy allows the organization to achieve a local competitive advantage, even if it does not achieve competitive advantage in the marketplace overall. (See Cost Strategy, Differentiation Strategy.)

Folksonomy: Collaboratively creating and managing a structure for any type of collection, such as a collection of ideas, data, or documents. The term is the merger of "folk" and "taxonomy," meaning that it is a user-generated taxonomy.

Functional view: The view of an organization based on the functional departments, typically including manufacturing, engineering, logistics, sales, marketing, finance, accounting, and human resources. (See Process View.)

Gigabit (Gb): 1 billion bits.

Gigabyte (GB): 1 billion bytes.

Governance (in the context of business enterprises): Making decisions that define expectations, grant power, or verify performance

Groupware: Software that enables a group to work together on a project, whether in the same room, or from remote locations, by allowing them simultaneous access to the same files. Calendars, written documents, e-mail messages, discussion tools, and databases can be shared.

GUI (Graphical User Interface): The term used to refer to the use of icons, windows, colors, and text as the means of representing information and links on the screen of a computer. GUIs give the user the ability to control actions by clicking on objects rather than by typing commands to the operating system.

Hard drive: A set of rotating disks used to store computer data. Because hard drives typically have much greater capacity than RAM, they are often also referred to as "mass storage."

Hypercompetition: A theory about industries and marketplaces that suggests that the speed and aggressiveness of moves and countermoves in any given market create an environment in which advantages are quickly gained and lost. A hypercompetitive environment is one in which conditions change rapidly.

HyperText Markup Language (HTML): The language used to write pages for the **Internet.** It was created by a researcher in Switzerland in 1989 and is part of an Internet standard called the HyperText Transport Protocol (the "http" at the beginning of Internet addresses), which enables the access of information stored on other Internet computers. "Hypertext" itself is another name for the "links" (or "hyperlinks," "hot links," or "hot spots") found on Web pages.

Informate: A term coined by S. Zuboff to imply adding information to a job or task. The alternative to informate is automate, where the tasks done are simply put on a computer to increase speed and accuracy and to cut costs. Informate, on the other hand, means to bring out the information aspects of the job to assist in assessment, monitoring, and decision making.

Information Model: A framework for understanding what information will be crucial to the decision, how to get it, and how to use it.

Information Resource: The available data, technology, people, and processes within an organization to be used by the manager to perform business processes and tasks.

Information System: The *combination* of technology (the "what"), people (the "who"), and process (the "how") that an organization uses to produce and manage information

Information Systems (IS) Strategy: The plan an organization uses in providing information services.

Information Systems Strategy Triangle: The framework connecting business strategy, information system strategy, and organizational systems strategy.

Information Technology: All forms of technology used to create, store, exchange, and use information.

Information: Data endowed with relevance and purpose; data in a context.

Infrastructure: Everything that supports the flow and processing of information in an organization, including hardware, software, data, and network components

Insourcing: The situation in which a firm provides IS services or develop IS from its own in-house IS organization.

Intellectual capital: The knowledge that has been identified, captured, and leveraged to produce higher-value goods or services or some other competitive advantage for the firm.

Internet: The system of computers and networks that together connect individuals and businesses worldwide. The Internet is a global, *inter*connected *net*work of millions of individual host computers.

Intranet: A network used within a business to communicate between individuals and departments. An Intranet is an application on the Internet, but limited to internal business use. It is a password-protected set of interconnected nodes that is under the company's administrative control. (See Extranets.)

IS (Information Systems): The technology (hardware, software, networking, data), people, and processes that an organization uses to manage information.

ISDN (Integrated Services Digital Network): A standard for transmission of digital signals over ordinary telephone lines at up to 128 kilobits per second.

ISP (Internet Service Provider): A company who sells access to the Internet. Usually, the service includes a direct line or dial-up number and a quantity of time for using the connection. The service often includes space for hosting subscriber Web pages and e-mail.

IT (Information Technology): The technology component of the information system, usually consisting of the hardware, software, networking, and data.

IT governance: Specifying the decision rights and accountability framework to encourage desirable behavior in using IT

JAVA: An object-oriented programming language designed to work over networks and commonly used for adding features into Web pages.

Kilobit (kb): Approximately 1 thousand bits (i.e., 1024 bits).

Kilobyte (kB): Approximately 1 thousand bytes (i.e., 1024 bytes).

Knowledge management: The processes necessary to capture, codify, and transfer knowledge across the organization to achieve competitive advantage.

Knowledge map: A list of people, documents, and databases telling employees where to go when they need help. A good knowledge map gives access to resources that would otherwise be difficult or impossible to find. Maps may also identify knowledge networks or communities of practice within the organization. A knowledge map serves as both a guide to where knowledge exists in an organization and an inventory of the knowledge assets available.

Knowledge repository: A physical or virtual place where documents with knowledge embedded in them, such as memos, reports, or news articles, are stored so they can be retrieved easily.

Knowledge: Information synthesized and contextualized to provide value.

LAN (Local Area Network): A network of interconnected (often via Ethernet) workstations that reside within a limited geographic area (typically within a single building or campus). LANs are typically employed so that the machines on them can share resources such as printers or servers and/or so that they can exchange e-mail or other forms of messages (e.g., to control industrial machinery).

Legacy System: Older, mature information system (often 20 to 30 years old)

List Server: A type of e-mail mailing list where users subscribe, and when any user sends a message to the server, a copy of the message is sent to everyone on the list. This allows for restricted-access discussion groups: Only subscribed members can participate in or view the discussions because they are transmitted via e-mail.

Mainframe: A large, central computer that handles all the functionality of the system

Managerial Levers: Organizational, control, and cultural variables that are used by decision makers to effect changes in their organizations.

Marketspace: A virtual market where the transactions taking place are all based on information exchange, rather than the exchange of goods and services.

Mashup: A term used in the Web2.0 community to mean the combination of data from multiple sources into one Web page, for example, combining Google Maps with real estate data to produce a diagram showing home price ranges for certain neighborhoods.

Megabit (Mb): 1 million bits.

Megabyte (MB): 1 million bytes.

Modem: A device that translates a computer's digital data into an analog format that can be transmitted over standard telephone lines, and vice versa. Modems are necessary to connect one computer to another via a phone line.

Nearshoring: Sourcing service work to a foreign, lower-wage country that is relatively close in distance or time zone (or both).

Network Effect: The value of a network node to a person or organization in the network increases when another joins the network.

Newsgroup: A type of electronic discussion in which the text of the discussions typically is viewable on an Internet or intranet Web page rather than sent through e-mail. Unless this page is shielded with a firewall or password, outsiders are able to view and/or participate in the discussion.

Open Source Software (OSS): Software released under a license approved by the Open Source Initiative (OSI).

Operating System (OS): A program that manages all other programs running on, as well as all the resources connected to, a computer. Examples include Microsoft Windows, DOS, and UNIX.

Oracle: A widely used database program.

Organizational Systems: The fundamental elements of a business including people, work processes, structure, and the plan that enables them to work efficiently to achieve business goals.

Outsourcing: The business arrangement where third-party providers and vendors manage the information systems activities. In a typical outsourced arrangement, the company finds vendors to take care of the operational activities, the support activities, and the systems development activities, saving strategic decisions for the internal information systems personnel.

Password: A string of arbitrary characters that is known only to a select person or group, used to verify that the user is who he says he is.

Platform: The hardware and software on which applications are run. For example, the iPhone is considered a platform for many applications and service that can be run on it.

Portal: Easy-to-use Web sites that provide access to search engines, critical information, research, applications, and processes that individuals want.

Process View: The view of a business from the perspective of the business processes performed. Typically the view is made up of cross-functional processes that transverse disciplines, departments, functions, and even organizations. (See Functional View.)

Processes: An interrelated, sequential set of activities and tasks that turn inputs into outputs and have a distinct beginning, a clear deliverable at the end, and a set of metrics that are useful to measure performance.

Project Management Office (PMO): The organizational unit within which resides the expertise for managing projects.

Protocol: A special, typically standardized, set of rules used by computers to enable communication between them.

Prototyping: An evolutionary development method for building an information system. Developers get the general idea of what is needed by the users, and then build a fast, high-level version of the system as the beginning of the project. The idea of prototyping is to quickly get a version of the software in the hands of the users, and to jointly evolve the system through a series of cycles of design and build, then use and evaluate.

RAD (Rapid Application Development): This process is similar to prototyping in that it is an interactive process, where tools are used to speed up development. RAD systems typically have tools for developing the user, reusable code, code generation, and programming language testing and debugging. These tools make it easy for the developer to build a library of a common, standard set of code that can easily be used in multiple applications.

RAM (Random Access Memory): Computer memory that can be accessed at random, read from, and written to by the CPU. Sometimes also called "main memory," it is typically used to store currently running programs and their data. RAM requires power to maintain data.

Reengineering: The management process of redesigning business processes in a relatively radical manner. Reengineering traditionally meant taking a "blank piece of paper" and designing (then building) a business process from the beginning. This was intended to help the designers

eliminate any blocks or barriers that the current process or environment might provide. This process is sometimes called BPR, Business Process Redesign or Reengineering or Business Reengineering.

Really Simple Syndication or RSS (also called Web feeds): Refers to a structured file format for porting data from one platform or information system to another.

SAP: The company that produces the leading ERP software. The software, technically named "SAP R/3," is often simply referred to as SAP.

SDLC (Systems Development Life Cycle): The process of designing and delivering the entire system. SDLC usually means these seven phases: initiation of the project, requirements definition phase, functional design phase, technical design and construction phase, verification phase, implementation phase, and maintenance and review phase.

Security Validators: Web sites that validate the security level of other sites and provide a "seal of approval" that a particular Web site is protected.

Server: A software program or computer intended to provide data and/or instructions to another software program or computer. The hardware on which a server program runs is often also referred to as "the server."

Service-Oriented Architecture (SOA): This is the term used to describe the architecture where business processes are built using services delivered over a network (typically the Internet). Services are software that are distinct units of business functionality residing on different parts of a network and can be combined and reused to create business applications.

Smart Card: A plastic card with an embedded microchip that can be loaded with data, used for telephone calling, electronic cash payments, and other applications, and then periodically "recharged" for additional use.

Social Contract Theory: A theory used in business ethics to describe how managers act. The social responsibilities of corporate managers by considering the needs of a society with no corporations or other complex business arrangements. Social contract theorists ask what conditions would have to be met for the members of such a society to agree to allow a corporation to be formed. Thus, society bestows legal recognition on a corporation to allow it to employ social resources toward given ends.

Social networking site: A Web site available from a Web-based service that allows members of the service to create a public profile within a bounded system, list other users with whom they share a connection, and view and interact with their list of connections and those made by others within the system. Examples are MySpace, Facebook, and LinkedIn.

Software-as-a-Service (SaaS): This term is used to describe a model of software deployment that uses the Web to deliver applications on an "as-needed" basis. Often when software is delivered as a service, it runs on a computer on the Internet, rather than on the customer's computer, and is accessed through a Web browser.

Stakeholder Theory: A theory used in business ethics to describe how managers act. This theory suggests that managers, although bound by their relation to stockholders, are entrusted also with a fiduciary responsibility to all those who hold a stake in or a claim on the firm, including employees, customers, vendors, neighbors, and so forth.

Standardization: The process of agreeing on technical specifications that will be followed throughout the infrastructure. Often standards are agreed on for development processes, technology, methods, practices, and software.

Stockholder Theory: A theory used in business ethics to describe how managers act. Stockholders advance capital to corporate managers who act as agents in advancing their ends. The nature of this contract binds managers to act in the interest of the shareholders (i.e., to maximize shareholder value).

Tacit Knowledge: Personal, context-specific, and hard to formalize and communicate. It consists of experiences, beliefs, and skills. Tacit knowledge is entirely subjective and is often acquired through physically practicing a skill or activity. (See Explicit Knowledge.)

Telecommuting: Combining telecommunications with commuting. This term usually means individuals who work from home instead of commuting into an office. However, it is often used to mean anyone who works regularly from a location outside their company's office.

T-Form Organization: An organizational form in which conventional design variables, such as organizational subunits, reporting mechanisms, flow of work, tasks, and compensation are combined with technology-enabled components, such as electronic linking, production automation, electronic work flows and communications, and electronic customer/supplier relationships.

Thick Client: A full-function stand-alone computer that is used, either exclusively or occasionally, as a client in a client/server architecture. Thick clients are typically standard PCs equipped with disk drives and their own copies of commonly used software.

Thin Client: Computer hardware designed to be used only as a client in a client/server architecture. Thin clients are also referred to as NCs (Network Computers) or NetPCs (Network PCs) and typically lack disk drives, CD ROM drives, and expansion capability.

Total Quality Management (TQM): A management philosophy in which quality metrics drive performance evaluation of people, processes, and decisions. The objective of TQM is to continually, and often incrementally, improve the activities of the business toward the goal of eliminating defects (zero defects) and producing the highest quality outputs possible.

Unified Communications (UC): An evolving communications technology architecture that automates and unifies all forms of human and device communications in context and with a common experience.

Value Net: The set of players in a co-opetitive environment. It includes a company and its competitors and complementors, as well as their customers and suppliers, and the interactions among all of them. (See Complementor.)

Video Teleconference (also called video-conference): A set of interactive telecommunication technologies that allow two or more locations to interact via two-way video and audio transmissions simultaneously.

Virtual Corporation: A temporary network of companies who are linked by information technology to exploit fast-changing opportunities.

Virtual Organization: An organization made up of people living and working from anywhere in the world. The virtual organization may not even have a company headquarters or company building, but functions much like any other organization. Employees typically use an information systems infrastructure to communicate, collaborate, and carry out company business.

Virtual Private Network (VPN): A private network that uses a public network such as the Internet to connect remote sites or users. It maintains privacy through the use of a tunneling protocol and security procedures.

Virtual Team: Geographically and/or organizationally dispersed coworkers that are assembled using a combination of telecommunications and information technologies to accomplish an organizational task.

Virtual World: A computer-based simulated environment intended for its users to inhabit and interact via avatars.

Voice over Internet Protocol (VoIP): A method for taking analog audio signals, like the kind you hear when you talk on the phone, and turning them into digital data that can be transmitted over the Internet

WAN (Wide Area Network): A computer network that spans multiple offices, often dispersed over a wide geographic area. A WAN typically consists of transmission lines leased from telephone companies.

Web 2.0: The term given to the Internet and its applications that support collaboration, social networking, social media, RSS, mashups, and a number of other information sharing tools. The term is used to distinguish it from Web1.0, which was mostly used for transactions and information dissemination. Web 2.0 is not about different technical specifications, but about using the Internet in different ways from Web 1.0.

Web Logs (Blogs): Online journals that link together into a very large network of information sharing.

Web Services: The software systems that are offered over the Internet and executed on a third party's hardware. Often Web services refer to a more fundamental software that use XML messages and follow SOAP (simple object access protocol) standards.

Wiki: Software that allows users to work collaboratively to create, edit, and link Web pages easily.

WWW (World Wide Web): A system for accessing much of information on the Internet, via the use of specially formatted documents. WWW is used interchangeably with the term "Internet."

Zero Time Organization: An organization designed around responding instantly to customers, employees, suppliers, and other stakeholder demands.

Index